SOCIAL ISSUES, JUSTICE AND STATUS

HANDBOOK ON BULLYING

PREVALENCE, PSYCHOLOGICAL IMPACTS AND INTERVENTION STRATEGIES

SOCIAL ISSUES, JUSTICE AND STATUS

Additional books in this series can be found on Nova's website under the Series tab.

Additional e-books in this series can be found on Nova's website under the e-books tab.

SOCIAL ISSUES, JUSTICE AND STATUS

HANDBOOK ON BULLYING

PREVALENCE, PSYCHOLOGICAL IMPACTS AND INTERVENTION STRATEGIES

PHOEBE TRIGGS
EDITOR

nova publishers
New York

For permission to use material from this book please contact us:
Telephone 631-231-7269; Fax 631-231-8175
Web Site: http://www.novapublishers.com

LIBRARY OF CONGRESS CATALOGING-IN-PUBLICATION DATA

ISBN: 978-1-63463-023-8

Published by Nova Science Publishers, Inc. † New York

CONTENTS

PREFACE

Bullying is one of today's biggest problems. Bullying is the intentional repeated aggression directed at a target individual. There is substantial evidence of the negative psychological and health outcomes associated with bullying. It occurs very frequently, especially in adolescence, and action is needed to lessen its causes and alleviate its consequences. Research has shown that behavior problems usually interact with other risk and protection factors, as well as with factors of etiological development. This book discusses the prevalence, psychological impacts and intervention strategies of bullying.

Peer victimization occurs when an individual is a repeated target of intentional aggression by one or more peers. Bullying is the intentional repeated aggression directed at a target individual. There is substantial evidence of the negative psychological and health outcomes associated with bullying and peer victimization. In Chapter 1, the authors review literature demonstrating the association between bullying/peer victimization and psychological problems (e.g., depression, anxiety, PTSD symptoms). The authors then consider how peer victimization/ bullying impacts the way people think about and process their experiences (particularly their social interactions) as well as how their self-concept is affected. Being bullied affects people's social relationship schemas as well as their cognitive processing. For example, literature indicates that people who are rejected by peers are higher on rejection sensitivity (e.g., anxious expectations about future rejection) and are more likely to engage in dsyregulated emotional processing compared to people who are accepted by peers. They also consider how this psychological impact of bullying on cognitions affects an individual's mental health status. Finally, the authors consider possible avenues for bullying interventions/prevention programs.

As witnessed in popular media, reports of violence and aggression – both on and off the field – is often associated with athletes such as football players. The emphasis on these reports creates a skewed perception of male athletes, and subsequently the non-violent behavior of countless other male athletes is often discounted and ignored. Nonetheless, there is evidence to suggest that male athletes may be more likely to engage in violence than their non-athlete male peers. Research aimed at studying this phenomenon has suggested that there is, "a continuum of physical contact and masculinity whereby highly masculinized contact sports increase the risks of violence". This raises the question: Are boys who participate in certain sports being taught to be violent? After critically examining the theories and research addressing this question, in this chapter the authors will look at the societal stereotype of the "jock bully" as it appears in both popular culture and academic writings. The authors will then use this psychologically-oriented lens to examine the 2013 Miami Dolphins controversy involving Jonathan Martin and Richie Incognito, where they will apply relevant literature on bullying and masculinity. Lastly, the authors will discuss future implications for research and clinical work. Prevention is the most desirable form of intervention and future research should therefore assess the effectiveness of violence and abuse prevention initiatives. Professionals working in school, athletic, and occupational settings can use the information in Chapter 2 to inform their efforts to create an environment that can address bullying dynamics.

Chapter 3 explains that bullies are individuals who use a superior force, whether it is physical or mental, to assert dominance over others in an effort to do what they ordinarily wouldn't. Recently, technology has become a fundamental part of life. People can't seem to escape technology without having to cut off all communication from the world. Access to the Internet has become more readily available through new technology such as tablets and mobile phones. As the need for physical communication decreases, use of cyberbullying as an alternative form of traditional bullying has become devastatingly prevalent. Cyberbullying is becoming more frequent throughout the world with advances in technology rapidly changing the traditional definition of bullying. Cyberbullying has become a way for those who typically would not bully, to terrorize without consequence, so it is not only affecting those who would have traditionally bullied, but it is also affecting a broader range of individuals including all ages through childhood, adolescents, and adulthood. Those who are bullied generally show more cognitive and affective empathy. Further, students who have pro-victim attitudes (i.e., the belief that bullying is unacceptable, victims are acceptable, and defending victims is valued) are less likely to be bullied than other students. Unfortunately, there are many dimensions to cyberbullying that make it easier to attempt than traditional bullying. One of these is the absence of physical strength. Those who were not strong enough to bully in a traditional setting, find it easier to bully via the Internet. Cyberbullying also decreases the level of awareness of the victim's distress. Another factor that makes cyberbullying easier is the ability to be anonymous to some extent over the Internet. There is a method of indirectly bullying people over the Internet as well. By tortuously posting a picture or statement on a social media page, cyberbullying can directly affect the victim without the bullying needing to target a specific person. Further, there is a lack of fear in cyberbullies, and they are often unaware or less aware of the consequences for their behaviors. Some cyberbullying attempts are even based on the ability of a teacher to intervene on traditional bullying attempts giving the bully an outlet with fewer consequences. Cyberbullying has the same side effects and consequences as traditional bullying. Low self-esteem and depression have been more consistent in victims rather than non-victims. In the past, bullying took place in specific environments such as school, work, home; places that are supposed to offer a sense of safety. Cyberbullying completely diminishes the idea of safety for victims of bullying. Victims are often unable to find a place of security due to the accessibility of technology and other people. However, many programs and organizations have worked to put an end to bullying by implementing constant awareness and guidelines within schools, workplaces, and social media.

Bullying has been defined as recurrent harassment of a student or group of students by another student or group. More specifically, bullying encompasses repeated negative actions with an intention to harm or disturb that involves a differential of power, where the more powerful individual attacks or harasses the individual who is less powerful individual. Studies have shown that bullying may lead to long-term negative effects, such as violence and depression, for the both perpetrator and the victim. Therefore, the development and examination of bullying interventions and their effectiveness is important in order to gain an understanding of which interventions may be the most effective in reducing bullying behavior. In general, school-based and/or whole-school approach to anti-bullying programs have been found to be the most empirically-supported intervention technique. However, other interventions, such as interventions aimed at changing the social norms around bullying behavior, have also been shown to be effective. Chapter 4 provides a thorough review of theoretically diverse bullying interventions that have been shown to be empirically effective at reducing bullying behaviors.

Bullying is defined by American Psychological Association as an aggressive behavior which is intended to cause distress or harm and that involves an imbalance of power or strength between the aggressor and the victim as explained in Chapter 5. Bullying in the workplace is angering enough people these days to be fueling a nationwide grass-roots legislative effort to force companies to draft and enforce policies aimed at stopping it. Requiring such policies, according to those pushing the legislation, is not an attempt to spawn lawsuits, but an effort to force organizations to deal with the problem. Bullying is blamed for unnecessarily creating high costs of turnover, insurance claims and thwarted productivity. Disruptive behavior has been observed in almost all members of the healthcare team from physicians and nurses to pharmacy, radiology, and laboratory staff members. Physician behavior, however, may have the greatest impact because of the position of authority that doctors hold as members of the healthcare team. A team member may, from fear of intimidation or patronization, withhold valuable or even critical input, such as a medication error or a breakdown in adherence to safety protocols. Hospitals, departments and individual personnel need to develop a higher level of awareness of the problem both in others and in them. Anti-bullying policies should be given a higher profile.

Youths in the 21st century are raised in a digital world where blogs, social networking sites, and instant messaging are part of their everyday life. These youths have been immersed in a digital world for as long as they can remember. As a result of this immersion, youths are at risk for cyberbullying, which has increased in intensity over the years.

Cyberbullying has become a major focus of not only youths, educators, and researchers, but also among the general population, due to high profile cases of cyberbullying victimization involving suicide. This chapter drew on literature utilizing cross-sectional, longitudinal, qualitative, and quantitative research methodologies to describe cyberbullying.

Chapter 6 provided an overview of cyberbullying, including the tools, technologies, and forms, along with the prevalence rates, correlates, and the emotional and behavioral consequences. Also discussed are the cultural differences in these behaviors, and theoretical underpinnings. The chapter concluded with recommendations for future research and public policy.

Bullying is one of today's biggest problems in Public Health. It occurs very frequently, especially in adolescence, and action is needed to lessen its causes and alleviate its consequences. Research has shown that behavior problems usually interact with other risk and protection factors, as well as with factors of etiological development. The objective of this investigation was to establish a hypothetical relationship between personal self-regulation, resilience, coping strategies and engagement-burnout, which would serve as a foundation for new lines of intervention at university.

A total of 253 university students participated in this research. Assessment questionnaires for personal self-regulation, coping strategies, resilience and positive-negative emotionality were completed on an anonymous, voluntary basis during class time, at different points during the 2012-2013 academic year. Correlation analyses and structural analysis were performed, using an ex post-facto design.

Results presented in Chapter 7 showed significant association relationships between self-regulation and resilience, between resilience and type of coping strategies used to cope with stress, and between resilience and burnout-engagement.

Greater personal self-regulation is significantly associated and interdependent with a greater level of resilient behavior, and resilient behavior in turn is similarly related to more problem-focused coping strategies, and more engagement behavior in dealing with stressful situations. The results suggest a line of research for skill-training programs as a means to deal with bullying. This evidence should be applied to intervention programs, both for training in personal self-regulation, and for implementing resilient behaviors and coping strategies with engagement behavior for managing this type of stressful situation. Future investigations should explore this line of work, which has not been fully considered to date.

In the last 15 years literature on bullying has emphasized the role of systemic processes in aggressive interactions, as well as the interplay of cognitive and emotional mechanisms leading to antisocial behaviors. Indeed, as adolescents interact with a varied social world, their development entails the formation of different but systematic types or domains of social reasoning. Social situations require a balancing and coordination of different social, individual and moral considerations related to features of the context. In Chapter 8, the authors suggest a broader view of moral reasoning trough the investigation of individual, culturally influenced, life values. In the authors' non-representative sample of 801 Italian students the prevalence students who witnessed episodes of school bullying was around 75% and the most common type was direct, either verbal (offending, teasing, threating) or physical aggression. Participating roles in bullying were coded into uninvolved (neutral) bystanders (56.8%), victims (37.1%) and bully/bully-victims (6.1%). Moreover, when the authors examined the relation between aggression and life values, their results evidenced, in addition to a general individualistic tendency for personal success, richness, and ambition; some values specifically pertained to adolescent bullies, as evidenced by little consideration for others' needs and desires, low respect of societal norms and little importance attributed to honesty. Bullies' self-assertion tendencies appeared even stronger in female than in males. These values may be supported by expectations of positive outcomes from the bullying behavior openly expressed by the peers' group or perceived by the bullies. Only by taking into consideration the interplay between personal goals, life and cultural values a fuller theoretical understanding of peer aggression can be reached. Integrative models are thus needed to investigate both moral cognition and moral affect in children in relation to their participant roles in different forms of bullying.

Cyberbullying refers to an indirect and covert form of aggression, carried out through the use of new technologies, and exhibiting distinct features from those found present in traditional bullying, and has been acquiring its own space of analyses and research; still, it maintains an inevitable proximity with the second, namely, the negative impact on the victim, both the person and the student, with consequences on academic performance, among other aspects.

Chapter 9 reviews some of the most relevant studies on cyberbullying, its assessment and relation with personal (self-esteem, age, sex, ethnicity and type of aggression) and contextual (family, school context and peer group) variables, as well as with several aspect related to academic context, particularly, students' engagement in school and academic success. Considering the expected link between bullying and cyberbullying, some studies on the first form of aggression were included in this review, as they may be considered a theoretical referential in this subject.

Cyberbullying is a recent and important phenomenon, linked to the inclusion of new technologies in daily life. There are, however, some gaps in research carried out on this issue, which presents different features from those that characterize traditional bullying. Similarly to bullying, studies suggest that cyberbullying presents negative impact both on students and academic success. Students' engagement in school plays an import role in the occurrence of aggression-victimization behaviors and appears to be a valorous strategy in cyberbullying prevention.

Previous research has revealed the existence of a transfer from bullying to cyberbullying of the roles of aggressor and victim. However, the interaction of physical and cyber environments in adolescents not only fosters this transfer or co-occurrence but also accentuates the adoption of more complex roles such as that of aggressive-victim. This profile, simply defined in traditional bullying situations, takes on new dimensions with the many combinations that arise from the co-existence of the phenomena of bullying and cyberbullying.

The aim of Chapter 10 is to contribute to knowledge of the aggressive-victim profile in the different categories resulting from physical and cyberspace bullying situations. To this end, the authors considered two questions to answer. The first was to ask what is the actual prevalence of the aggressive-victim in the various forms that this role might be found in the context of bullying and cyberbullying, and then to analyse the behaviours that it involves. The second concerns the variability of these manifestations according to the mode and frequency of the abuses suffered in the two contexts: physical and cyberspace. To answer these questions by presenting the results of research with 1648 Spanish adolescents (aged from 12 to 16 years).

The most relevant contributions of the chapter reside in the identification of variables that modulate the type of abuse that the different categories of aggressive-victims commit against their peers. Gender, mode and frequency of the abuses suffered by aggressive victims are the three variables that influence in the type of violent behavior that they manifest. Also, the results show the victims of aggression in physical or virtual environments tend to use the same context to in turn abuse their peers.

Chapter 11 synthesized recent research on bullying and victimization in educational settings. The chapter drew on literature related to the impact of the school context, particularly school climate and school characteristics, on youths' involvement in bullying, as victims and perpetrators. This section of the chapter discussed studies on the effect of school size, class size, racial and ethnic minority composition, and school location on school bullying. School climate was also examined, specifically teachers' attitudes and students' perceptions of teachers' attitudes, and how such climates relate to school bullying. At the end of this section, school-based preventive intervention programs are described, highlighting the effective components of these programs. The second part of this chapter focused on peers' roles in school bullying. It also covered bystanders, peer clustering, peer ecology, and peer status, and how these impact school bullying involvement. This section concludes with the effectiveness of peer-based preventive intervention programs. The final section of the chapter provided recommendations for schools, parents, and youths. The research shared in this chapter utilized cross-sectional, longitudinal, qualitative, and quantitative research methodologies. It also incorporated research across multiple disciplines, including psychology, sociology, education, social work, and anthropology. The research featured is also international to provide a broad overview of school bullying across the world.

Chapter 12 examines special developmental features of the terrorist demoralization syndrome; it discerns terrorism in the classification of destructive social epidemics highlights mechanisms of manipulations with human consciousness in extremist organizations and formulates the characteristics of mental paradigm of national security. It also offers a synergetic bio-psycho-socio-spiritual system for preventive and correctional activities based on the mental medicine methodology.

Chapter 13 aims to address the lack of research exploring differences between male adult prisoners and male juvenile training school students in relation to their bullying behavior.

A training school is a correctional facility that is used for the custody and re-education of juvenile offenders. Training schools are a part of the educational system in Estonia and they are used to prepare incarcerated youth for returning to society. The first sample of this study consists of all 53 male adolescent offenders (13–17 years old with average age 14.7 years) at the only maximum security male juvenile training school in Estonia, and the second sample consists of 105 male adult offenders (21–66 years old with average age 33.1 years) at one of four maximum security male prisons in Estonia.

The present study used a self-reported questionnaire developed by Ireland and Archer (1996) to provide not only a descriptive analysis of the nature and extent of bullying among adolescents in training school and among adults in prison, but also a comparison between two study group to assess the hypothesis that adolescents' bullying would involve a greater proportion of direct forms than adults' would, and that adults' bullying would display a greater proportion of indirect forms than youth' would.

The perceived extent of bullying was higher in prison compared with juvenile training school. Bullying in the juvenile training school was predominately physical (direct) but adult reported a higher frequency of indirect bullying in prison. A particular characteristic of individuals (e.g., vulnerable) was viewed as being predisposed to become a victim of bullying and various reasons (e.g., victims are easy targets) were suggested as to why a person was bullied, but adults in prison were significantly more likely than juveniles in training school to suggest sex offenders, and adolescents more likely than adults the physical weakness of victim. Bullying was seen to occur at locations out of sight of staff but more in living areas in the prison and more at school and private areas in the juvenile training school. More juveniles at training school then prison inmates reported that both they and staff were willing to help the victims of bullying. A relatively higher percentage of inmates in both institutions - prison and training school, admitted to being bullies, victims and bully/victims with on average 2 to 4 bullying incidents in previous week.

Cyberbullying is widely recognised as a serious social menace which affects millions of people around the world, especially teenagers and adolescents. In Chapter 14, the authors present the results of an online survey, which is conducted to understand and differentiate between real cyberbullying and cyberbullying-like instances in user-generated content. The authors study the subtle differences between the motives of the sender of messages similar to cyberbullying, and how messages are perceived by the recipient. In particular, the authors investigate forms, prevalence, and key indicators of cyberbullying within written contents. Firstly three variants of cyberbullying are introduced, namely: 'direct', 'indirect' and 'misinterpreted' forms of cyberbullying, based on the involvement of the recipient in these types of cyberbullying. Then the authors validate the key indicators which make written contents becomes cyberbullying, based on users' online experiences and the frequency with which they received and/or sent cyberbullying messages.

The findings reveal that: i) For direct cyberbullying, 'presence of loud language' and 'teasing - repeated comments or messages that may upset someone' are the main indicators in social networks. ii) For indirect cyberbullying, 'bullied or picked on by someone indirectly, as a third person, while online', 'been talked about online in ways that make you feel uncomfortable or upset', and 'been mentioned in a message to someone else in a way that is mocking or otherwise makes you feel uncomfortable or upset' are the main indicators. iii) For misinterpreted form of cyberbullying, 'bullied or picked on a friend or relative while online', 'been talked about online by a friend or relative, in ways that make you feel uncomfortable or upset' and 'been mentioned in a message to a friend or relative in a way that is mocking or otherwise makes you feel uncomfortable or upset' are the main indicators. These results are discussed in the light of the relatively limited cyberbullying detection research undertaken to date.

Nowadays, cyberbullying is becoming an increasingly obvious concern, especially among children and teenagers. Cyberbullying can have an extremely negative impact on victims and in the worst scenarios, it can actually result in suicidal attempts.

In Chapter 15, the authors present the results of an online survey, which is conducted to study the sources, motives and reaction to cyberbullying. The study focuses on obtaining feedback on the nature and prevalence of cyberbullying from the Internet users of different age groups and genders, based on the frequency of offensive posts received. Findings reveal that in social networking websites, instance messaging and chat rooms are the main sources of cyberbullying. Items 'to show hate', 'to make fun of someone', and 'to copycat others in cyberbullying activities' are the main motives of cyberbullying. The main reactions to cyberbullying are 'replied in a bullying manner', 'never replied' and 'blocked someone'. To differentiate real bullying from cyberbullying-like or non-bullying messages, the frequency between sender and receiver over a long period of a time can be seen to demonstrate whether it is an unusual (intentional) act of teasing, or a usual (unintentional) act that generally exists between good friends or those in close relationships. However, it is important to note that a frequent pattern should not be confused with frequent coarse language at one particular time. The unusual patterns over a long period of time should be considered as clear indicators of true bullying.

In: Handbook on Bullying
Editor: Phoebe Triggs

ISBN: 978-1-63463-023-8

Chapter 1

COPING STRATEGIES AND COGNITIVE PROCESSES RELATED TO PEER VICTIMIZATION AND THE ROLE OF INTERVENTION PROGRAMS

***Jennifer M. Knack*[1,*], *Madeline Rex-Lear*[2], *Alanna Wormwood*[1] and *Aaliyah Gibbons*[1]**
[1]Clarkson University, Potsdam, New York, US
[2]University of Texas at Arlington, Arlington, Texas, US

Abstract

Peer victimization occurs when an individual is a repeated target of intentional aggression by one or more peers (Olweus, 1999). Bullying is the intentional repeated aggression directed at a target individual. There is substantial evidence of the negative psychological and health outcomes associated with bullying and peer victimization. In this chapter, we review literature demonstrating the association between bullying/peer victimization and psychological problems (e.g., depression, anxiety, PTSD symptoms). We then consider how peer victimization/bullying impacts the way people think about and process their experiences (particularly their social interactions) as well as how their self-concept is affected. Being bullied affects people's social relationship schemas as well as their cognitive processing. For example, literature indicates that people who are rejected by peers are higher on rejection sensitivity (e.g., anxious expectations about future rejection) and are more likely to engage in dsyregulated emotional processing compared to people who are accepted by peers. We also consider how this psychological impact of bullying on cognitions affects an individual's mental health status. Finally, we consider possible avenues for bullying interventions/prevention programs.

Introduction

Developing and maintaining positive peer relationships predicts healthy emotional and developmental well-being in people of all ages. Positive peer relationships are particularly important in children and adolescents as childhood creates a framework for later thoughts and

* E-mail address: jknack@clarkson.edu (Corresponding author)

perceptions of the social world and influences adult behavior. Because most people have an innate desire to create and maintain meaningful interpersonal relationships with others (Baumeister and Leary, 1995), peer victimization can negatively affect an individual. Peer victimization is defined as the perpetual, intentional aggression of a person(s) of higher power directed at someone of lower power (Olweus, 1993). A plethora of problems arise as people try to cope with peer victimization. These coping strategies can manifest as adjustment problems (i.e., internalizing and externalizing problems), symptoms of post-traumatic stress disorder (PTSD), and loneliness. Despite the negative implications of peer victimization, intervention strategies and anti-bullying campaigns in the United States have limited empirical evidence supporting their effectiveness.

We begin this chapter by reviewing the association between peer victimization and these negative outcomes. We then present several cognitive biases and assumptions that may contribute to the association between peer victimization and these negative outcomes and consider the role that social cognition and social information processing play. We conclude by reviewing some of the intervention and prevention strategies and argue that there is a clear and growing need for more effective prevention programs.

Peer Victimization and Adjustment Problems

Peer relationships are an important indicator of emotional development and adjustment both concurrently and later in life (e.g., Rigby, 2000; La Greca and Prinstein, 1999). When peer victimization occurs, the social pain experienced by the victim can manifest as adjustment problems (Perren, Ettekal, and Ladd, 2012). Some people who experience peer victimization externalize their problems (e.g., disruptive behavior, hyperactivity, aggressive symptomology) whereas other people internalize their problems (e.g., anxiety, depression, loneliness; Cicchetti and Toth, 1991). In many cases externalizing and internalizing problems predict further peer victimization and/or intensifies emotional pain (Kochenderfer-Ladd and Skinner, 2002). In this section, we consider the association between peer victimization, externalizing problems, internalizing problems, and other negative outcomes related to mental health.

Externalizing Problems

Externalizing problems are characterized by disruptive, oppositional, and/or aggressive behaviors, a lack of regulation and control, attention deficiency, hyperactivity, or impulsivity (Chan et al., 2008; Eisenburg et al., 2000; Olson et al., 1999; Prinstein et al., 2009). Externalizing problems are typical psychopathological responses used to adapt to social situations (Ollendick and King, 1994; Prinstein et al., 2009).

Numerous longitudinal studies have demonstrated that peer rejection is robustly associated with externalizing problems later in life (i.e., delinquency, conduct disorders, attention-deficit/hyperactivity disorder) and that externalizing problems occur most frequently when rejection is experienced repeatedly (Laird et al., 2001; Prinstein et al., 2009). Troop-Gordon and Ladd (2005) ascertained that peer victimization exacerbates social dysfunction in ways that intensify externalizing problems. In addition, externalizing problems typically further compound antisocial behavior or poor social skills that may put people at risk for future peer victimization (Dodge and Pettit, 2003; Fox and Boulton, 2005; Kochenderfer-Ladd and Skinner, 2002).

Internalizing Problems

Peer victimization can also lead to internalizing problems such as depression and anxiety (Ollendick et al., 1994; Zwierzynska et al., 2013). Individuals who have been indirectly victimized (e.g., gossiped about) are more likely to internalize problems than individuals who have been directly victimized (e.g., hit, called names; Benjet et al., 2010). There is a complex bi-directional dynamic as internalizing problems can be the result of peer victimization and can also be a risk factor for peer victimization (Zwierzynska et al., 2013).

Depression

One of the most common consequences of peer victimization is depression (Hawker and Boulton, 2000). There is a cognitive triad associated with depression in which depressed individuals have negative perspectives of themselves, their world, and their future (Beck, 1987; Leahy, 2002). Researchers have shown that severe or frequent peer victimization increased the likelihood of having depressive symptoms in adulthood (Gladstone et al., 2006; Lund et al., 2009), although girls who have been both directly and indirectly victimized were more likely than boys to show depressive symptoms concurrently (van der Wal et al., 2003). Zwierzynska et al.'s (2013) longitudinal study of 3,962 children and parents demonstrated that children who were peer victimized were not only more likely to internalize problems but they were also more likely to show persistent depressive symptoms two years later. Though there is some debate about the direction of influence between peer victimization and depression, Barchia and Bussey (2010) proposed that rumination, school efficacy, and self-efficacy to find support against bullying may mediate the link between peer victimization and depression. In their study of 1,167 school children, Barchia and Bussey (2010) found that individuals who were frequently peer victimized tended to ruminate more than children who were infrequently victimized; this increased rumination predicted depressive symptoms. Children who were bullied were also less likely to believe that school officials and other individuals could provide support and were therefore less likely to seek support which also predicted increased depressive symptoms.

Anxiety

Anxiety is another consequence of peer victimization. Because anxiety can lead to social withdrawal, it can affect the formation of successful interpersonal relationships, lead to disorders or phobias, and be a precursor to negative self-medication tactics like alcohol or substance abuse (La Greca and Mackey, 2007; Moutier and Stein, 1999). Siegel et al. (2009) examined the short-term longitudinal relationships between peer victimization (i.e., overt, relational, and reputational) and social anxiety in adolescents from November (Time 1) to January (Time 2) of the same school year. They found that all types of peer victimization at Time 1 were associated with social anxiety at Time 2. This relationship was stronger for relational victimization; the more an individual was relationally victimized, the more socially anxious they were. Relational victimization at Time 1 predicted an increase in social anxiety over time but this relationship was stronger for girls than boys. In addition, social anxiety was also a predictor of relational victimization. Anxiety at Time 1 increased the likelihood of being relationally victimized at Time 2.

Again, this pattern of findings suggests that the association between anxiety and peer victimization is bidirectional in nature (La Greca, 2001). Since anxiety, if unchecked, can lead to major depressive disorder, developing intervention techniques might be particularly helpful if employed in anxious victims before depressive symptoms form.

Other Related Negative Outcomes of Peer Victimization

In addition to adjustment problems, being bullied has been associated with other mental health and developmental problems. For example, children (e.g., Idsoe, Dyregrov, and Idsoe, 2012) and adults (e.g., Matthiesen and Einarsen, 2004) who are bullied are more likely to exhibit symptoms of Post-Traumatic Stress Disorder (PTSD) than their counterparts who are not bullied. PTSD was considered to be an anxiety disorder in the DSM-IV-TR (American Psychiatric Association, 2000) and is now listed in the Trauma- and Stressor-Related Disorders section of the DSM-5 (American Psychiatric Association, 2013). PTSD develops after an individual is exposed to an extreme traumatic event (e.g., actual/threatened death, serious injury, sexual violation). Mikkelsen and Einarsen (2002) found that victims of bullying who met all of the diagnostic criteria for PTSD were more likely to report adverse events other than bullying compared to victims of bullying who met some, but not all, of the diagnostic criteria for PTSD.

Although an estimated 29% - 42.6% of victims of bullying meet all diagnostic criteria for PTSD, between 47% - 54.1% of people who were bullied failed to meet A1 diagnostic criterion (i.e., exposure to event(s) that involve actual or threatened death/serious injury or a threat to own or others' physical integrity) but met the other diagnostic criteria for PTSD (Mikkelsen and Einarsen, 2002; Rodríguez-Muñoz et al., 2010). In addition to having more symptoms of PTSD, people who were bullied at work had more negative views of themselves, others, and the world compared to those who were not bullied.

Loneliness is also associated with peer victimization. Loneliness is the feeling experienced when an individual's current peer relationships are thought to be less than what the individual feels they should be (Peplau and Perlman, 1982). Loneliness is predicted by the *perception* of relationship quality rather than the actual quality of relationships (Peplau and Perlman, 1982). The size of the social group is not important, but lower quality friendships are more likely to be associated with feelings of loneliness than are higher quality friendships (Jones, 1982; Parker and Asher, 1993). According to Kochenderfer-Ladd and Wardrop's (2001) longitudinal study of elementary school children, when children were bullied their loneliness increased and social satisfaction decreased over time.

Even children who made the transition from victim to nonvictim did not see a significant decrease in their feelings of loneliness or an increase in their social satisfaction over time. Individuals who were chronically lonely were more likely to have trouble in school or become a delinquent during childhood than those who were not lonely (Brennan, 1982).

Although teachers may attempt to intervene to stop bullying, these interventions are not always perceived as effective and may contribute to children's prolonged feelings of loneliness (Berguno et al., 2004). Loneliness can also be a precursor to a number of psychiatric disorders including Social Anxiety Disorder and Major Depression (American Psychiatric Association, 2000). In addition to increased loneliness, people who are bullied are also more likely to have more suicidal thoughts (Klomek et al., 2008; Rigby and Slee, 1999) and suicide attempts (Hinduja and Patchin, 2010) compared to people who bully others and those who are not bullied.

As briefly reviewed in this section, the association between being bullied and adjustment problems and other negative outcomes has been robustly demonstrated. Moreover, this association is bidirectional such that being bullied predicts further adjustment problems and negative outcomes which in turn is a risk factor for future peer victimization. We suggest that this cyclical relationship is difficult to break, in part, due to the cognitions associated with being bullied and adjustment problems/poor mental health.

Social Cognition and Peer Victimization

In this section, we consider some of the social cognitive biases that may contribute to the cyclical relationship between bullying involvement and negative outcomes. We also review literature demonstrating that social cognition both influences and is affected by social interactions. Social cognition is the study of how people think about others and themselves as well as how they process social situations (Baldwin, 1992; Fiske, 2014, Chapter 3). It is worth noting that social cognition is unlikely to be the only component that affects the link between bullying involvement and adjustment or developmental problems. We focus on social cognition because despite evidence that social cognition affects how we attend to, process, and respond to the general social environment, there is little research examining how being bullied is associated with specific changes in cognitive processing.

Cognitive Biases and Assumptions

People generally want to accurately perceive their world as well as see themselves in a positive and consistent manner (Taylor and Brown, 1988; Taylor and Brown, 1994). However, there are cognitive mechanisms that impede accuracy. These cognitive components may affect the relationship between being bullied and adjustment problems. For example, schemas and scripts affect what information people attend to in the environment and how the information is interpreted (Baldwin, 1992). Schemas are mental representations of objects or categories; scripts are mental representations of situations or events. These schemas and scripts are formed based on a combination of personal experiences and general knowledge. They help people make sense of experiences by creating templates for what to anticipate during a similar experience. Schemas and scripts are especially useful in ambiguous situations to interpret ambiguous information. In the classic "Donald study," Higgins, Rholes, and Jones (1977) primed participants with words to activate either a positive, adventurous schema or a negative, reckless schema. Participants then read a description of Donald and subsequently rated their perception of Donald. Participants who were primed with positive words rated Donald more positively than participants who were primed with negative words. Because all participants read the same description of Donald, these results suggested that schemas influence what information we attend to and how we interpret the information. Over time and situations, people rely on some schemas/scripts more than others (i.e., chronic accessibility; Breckler, Olson, and Wiggins, 2006, Chapter 3).

The way schemas and scripts affect how people attend to and interpret information in the environment is important because this information is used to make attributions about others' behavior and determine one's own behavior. For example, when responding to ambiguous scenarios that could be interpreted as either aggressive/intended to be hurtful or non-aggressive/not meant to be hurtful, children classified as bully-victims (i.e., were both bullied and bully others) were more likely to blame and be angry with the perpetrator and retaliate than children not involved in bullying (Camodeca et al., 2003). Camodeca and colleagues concluded that bully-victims interpreted the cues within the ambiguous scenario as being malicious/hurtful rather than attributing the perpetrator's actions as being accidental/non-hurtful. In contrast, people who are habitually aggressive tended to attribute ambiguous behavior as being aggressive; this tendency is known as the hostile attribution bias (Fiske, 2014, Chapter 10). In play groups of 8-year-old boys, peer victimization was associated with submissive behavior, hostile attribution bias, and reactive aggression (Schwartz et al., 1998). Boys who were bullied also had negative expectations about the outcomes of aggression and assertion. According to Fiske (2014), this tendency to attribute ambiguous behaviors as being aggressive rather than benign is partially a function of people's daily experiences and the schemas/scripts that are developed.

Classical and operant conditioning may also affect the relationship between being bullied and adjustment problems. Classical conditioning occurs when people learn that two events in the environment are associated. A well-known example of classical conditioning is Pavlov's dogs learning to salivate at the sound of a bell. Operant conditioning occurs when people learn that their behavior elicits consequences (i.e., reward or punishment). For example, a child might learn that hitting a playmate leads to being put in time out whereas sharing with a playmate leads to extra playtime. MacDonald, Borsook, and Spielmann (2011) argued that perceived rewards and punishments within social relationships affect people's behaviors. MacDonald et al. suggested that perceived rewards of social interactions could include anticipating comfortable self-disclosure, making new friends, and developing meaningful connections whereas perceived punishments or risks of social interactions could include social anxiety, the potential of not being liked, and being embarrassed. As people who are bullied begin to anticipate negative outcomes from social interactions, they may begin to overestimate the likelihood of further negative outcomes (e.g., rejection) and underestimate the positive outcomes (e.g., acceptance; MacDonald, Borsook, and Spielmann, 2011). Indeed, Storch and Masia-Warner (2004) found that being bullied was correlated with fear of negative evaluation as well as social avoidance and loneliness. In contrast, people who bullied others felt more secure and less anxious when bullying (Batsche and Knoff, 1994). Bullying behaviors are often reinforced through achieving goals (e.g., controlling others, gaining power) or removing threats from others (Batsche and Knoff, 1994; Vaillancourt, Hymel, and McDougall, 2003).

Dual Cognitive Processing Systems and Social Information Processing

There is consensus within the cognitive psychology field that at least two cognitive processing systems exist (Evans, 2008). The rational cognitive processing system (also referred to as the controlled, systematic, or analytic system) is characterized by reason and logic. Processing within this system is conscious, analytical, relatively slow, and effortful (Evans, 2008; Pacini and Epstein, 1999). In contrast, the experiential cognitive processing system (also referred to as the automatic, heuristic, or intuitive system) is characterized by automatic and instinctual responses. Processing within this system is unconscious, intuitive, relatively rapid, implicit, and low effort (Evans, 2008; Pacini and Epstein, 1999). These two processing systems typically operate in a synchronous manner to allow people to adjust to social situations.

In order to understand how people use and process information from social experiences to determine behavioral responses, Crick and Dodge (1994) proposed that social information processing consisted of six steps: (1) encoding the cues from the social interaction, (2) interpreting the cues, (3) clarifying goals, (4) accessing or constructing a response, (5) deciding how to respond, and (6) executing the behavioral response. Crick and Dodge's model accounted for past experiences, social schemas, and knowledge of social rules affecting each step of social processing. Although Crick and Dodge's model is comprised of specific discrete steps in social information processing, much of the research examining how social information is processed during negative social interactions includes multiple steps rather than specific discrete steps. Below we review some of this literature to provide a brief overview of how negative social experiences such as being bullied affect cognitive processing (Bernstein et al., 2008).

Attention to and Interpretation of Social Information

Attention to social cues increases after being socially rejected (Bernstein et al., 2008) and may be an attempt to successfully reestablish social connections (Hess and Pickett, 2010). Individuals who are periodically bullied or excluded from a group were better at interpreting the non-verbal cues of others. For example, people who were periodically bullied were more accurate in assessing facial expressions and emotions compared to people who were not periodically bullied (Bernstein et al., 2010). This heightened awareness of social surroundings suggests that a change in rational cognitive processing may occur due to an individual's willingness to adapt to social situations in order to cope with social rejection. Increased attention to social cues may also be due to an increase in depressive symptoms (which have been shown to reduce rational processing) that often accompanies peer victimization (Gibb et al., 2004; Pacini and Epstein, 1999). Individual differences in rejection sensitivity may also affect how people attend to and process social information, especially in situations where rejection cues are ambiguous. Individuals high on rejection sensitivity anxiously expect, readily perceive, and overreact to rejection (Downey, Feldman, Khuri, and Friedman, 1994; Feldman and Downey, 1994). For example, Downey and Feldman (1996) manipulated feedback provided to participants following a 10-minute interaction with a confederate (participants were expecting a subsequent 5-minute interaction; Study 2). Participants were either told that the confederate did not want to continue the study (i.e., ambiguous rejection information) or that there was not enough time for the second interaction. Individuals high on rejection sensitivity were more likely to report higher levels of perceived rejection compared to people low on rejection sensitivity. Zimmer-Gembeck et al. (2013) also demonstrated that adolescents who overestimated their peer victimization (i.e., had higher self-reported peer victimization compared to their peer-reported peer victimization) were high on rejection sensitivity.

Moreover, the specific types of attributions people make regarding why they are bullied affect the strategies used to cope with being bullied. For example, children who attributed being bullied to their race were less likely to seek out support from friends, whereas boys, but not girls, who attributed being bullied to not being cool were likely to seek support from friends (Visconti, Sechler, and Kockenderfer-Ladd, 2013). In addition, children who attributed being bullied to their own behavior were less likely to attempt to problem solve and more likely to retaliate. The variation in attributions made in response to bullying suggests that emotional cues can trigger a specific set of behavioral response tendencies that differ among individuals (Gross and John, 2003).

Forming and Clarifying Social Goals

In addition to attributions about the intent of behaviors, the broader social goals people have are related to involvement in bullying and how people behave during ambiguous and negative social interactions. For example, Smalley and Banergee (2013) found that low concern about getting along with a perpetrator in ambiguous scenarios was related to physical and relational bullying (even after accounting for affect and attributions). Avoiding the perpetrator was associated with both relational bullying and physical victimization; in addition, submissiveness predicted relational victimization. Rudolph et al. (2011) found that children's broader social goals predicted situation-specific goals. Children who wanted to develop harmonious, high-quality relationships were more likely to report adaptive responses (e.g., want to cooperate and reduce conflict, less likely to want to retaliate and control others), whereas children who wanted to obtain positive judgments were more likely to have maladaptive responses (e.g., less likely to want to cooperate, more likely to want to retaliate and control others).

Behavioral Responses

Involvement in bullying also affects behavioral responses. Researchers have demonstrated that children who are repeatedly bullied often have inappropriate and/or ineffective responses to negative social situations (Crick and Dodge, 1996; Olweus, 1978; Rosen et al., 2007; Schwartz et al., 1993; Schwartz et al., 2001). For example, peer victimized children can engage in behaviors that elicit further victimization (e.g., submissive behaviors, angry but ineffectual retaliation, aggression; Perry et al., 2001; Perry et al., 1990). Boys who responded to provocation by fighting back were more likely to continue to be bullied, whereas boys who had a friend help during provocation were less likely to continue to be bullied (Kochenderfer and Ladd, 1997). In a hypothetical provocative scenario, Camodeca et al. (2003) examined how children responded to situations that clearly involved a perpetrator being intentionally aggressive to a child. Children who were bullied and who bullied others responded in less assertive ways than children who were not involved in bullying (however, no differences were found in use of aggression, help, avoidance, or irrelevant strategies).

There is also evidence that negative self-views predicted social disengagement which in turn predicted interpersonal stress, more negative self-views, and social disengagement (Caldwell, Rudolph, Troop-Gordon, and Kim, 2004). Another common behavioral response, especially among girls, is co-rumination. Co-rumination occurs when two friends repetitively and excessively discuss problems and negative moods (Rose, 2002; Rose, Carlson, and Waller, 2007). Co-rumination is both a protective measure against and a risk factor for adjustment problems. On one hand, co-rumination predicted increased satisfaction in friendships and higher perceived friendship quality. On the other hand, it predicted more symptoms of depression and anxiety, particularly in girls (Rose, Carlson, and Waller, 2007; Stone, Hankin, Gibb, and Abela, 2011). In boys, co-rumination appeared to be indicative of symptoms of depression and anxiety but did not increase these symptoms. Moreover, co-rumination (but not normal self-disclosure of problems) mediated the spread of internalizing problems between friends (Schwartz-Mette and Rose, 2012). Rumination, defined as repetitively thinking about one's negative mood (Smith and Alloy, 2009), is also associated with negative outcomes. For example, rumination predicts future peer victimization, particularly among adolescents who have high levels of depression (Shapero et al., 2013) and is considered to be a risk factor for depression (Erdur-Baker, 2009; Smith and Alloy, 2009).

As reviewed in the above sections, the robust association between peer victimization and negative outcomes is well documented. Given the number of students who are either the recipients or perpetrators of bullying and the negative coping mechanisms employed when individuals are confronted with peer victimization, the next step is to understand and implement systems that can potentially offset the negative consequences.

Bullying Prevention Strategies

Over the last 20 years bullying prevention research has been slow to accumulate in the United States, whereas in Europe, Australia, and Canada, intervention innovation has been addressed for several decades (Swearer, Espelage, and Napolitano, 2009). Despite the large body of work on the description and analysis of bullying issues in many different social contexts, the United States has only recently accumulated enough empirical research to effectively evaluate these US based programs. These evaluations have a potential impact on public policy making and educational programming decisions. However, sound social structures for bullying prevention/intervention are scarce. Even though various state laws have provided some structure to prevent bullying and protect children, each state addresses bullying differently, so uniform policies have not been adopted throughout the education system. This lack of uniform policy leaves huge gaps in services provided for many children involved in bullying across the United States. As a result, many individual schools have been left to create programs without clear guidelines of what to do. Moreover, there are some specific factors that may actually increase bullying in the school environment (Clarke and Kiselica, 1997).

For example, inadequate staffing promotes less than optimal supervision during recreational and instructional periods and prevents adequate monitoring of student behaviors across the school campus. Many schools are very large and the physical structure of the school can contribute to poor monitoring of student behaviors. This is not to suggest that bullying is exclusively a product of large schools and classes, as this hypothesis is not supported by empirical data (e.g., Olweus, 2003). Some schools may actually encourage bullying and violence when they fail to acknowledge that bullying, victimization, and aggression are potential problems. The attitudes and behaviors of principals and teachers are crucial in determining the bullying behaviors that manifest within the school environment (Olweus, 2003). One of the best predictors of implementing school based anti-bullying programs has been the active involvement of teachers as the key agents of change within the school setting (Kallestad and Olweus, 2003). The following section explores a range of evaluated programs and research that provides a glimpse of potential interventions for different social situations. The programs discussed here focus on children in school, because schools act as a microcosm of the larger social framework and are training grounds of social norm development and future behaviors.

Background of Intervention Programs

In the 1970's as a response to increasing societal concerns over bullying problems among school children, Norway introduced the first large scale anti-bullying program. This program was followed by a nation-wide intensive program known as the Olweus Bullying Prevention Program (OBPP) which was implemented and evaluated in the early 1990's (Olweus, 1991). The OBPP is a long term, system-wide program that focuses on change in four key areas of children's lives: the individual level, the classroom level, the school level, and the community level. It builds on principles derived from research on development and identification of problem behaviors, especially aggressive behaviors. The objective of the OBPP program is to substantially reduce, if not eliminate, existing bully/victim issues in and outside the school setting, prevent the development of new bully/victim problems, and improve peer relations among bullies and victims. Rather than concentrating on changing behavior at any one specific level to accomplish these objectives, the criteria focuses on restructuring the social environment. In other words, focusing on protecting the victim only and/or punishing the bully only is not seen as an efficient or effective approach to dealing with bullying issues. The OBPP philosophy includes creating a school (and ideally, a home) environment characterized by warmth, positive interest, and involvement with adults; firm limits on unacceptable behavior; consistent application of non-punitive, non-physical sanctions for unacceptable behavior or violations of rules; and adults who act as authorities and positive role models (Olweus, 1993; 1999; 2004; Olweus and Limber, 2010). By creating specific measures for classroom use and beyond, these concepts have been assessed in multiple ways at the school, classroom, and individual level. The core components of the OBPP include: a) school-level components (e.g., establishing an bullying prevention committee, introduce clear anti-bullying rules, and train committee and staff members), b) individual-level components (e.g., hold meetings with parents of involved children, supervise students' activities, intervene on the spot when bullying occurs, c) classroom-level components (e.g., post and enforce school-wide rules against bullying, hold regular class meetings, and d) community-level components (e.g., help to spread anti-bullying messages and principles of best practice in the community) (Olweus Bullying Prevention Program violencepreventionworks.org, 2014).

The success of these types of programs hinges on restructuring social environments so that opportunity and reward structures for bullying are disrupted (e.g., less prestige or peer support for maintaining negative social behaviors; Olweus, 1992). The OBPP program initially evaluated 2,500 boys and girls in multiple schools and found dramatic reductions in bully/victims problem behaviors by over 50%, (at 20 months after interventions) along with reductions in several anti-social behaviors. School life satisfaction among students increased and overall classroom social climate improved. The OBPP has been tested and refined for over 35 years and has provided a blueprint for anti-bullying programs in other countries, including the United States and has been adapted and implemented in schools, the workplace, and senior living institutions (Olweus, 1993, 1999).

The Sheffield Study

Based on the OBPP philosophy of creating a whole-school policy approach on bullying, the Sheffield Study conducted in the United Kingdom in 1994 found some success in reducing reports of both bullying and being bullied (Smith, 1997). The program was tailored to individual school needs but laid out clear directions from the top level supervision all the way through to individual student and staff levels. Additional measures included reconfiguring playgrounds to facilitate improved staff supervision where required; using videos, stories and drama to instill an anti-bullying ethos across the school; and providing assertiveness training for victims and tolerance training for bullies. Smith and colleagues (1997) assessed 27 different schools (23 intervention groups, 4 control groups, approximately 8, 380 students) and after two years found a 12% decrease in bullying behaviors both at elementary and secondary school levels and a 14% increase in the control schools.

KiVa Program

The KiVa program was designed and developed in Finland in the 1990's to combat growing concerns for the ramifications of bullying even for those who are not directly involved in bullying scenarios (e.g., bystanders or victims' friends) (Salmivalli, Kärnä, and Poskiparta, 2011). As the researchers behind this program development considered bullying a group phenomenon, the program employed a multi-faceted approach to reduce bullying behaviors (Salmivalli et al., 2011). The KiVa anti-bullying program became nationalized in Finland in 2009 and currently about 2700 schools implement it. They utilize student lessons such as discussion, video films, and exercises in dyads. For secondary school children they also include visual learning tools such as video games involving bullying and an Internet forum (KiVa Street) aimed at changing students' attitudes and ultimately preventing bullying. Program evaluation involved studies of different grades and different types of bullying/ victimization behaviors. Researchers found significant reduction in bullying and adjustment problems among perpetrators and targets and reduced negative behaviors in bystanders (Salmivalli, et al., 2011; Williford, Boulton, Noland, Kärnä, Little, and Salmivalli, 2012). As this program took a whole-school approach the researchers concluded that those teachers and schools who were more involved in the program gained more in terms of reducing victimization overall. Due to the program's ongoing success, it has been translated into several different languages, and evaluation and studies of KiVa based programs are ongoing in the United States.

Safety Training

In the United States one particular study found that providing *safety skill training* to third grade students elevated their knowledge of recognizing and increasing their awareness of bullying behaviors and how to prevent being a target and a potential perpetrator of bullying later on (Kid Power Safety Report, 2011). In programs targeting safety skill training, the main themes focus on building self-confidence and self-esteem among children. Children participate in multiple activities to teach positive, practical, and effective ways to deal with personal safety situations including abuse, abduction, and bullying. Some of the core concepts of the programs include how to set clear and appropriate boundaries; how to advocate for oneself and others; how to act aware, remain be calm and confident to help prevent being chosen as a victim; how to take charge of a situation if it becomes threatening or dangerous; how to effectively get help and persist in getting help when needed; how to stop unwanted teasing and touching; and how to create effective safety plans anywhere one goes (Kid Power Safety Report, 2011).

The initial study was conducted with 238 third graders from 14 different elementary schools throughout Santa Cruz, California in 2010. From initial pretest to a 3 month follow up, the study demonstrated that over 31% of students who received safety training had improved safety knowledge versus a control group who did not receive training. These training programs have gained popularity as the core concepts included can be applied in many different social settings.

Kid Power Personal Safety Skills Project of Colorado Springs (2010), an affiliate of Kid Power International, conducted a similar study to evaluate whether a safety training program would be effective in reducing and/or preventing bullying and abuse of developmentally disabled children from K-12 grades over a 3 year period. They concluded that in general, students, parents, and teachers demonstrated greater knowledge of skills relating to personal safety that could be used in multiple settings. By empowering children with revised schemas and scripts of how to behave appropriately, the Kid Power studies have provided evidence that practical school-based safety training programs can enhance resiliency in individuals and groups when dealing with aversive situations.

Steps to Respect Bullying Prevention Program (STR)

Steps to Respect (STR: Committee for Children, 2005) is a school wide bullying prevention program in the United States. First the school administration assesses the bullying/victimization policies and procedures of the school, then *all* adults within the school workforce (including staff from outside the classroom e.g., bus drivers and cafeteria workers) are trained to recognize and deal with bullying when it arises (Committee for Children, 2005). Classroom instruction includes multiple tools for identifying, coping with, and doing something about bullying when/if it occurs. An initial review of the STR program reported a 25% reduction in bullying behaviors and a 31% reduction over a two year period (Frey et al., 2005, 2009). Recently Brown et al. (2011) evaluated the Steps To Respect bullying prevention program and corroborated this program's positive effects on reducing bullying behaviors and improving school social climate within one year of implementation, and teachers reported students were 33% less likely to engage in bullying behaviors than those who did not receive the training.

Multimodal Training

In addition to school and general safety training programs it may also be important to recognize when children are involved in family disruptions. For example, adolescents with divorced parents exhibit higher levels of risky and aggressive behaviors including, but not limited to, bullying (World Health Organization: WHO, 2010). Also, internalizing behaviors such as depression can be a risk factor for becoming a victim of aggression and bullying (Williams, Chambers, Logan, and Robinson, 1996; Williford et al., 2011, 2012). The WHO has emphasized interventions for both parents and children in divorce settings to teach cognitive coping skills, anger control, problem solving, communication skills, and identification and expression of emotions, which in turn fosters social support, and reduces feelings of isolation and loneliness. These factors can often influence positive mental health and reduce risk factors of emotional and behavioral problems. Research has found that these programs assist with reduced depression and behavioral problems one year later (Wolchik et al., 2002). The Good Behavior Game that promotes positive behavior and rule compliance in the classroom showed significant reductions in aggressive behaviors up to five years after the intervention (Kellam, Rebok, Ialongo, and Mayer, 1994). Other programs such as I Can Problem Solve (Shure, 1997) include measures to provide children with cognitive skills such as listening, empathy, interpersonal problem solving, and anger management. These types of programs have improved behaviors for up to one year post intervention. The Child Development Project (Battistich, Schaps, Watson, and Solomon, 1996) provides both children and caregivers with improved behavioral skills to effectively develop prosocial behaviors and has been shown to reduce aggressive behaviors, including bullying, in the school setting.

Youth Matters Prevention Program (YM)

There is substantial evidence that bullying behaviors continue from elementary school to middle school, with some researchers finding stable patterns across the transition (Scholte, Engels, Overbeck, de Kemp, and Haselager, 2007). Conversely, other researchers have found a decrease during the latter two years of elementary school and then a fluctuation throughout the middle school years (Nylund, Bellmore, Nishina and Graham, 2007; Schäfer, Korn, Brodbeck, Wolke and Schulz, 2005; Williford, Brisson, Bender, Jenson, and Forrest-Bank, 2011). Youth Matters is a school-based bullying prevention program that builds training modules into the curriculum with interactive instruction to teach upper elementary school students skills for dealing with bullying in and out of school.

By developing important social competency skills and resistance to bullying techniques, YM emphasizes the negative impact of bullying behaviors while attempting to strengthen peer and social norms against them (Jenson and Dieterich, 2007). One evaluation of the program assessed the transitional bullying effects on students in grades 4-6 and found children involved in bullying did indeed show positive effects of the YM program especially in the first year of intervention (grade 4) and during the first year of middle school (grade 6)

(Jensen, Brisson, Bender, and Williford, 2013). Anti-bullying programs may be particularly effective during the latter years of elementary school by providing children with more information and tools to reduce aggression and bullying as they transition into very diverse and often overwhelming school and peer environments.

What the Evidence Suggests

In 2008, Merrell, Gueldner, Ross, and Isava conducted an exploratory meta-analysis of a variety of intervention programs from Europe and the United States spanning a 25 year period. Overall, they found very weak effect sizes for successful bullying interventions suggesting that these programs are more likely to influence knowledge, attitudes, and perceptions rather than specific bullying behaviors. Recently, Ttofi and Farrington (2011) conducted a meta-analysis on the effectiveness of 53 different international school based programs aimed at reducing bullying among children from kindergarten to high school. Again, the results provide a mixed picture on the success of many anti-bullying programs. Overall, Ttofi and Farrington concluded that on average bullying decreased by 20 - 23% with successful programs. The effects were highest in age cohort designs and lowest in randomized experiments (potentially due to validity problems).

A continued dilemma exists over what works and why. Since this research is difficult to conduct and compare due to the vast differences among education systems, there will be a continued challenge to find, evaluate, and implement solid programs that make a difference in the bullying phenomenon. However, the overarching message suggested is that school based anti-bullying programs can be effective depending on the intensity, duration, and types of elements they engage. Ttofi and Farrington concluded that programs influenced by Dan Olweus were the most successful. Those that were more intensive programs that included different social groups such as meetings with parents, improved playground supervision, and firm, consistent disciplinary methods were associated with decreased bullying. Conversely, work with peers (such as peer mentoring, peer mediation and encouraging bystander intervention) was associated with an increase in bullying behaviors.

Bullying is increasingly being considered as a group process that is enabled by many individuals in addition to the specific victims and perpetrators (e.g., Craig, Pepler, and Blais, 2007) and highlights the need for adults to support students in dealing with ongoing bullying issues. As a response, more holistic intervention programs are being considered and implemented. The whole-school approach seems to be drawing more attention, but in the United States one still has to consider the vast cultural, socioeconomic, and ideological differences that exist across the nation – a one size fits all approach will not likely be successful if planners, policymakers, and education decision makers do not recognize these individual differences and tailor programs accordingly (Smith, Schneider, Smith, and Ananiado, 2004).

However, a consistent factor across successful programs is effective and sufficient training of adults who are responsible for initiating and carrying out bullying prevention programs. Any substantial success with anti-bullying programs requires strong consistency and conviction of implementation from the administration all the way through the school environment to bus drivers and caretakers (Durlak and DuPre, 2008; Low, Van Ryzin, Brown, Smith, and Haggerty, 2013). In sum, programs that approach bullying prevention comprehensively while still acknowledging the unique needs of individuals in differing environments are the most effective (Clark and Kiselica, 1997; Espelage and Swearer, 2003: Olweus, 1991). Without full understanding, cooperation, and oversight from all involved, these programs will reap only moderate - if any - results at reducing or eliminating the bullying behaviors that exist in the school and beyond.

Conclusion

As we have documented, there are multiple psychological and cognitive factors affecting children's and adults' socialization when exposed to peer victimization. Those individuals who are left to manage such aversive situations on their own may be prone to mental health issues later in life including anxiety, depression, and suicide ideation. It is not only important to recognize these potential issues but also to determine best practices for reducing or eliminating the effects. Comprehensive and consistent interference in environments that support bullying is required, and strong support of those individuals who are both recipients and perpetrators are key factors in reducing or eliminating bullying behaviors.

References

American Psychiatric Association (2000). *Diagnostic and statistical manual of mental disorders* (4th Ed.). Washington, DC: American Psychiatric Publishing.

American Psychiatric Association. (2013). *Diagnostic and statistical manual of mental disorders* (5th Ed.). Arlington, VA: American Psychiatric Publishing.

Baldwin, M. W. (1992). Relational schemas and the processing of social information. *Psychological Bulletin*, 112(3), 461-484. doi: 10.1037/0033-2909.112.3.461.

Barchia, K. and Bussey, K. (2010). The psychological impact of peer victimization: Exploring social-cognitive mediators of depression. *Journal of Adolescence*, 33(5), 615-623. doi: 10.1016/j.adolescence.2009.12.002.

Batsche, G. M. and Knoff, H. M. (1994). Bullies and their victims: Understanding a pervasive problem in the schools. *National Association of School Psychologist*, 23(2), 165-174.

Battistich, V., Schaps, E., Watson, M., and Solomon, D. (1996). Prevention effects of the child development project: Early findings from an ongoing multisite demonstration trial. *Journal of Adolescent Research*, 11(1), 12-35. doi: 10.1177/0743554896111003.

Baumeister, R. F. and Leary, M. R. (1995). The need to belong: Desire for interpersonal attachments as a fundamental human motivation. *Psychological Bulletin*, 117(3), 497-529. doi: 10.1037/0033-2909.117.3.497.

Beck, A. T. (1987). Cognitive models of depression. *Journal of Cognitive Psychotherapy: An International Quarterly*, 1, 5-37.

Benjet, C., Thompson, R. J. and Gotlib, I. H. (2010). 5-HTTLPR moderates the effect of relational peer victimization on depressive symptoms in adolescent girls. *Journal of Child Psychology and Psychiatry*, 51(2), 173-179. doi: 10.1111/j.1469-7610.2009.02149.x.

Berguno, G., Leroux, P., McAinsh, K., and Shaikh, S. (2004). Children's experience of loneliness at school and its relation to bullying and the quality of teacher interventions. *The Qualitative Report*, 9(3), 483-499.

Bernstein, M. J., Sacco, D. F., Brown, C. M., Young, S. G., and Claypool, H. M. (2010). A preference for genuine smiles following social exclusion. *Journal of Experimental Social Psychology,* 46(1), 196-199. doi: 10.1016/j.jesp.2009.08.010.

Bernstein, M. J., Young, S. G., Brown, C. M., Sacco, D. F., and Claypool, H. M. (2008). Adaptive responses to social exclusion: Social rejection improves detection of real and fake smiles. *Psychological Science,* 19(10), 981-983. doi: 10.1111/j.1467-9280.2008.02187.x.

Breckler, S. J., Olson, J. and Wiggins, E. (2006). *Social psychology alive.* Belmont, CA: Wadsworth.

Brennan, T. (1982). Loneliness at adolescence. In: L. A. Peplau and D. Perlman (Eds.), *Loneliness: A sourcebook of current theory, research and therapy* (pp. 269-290). New York: Wiley.

Brown, E. C., Low, S., Smith, B. H., and Haggerty, K. P. (2011). Outcomes of a randomized controlled trial of Steps to Respect: A bullying prevention program. *School Psychology,* 40(3), 423-443.

Caldwell, M. S., Rudolph, K. D., Troop-Gordon, W., and Kim, D. (2004). Reciprocal influences among relational self-views, social disengagement, and peer stress during early adolescence. *Child Development,* 75(4), 1140-1154. doi: 10.1111/j.1467-8624.2004.00730.x.

Camodeca, M., Goossens, F. A., Schuengel, C., and Terwogt, M. M. (2003). Links between social information processing in middle childhood and involvement in bullying. *Aggressive Behavior,* 29(2), 116-127. doi: 10.1002/ab.10043.

Chan, Y. F., Dennis, M. L. and Funk, R. R. (2008). Prevalence and comorbidity of major internalizing and externalizing problems among adolescents and adults presenting to substance abuse treatment. *Journal of Substance Abuse Treatment,* 34(1), 14-24. doi: 10.1016/j.jsat.2006.12.031.

Cicchetti, D. and Toth, S. L. (1991). *Internalizing and externalizing expressions of dysfunction* (Volume 2). New York, NY: Lawrence Earlbaum Associates, Inc.

Clarke, E. A. and Kiselica, M. S. (1997). A systemic counseling approach to the problem of bullying. *Elementary School Guidance and Counseling,* 31(4), 310-326.

Committee for Children (2005). *Steps to Respect: A Bullying Prevention Program.* Seattle, WA.

Craig, W., Pepler, D. and Blais, J. (2007). Responding to bullying: What works? *School Psychology International,* 28(4), 465-477. doi: 10.1177/0143034307084136.

Crick, N. R. and Dodge, K. A. (1996). Social information-processing mechanisms in reactive and proactive aggression. *Child Development,* 67(3), 993-1002. doi: 10.2307/1131875.

Dodge, K. A. and Pettit, G. S. (2003). A biopsychosocial model of the development of chronic conduct problems in adolescence. *Developmental Psychology,* 39(2), 349-371. doi: 10.1037/0012-1649.39.2.349.

Downey, G. and Feldman, S. (1996). Implications of rejection sensitivity for intimate relationships. *Journal of Personality and Social Psychology,* 70(6), 1327-1343. doi: 10.1037/0022-3514.70.6.1327.

Downey, G., Feldman, S., Khuri, J., and Friedman, S. (1994). Maltreatment and child depression. In: W. M. Reynolds and H. F. Johnson (Eds.), *Handbook of depression in children and adolescents* (pp. 481-508). New York, NY: Plenum.

Durlak, J. A. and DuPre, E. P. (2008). Implementation matters: A review of research on the influence of implementation on program outcomes and the factors affecting implementation. *American Journal of Community Psychology,* 41(3-4), 327-350. doi: 10. 1007/s10464-008-9165-0.

Eisenberg, N., Guthrie, I. K., Fabes, R. A., Shepard, S., Losoya, S., Murphy, B., ... and Reiser, M. (2000). Prediction of elementary school children's externalizing problem behaviors from attentional and behavioral regulation and negative emotionality. *Child Development,* 71(5), 1367-1382. doi: 10.1111/1467-8624.00233.

Erdur-Baker, O. (2009). Peer victimization, rumination, and problem solving as risk contributors to adolescents' depressive symptoms. *Journal of Psychology,* 143(1), 78-90, doi: 10.3200/JRLP.143.1.78-90.

Espelage, D. L. and Swearer, S. M. (2003). Research on school bullying and victimization: What have we learned and where do we go from here? *School Psychology Review,* 32, 365-384.

Evans, J. S. B. T. (2008). Dual-processing accounts of reasoning, judgment, and social cognition. *Annual Review of Psychology,* 59, 255-278. doi: 10.1146/annurev.psych.59. 103006.093629.

Feldman, S. and Downey, G. (1994). Rejection sensitivity as a mediator of the impact of childhood exposure to family violence on adult attachment behavior. *Development and Psychopathology,* 6(1), 231-247. doi: 10.1017/S0954579400005976.

Fiske, S. T. (2014). *Social beings: Core motives in social psychology.* (3rd Ed). New York, NY: Wiley.

Fox, C. L. and Boulton, M. J. (2005). The social skills problems of victims of bullying: Self, peer, and teacher perceptions. *British Journal of Educational Psychology,* 75(2), 313-328. doi: 10.1348/000709905X25517.

Frey, K. S., Hirschstein, M., Edstrom, L., and Snell, J. (2009). Observed reductions in school bullying, non-bullying aggression, and destructive bystander behavior: A longitudinal evaluation. *Journal of Educational Psychology, 101*(2), 466-481.

Frey, K. S., Hirschstein, M., Snell, J. L., Edstrom, L. V., MacKenzie, E. P., and Broderick, C. J. (2005). Reducing playground bullying and supporting beliefs: An experimental trial of the *Steps to Respect* program. *Developmental Psychology, 41*(3), 479-491. doi: 10.1037/ 0012-1649.41.3.479.

Gibb, B. E., Abramson, L. Y. and Alloy, L. B. (2004). Emotional maltreatment from parents, verbal peer victimization, and cognitive vulnerability to depression. *Cognitive Therapy and Research,* 28(1), 1-21. doi: 10.1023/B:COTR.0000016927.18027.c2.

Gladstone, G. L., Parker, G. B. and Malhi, G. S. (2006). Do bullied children become anxious and depressed adults? A cross sectional investigation of the correlates of bullying and anxious depression. *The Journal of Nervous and Mental Disease,* 194(3), 201-208. doi: 10.1097/01.nmd.0000202491.99719.c3.

Gross, J. J. and John, O. P. (2003). Individual differences in two emotion regulation processes: Implications for affect, relationships, and well-being. *Journal of Personality and Social Psychology,* 85(2), 348-362. doi: 10.1037/0022-3514.85.2.348.

Hawker, D. S. and Boulton, M. J. (2000). Twenty years' research on peer victimization and psychosocial maladjustment: A meta-analytic review of cross-sectional studies. *Journal of Child Psychology and Psychiatry,* 41(4), 441-455. doi: 10.1111/1469-7610.00629.

Hess, Y. D. and Pickett, C. L. (2010). Social rejection and self- versus other-awareness. *Journal of Experimental Social Psychology,* 46(2), 453-456. doi: 10.1016/j.jesp.2009.12.004.

Higgins, E. T., Rholes, W. T. and Jones, C. R. (1977). Category accessibility and impression formation. *Journal of Experimental Social Psychology,* 13(2), 141-154. doi: 10.1016/S0022-1031(77)80007-3.

Hinduja, S. and Patchin, J. W. (2010). Bullying, cyberbullying, and suicide. *Archives of Suicide Research,* 14(3), 206-221. doi: 10.1080/13811118.2010.494133.

Idsoe, T., Dyregrov, A. and Idsoe, E. C. (2012). Bullying and PTSD symptoms. *Journal of Abnormal Child Psychology,* 40(6), 901-911. doi: 10.1007/s10802-012-9620-0.

Jensen, J. M., Brisson, D., Bender, K. A., and Williford, A. P. (2013). Effects of the *Youth Matters Prevention Program* on patterns of bullying and victimization in elementary and middle school. *Social Work Research,* 37(4), 361-372. doi: 10.1093/swr/svt030.

Jenson, J. M. and Dieterich, W. A. (2007). Effects of a skills-based prevention program on bullying and bully victimization among elementary school children. *Prevention Science,* 8(4), 285-296. doi: 10.1007/s11121-007-0076-3.

Jones, W. H. (1982). Loneliness and social behavior. In: L. A. Peplau and D. Perlman (Eds.), *Loneliness: A sourcebook of current theory, research and therapy* (pp. 238-252). New York: Wiley.

Kallestad, J. H. and Olweus, D. (2003). Predicting teachers' and schools' implementation of the Olweus Bullying Prevention Program: A multilevel study. *Prevention and Treatment,* 6(1), 21a. doi: 10.1037/1522-3736.6.1.621a.

Kellam, S., Rebok, G., Ialongo, N., and Mayer, L. (1994). The course and malleability of aggressive behavior from early first grade into middle school: Results of a developmental epidemiologically-based preventive trial. *Journal of Child Psychology and Psychiatry and Allied Disciplines,* 35(2), 259-281. doi: 10.1111/j.1469-7610.1994.tb01161.x.

Kid Power Safety Report. (2011). *The effects of Kid Power everyday safety skills program on third grade children in Santa Cruz County*. California: Shattuck Applied Research and Evaluation.

Kid Power Personal Safety Skills Project. (2010). (Report). Denver, CO: JVA Consulting.

Klomek, A. B., Marrocco, F., Kleinman, M., Schonfeld, I. S., and Gould, M. S. (2008). Peer victimization, depression, and suicidality in adolescents. *Suicide and Life Threatening Behavior,* 38(2), 166-180. doi: 10.1521/suli.2008.38.2.166.

Kochenderfer, B. J. and Ladd, G. W. (1997). Victimized children's responses to peers' aggression: Behaviors associated with reduced versus continued victimization. *Development and Psychopathology*, 9(1), 59-73. doi: 10.1017/S0954579497001065.

Kochenderfer-Ladd, B. and Skinner, K. (2002). Children's coping strategies: Moderators of the effects of peer victimization. *Developmental Psychology,* 38(2), 267-278. doi: 10.1037/0012-1649.38.2.267.

Kochenderfer-Ladd, B. and Wardrop, J. (2001). Chronicity and instability of children's peer victimization experiences as predictors of loneliness and social satisfaction trajectories. *Child Development,* 72(1), 134-151. doi: 10.1111/1467-8624.00270.

La Greca, A. M. (2001). The peer group: Friends or foes? In: W. K. Silverman and P. A. Treffers (Eds.), *Anxiety disorders in children: Theory, research and practice*. London: Cambridge University Press.

La Greca, A. M. and Mackey, E. R. (2007). Adolescents' anxiety in dating situations: The potential role of friends and romantic partners. *Journal of Clinical Child and Adolescent Psychology,* 36(4), 522-533. doi: 10.1080/15374410701662097.

La Greca, A. M. and Prinstein, M. J. (1999). The peer group. In: W. K. Silverman and T. H. Ollendick (Eds.), *Developmental issues in the clinical treatment of children and adolescents* (pp. 171-198). Needham Heights, MA: Allyn and Bacon.

Laird, R. D., Jordan, K. Y., Dodge, K. A., Pettit, G. S., and Bates, J. E. (2001). Peer rejection in childhood, involvement with antisocial peers in early adolescence, and the development of externalizing behavior problems. *Development and Psychopathology,* 13 (2), 337-354. doi: 10.1017/S0954579401002085.

Leahy, R. L. (2002). An investment model of depressive resistance. In: R. L. Leahy and E. T. Dowd (Eds.), *Clinical advances in cognitive psychotherapy: Theory and application* (pp. 170-188). New York, NY: Springer Publishing Company, Inc.

Low, S., Van Ryzin, M. J., Brown, E. C., Smith, B. H., and Haggerty, K. P. (2014). Engagement matters: lessons from assessing classroom implementation of Steps to Respect: a bullying prevention program over a one-year period. *Prevention Science,* 15 (2), 165-176.doi: 10.1007/s11121-012-0359-1.

Lund, R., Nielsen, K. K., Hansen, D. H., Kriegbaum, M., Molbo, D., Due, P., Christensen, U. (2009). Exposure to bullying at school and depression in adulthood: A study of danish men born in 1953. *European Journal of Public Health,* 19(1), 111-116. doi: 10.1093/ eurpub/ckn101.

MacDonald, G., Borsook, T. K. and Spielmann, S. S. (2011) Defensive avoidance of social pain via perceptions of social threat and reward. In: G. MacDonald and L. A. Jensen-Campbell (Eds.), *Social pain: Neuropsychological and health implications of loss and exclusion* (pp. 141-160). Washington, DC: American Psychological Association.

Matthiesen, S. B. and Einarsen, S. (2004). Psychiatric distress and symptoms of PTSD among victims of bullying at work. *British Journal of Guidance and Counseling,* 32(3), 335-356. doi: 10.1080/03069880410001723558.

Merrell, K. W., Gueldner, B. A., Ross, S. W., and Isava, D. M. (2008). How effective are school bullying intervention programs? A meta-analysis of intervention research. *School Psychology Quarterly,* 23(1), 26-42. doi 10.1037/1045-3830.23.1.26.

Mikkelsen, E. G. and Einarsen, S. (2002). Basic assumptions and symptoms of post-traumatic stress among victims of bullying at work. *European Journal of Work and Organizational Psychology,* 11, 87-111. Doi: 10.1080/13594320143000861.

Moutier, C. Y. and Stein, M. B. (1999). The history, epidemiology, and differential diagnosis of social anxiety disorder. *The Journal of Clinical Psychiatry,* 60(9), 4-8.

Nylund, K., Bellmore, A., Nishina, A., and Graham, S. (2007). Subtypes, severity, and structural stability of peer victimization: What does latent class analysis say? *Child Development,* 78(6), 1706-1722. doi: 10.1111/j.1467-8624.2007.01097.x.

Ollendick, T. H. and King, N. J. (1994). Diagnosis, assessment, and treatment of internalizing problems in children: The role of longitudinal data. *Journal of Consulting and Clinical Psychology,* 62(5), 918-927. doi: 10.1037/0022-006X.62.5.918.

Olson, S. L., Schilling, E. M. and Bates, J. E. (1999). Measurement of impulsivity: Construct coherence, longitudinal stability, and relationship with externalizing problems in middle childhood and adolescence. *Journal of Abnormal Child Psychology,* 27(2), 151-165. doi: 10.1023/A:1021915615677.

Olweus, D. (1978). Aggression in the schools: Bullies and their whipping boys. *European Journal of Psychology,* 10(1), 101.

Olweus, D. (1991). Bully/victim problems among schoolchildren: Basic facts and effects of a school based intervention program. In: D. J. Pepler and K. H. Rubin (Eds.), *The development and treatment of childhood aggression* (pp. 411-448). Hillside, NJ: Erlbaum.

Olweus, D. (1992). Bullying among schoolchildren: Intervention and prevention. In: R. D. Peters, R. J. McMahon and V. L. Quincy (Eds). *Aggression and violence throughout the lifespan.* Newbury Park, CA: Sage.

Olweus, D. (1993). *Bullying at school: What we know and what we can do*. Cambridge, MA: Blackwell Publishing.

Olweus, D. (1999). Norway. In: P. K. Smith, Y. Morita, J. Junger-Tas, D. Olweus, R. Catalano, and P. Slee (Eds.), *The nature of school bullying: A cross-national perspective* (pp. 28-48). New York, NY: Routledge.

Olweus, D. (2003). A profile of bullying at school. *Educational leadership*, 60(6), 12-17.

Olweus, D. (2004). Bullying at school: Prevalence estimation, a useful evaluation design, and a new national initiative in Norway. *Association for Child Psychology and Psychiatry Occasional Papers*, 23, 5-17.

Olweus, D. and Limber, S. P. (2010). Bullying in school: Evaluation and dissemination of the Olweus bullying prevention program. *American Journal of Orthopsychiatry,* 80(1), 124-134. doi: 10.1111/j.1939-0025.2010.01015.x.

Olweus Bullying Prevention Program (n.d). Retrieved on May 12, 2014 from http://www.violencepreventionworks.org/public/olweus_scope.page.

Pacini, R. and Epstein, S. (1999). The relation of rational and experiential information processing styles to personality, basic beliefs, and the ratio-bias phenomenon. *Journal of Personality and Social Psychology,* 76(6), 972-987. doi: 10.1037/0022-3514.76.6.972.

Parker, J. G. and Asher, S. R. (1993). Friendship and friendship quality in middle childhood: Links with peer group acceptance and feelings of loneliness and social dissatisfaction. *Developmental Psychology,* 29(4), 611-621. doi:10.1037/0012-1649.29.4.611.

Peplau, L. A. and Perlman, D. (1982). Perspectives on loneliness. In: L. A. Peplau and D. Perlman (Eds.), *Loneliness: A sourcebook of current theory, research and therapy* (pp. 1-18). New York: Wiley.

Perren, S., Ettekal, I. and Ladd, G. (2013). The impact of peer victimization on later maladjustment: Mediating and moderating effects of hostile and self-blaming attributions. *Journal of Child Psychology and Psychiatry,* 54(1), 46-55. doi: 10.1111/j.1469-7610.2012.02618.x.

Perry, D., Hodges, E. and Egan, S. (2001). Determinants of chronic victimization by peers: A review and a new model of family influence. In: J. Juvionen and S. Graham (Eds.), *Peer harassment in school: The plight of the vulnerable and victimized* (pp. 73-104). New York, NY: Guilford Press.

Perry, D. G., Perry, L. C. and Boldizar, J. P. (1990). Learning of aggression. In: *Handbook of developmental psychopathology* (pp. 135-146). Springer US.

Prinstein, M. J., Rancourt, D., Guerry, J. D., and Browne, C. B. (2009). Peer reputations and psychological adjustment. In: K. H. Rubin, W. M. Bukowski and B. P. Laursen (Eds.), *Handbook of peer interactions, relationships, and groups* (pp. 548-567). New York, NY: Guilford Press.

Rigby, K. (2000). Effects of peer victimization in schools and perceived social support on adolescent well-being. *Journal of Adolescence,* 23(1), 57-68. doi: 10.1006/jado.1999. 0289.

Rigby, K. and Slee, P. (1999). Suicidal ideation among adolescent school children, involvement in bully-victim problems, and perceived social support. *Suicide and Life Threatening Behavior,* 29(2), 119-130. doi: 10.1111/j.1943-278X.1999.tb01050.x.

Rodriguez-Muñoz, A., Moreno-Jimenez, B., Sanz Vergel, A. I., and Hernandez, E. G. (2010). Post-traumatic symptoms among victims of workplace bullying: Exploring gender differences and shattered assumptions. *Journal of Applied Social Psychology,* 40 (10), 2616-2635. doi: 10.1111/j.1559-1816.2010.00673.x.

Rose, A. J. (2002). Co-rumination in the friendships of girls and boys. *Child Development,* 73 (6), 1830-1843. doi: 10.1111/1467-8624.00509.

Rose, A. J., Carlson, W. and Waller, E. M. (2007). Prospective associations of co-rumination with friendship and emotional adjustment: Considering the socioemotional trade-offs of co-rumination. *Developmental Psychology,* 43(4), 1019-1031. doi : 10.1037/0012-1649. 43.4.1019.

Rosen, P. J., Milich, R. and Harris, J. M. (2007). Victims of their own cognitions: Implicit social cognitions, emotional distress, and peer victimization. *Journal of Applied Developmental Psychology,* 28(3), 211-226. doi: 10.1016/j.appdev.2007.02.001.

Rudolph, K. D., Abaied, J. L., Flynn, M., Sugimura, N., and Agoston, A. M. (2011). Developing relationships, being cool, and not looking like a loser: Social goal orientation predicts children's responses to peer aggression. *Child Development,* 82(5), 1518-1530. doi: 10.1111/j.1467-8624.2011.01631.x.

Salmivalli, C., Kärnä, A. and Poskiparta, E. (2011). Counteracting bullying in Finland: The KiVa program and its effects on different forms of being bullied. *International Journal of Behavioral Development,* 35(5), 405-411. doi 10.1177/0165025411407457.

Schäfer, M., Korn, S., Brodbeck, F. C., Wolke, D., and Schulz, H. (2005). Bullying roles in changing contexts: The stability of victim and bully roles from primary to secondary school. *International Journal of Behavioral Development,* 29(4), 323-335. doi: 10.1177/ 01650250544000107.

Scholte, R. H., Engels, R., Overbeek, G., de Kemp, R., and Haselager, G. (2007). Stability in bullying and victimization and its association with social adjustment in childhood and adolescence. *Journal of Abnormal Child Psychology,* 35(2), 217-228. doi: 10.1007/s 10802-006-9074-3.

Schwartz, D., Dodge, K. A. and Coie, J. D. (1993). The emergence of chronic peer victimization in boys' play groups. *Child Development,* 64(6), 1755-1772. doi: 10.1111/j. 1467-8624.1993.tb04211.x.

Schwartz, D., Dodge, K. A. and Coie, J. D., Hubbard, J. A., Cillessen, A. H. N., Lemerise, E. A., and Bateman, H. (1998). Social-cognitive and behavioral correlates of aggression and victimization in boys' play groups. *Journal of Abnormal Child Psychology,* 26(6), 431-440. doi: 10.1023/A:1022695601088.

Schwartz, D., Proctor, L. and Chien, D. (2001). The aggressive victim of bullying: Emotional and behavioral dysregulation as a pathway to victimization by peers. In: J. Juvonen and S. Graham (Eds.), *Peer harassment in school: The plight of the vulnerable and victimized* (pp. 147-174) New York, NY: Guilford Press.

Schwartz-Mette, R. A. and Rose, A. J. (2012). Co-rumination mediates contagion of internalizing symptoms within youths' friendships. *Developmental Psychology,* 48(5), 1355-1365. doi: 10.1037/a0027484.

Shapero, B. G., Hamilton, J. L., Liu, R. T., Abramson, L. Y., and Alloy, L. B. (2013). Internalizing symptoms and rumination: The prospective prediction of familial and peer emotional victimization experiences during adolescence. *Journal of Adolescence,* 36(6), 1067-1076. doi: 10.1016/j.adolescence.2013.08.011.

Shure, M. B. (1997). Interpersonal cognitive problem solving: Primary prevention of early high-risk behaviors in the preschool and primary years: In: G. W. Albee and T. P. Gullotta (Eds.), *Primary prevention works. Issues in children's and families' lives.* (Voume 6). Thousand Oaks, CA: Sage Publications, Inc.

Siegel, R. S., La Greca, A. M. and Harrison, H. M. (2009). Peer victimization and social anxiety in adolescents: prospective and reciprocal relationships. *Journal of Youth and Adolescence,* 38(8), 1096-1109. doi: 10.1007/s10964-009-9392-1.

Smalley, D. and Banerjee, R. (2013). The role of social goals in bullies' and victims' social information processing in response to ambiguous and overtly hostile provocation. *Social Development,* doi: 10.1111/sode.12067.

Smith, J. D., Schneider, B. H., Smith, P. K., and Ananiadou, K. (2004). The effectiveness of whole-school bullying programs: A synthesis of evaluation research. *School Psychology Review,* 33(4), 547-560.

Smith, J. M. and Alloy, L. B. (2009). A roadmap to rumination: A review of the definition, assessment, and conceptualization of this multifaceted construct. *Clinical Psychology Review,* 29(2), 116-128. doi: 10.1016/j.cpr.2008.10.003.

Smith, P. (1997). Bullying in schools: The UK experience and the Sheffield anti-bullying project. *Irish Journal of Psychology,* 18(2), 191-201. doi: 10.1080/03033910.1997.10558139.

Stone, L. B., Hankin, B. L., Gibb, B. E., and Abela, J. R. Z. (2011). Co-rumination predicts the onset of depressive disorders during adolescence. *Journal of Abnormal Psychology,* 120(3), 752-757. doi: 10.1037/a0023384.

Storch, E. and Masia-Warner, C. (2004). The relationship of peer victimization to social anxiety and loneliness in adolescent females. *Journal of Adolescence,* 27(3), 351-362. doi: 10.1016/j.adolescence.2004.03.003.

Swearer, S. M., Espelage, D. L. and Napolitano, S. A. (2009). *Bullying prevention and intervention: Realistic strategies for schools.* New York, NY: Guilford Press.

Taylor, S. E. and Brown, J. D. (1988). Illusion and well-being: A social psychological perspective on mental health. *Psychological Bulletin,* 103(2), 193-210. doi: 10.1037/0033-2909.103.2.193.

Taylor, S. E. and Brown, J. D. (1994). Positive illusions and well-being revisited: Separating fact from fiction. *Psychological Bulletin,* 116(1), 21-27. doi: 10.1037/0033-2909.116.1.21

Troop-Gordon, W. and Ladd, G. W. (2005). Trajectories of peer victimization and perceptions of the self and schoolmates: precursors to internalizing and externalizing problems. *Child Development,* 76(5), 1072-1091. doi:10.1111/j.1467-8624.2005.00898.x.

Ttofi, M. and Farrington, D. P. (2011). Effectiveness of school-based programs to reduce bullying: A systematic and meta-analytic review. *Journal of Experimental Criminology,* 7 (1), 27-56. doi 10.1007/s11292-010-9109-1.

Vaillancourt, T., Hymel, S. and McDougall, P. (2003). Bullying is power: Implications for school-based intervention strategies. *Journal of Applied School Psychology,* 19(2), 157-176. doi: 10.1300/J008v19n02_10.

Van der Wal, M. F., de Wit, C. A. M. and Hirasing, R. A. (2003). Psychosocial health among young victims and offenders of direct and indirect bullying. *Pediatrics,* 111(6), 1312-1317.

Visconti, K. J., Sechler, C. M. and Kochenderfer-Ladd, B. (2013). Coping with peer victimization: The role of children's attributions. *School Psychology Quarterly.* 28(2), 122-140. doi: 10.1037/spq0000014.

Williams, K., Chambers, M., Logan, S., and Robinson, D. (1996). Association of common health symptoms with bullying in primary school children. *British Medical Journal,* 313 (7048), 17-19.

Williford, A., Boulton, A., Noland, B., Kärnä, A., Little, T., and Salmivalli, C. (2012). Effects of the kiva anti-bullying program on adolescents' depression, anxiety, and perception peers. *Journal of Abnormal Child Psychology,* 40(2), 289-300. doi: 10.1007/s10802-011-9551-1.

Williford, A. P., Brisson, D., Bender, K. A., Jenson, J. M., and Forrest-Bank, S. (2011). Patterns of aggressive behavior and peer victimization from childhood to early adolescence: A latent class analysis. *Journal of Youth and Adolescence*, 40(6), 644-655. doi: 10.1007/s10964-010-9583-9.

World Health Organization (2010). *Prevention of mental disorders: effective interventions and policy options: A report of the World Health Organization Department of Mental Health and Substance Abuse in collaboration with the Prevention Research Centre of the Universities of Nijmegen and Maastricht.* World Health Organization.

Wolchik, S. A., Sandler, I. N., Millsap, R. E., Plummer, B. A., Greene, S. M., Anderson, E. R., ... and Haine, R. A. (2002). Six-year follow-up of preventive interventions for children of divorce: A randomized controlled trial. *Journal of American Medical Association*, 288(15), 1874-1881. doi: 10.1001/jama.288.15.1874.

Zimmer-Gembeck, M. J., Nesdale, D., McGregor, L., Mastro, S., Goodwin, B., and Downey, G. (2013). Comparing reports of peer rejection: Associations with rejection sensitivity, victimization, aggression, and friendship. *Journal of Adolescence,* 36(6), 1237-1264. doi: 10.1016/j.adolescence.2013.10.002.

Zwierzynska, K., Wolke, D. and Lereya, T. (2013). Peer victimization in childhood and internalizing problems in adolescence: a prospective longitudinal study. *Journal of Abnormal Child Psychology,* 41(2), 309-323. doi: 10.1007/s10802-012-9678-8.

In: Handbook on Bullying
Editor: Phoebe Triggs

ISBN: 978-1-63463-023-8

Chapter 2

BULLYING AMONG MALE ATHLETES: A CONTEXTUAL EXAMINATION

Jesse A. Steinfeldt, Ph.D.*, Nicole T. Gabana, M.S. and Matthew D. Powless, M.S.
Indiana University-Bloomington, Bloomington, Indiana, US

Abstract

As witnessed in popular media, reports of violence and aggression-both on and off the field-is often associated with athletes such as football players. The emphasis on these reports creates a skewed perception of male athletes, and subsequently the non-violent behavior of countless other male athletes is often discounted and ignored. Nonetheless, there is evidence to suggest that male athletes may be more likely to engage in violence than their non-athlete male peers (Kreager, 2007; Messner, and Sabo, 1994; Mutz, 2012). Research aimed at studying this phenomenon has suggested that there is, "a continuum of physical contact and masculinity whereby highly masculinized contact sports increase the risks of violence" (Kraeger, 2007, p. 717). This raises the question: Are boys who participate in certain sports being taught to be violent (e.g., Kotler, 2008)? After critically examining the theories and research addressing this question, in this chapter we will look at the societal stereotype of the "jock bully" as it appears in both popular culture and academic writings. We will then use this psychologically-oriented lens to examine the 2013 Miami Dolphins controversy involving Jonathan Martin and Richie Incognito, where we will apply relevant literature on bullying and masculinity. Lastly, we will discuss future implications for research and clinical work. Prevention is the most desirable form of intervention and future research should therefore assess the effectiveness of violence and abuse prevention initiatives (Stirling, 2008). Professionals working in school, athletic, and occupational settings can use the information in this chapter to inform their efforts to create an environment that can address bullying dynamics.

* E-mail address: jesstein@indiana.edu; Tel: 812 856-8331; Fax: 812 856-8333; Address: Indiana University, EDUC 4064, 201 N. Rose Avenue, Bloomington, IN, 47401, US; (Corresponding author)

Introduction

The dynamic of violence and bullying among male athletes is not only a relevant topic of interest in the psychological study of masculinity and sport, but this topic is also omnipresent in contemporary society. Media reports of male athletes engaging in violence often capture the attention of the viewing audience (Associated Press, 2007; Associated Press, 2012; Smith, 2014). However, these reports represent the minority experience of most athletes-the stories about the myriad of male athletes who do not engage in violent acts do not readily make the front pages. Subsequently, society is left with a skewed perspective, but the question remains: are male athletes more violent than non-athletes?

While there are more non-violent male athletes than violent male athletes, there is some evidence to suggest that male athletes might be more likely to engage in violent acts in relation to men who don't play organized sports (Kreager, 2007; Messner, and Sabo, 1994; Mutz, 2012). Mutz (2012) found that, when compared to their non-athlete male peers, male adolescents in certain sports (i.e., combat sports, bodybuilding activities) engaged in more physically violent acts and more readily endorsed violence beliefs. Specifically, Kreager (2007) reported that male athletes who participate in contact sports (e.g., football, wrestling) were more likely to engage in violent acts, with high school football players being 40% more likely to get in a serious fight when compared to their non-athlete peers. In sum, Kreager purported that there exists, "a continuum of physical contact and masculinity whereby highly masculinized contact sports increase the risks of violence" (2007, p. 717).

While these studies do not present a definitive answer to the original question (are male athletes more violent than non-athletes?), they do raise a related sub-question: Are boys who participate in certain sports being taught to be violent (e.g., Kotler, 2008)? However, this is a nuanced and complicated issue that requires critical thought and examination. Rather than arrive at the oversimplified (and potentially inaccurate) explanation that sports like football make boys more violent, a critical analysis of this issue should be guided by multiple perspectives, most notably the notion of a) instrumental aggression and b) self-selection.

In and of itself, football is a place where young boys are socialized to learn values and behaviors (e.g., competition, toughness, winning-at-all costs) that are considered to be socially desirable aspects of masculinity (Messner, 1996; Steinfeldt and Steinfeldt, 2012). Specifically, contact sports like football encourage and teach instrumental aggression, which allows for a functional need for aggression and even violence to facilitate success on the football field (Messner, 1990, 2002). A football player must hit, dominate, and overpower his opponent in order to be successful. If he does not, that player will be overpowered, hit, and dominated.

As a result, violence can be conceptualized as something that exists within the rules and nature of a sport like football, and boys and young men are rewarded for their successful engagement with functional aggression and violence on the field of play. However, "Reinforcement of masculine gender norms through strict football rituals in team practice creates a behavioral repertoire that may extend to other contexts, with gender norms also informing the interpersonal relationships that athletes form off the field" (Gage, 2008, p. 1016). Thus, it is imperative to teach football players to compartmentalize their aggression and keep it on the field and "between the lines" (e.g. Steinfeldt, Foltz, et al., 2011).

Additionally, the dynamics of self-selection need to be examined in order to shed additional light on this issue, particularly in terms of directionality of influence. Instead of a simplified explanation of "football teaches boys to be violent" there is value in exploring the types of boys that are attracted to play football. In an early examination of "non conforming males" (e.g., juvenile offenders), Donnelly (1981) identified this self-selection dynamic by concluding that certain types of boys might be drawn to contact sports. For boys who might desire activities that involve risk or other forms of physical aggression, football could provide them with the outlet to physically aggress against other boys, but in a regulated and socially desirable environment. So in sum, through a more contextual examination involving instrumental aggression and self-selection, we can arrive at a more nuanced conclusion than the thought-provoking yet misleading question, "Are sports making our children more violent?" (e.g., Kotler, 2008).

Bullying among Male Athletes

While this nuanced examination provides some contextual understanding of the issue, it doesn't fully address the reality that some male athletes do engage in violent behaviors off the field (or what we should do about this). While getting into fights off the field is an area of concern, another subset of violence that garners considerable attention in society is bullying. And related to the perception of violent male athletes is the existence of a familiar archetype in American movies and television: the "jock bully" (e.g., Steinfeldt, LaFollette, Vaughan, and Steinfeldt, 2012). This stereotypic representation of a character is often a member of the football team who uses his social and physical influence to harass and bully other students, often peers who are not part of the popular crowd. Movies such as *Revenge of the Nerds* and *The Karate Kid* gave children of the 80s the everlasting "jock bully" images of Ogre and Stan Gable from the Adams College Atoms football team and Johnny Lawrence from the Cobra Kai. Younger folks may resonate more with the image of slushings at the hands of Azimio and Dave Karofsky from the football team in *Glee*. Regardless of preferred genre, these references all conjure up images of characters that are stereotypically represented in popular culture-the stereotype of the jock bully has become firmly entrenched in our minds.

This stereotypic image of the jock has recently emerged in academic writings. Miller (2009) attempted to distinguish the "jock" identity from "athlete" identity, two concepts which have traditionally been interpreted as interchangeable in popular culture. Miller suggested that for athletes who self-identify with this "jock" identity, the link between masculinity and sport-related identity is stronger than for those who self-identify with the "athlete" role. Furthermore, Miller hypothesized that negative behavior associated with athletic status is more commonly attributed to the "jock" identity. This behavior includes problem drinking (Miller et al., 2003), academic misconduct (Miller, Melnick et al., 2005), unsafe sex (Miller, Farrell, Barnes, Melnick, and Sabo, 2005), delinquency (Miller et al., 2007), and interpersonal violence (Miller, Melnick, Farrell, Sabo, and Barnes, 2006). Miller and Hoffman (2009) also found "jock" identity to be related to attempted suicide. Based on these findings, Miller (2009) coined the term "toxic jock" in an attempt to suggest that the strength of identification with this role impacts the athlete's likelihood of an athlete engaging in negative health-risk behaviors.

Miller, Sabo, et al. (2006) suggested that the "jock" identity is more prominent in high-profile sports which contain some degree of structured physical violence. In such sports, masculinity is emphasized, with football being the epitomic environment for typical "jock" behavior.

Additionally, the "jock" identity was positively associated with status, perceived popularity, institutional support, and overall sport rating (Miller, 2009). Conventional masculine norms such as propensity toward violence, emphasis on risk-taking and winning, a "playboy" attitude toward sexual relationships, and interpersonal dominance were positively predicted by the strength of the "jock" identity. Finally, "jock" identity was significantly related to an ego-focused goal orientation which values the outperformance of competitors by any means possible (Miller, 2009).

Consistent with Miller's (2009) findings linking social status with this "jock" identity, certain activities (e.g., playing high profile sports) in school settings are linked to high levels of social status (Peguero, 2008). Furthermore, most research on bullying has found that those with high status within peer groups are generally perceived to be the aggressors and bullies (Cillessen and Mayeux, 2007; Pokhrel, Sussman, Black, and Sun, 2010; Prinstein and Cillessen, 2003). Bullying is often used by individuals to either gain status and/or to intimidate others in order to maintain high status, which would explain why bullying is so easily associated with high status groups such as football players (Dijkstra, Cillessen, Lindenberg, and Veenstra, 2010; Caravita Di Blasio and Salmivalli, 2009). These associations occur even before the high school years, when sports begin to take on a greater role for their participants. In a study of adult (i.e., teachers, administrators, counselors) and student perceptions of bullying victimization in a middle school, it was found that adults and students most often identified popular students and athletes as the school bullies (Dranoff, 2008).

Although research has examined the relationship between social status in schools, athletic involvement, and bullying, there has been a dearth of research that has directly investigated specific bullying behaviors and attitudes of athletes. Steinfeldt et al. (2012) conducted a study that directly examined bullying beliefs of high school football players. The authors investigated the role of moral atmosphere (i.e., influence of teammates and their most influential male figure) and the role of adherence to male norms (e.g., Meanings of Adolescent Masculinity; Oransky and Fisher, 2009) in the development and potential activation of these bullying beliefs. Results indicated that an adherence to male norms and teammate influence were significantly related to bullying beliefs. The perception of the views of the players' most influential male (e.g., father, coach, brother) was the strongest predictor of bullying among those boys who reported having engaged in bullying behaviors (after controlling for social desirability).

Beyond these findings, the results also indicated that these high school football players did not report a high degree of involvement with any of the four specific bullying behaviors (i.e., physical; verbal threat; homophobic; relational cyberbullying). In fact, the majority (85%) of high school football players in this study reported that *they have never* (69%) or that *they have rarely* (16%) engaged in any of the bullying behaviors (Steinfeldt et al., 2012). Thus, in spite of prevalent social stereotypes (i.e., "jock bully"), these results indicate that these high school football players do not engage in bullying behaviors at a rate consistent with these societal stereotypes.

Application of Bullying Dynamics to a Case Study

The previous pages of this chapter have been devoted to providing context and perspective on perceptions-both societal and empirical, albeit limitedly so-on the dynamic of bullying among male athletes, particularly those who play the contact sport of football. At this point, we will provide an example that highlights some of the dynamics of bullying, while also illustrating aspects of bullying that do not fully conform with our emerging understanding of bullying among male athletes.

In 2013 the male "jock bully" stereotype was simultaneously reinforced and challenged. The events surrounding the Miami Dolphins of the NFL provided interesting perspectives on bullying, particularly from the victim's perspective. Jonathan Martin, an offensive lineman, accused his teammate, Richie Incognito, of bullying. These two men both weigh over 300 pounds and play a physically demanding position (i.e., offensive line) in the "masculinized" (e.g., Richman and Shaffer, 2000) and often violent sport of professional football. While Incognito readily fit the social stereotype of the jock bully, Martin clearly did not fit the profile of a bullying victim: how could a 300-pound professional football player possibly be bullied? The media coverage was intense, and subsequently the incident generated an interesting public dialogue about bullying, power, masculinity, and other related issues, including conversations about "what it means to be a real man" (e.g., Fagan, 2013).

The circumstances surrounding the Martin and Incognito controversy are interesting for a number of reasons, primarily because these events occurred within a culture that exists in a football locker room that is foreign-and even antithetical-to most, if not all, other workplaces. However, a full investigation was ordered and carried out by an impartial investigator, who released the facts in a 144-page report that was filed with the NFL (Wells, Karp, Birenboim, and Brown, 2014), so we can sort through the report and attempt to interpret the situation through a psychologically-oriented lens.

As we present this case study, there are three important factors in this story that relate to relevant literature on bullying and masculinity that contributed to Martin's withdrawal from professional football. Those factors – which will be the focus of this section – are: a) the victim (i.e., Martin); b) the bully (i.e., Incognito); and c) the social climate within the Dolphins football team and locker room.

The Victim

The victim, Jonathan Martin, was a second year NFL player who was a starting offensive lineman for Miami, but after approximately a year and a half of being bullied and harassed by teammates, decided to leave the Dolphins organization and check himself into a hospital for psychological treatment in the middle of the 2013 NFL season.

Despite being a large, athletic man who successfully played the popular sport of football, Martin reported that he was bullied all through middle school and most of high school (Wells et al., 2014). Evidence has shown that even though bullying victimization decreases as children get older, being a victim of bullying can still be stable across ages for some children (Arseneault, Bowes, and Shakoor, 2009). This was true for Martin as well.

Despite always being large for his age and athletically gifted, Martin was described as being reserved, having low self-esteem, and having low levels of self-confidence, which are often characteristics of children who are bullied (Egan and Perry, 1998). Martin claims that the bullying he experienced in middle school and high school gave him trouble with social adjustment and caused self-diagnosed bouts of depression throughout his teenage and college years (Wells et al., 2014).

While playing professional football for the Dolphins, Martin was harassed primarily by three teammates: Incognito, John Jerry, and Mike Pouncey, with Incognito being the ringleader of the trio. The harassment Martin endured from his teammates came in the form of cyber bullying, verbal bullying, and even physical bullying. The content of what his teammates said and did to verbally harass him included racial slurs, derogatory language, suggestive sexual advances toward members of his family (i.e., sister, mother), homophobic remarks, and slights at Martin's masculinity (Wells et al., 2014).

A graduate of the academically prestigious Stanford University, Martin believes he was bullied because he was different from a lot of other players due to his intellectual interests (i.e., reading books) and quiet nature. This is a valid assumption given that bullying is usually more acceptable when it is directed at someone not a member of the in-group or individuals who are shy or reserved (Duffy and Nesdale, 2009; Ojala and Nesdale, 2004). Martin reported that the bullying by his teammates and his inability to make them stop eventually drove him to depression, resulting in his contemplating suicide on at least two occasions (Wells et al., 2014). Therefore, while Martin may not fit into society's perception of the typical victim of bullying, the effect bullying has had on his mental health is common for victims of bullying. All of the mental health issues Martin says he has faced due to being bullied (i.e., social anxiety, lower self-esteem, depression, hopelessness, suicidal ideation) are consistent with the psychological literature on victims of bullying (Coggan, Bennett, Hooper, and Dickinson, 2003; Dukes, Stein, and Zane, 2009; Espelage and Holt, 2001; Jankauskiene, Kardelis, Sukys, and Kardeliene, 2008; Kim and Leventhal, 2008; Storch, Bagner, Geffken, and Baumeister, 2004).

The Bully

We have examined the victim of this situation and now we will turn our attention to the perpetrator: Richie Incognito. According to news reports, Incognito had "run-ins with bullies as a boy" (Wells et al., 2014, p. 59). If that is accurate, Incognito could be grouped into part of a small percentage of victims of bullying who externalize problems, going on to bully others and exhibit violent behaviors later in life (Scholte, Engels, Overbeek, de Kemp, and Haselager, 2007; Arseneault et al., 2009). Previous research on adolescents has shown that those who have been both bullies and victims (a.k.a., bully-victims) exhibit much more conduct problems than either bullies or victims (Juvonen, Graham, and Schuster, 2006).This research fits the profile of Incognito who, as mentioned earlier, fits the stereotypical depiction of the "jock bully."

Before playing for the Dolphins, Incognito was a college football standout at the University of Nebraska, where he would start to develop his "bad boy" reputation. Incognito's college career was filled with behavioral problems on and off the field. Incognito fought on the field, leading to suspensions and even an ejection from a game, was charged with three accounts of assault off the field, and struggled with drug and alcohol issues (i.e., failed drug tests), which he would later admit he abused for a decade (Wells et al., 2014). After a positive drug test for marijuana use and a shoving match with a teammate in the locker room, Incognito was suspended indefinitely from Nebraska's football team. He then transferred to the University of Oregon, but was kicked off their football team after one week for violating team policies. Incognito's alcohol and drug use, conduct problems, and violence off the field were all problems associated with being a bully, as well as pressure to conform to masculine norms (Curry, 2000; Kreager, 2007; Juvonen et al., 2006; Storch et al., 2004).

Even though Incognito may fit society's idea of what a prototypical bully is, to those in the world of professional football, his behavior can sometimes be perceived as only mildly appropriate, if at all. While football teaches instrumental aggression to succeed, Incognito has often been excessive with his aggression and unable to keep it "between the lines." Before the Dolphins, Incognito played for the St. Louis Rams for five seasons from 2005-2009. In those five seasons, he played 44 regular season games in which he committed 38 penalties, 7 of which were for unnecessary roughness. In 2009, he was deemed the "Dirtiest Player in the NFL," by *The Sporting News* (Wells et al., 2014). Incognito's anti-social behavior extended beyond the football field as well. When interacting with Martin, Incognito reported that he intentionally tried to "break" Martin through verbal harassment (i.e., racial slurs, sexual comments about his mother and sister) on a regular basis, although he claimed this was never meant to cause lasting emotional harm to Martin (Wells et al., 2014). Additionally, Martin claimed that at a Christmas party in 2012, he and Incognito were inoffensively pushing and shoving one another but it escalated quickly when Incognito took of his shirt, tackled Martin onto the sofa, and began punching him in the body and face. This incident humiliated Martin and contributed to the pattern of treatment that led to his departure (Wells et al., 2014).

In addition to being overly aggressive both on and off the field, Incognito has been described by his teammates as "inappropriate," "vulgar," "crazy," "someone who has no filter," and, "the kind of guy who has to be the alpha male" (Wells et al., 2014, p. 65). When considering self-selection dynamics in football, it seems plausible that someone like Incognito would be drawn to the sport because it provides a space where his physically aggressive behavior would be productive, his incessant taunting would be acceptable (i.e., "trash talking"), and his desire to be the alpha male would serve him well in trying to both dominate his opponents and motivate his teammates toward instrumentally aggressive behaviors that can help the team win.

So far we have focused on the characteristics of a stereotypic "jock bully" that aptly describe and fit Richie Incognito, but the flip side of that stereotype provides a question that still remains: How could another physically imposing, 300 pound man---who had also been socialized in the same context of football his whole life--also be the victim of bullying? Part of this answer resides in an analysis of relational power. When Incognito harassed Martin, he was using his relational power to his advantage, which is common in cases of bullying in any workplace (Hodson, Roscigno, and Lopez, 2006). Incognito and Mike Pouncey were regarded as the leaders of the offensive line, if not the entire offense, and even served on the Dolphins' *Leadership Council*, a group of players who serve as representatives to the head coach, Joe Philbin, despite their anti-social behaviors (Wells et al., 2014). Martin was a young player and Incognito was considered to be a superior member of the team to him due to his appointed leadership status. Additionally, there was an incident in which Martin got in a fight with a Dolphins defensive lineman and Incognito came to his defense (Wells et al., 2014). These circumstances placed Incognito in a more powerful position than Martin, leaving Martin to be more vulnerable to bullying. Furthermore, there was a lack of visibility of Incognito's bullying behavior to many of the staff members in the Dolphins organization, and this lack of visibility helps allow bullying behaviors to occur relatively unfettered in the workplace (Hodson et al., 2006).

Social Climate

An NFL locker room is a workplace, albeit a workplace unlike any other professional venue. Like many other football teams, the Dolphins have a unique locker room culture that is insulated from certain social controls and pressures, which allows for antisocial behavior to occur that would not be allowed elsewhere (Messner, 2002; Wells et al., 2014). While Incognito and other linemen on the Dolphins have acknowledged that their behavior towards Martin and others was harsh (and unacceptable in other places in society), they considered it to be a part of joking and bonding that comes with being on a football team. This aligns with previous research that bullying behavior increases when it is endorsed by group norms and is more acceptable in places where there exists a climate of low level of moral functioning (Duffy and Nesdale, 2009; Gini, 2008; Ojala and Nesdale, 2004; Steinfeldt et al., 2012).

In regard to this climate of low moral functioning, one of the coaches of the Dolphins was reported to have joined players in making homophobic jokes toward another teammate ("Player A" as he is listed in the report; Wells et al., 2014). As mentioned earlier, research has shown that the strongest predictor for bullying behaviors among football players is their perception of whether the most influential male figure in their life (e.g., father, coach) would approve of this bullying behavior (Steinfeldt et al., 2012). These men have been socialized in the culture of football where players respect coaches and even revere them in their position of authority. Therefore, it is likely that the coach's participation in this bullying facilitated and enabled the maintenance of an environment that endorsed norms that allowed bullying behaviors.

Additionally, there existed an accepted cultural norm amongst the Dolphins players for "no snitching." This rule was especially important to the offensive linemen who had a "Judas" code, introduced by the coach who also joined in on the homophobic bullying behaviors. The "Judas" code was created for film sessions to prevent linemen from "snitching" on other linemen. If a lineman missed an assignment and was criticized during a film session by this coach, but then pointed out that the botched play or missed assignment was another lineman's fault, then he would be labeled a "Judas" and have a fine imposed on him by another teammate. With this in mind, Martin refused to seek help out of fear for being labeled a "Judas," (Wells et al., 2014).

The reaction by players to the Martin case was interesting--in fact, many players defended Incognito and chided Martin for not having thick enough skin. Martin violated a code of the locker room by snitching and "not taking care of his business." However, after Martin left the team midseason, several players have since admitted that Incognito's behavior toward Martin and even other players was inappropriate.

One player confided that most players did not intervene when Incognito bullied and harassed Martin or others because they did not want to become the target of harassment themselves. Even Martin participated in making homophobic jokes about another player ("Player A") with Incognito (Wells et al., 2014), likely in an attempt to align with the bully and deflect the harassment that was usually directed his way. This lack of intervention by the other players is consistent with findings in the psychological literature that suggests boys will tease and even bully other boys in order to avoid being victimized themselves (Steinfeldt et al., 2012). Although the verbal abuse that Martin endured was considered to be normal by many Dolphins players, these behaviors were in direct violation of the team's formal anti-harassment policies. In 2013, prior to Martin's departure, the Dolphins players were given a workplace conduct policy that strictly prohibits the type of behavior that occurred.

Additionally, Coach Philbin publicly strived to promote integrity within the Dolphins organization and was found to be completely unaware of either Incognito's behavior or Martin's mental health ailments (Wells et al., 2014). However, consistent with culture of football locker rooms and traditional norms of hegemonic masculinity (e.g., Connell and Messerschmidt, 2005), this bullying behavior (e.g., homophobic slurs, insinuation of having sex with one's mother or sister, chiding one's manhood) can be inappropriately dismissed as "boys just being boys," particularly within the context of a football locker room, a dismissal that can allow bullying behaviors to flourish.

Conclusion

In spite of societal misperceptions that a 300-pound male professional football player should be immune to bullying, research has shown that there is almost no demographic which can completely shield someone from becoming a victim of bullying (Dane-Staples, Lieberman, Ratcliff, and Rounds, 2013).Although Martin would have been justified in seeking help, the culture of the Dolphins football team led him to believe that he would be wrong in doing so. Players should not be discouraged to seek professional help when it is needed because, "even the largest, strongest and fleetest person may be driven to despair by bullying, taunting and constant insults," (Wells et al., 2014, p. 140). This incident shows the importance of regulating what is acceptable behavior in a school, locker room, or workplace. Many teams purport to promote a healthy locker room culture, but the regulation of a football locker room is often considered to be the responsibility of the players, which can present a conflict of interest when the bully is in charge.

In sum, if bullying is considered to be, "behavior that is intended to inflict harm or stress, occurs repeatedly over a period time, and involves an inequity of strength or power," (Steinfeldt, LaFollette et al., 2012, p. 341) then it becomes clear that this situation represents an interesting example of bullying. Incognito claims he never intended to cause Martin harm, yet intent does not always equal outcome. Given the unique nature of the football locker room, was this simply a part of football culture that Martin was unable to cope with? Wells et al. (2014) ultimately decided that Incognito's friendship with Martin and the culture of the Dolphins football team did not excuse the harassment directed at Martin. This was a case of bullying, even if the victim is as atypical as the perpetrator is typical, and all of this occurred in an environment (i.e., football locker room) that can be conceptualized as a breeding ground for potential bullying behaviors.

Future Research Implications

One of the conclusions of the Wells Report (Wells et al., 2014) was that bullying is an omnipresent problem that transcends athletic environments across the high school, college, and professional domains. Researchers and clinicians need to recognize that even NFL-caliber 300-pound seemingly superhuman athletes are still people who can be deeply affected by bullying, taunting, and insults. For this and many other reasons, a culture of respect must be promoted and enforced within the professional sport workplace. This includes establishing guidelines, rules, and consequences for bullying behaviors, just as it is expected in non-sport workplace and personal contexts. The culture of the player-regulated locker room needs to be addressed and incorporated into this process.

Furthermore, a holistic perspective of the athlete as a human being who also happens to be a contact sport participant (e.g., football player) may help to dispel the notion that bullying or violence is more acceptable or even condonable in sport. Beyond this perspective, there are a number of research questions that need to be addressed concerning bullying and violence among male athletes, particularly those who play contact sports.

Mutz (2012) found that different types of sports have differing impacts on pro-social or antisocial outcomes in youth sport participants, in relation to sport involvement and the approval and use of violence. More research regarding this relationship is needed, as the literature in this area is sparse. Although research has found that boys do not have a tendency to act aggressively prior to practicing combat sports (Endresen and Olweus, 2005; Reynes and Lorant, 2001), more research should be conducted to examine whether a predisposition to violence prompts engagement in combat sports, or whether combat sports initiate and foster aggression, leading to violent behavior. Mutz (2012) also suggests that future studies in violence in combat sports should examine the subtle differences among sports disciplines (e.g., karate vs. boxing). Moral climate and moral expectations of coaches are also worth examining in relation to aggressive and violent behaviors and attitudes (e.g., Steinfeldt et al., 2012).

As we have discussed, violence and bullying is commonly associated with contact sports such as football. When the aggressive behavior that is often praised in sport performance transcends the boundaries of the playing field (Gage, 2008), measures must be taken to prevent and address this transfer when it occurs. While Steinfeldt, Foltz, et al. (2011) highlight the importance of teaching football players to compartmentalize their aggression, Stirling (2008) suggests that future research focus on the implementation of violence and abuse prevention initiatives in order to assess their effectiveness. This includes identifying the nature of the problem, clarifying risk and protective factors, designing and testing interventions, conducting clinical trials to evaluate the interventions, and facilitation of implementation on the grand scale (Stirling, 2008). Stirling also calls for the examination of how maltreatments occur, as well as the short-term and long-term effects on the athlete's personal and professional well-being. Specifically, the varying types of maltreatment (e.g., hazing, verbal abuse, physical abuse) should be explored comparatively and longitudinally, and in relation to prevention and intervention initiatives. The maltreatment experiences of athletes should be examined within a broader research perspective (Shannon, 2013; Stirling, 2008). Identifying risk and resiliency factors would also be valuable to the literature in this area, as specifically related to age, race, gender, ethnicity, sexuality, disability, sport type, career stage, period of competitive season, and level of competition (Messner, 1990). Additionally, Stirling (2008) asks that relationships among coaches, parents, and teammates be examined in relation to the athlete's vulnerability to maltreatment. Such relationships have been found to be influential in the endorsement of group norms and the level of moral atmosphere, i.e., whether or not bullying behavior is acceptable on and off the field (Duffy and Nesdale, 2009; Gini, 2008; Ojala and Nesdale, 2004; Steinfeldt et al., 2012).

In the broader context of bullying in schools, Shannon (2013) suggested that the knowledge on bullying behavior in respective social worlds (e.g., extracurricular activities such as sport) would be benefited by interviewing youths regarding their perceptions and experiences of bullying behavior. This could also lead to the development of structural preventative bullying measures in youth sport, depending on the wealth of support. Concurrently, the perceived systemic and organizational barriers to addressing bullying would add to the literature and clinical implications for prevention. Steinfeldt et al. (2012) suggest that future research is needed to explore bullying dynamics specifically in the sport environment, in order to connect their findings with previous bullying literature. The relationship between bullying and social teasing is also worth investigating. As seen in the Martin case, many players accused him of not having "thick enough skin." Other players confessed that they didn't want to defend Martin when he was being bullied because they didn't want to become the target of the teasing (Wells et al., 2014).

More research is needed to determine what drives bullying behavior and social compliance. Findings have linked having a high status within peer groups to aggression and bullying (Cillessen and Mayeux, 2007; Pokhrel, Sussman, Black and Sun, 2010; Prinstein and Cillessen, 2003). Furthermore, bullying may be a means to maintain this status, which may be why it shows up traditionally high status groups such as football players (Dijkstra, Cillessen, Lindenberg, and Veenstra, 2010; Caravita Di Blasio, and Salmivalli, 2009). This may be one area of exploration for future research. Aligning with this "jock" identity, Miller (2007) suggests that future longitudinal research is needed to examine the relationships between sport-related identity and variables such as masculine norms and goal orientation.

While Miller and Hoffman (2009) reported a correlation between athletic involvement and risk for suicidality, future research should seek to further tease out this relationship, as more empirical support is needed to make such conclusions. In line with the findings of Miller and Hoffman (2009), future research should combine both quantitative and qualitative analyses of sport-related identities, so as to harness their complexities and variation. Overall, there are substantial areas for growth in bullying research, especially as it relates to athletics and specifically to combat sports such as football. Focusing efforts on testing the effectiveness of prevention and intervention strategies, while further clarifying the factors that contribute to bullying, would be valuable in increasing the literature base in this area.

Future Clinical Implications

In addition to the recommendations for future research, it is also important to consider the clinical implications pertaining to the current literature in bullying in sport. Stirling (2008) proposes a model for the implementation of prevention and intervention initiatives aimed at advocacy, policy, education and research. The importance of empirical support for these types of initiatives is stressed throughout the literature. This includes pilot testing of established interventions as well as evaluation of their effectiveness over time.

Mutz (2012) also stresses the importance of concept education and evaluation of implementation programs for bullying prevention within sports contexts. He purports that identification of the specific factors that make these types of programs successful is essential to the development of effective clinical implementation. Particularly, Mutz mentions that coaches should not promote a "win at all costs" mentality, but rather emphasize respect, fairness, discipline, and team spirit both on and off the playing field, as to counter a possible ego-focused goal orientation. Team morals and values are often influential in sport-related identification, behavior, and attitude. Mutz suggests that the education, implementation, and practice of these values are even more important within combat sport contexts, which contain an emphasis on physical supremacy and should be accompanied by a high level of self-control (Mutz, 2012).

In further reference to the implementation of anti-bullying programs, Shannon (2013) suggests that the development of a clear statement of an organization's commitment to a safe and positive sport environment is the first step to bullying prevention. Furthermore, policies for both prevention and response to bullying incidents should be established from the get-go. Situational factors in which the likelihood for bullying may be increased must be identified within the respected organizational context. Shannon also states that staff should be educated on the topic of bullying, including prevention methods and how to recognize its occurrence. Closing the gap between bullying prevention and intervention in schools vs. sport environments would also be helpful in reducing the occurrence of incidents in either context. This requires communication, organization, and implementation of appropriate procedures in both systems, as well as consistency in terms of expectations, response, and consequences for bullying behavior. Climates that support and encourage positive peer relationships are most beneficial for bullying prevention (Shannon, 2013).

In addition to the organizational aspects of bullying prevention, it is also important to consider the factors at play for the victims themselves. Stafford, Alexander, and Fry (2013) reported that children were unlikely to speak up to adults regarding issues affecting their physical safety and well-being in the sport context. This stresses the need for athletes' input when planning and implementing bullying education, prevention, and intervention programs. Stafford et al. also place responsibility with the coaches for creating and modeling an atmosphere of positive behavior. We currently live in a society which commonly practices and condones aggressive verbal and/or physical coaching methods; this plays a role in the prevalence and permission of violence and aggression among players. It is worth examining the coaches' attitudes and behaviors toward these types of behaviors in depth, in order to determine how much their influence contributes to bullying incidents. It is likely that a coach may be the most influential male in a young [male] athlete's life, a role which has been shown to be the strongest predictor of immoral attitude and behavior (Steinfeldt et al., 2012).

The environmental, social, and cultural factors surrounding bullying behavior should also be taken into consideration for clinical application. Messner (1990) suggested that poor, ethnic minority males are most likely to be disproportionately directed into sports careers due to poverty, institutionalized racism, and scarcity of other career options. Messner stated that due to these issues, athletes with these types of demographic characteristics are more likely to place a higher value on their athletic identity, whereas privileged white males participate in sport primarily for status and are less likely to persist to high-level competition. While this relationship may have shifted in the past two and a half decades, the role of socio, cultural, and economic factors in sport transcends various issues and should be examined in relation to bullying as well. A multicultural approach should be considered for future clinical prevention and intervention of bullying in sport.

References

Arseneault, L., Bowes, L. and Shakoor, S. (2009). Bullying victimization in youths and mental health problems: 'Much ado about nothing?' *Psychological Medicine,* 40, 717-729.

Associated Press (2007). *Kings suspend Artest after domestic violence arrest.* Retrieved from http://sports.espn.go.com/nba/news/story?id=2788871.

Associated Press (2012). *Chad Johnson gets probation.* Retrieved from http://espn.go.com/nfl/story/_/id/8406775/chad-johnson-gets-probation-domestic-battery-case.

Caravita, S. C. S., Di Blasio, P. and Salmivalli, C. (2009). Unique and interactive effects of empathy and social status on involvement in bullying. *Social Development,* 18, 140-163.

Cillessen, A. H. N. and Mayeux, L. (2007). Expectations and perceptions at school transitions: The role of peer status and aggression. *Journal of School Psychology,* 45 (5), 567-586.

Coggan, C., Bennet, S., Hooper, R., and Dickinson, P. (2003). Association between bullying and mental health status in New Zealand adolescents. *The International Journal of Mental Health Promotion*, 5, 16-22.

Connell, R. W. and Messerschmidt, J. W. (2005). Hegemonic masculinity: Rethinking the concept. *Gender and Society*, 19, 829-859. doi: 10.1177/0891243205278639.

Curry, T. J. (2000). Booze and bar fights: A journey to the dark side of college athletics. In: J. McKay, M. A. Messner and D. Sabo (Eds.), *Masculinities, gender relations and sport* (pp. 162-175). Thousand Oaks, CA: Sage.

Dane-Staples, E., Lieberman, L., Ratcliff, J., and Rounds, K. (2013). Bullying experiences of individuals with visual impairment: The mitigating role of sport participation. *Journal of Sport Behavior,* 36, 365-386.

Dijkstra, J. K., Cillessen, A. H. N., Lindenberg, S., and Veenstra, R. (2008). Beyond the class norm: Bullying behavior of popular adolescents and its relation to peer acceptance and rejection. *Journal of Abnormal Child Psychology,* 36, 1289-1299.

Donnelly, P. (1981). Athletes and juvenile delinquents: A comparative analysis based on a review of literature. *Adolescence*, 16(62), 415-432.

Dranoff, R. (2008). Teacher and student perceptions of bullying and victimization in a middle school. (Order No. AAI3272789), *Dissertation Abstracts International Section A: Humanities and Social Sciences,* 2826. Retrieved from http://ezproxy.lib.indiana.edu/login?url=http://search.proquest.com/docview/621715930?accountid=11620. (621715930; 2008-99010-525).

Duffy, A. L. and Nesdale, D. (2009). Peer groups, social identity, and children's bullying behavior. *Social Development,* 18, 121-139.

Dukes, R. L., Stein, J. A. and Zane, J. I. (2009). Effect of relational bullying on attitudes, behavior and injury among adolescent bullies, victims, and bully-victims. *The Social Science Journal*, 46, 671-688.

Egan, S. K. and Perry, D. G. (1998). Does low self-regard invite victimization? *Developmental Psychology,* 34, 299-309.

Endrensen, I. M. and Olweus, D. (2005). Participation in power sports and antisocial involvement in preadolescent and adolescent boys. *Journal of Child Psychology and Psychiatry*, 46(5), 468-478. doi: 10.1111/j.1469-7610.2005.00414.x.

Espelage, D. L. and Holt, M. K. (2001). Bullying and victimization during early adolescence: Peer influences and psychosocial correlates. *Journal of Emotional Abuse*, 2, 123-142.

Fagan, K. (2013). *So, what defines a 'real man' in sports?* Retrieved online on Nov. 13, 2013: http://espn.go.com/espnw/news-commentary/article/9937514/espnw-jonathan-martin-richie-incognito-incident-raises-questions-means-real-man-sports.

Gage, E. A. (2008). Gender attitudes and sexual behavior. *Violence Against Women*, 14, 1014-1032. doi:10.1177/1077801208321987.

Gini, G. (2008). Italian elementary and middle school students' blaming the victim of bullying and perception of school moral atmosphere. *The Elementary School Journal*, 108, 335-354. doi:10.1086/528975.

Jankauskiene, R., Kardelis, K., Sukys, S., and Kardeliene, L. (2008). Associations between school bullying and psychosocial factors. *Social Behavior and Personality*, 36, 145-162.

Juvonen, J., Graham, S. and Schuster, M. A. (2006). Bullying among adolescents: The strong, the weak, and the troubled. *Pediatrics,* 112, 1231-1237.

Hodson, R., Roscigno, V. J. and Lopez, S. H. (2006). Chaos and the abuse of power: Workplace bullying in organizational and interactional context. *Work and Occupations*, 33, 382-416. doi: 10.1177/0730888406292885.

Kim, Y. S. and Leventhal, B. (2008). Bullying and suicide. A review. *International Journal of Adolescent Medicine and Health*, 20, 133-154.

Kotler, S. (2008). *Are sports making our children more violent?* Retrived online on January 4, 2014 from http://www.psychologytoday.com/blog/the-playing-field/200807/are-sports-making-our-children-more-violent.

Kraeger, D. A. (2007). Unnecessary roughness: School sports, peer networks, and male adolescent violence. *American Sociological Review,* 72, 705-724.

Messner, M. A. (1990). When bodies are weapons: Masculinity and violence in sport. *International Review for Sociology of Sport*, 25, 203-220. doi: 10.1177/101269029002500303.

Messner, M. A. (1996). Masculinities and athletic careers. In: E. N. Chow, D. Wilkinson and M. Baca Zinn (Eds.), *Race, class and gender: Common bonds, different voices* (pp. 70-86). Thousand Oaks, CA: Sage.

Messner, M. A. (2002). *Taking the field: Men, women, and sports*. Minneapolis, MN: University of Minnesota Press.

Messner, M. A. and Sabo, D. F. (1994). *Sex, violence and power in sports: Rethinking masculinity*. Freedom, CA: The Crossing Press.

Miller, K. E. (2009). Sport-related identities and the "Toxic Jock". *Journal of Sport Behavior,* 32, 69-91.

Miller, K. E. and Hoffman, J. H. (2009). Mental well-being and sport-related identities in college students. *Sociology of Sport Journal*, 26, 335-356.

Miller, K. E., Hoffman, J. H, Barnes, G. M., Farrell, M. P., Sabo, D. F., and Melnick, M. J. (2003). Jocks, gender, race, and adolescent problem drinking. *Journal of Drug Education*, 33(4), 445-462.

Miller, K. E., Farrell, M. P., Barnes, G. M., Melnick, M. J., and Sabo, D. F. (2005). Gender/ racial differences in jock identity, dating, and adolescent sexual risk. *Journal of Youth and Adolescence*, 34, 123-136.

Miller, K. E., Melnick, M. J., Barnes, G. M., and Farrell, M. P., and Sabo, D. F. (2005). Untangling the links among athletic involvement, gender, race, and adolescent academic outcomes. *Sociology of Sport Journal*, 22, 178-193.

Miller, K. E., Melnick, M. J., Barnes, G. M., Sabo, D. F., and Farrell, M. P. (2007). Athletic involvement and adolescent delinquency. *Journal of Youth and Adolescence*, 36, 711-723. doi: 10.1007/s10964-006-9123-9.

Miller, K. E., Melnick, M. J., Farrell, M. P., Sabo, D. F., and Barnes, G. M., (2006). Jocks, gender, binge drinking, and adolescent violence. *Journal of Interpersonal Violence*, 21, 105-120.

Miller, K. E., Sabo, D. F., Melnick, M. J., Farrell, M. P., and Barnes, G. M. (2006). *Jocks and athletes: College students' reflections on identity, gender, and high school sports*. Paper presented at the American Sociological Association annual meeting. Montreal, Quebec, Canada.

Mutz, M. (2012). Athletic participation and the approval and use of violence: A comparison of adolescent males in different sport disciplines. *European Journal for Sport and Society*, 9(3), 177-201.

Ojala, K. and Nesdale, D. (2004). Bullying and social identity: The effects of group norms and distinctiveness threat on attitudes toward bullying. *British Journal of Developmental Psychology,* 22, 19-35.

Oransky, M. and Fisher, C. (2009). The development and validation of the meanings of adolescent masculinity scale. *Psychology of Men and Masculinity*, 10, 57-72. doi:10. 1037/a0013612.

Peguero, A. A. (2008). Bullying victimization and extracurricular activity. *Journal of School Violence,* 7, 71-85.

Pokhrel, P., Sussman, S., Black, D., and Sun, R. (2010). Peer group self-identification as a predictor of relational and physical aggression among high school students. *Journal of School Health,* 80, 249-258.

Prinstein, M. J. and Cillessen, A. H. N. (2003). Forms and functions of adolescent peer aggression associated with high levels of peer status. *Merrill-Palmer Quarterly* 49(3) 310-342.

Reynes, E. and Lorant, J. (2001). Do competitive martial arts attract aggressive children? *Perceptual and Motor Skills*, 93, 382-386. doi: 10.2466/pms.2001.93.2.382.

Richman, E. L. and Shaffer, D. R. (2000). "If you let me play sports." *Psychology of Women Quarterly*, 24, 189-199.

Shannon, C. S. (2013). Bullying in recreation and sport settings: Exploring risk factors, prevention efforts, and intervention strategies. *Journal of Park and Recreation Administration,* 31, 15-33.

Scholte, R. H., Engels, R. C., Overbeek, G., de Kemp, R. A., and Haselager, G. J. (2007). Stability in bullying and victimization and its association with social adjustment in childhood and adolescence. *Journal of Abnormal Child Psychology,* 35, 217-228.

Smith, L. C. (2014). This is the way the case crumbles. *ESPN The Magazine*. Retrieved from http://espn.go.com/nfl/notebook/_/id/10566795/breaking-aaron-hernandez-case-eight-months-arrest-espn-magazine.

Stafford, A., Alexander, K. and Fry, D. (2013). Playing through pain: Children and young people's experiences of physical aggression and violence in sport. *Child Abuse Review*, 22, 287-299. doi: 10.1002/car.2289.

Steinfeldt, J. A., Foltz, B. D., Mungro, J., Speight, Q. L., Wong, Y. J., and Blumberg, J. (2011). Masculinity socialization in sports: Influence of college football coaches. *Psychology of Men and Masculinity,* 12, 247-259. doi:10.1037/a0020170.

Steinfeldt, J. A., LaFollette, J. R., Vaughan, E. L., and Steinfeldt, M. C. (2012). Bullying among adolescent football players: Role of masculinity and moral atmosphere. *Psychology of Men Masculinity,* 13, 340-353.

Steinfeldt, M. S. and Steinfeldt, J. A. (2012). Athletic identity and conformity to masculine norms among college football players. *Journal of Applied Sport Psychology*, 24, 115-128. doi: 10.1080/10413200.2011.603405.

Stirling, A. E. (2008). Definition and constituents of maltreatment in establishing a conceptual framework for research practitioners. *British Journal of Sports Medicine,* 43, 1091-1099.

Storch, E. A., Bagner, D. M., Geffken, G. R., and Baumeister, A. L. (2004). Association between overt and relational aggression and psychosocial adjustment in undergraduate college students. *Violence and Victims*, 19, 689-700.

Wells, Jr., T. V., Karp, B. S., Birenbroim, B., and Brown, D. W. (2014). *Report to the National Football League concerning issues of workplace conduct at the Miami Dolphins*. Retrieved from: http://63bba9dfdf9675bf3f10-68be460ce43dd2a60dd64ca5eca4ae1d.r37.cf1.rackcdn.com/PaulWeissReport.pdf.

In: Handbook on Bullying
Editor: Phoebe Triggs
ISBN: 978-1-63463-023-8

Chapter 3

CYBERBULLYING

Caleb McCoy, Marisa Potate and Cliff McKinney *
Mississippi State University, Mississippi, US

Abstract

Bullies are individuals who use a superior force, whether it is physical or mental, to assert dominance over others in an effort to do what they ordinarily wouldn't. Recently, technology has become a fundamental part of life. People can't seem to escape technology without having to cut off all communication from the world. Access to the Internet has become more readily available through new technology such as tablets and mobile phones. As the need for physical communication decreases, use of cyberbullying as an alternative form of traditional bullying has become devastatingly prevalent. Cyberbullying is becoming more frequent throughout the world with advances in technology rapidly changing the traditional definition of bullying. Cyberbullying has become a way for those who typically would not bully, to terrorize without consequence, so it is not only affecting those who would have traditionally bullied, but it is also affecting a broader range of individuals including all ages through childhood, adolescents, and adulthood. Those who are bullied generally show more cognitive and affective empathy. Further, students who have pro-victim attitudes (i.e. the belief that bullying is unacceptable, victims are acceptable, and defending victims is valued) are less likely to be bullied than other students. Unfortunately, there are many dimensions to cyberbullying that make it easier to attempt than traditional bullying. One of these is the absence of physical strength. Those who were not strong enough to bully in a traditional setting, find it easier to bully via the Internet. Cyberbullying also decreases the level of awareness of the victim's distress. Another factor that makes cyberbullying easier is the ability to be anonymous to some extent over the Internet. There is a method of indirectly bullying people over the Internet as well. By tortuously posting a picture or statement on a social media page, cyberbullying can directly affect the victim without the bullying needing to target a specific person. Further, there is a lack of fear in cyberbullies, and they are often unaware or less aware of the consequences for their behaviors. Some cyberbullying attempts are even based on the ability of a teacher to intervene on traditional bullying attempts giving the bully an outlet with fewer consequences. Cyberbullying has the same side effects and consequences as traditional bullying. Low self-esteem and depression have been more consistent in victims rather than

* E-mail address: cmckinney@psychology.msstate.edu; Tel: 662-325-3782; Fax: 662-325-7212; Address: Mississippi State University, Department of Psychology, P.O. Box 6161, Mississippi State, Mississippi 39762, US. (Corresponding author)

non-victims. In the past, bullying took place in specific environments such as school, work, home; places that are supposed to offer a sense of safety. Cyberbullying completely diminishes the idea of safety for victims of bullying. Victims are often unable to find a place of security due to the accessibility of technology and other people. However, many programs and organizations have worked to put an end to bullying by implementing constant awareness and guidelines within schools, workplaces, and social media.

In general, children are seen as the most prominent source of internet bullying. Although they are not the only age group that can be a source of cyberbullying, most of the research in cyberbullying has been done on this age group. Children and adolescents in the present have been raised as part of an internet generation. However, children and adolescents aren't the only age group affected by cyberbullying. Adults have also been involved with sides; bullying and being bullied with the use of social media and technology. Therefore, it is of great importance to note the amount of cyberbullying that occurs among children, adolescents and adults. In this paper, cyberbullying will be compared with traditional bullying by reviewing the similarities, differences, perceptions, and characteristics of multiple forms cyberbullying. Also, this paper will discuss a few cases that involved victims of cyberbullying, and prevention plans that have recently been added to intervene.

Similarities and Differences between Cyberbullying and Bullying

First, it is of great importance to point out that cyberbullying is much different than traditional bullying. Although there is not a completely agreed upon definition of cyberbullying, it definitely lacks some components of traditional bullying that may have aided in decreasing ambiguity among the perpetrators and victims. For example, cyberbullying contains text that maybe easily misunderstood with no other types of communication to assist in meaning. When body language and eye contact are not taken into account, words can be easily twisted into different meanings than what was originally intended (Baruch, 2005). Because of this, cyberbullying can be much harder to identify than traditional bullying styles. Furthermore, text on the internet or through mobile devices may stay in cyberspace for unlimited amount of time or until someone takes the comments down, but the text may have gone viral at that point. There is no way to know for sure where text may end up on the internet. Spoken words may disappear, but hurtful comments through cyberspace may have a longer effect. In addition to this, some researchers are in disagreement as to whether or not this should be counted as repetition due to its lasting effect (Slonje & Smith, 2007). Another factor in cyberbullying that is different than in traditional bullying is that there is a certain amount of anonymity that comes with being a cyberbully.

Unfortunately, cyberbullies can mask their identities a number of different ways on the internet. A traditional bully may find masking themselves difficult. In fact, traditional bullies generally bully on the basis of physical strength whereas cyberbullies do not worry about appearance. Instead, they are able to focus more on emotional strength, ease of manipulation, and dominance (Ybarra & Mitchell, 2004). Further, the lack of exposure creates an environment where the bully has little chance of developing skills such as empathy because there are no consequences for the bully (Froese-Germain, 2008). This is contrary to traditional bullying where the bully is face to face with the victim. Even though cyberbullying is much different than traditional bullying, it is also similar when it comes to the motive for attempting to cyberbully someone else. The motive behind traditional bullying is generally to cause distress to another person because of jealousy or dislike. The motive for cyberbullying is generally the same.

Characteristics of Cyberbully Perpetrators and Victims

As far as a profile for child and adolescent cyberbully victims, a definite profile has been unclear. Some researchers claim that there is no significant difference between the rate of cyberbullying toward boys and girls (Li, 2006; Patchin & Hinduja, 2006; Slonje & Smith, 2007). Some other research has shown that girls may be more prone to being cyberbullied than boys are (Li, 2007; Smith, Mahdavi, Carvalho, & Tippet, 2006). This difference could possibly be due to demographic differences as well as several other factors. Another factor that has been disagreed upon in the literature is age. Some research has shown that the chances of being cyberbullied increases with age (Kowalski and Limber, 2007; Patchin and Hinduja, 2006). Some has shown that there is a decrease in the chances of being cyberbullied as children and adolescents grow older (Slonje & Smith, 2007). Still other research has shown that there has been neither an increase nor a decrease in cybervictimization as children grow older (Smith et al., 2006, 2008). Still other research has shown that the ages in which cyberbullying seems to be the biggest problem are ages 11 to 18 years (Baumand, 2007).

Further, there are many characteristics of internet usage that may play a role in cybervictimization or perpetration. Li (2007) found that there was no link between the amount of time spent on the internet and the amount of time users bullied or were victimized by bullies. However, Ybarra (2004) found that the amount of time on the internet and the use of instant messaging were significantly correlated with cybervictimization among females. Ybarra (2004) also found that the amount of internet use in males was a small predictor for internet harassment. Patchin and Hinduja (2006) had similar results, and they found that those who spent more time on the internet were more likely to experience online bullying. Juvonen and Gross (2008) even found that webcam use was correlated with a higher risk of repeated cyberbullying.

In addition to these characteristics, some studies also have shown that different psychological characteristics may have a relationship to cyberbullying. Unfortunately, it is difficult to tell whether these characteristics are causes or symptoms of cyberbullying. 42.5% of cyberbullying victims felt frustrated according to Patchin and Hinduja (2006). Similarly, 40% felt angry and 27% felt sad. These figures could be due to the fact that cyberbullying can cause these problems, but it is also possible that these individuals have these characteristics already, making them more susceptible to cyberbullying and even traditional bullying. One study of males found that they were 8 times more likely to be bullied if they had depressive symptoms (Ybarra, 2004). Also, Juvonen and Gross (2008) conducted a study where a positive relationship was shown between social anxiety and cyberbullying. Most of these studies also found that those who were prone to being bullied in the traditional style were also prone to being bullied through cyberbullying in up to one out of three cases (Deheu & Bolman, 2008; Juvonen & Gross, 2008; Li, 2007).

Perceptions of Cyberbullying

Cyberbullying clearly is a big problem, but it is unclear whether the perceptions of cyberbullying reflect this throughout each generation. In one study of children (Vandebosch & van Cleemput, 2009), when asked if they had been involved with cyberbullying, 11% said that they had been cyberbullied, 18% admitted to being the perpetrator in a cyberbullying situation, and 27.9% said that they were bystanders to a cyberbullying attempt. Further, 63.8% of respondents considered cyberbullying to be a big problem. These numbers come from when respondents were asked directly if they had been involved in bullying. However, when students were asked questions about specific types of cyberbullying but the word bullying was not used, there was a much greater response. It showed that 61.9% had been victims, 52.5% had been perpetrators, and 76.3% had been bystanders. On average, about 20% of people perceive themselves to be the victim of cyberbullying, but the reality is, that cyberbullying occurs much more often than that.

One of the most important factors of Cyberbullying is the perception of it by those who are perpetrators, victims, and bystanders. Many times, teachers are aware that cyberbullying and do not know how to effectively stop it from happening. One of the most difficult problems that administrators and educators face is the not infringing on first amendment rights by punishing students for cyberbullying that occurred outside the school (Willard, 2007). One study found that even when anti-bullying campaigns are promoted in schools, they are not necessarily effective (Ferguson, Miguel, Kilburn, and Sanchez, 2007). Many researchers have found that it is extremely difficult for a school to implement programs that effectively reduce cyberbullying (Merrell, Gueldner, Ross, & Isava, 2008; Smith, Schneider, Smith, & Ananiadou, 2004).

Online Gaming

A newer realm to cyberbullying has become an increasing problem: online gaming. This method is not as anonymous as some other methods (i.e., the cyberbully may have an identifiable in-game avatar), but can still give the perpetrator a sense of superiority over the victim. With the use of screen names or avatars instead of real names or face-to-face interactions, it is completely possible for a perpetrator to remain anonymous if they feel that it is necessary (i.e., a perpetrator can create multiple avatars ensuring anonymity). Unfortunately, online gaming has become one of the most popular leisure activities for adolescents (Gross, 2010), so it may be easier for a perpetrator to victimize youth playing these games. Also, the aggressive nature of video games may play a role in increasing aggression (Huesmann, 2010), which could be referenced to the observational learning theory proposed by Bandura (1973). Some video games even reward aggressive behavior (Polman, Orobio de Castro, & van Aken, 2008), and video game addictions have been associated with aggressive behavior (Anderson et al., 2010).

Video games have become one of the most popular leisure activities among adolescents. Because they are being exposed more to video games, they are also being exposed to what is included in the video games. Most video games contain aggression in some form. It has been concluded that video games promote aggression through observational learning (Bandura, 1973; Huesmann, 2010). Not only do video games promote cyberbullying, but they may also play a role in promoting traditional bullying through exposure to violence and aggression. Those who engage in violent video games are less likely to show empathy and are more likely to show aggressive tendencies (Anderson et al., 2010). Unfortunately video games may be to blame for much of the cyberbullying and traditional bullying that occurs among youth.

Adult Cyberbullying

Unfortunately, cyberbullying may even continue into adulthood. There has not been nearly as much literature on cyberbullying in adults as there has been on children and adolescents. Some researchers have tried to fill the gap in the literature, but there is still much to learn. Although the motives of bullying at this age are similar to those of younger children and adolescents and generally stem from jealousy and dislike, there are many more reasons that a person might be bullied. Another motivation for young adults to cyberbully is "trolling" or using cyberbullying as entertainment. One study found that up to 30% of adult perpetrators cyberbully purely for entertainment purposes (Rafferty & Vander Ven, 2014). One of the most common reasons for an adult to be cyberbullied or deal with cyber aggression is sexual orientation. One study explains that an increase in use of smart phones and social media by adults may be a cause for an increase of cyberbullying in adults (Lenhart, Purcell, Smith, & Zichuhr, 2010).

Among adults, cyberstalking seems to be a more prominent form of cyberbullying. Recent studies have shown that cyberstalkers tend to be more educated, struggle with internet addiction and are over the age of 16, which means that cyberstalking is much more prevalent among adults than children and adolescents (Reyns et al., 2012). Furthermore, cyberbullying in the workplace has become more common as technologies in businesses have advanced. One earlier study by Finn (2004) found that 10-15 percent of adults were victimized by some type of cyberbullying. Those numbers have increased greatly since that point. Walker, Sockman, and Koehn (2011) found that 56 percent of young adults had been victimized on social media sites like facebook, and 45 percent of young adults had been victimized through cell phones.

Adaptation of Bullying with Technology and Social Media

With the development of technology rapidly growing in today's society, technology has worked its way into our daily tasks. Landline phones, dial-up Internet, and bulky desktop computers have been replaced by cellphones, Wi-Fi, and tablets. As these devices become more accessible, the use of them as tools to bully has increased also. In the 1980s, the words "YouTube," "Facebook Post," and "Tweet" did not exist, but these words are almost inescapable in conversation presently among adolescents. These are only a few examples of social media that have affected the way traditional bullying has progressed. Traditional bullying required for the bully to be physically present to torment and manipulate the victim. However, with cyberbullying, the bully can be anywhere using technology and social media to manipulate the victim. Cyberbullying has been described as being cruel to others by sending or posting harmful material or engaging in other forms of social aggression using the Internet or other digital technologies (Willard, 2007).

There are many ways for bullies to use social media and technology to victimize. Willard (2007) explains 8 forms of cyberbullying. The term "flaming" is used to describe an online altercation using aggression and profanity. Flaming is not restricted to online social media such as Facebook and Twitter, but can also be done via text messaging and email. Once again, with the use of technology, people are able have arguments with each other without having to be physically present and without having to vocalize their aggression. If flaming develops into a common occurrence from the bully it becomes an even more problematic. "Harassment" is the repetition of sending vulgar and insulting messages after the initial situation(s) have occurred. This is seen in both traditional bullying and cyberbullying. The bully or bullies continually badger the victim(s) until they become submissive and more vulnerable. Both flaming and harassment can be unnoticed by other parties due to the lack of publicity. However, harassment can be made public directly and indirectly. "Denigration" is using social media to disrespect someone by posting horrid rumors and/or embarrassing pictures to hurt the friendships and reputation of the bullied. This is a method used by bullies to publically humiliate their victims and can commonly be done indirectly. The bully can publically post a distressing picture of the victim without "tagging" him or her to it. This will allow anyone to see it and the target not having to know the picture is being publicized.

"Impersonation" is the act of pretending to be someone else to send and post harmful material to incriminate or harm the person, friendships, and reputations. With the use of technology, the ease of accessing someone's social media profile and creating a fake, with the person's own pictures, has become an everyday occurrence. Often the bully doesn't have to create a fake profile; he or she can "hack" their victims' social media account and cause damage. Denigration and impersonation are two ways that bullies might "out" their victim. "Outing" is sharing someone's secret(s), embarrassing information, or private pictures online. This term is commonly heard in the LGBT community when someone who has not publically announced his or her sexuality is suddenly exposed as gay or lesbian. However, this term is universal when dealing with the exposure of personal information by a bully to harm or embarrass the victim. This type of exposure can be done directly or indirectly as well using deceit and manipulation. "Trickery" is the action of talking someone into revealing embarrassing information or images online. This is a method used by traditional bullies without the use of technology, usually by manipulation or blackmail. Another method used both online and offline is "exclusion." This occurs when the bullying party purposely and harshly omits someone from a group or event using rejection. Cyberbullies do this by excluding the victim from an exclusive online social group, causing the person to feel unwanted and unimportant. Online bullying takes an even more drastic progression from the traditional method of stalking to being able to stalk a victim without physically seeing or knowing the person. "Cyberstalking" is intense repetitive harassment towards someone using threats and denigration to bestow substantial fear.

Examples of Cyberbullying in the Media

Throughout advancements in technology there have been several cases in which people have been victimized by cyberbullies. There are several different ways that this is possible. In some cases bullies stalk their victims. In other cases they post hateful and rude comments and messages on social media sites and instant messaging. Cyberbullying happens everyday, but it goes unrecognized in most cases. However, there are some cases that have been brought to light by the news and social media.

Manti Te'o and Catfish

Perhaps one of the most devastating occurrences of cyberbullying is what is known as catfishing. Catfishing is the act of creating a false emotional relationship through an internet site with someone who believes that the relationship is with a real person. Most people who are considered catfish create fake profiles with real pictures that are stolen from a real person and made to look like a completely different person. In essence, an identity is stolen to create a fake relationship.

One of the most publicized times that this has happened was the instance of the Manti Te'o hoax. Manti Te'o was a football player at Notre Dame, and had begun to form a relationship with Lennay Kekua in his freshman year of college. At first it was a friendly relationship, but then it became much deeper. He began to form an emotional connection with her. There were times when he would attempt to meet her but his attempts would fail. There were also times when he would attempt to video chat but his attempts at that would also fail. This relationship went on for several months. At one point, Manti was informed that she had gotten into a terrible car accident and was left in a coma. When she was finally out of the coma, she was supposedly diagnosed with Leukemia. She was released from the hospital, and the next day Manti was informed that the she had passed just hours after his grandmother. Then he was informed that the entire relationship had been a hoax. Lennay had never existed, but the pain he felt was real. He had been a part of a cruel prank, and had lost someone that he really cared about and really thought existed. His story went viral, and became a high profile case. This kind of thing happens quite frequently, but his story was in the limelight because he was well known prior to the incident. The media ridiculed him and said that he was a liar and even went as far as to spread the theory that he might have used this story to gain publicity or even to hide that he was gay.

Not only did this prank hurt Te'o, but it also hurt his family and friends. It also hurt Diane O'Meara, the face of Lennay Kekua. Tuisasosopo, who had gone to school with Diane, had stolen pictures from her facebook and even asked her to record videos, so he could send them to Manti. Diane was unaware of what Tuisasosopo was really doing with her pictures and videos as he had told her that he was using them for awareness for his ill friend. After her face was plastered across the media, she faced many challenges. People accused her of setting the hoax up as well as playing a role in the entire prank. She denies that she had anything to do with it. She was just as much a victim as Manti was. As for the perpetrator, Tuisasosopo used the scandal to test his sexual orientation. He had a crush on Manti, and used this fake profile to form a relationship with Manti. Things like this happen every day to average people. There is really no way to stop it from happening. Even setting privacy blocks on websites was not enough for Diane O'Meara. There was also no way for Manti Te'o to know that this was all a hoax.

Richie Incognito and the Miami Dolphins

Richie Incognito was an offensive lineman for Miami Dolphins until he was released from the team in late October of 2013. His release was based on his past record of bullying other teammates, which he described as "toughening them up"(Sciullo, 2013). Jonathon Martin was a second year player for the Dolphins, until his lifestyle and the bullying from other teammates were causing him emotional distress. After an incident in the football team's cafeteria and because of the bullying from his teammates, particularly Incognito, Martin left the team. Afterwards, Martin's representative released a voicemail and other evidence of abuse from Incognito to the Dolphins. After leaving the team, Martin then began to face cyberbullying from other teammates and Incognito. Calling him a quitter and other harmful names, Martin's twitter account and phone began to receive all sorts of accusations of being a traitor to his team.

From this incident, a more thorough investigation was done on Incognito's past relationships with other teammates. His history of bullying goes back to 2002, when he was accused of bullying a walk-on offensive lineman, Jack Limbaugh. Incognito was only a freshman at the time, in Nebraska. More evidence appeared following the full investigation, where Incognito had been reported for bullying an Asian-American trainer as well. His history of abuse included harsh racial and sexual slander towards all those he bullied (Tracy, 2014). However, even after the proof of Incognito's bullying was exposed, his teammates defended him. The team blamed Martin for breaking the rules of locker room conduct by taking Incognito's jokes so personal. They viewed the text messages, voicemails, and verbal slurs as common horse-play. After the investigation was over, Incognito was taken off the non-football illness list and indefinitely released from the Miami Dolphins. Although he was released, he signed papers finalizing his retirement as a way to still receive an income and not be financially burdened.

The case between the Miami Dolphins and Richie Incognito did not lead to a tragic ending for Martin either. He was reunited with his first head coach after the Dolphins agreed to trade him for another draft pick with the San Francisco 49ers. This case opened a lot of closets, revealing cyberbullying and bullying among many professional athletics. This is only one case that shows how cyberbullying can affect adults rather than just children and adolescents.

New Jersey versus Dharun Ravi

Tyler Clementi was an 18-year-old individual who had recently graduated high school and was a freshman at Rutgers University. He was a prominent violinist and was an excellent student. The summer before his first semester at Rutgers University, Tyler Clementi told his parents that he was gay. His father was accepting and his mother was as well but was a little withdrawn. After coming out to his parents, Clementi posted on Twitter about this event and his newly found feelings. During this summer he was also assigned a roommate at the university. Both young men, Tyler Clementi and Dharun Ravi, used social media to learn a little about each other.

By visiting Clementi's Twitter page, Dharun Ravi discovered that his new roommate was gay. After reading this, he posted, "Just found out my roommate is gay." They went on as roommates with no evidence of animosity or detestation until Clementi asked to have the dorm room to himself on the night of September 19, 2010. Ravi complied with Clementi's request and left for the night, but not until he set up his webcam so that he could watch. Once Ravi left, he went to a friend's dorm room to watch what was happening in his own room. He had set up a live stream from his camera and was able to see Clementi and his date, in addition to broadcasting it to other friends. Ravi then posted on twitter, "Roommate asked for the room till midnight. I went into molly's room and turned on my webcam. I saw him making out with a dude. Yay."(Squawstar, 2012).

Clementi saw the post and reported this incident to the resident hall advisor as well as his beliefs that Ravi would again spy on him. Ravi's excuse for setting up the webcam was because he was worried about theft. The resident hall advisor showed little interest in the incident and Clementi left. Ravi posted early one day, "Anyone with iChat, I dare you to video chat me between the hours of 9:30 and 12. Yes it's happening again." Clementi then went and requested that he be assigned to a different dorm room, but nothing happened. After viewing Ravi's posts about seeing Clementi and his date engaged in romantic activities, Tyler Clementi walked to the George Washington Bridge and jumped off. Taking his own life at the age of 18, Clementi had felt humiliated and uncomfortable, because one person invaded his privacy and exposed it (O'Donnell, 2012)

Ravi was charged with 15 indictments, which included invasion of privacy and hate crimes, but not murder. He was found guilty on all counts and could have faced years in prison. However, Ravi was sentenced to 30 days in jail, 300 hours of community service, and 3 years of probation. He spent 20 days in jail before he was released. To the family of Tyler Clementi, this was far too tolerant and unjust. Since the incident, the Clementi family has created the Tyler Clementi foundation, which hopes to help teenagers and young adults against this type of bullying by promoting safe, inclusive, and respectful social environments.

What Should Be Done

The result of cyberbullying has shown devastating psychological consequences to the victim. With symptoms of depression, anxiety, and even suicidal thoughts, cyberbullying prevention plans have been brought forward to help spot victims of cyberbullying as well as identify the bullies. Almost all settings, workplace and educational, have strict policies against bullying and cyberbullying. Policies that restrict people from using social media and electronics as tools to bully are fairly new, considering the advancement of technology in the past decade. Preventing cyberbullying is different than preventing traditional bullying.

Because of the rapid use of social media and other electronics, it is close to impossible to keep the bullying messages away from the victim. Second, because of the ability to release a rumor or statement on the Internet to the entire world, it is impossible to see how many people have seen it. Lastly, the ability for the bully to remain anonymous with ease makes it difficult for officials to pinpoint the bully. Educational, workplace, and most other settings have now implemented policies to intervene between bullies and their victims. However, it is usually up to the individual(s) to come forward and report the incidents. For instance, if a student posts a humiliating video of another student off campus and after school hours, the school doesn't have the authority to fully punish the bully and must leave it up to local law enforcement to continue with the investigation.

Another problem that occurs is separating cyberbullying from just joking. This is up to the victim to decide. If the victim doesn't tell the cyberbully that their jokes are offending them, then the bully can say that he or she was just "joking". This does not include forward taunts or threats; those that are obviously causing harm cannot be passed off as joking. Cyberbullying cases are often passed off as simple joking or kids being kids, but through prevention programs and no bullying policies among schools and workplaces; it is more difficult to bully traditionally or through social media and with the use of technology. Federal and State governments have both implemented new policies to old bullying prevention methods, adjusting the way we view bullying and how we recognize victims (Jordan & Austin, 2012).

Since technology is growing more advanced every year, schools and offices have become more aware of what to look for when identifying possible victims of bullying. Almost all schools have implemented a no-bullying policy, which includes cyberbullying to a certain degree, and states have implemented laws that identify bullying as harassment (Goodno, 2011). These laws and policies help make it more difficult for bullies to succeed in victimizing others and overall find just for those that have been harmed, physically or mentally. However, with electronics and social media being around every corner, these laws and policies must consistently advance and adapt to new ways that cyberbullies impair others.

References

Anderson, C. A., Shibuya, A., Ihori, N., Swing, E. L., Bushman, B. J., Sakamoto, A., et al. (2010). Violent video game effects on aggression, empathy, and prosocial behavior in Eastern and Western countries: A meta-analytic review. *Psychological Bulletin,* 136(2), 151-173.

Bandura, A. (1973). Aggression: A social learning analysis. Englewood Cliffs, NJ: Prentice-Hall.

Baruch, Y. (2005). Bullying on the net: Adverse behavior on email and its impact. *Information and Management,* 42(2), 361–71.

Bauman, S. (2007). Cyberbullying: A virtual menace. Melbourne: Paper presented to the National Coalition against Bullying National Conference.

Christian Elledge, L. L., Williford, A., Boulton, A. J., DePaolis, K. J., Little, T. D., & Salmivalli, C. (2013). Individual and contextual predictors of cyberbullying: The influence of children's provictim attitudes and teachers' ability to intervene. *Journal of Youth and Adolescence*, 42(5), 698-710.

CNN. (2013, January 23). Face of Te'o girlfriend speaks out. [Video file]. Retrieved from https://www.youtube.com/watch?v=aEKb8tdi4tQ

CNN. (2013, January 30). Dr. Phil interviews the man who says he hoaxed Manti Te'o. [Video file]. Retrieved from https://www.youtube.com/watch?v=O7rEIqLBQ_I

Couric, K. (2013, January 24). Manti Te'o fake girlfriend hoax interview with Katie Couric. [Video file]. Retrieved from https://www.youtube.com/watch?v=O0wOgRVySgU

Deheu, F., & Bolman, C.V. (2008). Cyberbullying: Respondents' experiences and parental perception. *Cyberpsychology and Behavior,* 11(2), 217–23.

Ferguson, C. J., Miguel, C. S., Kilburn, J. C., & Sanchez, P. (2007). The effectiveness of school-based anti-bullying programs: A meta-analytic review. *Criminal Justice Review*, 32(4), 401 – 414.

Finn, J. (2004). A survey of online harassment at a university campus. *Journal of Interpersonal Violence*, 19, 468–483.

Froese-Germain, B. (2008). Bullying gets digital shot-in-the-arm. Retrieved May 5, 2014, from: http://www.cea-ace.ca/.

Goodno, N. H. (2011). How public schools can constitutionally halt cyberbullying: a model cyberbullying policy that considers first amendment, due process, and fourth amendment challenges. *Wake Forest Law Review*, 46, 641-700.

Gross, M. L. (2010). Advergames and the effects of game-product congruity. *Computers in Human Behavior, 26*(6), 1259-1265.

Huesmann, L. R. (2010). Nailing the coffin shut on doubts that violent video games stimulate aggression: Comment on Anderson et al. (2010). *Psychological Bulletin*, 136(2), 179-181.

Jordan, K., & Austin, J. (2012). A review of the literature on bullying in U.S. schools and how a parent–educator partnership can be an effective way to handle bullying. *Journal of Aggression, Maltreatment, & Trauma*, 21, 440-458.

Juvonen, J., & Gross, E. F. (2008) Extending the school grounds? Bullying experiences in cyberspace. *Journal of School Health*, 78(9), 496–505.

Kiriakidis, P., & Kavoura, A. (2010). Cyberbullying: A review of the literature on harassment through the internet and other electronic means. *Family Community Health*, 33(2), 82–93.

Kowalski, R. M., & Limber, S. P. (2007). Electronic bullying among middle school students. *Journal of Adolescent Health*, 41, 22–30.

Lenhart, A., Purcell, K. Smith, A., & Zichuhr, K. (2010). Social media and mobile internet use among teens and young adults. *Pew Internet and American Life Center*. Retrieved May 5, 2014 from (http://www.pewinternet.org/Reports/2010/Social-Media-and-Young-Adults.aspx).

Li, Q. (2006). Cyberbullying in schools. A research of gender differences. *School Psychology International*, 27(2), 157–170.

Li, Q. (2007). New bottle but old wine: A research of cyberbullying in schools. *Computers in Human Behavior* 23(4), 1777–1791.

Merrell, K.W., Gueldner, B. A., Ross, S.W., & Isava, D. M. (2008). How effective are school bullying intervention programs? A meta-analysis of intervention research. *School Psychology Quarterly*, 23(1), 26 – 42.

O'Donnell, M. (2012, June 27). Parents of Rutgers student who committed suicide change view of homosexuality. *Rock Center NBC News*. Retrieved from http://rockcenter.nbcnews.com/_news/2012/06/27/12437202-parents-of-rutgers-student-who-committed-suicide-change-view-of-homosexuality?lite

Patchin, J.W. and S. Hinduja (2006). Bullies move beyond the schoolyard. A preliminary look at cyberbullying. *Youth Violence and Juvenile Justice*, 4(2), 148–69.

Patchin, J.W., & Hinduja, S. (2010). Cyberbullying and self-esteem. *Journal of School Health*, 80(12), 614-621.

Pettalia, J. L., Levin, E., & Dickinson, J. (2013). Cyberbullying: Eliciting harm without consequence. *Computers in Human Behavior*, 29(6), 2758-2765.

Polman, H., Orobio de Castro, B., & van Aken, M. A. G. (2008). Experimental study of the differential effects of playing versus watching violent video games on children's aggressive behaviors. *Aggressive Behaviors,* 34, 256-264.

Rafferty, R., & Vander Ven, T. (2014). "I hate everything about you": A qualitative examination of cyberbullying and on-line aggression in a college sample. *Deviant Behavior,* 35(5), 364-377.

Reyns, B.W., Henson, B., & Fisher, B. (2012). Stalking in the twilight zone: Extent of cyberstalking victimization and offending among college students. *Deviant Behavior,* 33, 1-25.

Sciullo, M. (2013, October 31). In a digital age, Richie Incognito, is nothing but. *The Pittsburgh Post-Gazette.* Retrieved from http://www.post-gazette.com/business/ technology/2013/11/11/In-a-digital-age-Richie-Incognito-is-anything-but/stories/201311110016

Slonje, R. & Smith, P. K. (2007) Cyberbullying: Another main type of bullying? *Scandinavian Journal of Psychology* 49(2), 147–54.

Smith, J. D., Schneider, B. H., Smith, P. K., & Ananiadou, K. (2004). The effectiveness of whole-school anti-bullying programs: A synthesis of evaluation research. School Psychology Review, 33 (4), 547 – 560.

Smith, P. K., Mahdavi, J., Carvalho, M., & Tippett, N. (2006). An investigation into cyberbullying, its forms, awareness and impact, and the relationship between age and gender in cyberbullying', anti-bullying alliance. Retrieved from http://www.anti-bullyingalliance.org.uk/downloads/pdf/ cyberbullyingreportfinal230106_000.pdf

Squawstar. (2012, November 28). The Tyler Clementi Story [Video file]. Retrieved from http://www.youtube.com/watch?v=6EpFua8wyNs

Tracy, M. (2014, February 14). Why the Miami Dolphins bullying scandal indicts the whole NFL. *New Republic.* Retrieved from http://www.newrepublic.com/article/116642/miami-dolphins-jonathan-martin-bullied-richie-incognito-says-repor

Walker, C., Sockman, B., & Koehn, S. (2011). An exploratory study of cyberbullying with undergraduate university students. *TechTrends,* 55, 31-38.

Willard, N. (2007). *Educator's Guide to Cyberbullying and Cyberthreats.* www.accem.org /pdf/cbcteducator.pdf

Willard, N. E. (2007). The authority and responsibility of school officials in responding to cyberbullying. *Journal of Adolescent Health,* 41, 64 – 65.

Vandebosch, H., & Van Cleemput, K. (2009). Cyberbullying among youngsters: Profiles of bullies and victims. *New Media & Society,* 11(8), 1349-1371.

Ybarra, M. L., & Mitchell, K. J. (2004). Online aggressor/targets, aggressors, and targets: A comparison of associated youth characteristics. *Journal of Child Psychology and Psychiatry* 45(7), 1308–1316.

Ybarra, M. L. (2004) Linkages between depressive symptomatology and internet harassment among young regular internet users. *Cyberpsychology and Behavior* 7(2), 247–57.

In: Handbook on Bullying
Editor: Phoebe Triggs
ISBN: 978-1-63463-023-8

Chapter 4

BULLYING INTERVENTIONS

Mary Ward Pollard, Courtney Walker and Janet W. Kwan
Mississippi State University, Mississippi, US

Abstract

Bullying has been defined as recurrent harassment of a student or group of students by another student or group. More specifically, bullying encompasses repeated negative actions with an intention to harm or disturb that involves a differential of power, where the more powerful individual attacks or harasses the individual who is less powerful individual. Studies have shown that bullying may lead to long-term negative effects, such as violence and depression, for the both perpetrator and the victim. Therefore, the development and examination of bullying interventions and their effectiveness is important in order to gain an understanding of which interventions may be the most effective in reducing bullying behavior. In general, school-based and/or whole-school approach to anti-bullying programs have been found to be the most empirically-supported intervention technique. However, other interventions, such as interventions aimed at changing the social norms around bullying behavior, have also been shown to be effective. The current chapter provides a thorough review of theoretically diverse bullying interventions that have been shown to be empirically effective at reducing bullying behaviors.

Bullying has been defined as the recurrent harassment of a student or group of students by another student or group. More specifically, bullying encompasses repeated negative actions with an intention to harm or disturb that involves a differential of power, where the more powerful individual attacks or harasses the individual who is a less powerful (Olweus, 1993). Bullying can occur in person, or over the Internet, as social media and other online outlets are becoming more and more popular. Internet bullying is more commonly referred to as "cyberbullying" and involves the use of primarily mobile phones and the Internet in the forms of text messaging, emailing, chatting, picture imaging, and social networking (Smith, 2011). Through these outlets, bullies can act in the forms of threats/intimidating, hacking/impersonation, manipulation/blackmail, and disclosing secrets (O'Higgins, Norman, & Connolly, 2011).

Studies have shown that there are long-term negative effects that result from bullying, such as violence and depression, for the both perpetrator and the victim (Ttofi, Farrington, & Losel, 2012; Ttofi, Farrington, Losel, & Loeber, 2011). One study examining the impact of bullying found that even when accounting and controlling for child psychiatric and family hardships, child victims of bullying were more likely to continue to have emotional problems in adulthood. Moreover, children who did not have pre-existing problems were also more likely to have later emotional problems if they were bullied (Copeland &Wolke, 2013). In addition, the behaviors that bullies utilize at school, both internalizing and externalizing, can be disruptive to the learning process and threaten the already limited teaching time that is available to both the teachers and the students (Paul, Smith, & Blumberg, 2012).

Studying interventions and their effectiveness is important to gain an understanding of which interventions have been shown to be the most effective in reducing bullying behaviors. Typically, bullying intervention and prevention efforts have focused on the school, targeting school policies, protocols, and procedures for responses to bullying incidents. School-based or whole-school approaches to anti-bullying programs have been found to be the most empirically supported intervention techniques (Ttofi & Farrington, 2012; Wurf, 2012). Generally, these methods consist of administrative elements such as anti-bullying policies, close monitoring, raising bullying awareness, curriculum activities and established management plans for incidents of reported bullying (Smith, Pepler, Rigby, 2004). Programs differ across schools, states, and countries; as such, program theories shift but can be loosely associated with theories regarding social learning, social development, and social interaction (Farrington &Ttofi, 2009).

Veeram and Carroll (2007) conducted a systematic review of school-based interventions to prevent bullying. Interventions were categorized into different types, such as curriculum (e.g., lectures), whole-school or multidisciplinary (e.g., teacher training, individual counseling), and social skills groups (e.g., group training in behavior modification). Of the different types of intervention, more whole-school approaches were found to directly reduce bullying more than other approaches (i.e., curriculum and social skills groups approaches; Veeram & Carroll, 2007).

Similarly, Ttofi and Farrington (2011) conducted a large-scale meta-analysis of 40 school-based anti-bullying programs across various countries. The results of the systematic review were congruent with the aforementioned systematic reviews. That is, results indicated that both bullying and victimization decreased as a result of a whole-school intervention program. Key elements such as intensity of the program (i.e., duration of children's participation and teachers' training), inclusion of parent meetings and firm disciplinary methods were found to be particularly effective (Ttofi & Farrington, 2011). In addition, the review also found school-wide anti-bullying policies, information for parents, improved playground supervision and classroom management were associated with decreased bullying. Further, Lee, Kim, and Kim (2013) conducted a meta-analysis of the effect of school-based anti-bullying programs. Findings emphasized that effective school-based interventions included training in emotional control, peer counseling, and a school policy on bullying. Taken together, these reviews provide convincing evidence for the investment, development, and implementation of school-based anti-bullying programs.

Other studies have examined what students perceive to be the most effective approaches to managing traditional bullying and cyberbullying. A study by Paul, Smith, and Blumberg (2012) measured various student perceptions of individual coping strategies and school interventions for bullying and cyberbullying and discovered that the highest intervention item rations were for School Sanctions and Disciplinary Action, primarily permanent suspension from school as the consequence for bullying or cyberbullying. Following behind student ratings for these two intervention items were the Informal Approach and Support Approach, and rated the lowest was the Curricular Approach. In Paul et al.'s 2012 study, results showed that students rated the support of family members, predominantly parents, to be the most helpful coping strategy.

In general, whole-school approaches to anti-bullying programs consist of combined support from the school, teachers, students, and parents in both prevention and intervention efforts (Smith, Pepler, & Ribgy, 2004). As mentioned before, these efforts often translate to administrative elements of intervention such as school-wide anti-bullying policies, close monitoring, raising bullying awareness, curriculum activities and established management plans for incidents of reported bullying (Smith, Pepler, & Ribgy, 2004; Wurf, 2012). Further, although intervention theories may vary amongst schools, states, and countries, most school-based programs have an underlying model that can be loosely associated with theories regarding social learning, social development, and social interaction (Farrington &Ttofi, 2009). This underscores the interpersonal aspect of anti-bullying intervention in promoting social skills and positive peer relations.

One particularly prevalent aspect of school-based approach intervention is the Shared Concern method (SCm; Pikas, 1989, 2002). It is a five-phase bullying intervention conducted by a teacher or counselor within a school setting. Adhering to a conflict resolution model, the intervention elicits non-punitive discussion with students involved and follow-up monitoring. The essence of this model stresses problem solving amongst the students involved, as opposed to traditional methods in which students are questioned, judged and punished (Rigby, 2005). In fact, many school-based programs within Farrington and Ttofi's (2011) meta-analysis consisted of this approach.

According to a recent study conducted by Wurf (2012) in which SCm is applied to four Hong Kong International Schools, the following are the five phases of the intervention. Phase one involves a one-on-one discussion with the student(s) suspected of bullying. Similarly, phase two consists of one-on-one discussions but with victimized student(s) to provide individuals with support and empathy for the situation. It is important to note this phase allows for the teacher or counselor to question whether the victim(s) provoked the bullies' behaviors. During phrase three, another meeting is held with the student(s) who bullied to check their commitment to cease bullying behaviors. Then, phase four allows for the teacher or counselor to establish an agreement between both parties to prevent bullying. Lastly, phase five requires a follow-up to monitor whether bullying has ceased.

Importantly, the SCm has been found to be especially effective in bullying situations in which perpetrators consist of group involvement (Rigby, 2005). This is the case because it allows for a diffusion of responsibility such that the behavior of the group involved in bullying is addressed, as opposed to the behavior of one single perpetrator. In addition, this method emphasizes the importance of exploring group dynamics and individual motives for such behaviors.

In addition to the Shared Concern method, various other programs have been developed to target traditional bullying at school as whole-school approaches. The Bully Busters program was developed by Horne, Bortolomucci, and Newman-Carlson (2003) and provides teachers and administrators with ways to focus on raising awareness of the prevalence of bullying and to develop the essential skills for everyone involved at the school to deal with the problems that stem from bullying. Another focus of the Bully Busters program is to prevent bullying before it starts by showing both students and faculty how to be proactive by acquiring skills, knowledge, and self-efficacy. In addition, there is a parental component that allows parents to learn what they can to do reduce incidence of aggression and bullying.

Whole-school approaches can also be implemented to target cyberbullying. As the use of technology in school-aged children is increasing, and will most likely continue to increase, it is important to target cyberbullying in interventions. Various studies have shown that evidence suggests most students who are cyberbullied are also bullied in other traditional ways (Beran & Li, 2007; Pearce, Cross, Monks, Waters, & Falconer, 2011). Therefore, it may be the case that strategies to address noncyberbullying behaviors, like the whole-school approach, may also effectively target cyberbullying behaviors (Pearce et al., 2011). Other current cyberbullying programs are centered on logical approaches and practical beliefs about prevention instead of scientific evidence (Snakenborg, Van Acker, & Gable, 2011). In these programs, schools implement various interventions, such as teaching students how to prevent bullying and how to effectively address instances in which they might become the victim or the bystander of an incident. In addition, some schools will introduce strategies to their students, such as cooperative learning, peer mediation, and social skills. In particular, some schools may especially focus on emphasizing these strategies to students who are deemed to be more at risk for becoming cyberbullying victims. These students may be anxious, withdrawn, insecure, physically weak, or smaller in size than other students (Snakenborg et al., 2011). However, these aforementioned strategies for addressing cyberbullying, both by itself and as a branch of more traditional bullying, are designed by individual schools and not based on scientific evidence. Researchers have been advocating for studies designed to investigate attributes of both bullies and their victims in order to develop more empirically based interventions (Wong-Lo, Bullock, & Gable, 2009).

Although the whole-school approach mainly targets interventions for bullying, and occasionally cyberbullying, once incidents occur, other approaches have been developed that aim to target bullying before it even happens. Traditionally, research has focused on individual factors (e.g., psychopathology) as well as contextual factors (e.g., socioeconomic status) as potential predictors of bullying behavior. Although this research has provided much insight as to what may contribute to a child engaging in bullying behavior, factors such as social norms and the perceptions of social norms also may play a significant role in bullying. Broadly, research on social norms and the perceptions of these norms has demonstrated that individuals have a tendency to conform to the social norms of his/her group (Asch, 1956). This may be particularly true for children and adolescents as their peers significantly influence their actions. For example, children who perceive bullying as a socially normative behavior amongst their peer group are more likely to engage in the behavior themselves than children who do not perceive bullying as a normative behavior amongst their peers (Duffy & Nesdale, 2008). This social influence on bullying is not exclusive to physical bullying; in fact, a youth's individual beliefs and perceptions of the presence of bullying in their school has also been shown to be predictive of relational aggressive behaviors (Elsaesser & Gorman-Smith, 2013).

It is also important to note that social influence has been found to play a role in bystanding behavior. Specifically, children who perceive that their classmates expect active interventions (e.g., telling a teacher) in bullying situations are less likely to engage in passive by standing behavior (e.g., not telling a teacher and allowing the bullying to continue). Interestingly, this effect on by standing behavior was not influenced by teacher expectations (i.e., perceiving that the *teacher* expected the active intervention) and was stronger for children enrolled in middle school (Pozzoli, Gini, & Vieno, 2012).

These findings highlight the importance of social influence on bullying as well as by standing behavior. Overall, it would appear that if a child perceives bullying to be a socially abnormal behavior in his/her peer group or classroom, he/she might be less likely to engage in the behavior. In addition, if it is socially acceptable among a peer group to actively intervene in a bullying situation, a child may be more likely to intervene. This appears to be increasingly true for middle school aged children and may be due to the significant impact of social influence in their development. Specifically, adolescents may be more likely to adhere to their peer group's social norms in order to "fit-in." However, it is often the case that children and adolescents misperceive the actual norm of their school and communities. For example, a study observing health and well being in adolescents found that adolescents of a normal weight perceived themselves as being overweight and were more likely to experience a larger weight gain into young adulthood than those who did not have this misconception (Cuypers et al., 2012). In other words, adolescents held misconceptions of what constituted a normal weight and, as a result, were more likely to experience negative effects due to this belief. Thus, it may be that adolescents hold misconceptions about their peers' normative behaviors (e.g., high occurrences of bullying, few intervening behaviors) and that this misconception exacerbates the problem of bullying (Perkins, Craig, & Perkins, 2011). As such, interventions that attempt to alter perceptions of bullying as a socially normative behavior, as well as correct any misconceptions about the prevalence of bullying, may be more effective in reducing the behavior long term.

Perkins et al. (2011) developed a research intervention based on the premise that bullying is a function of conforming to peer norms as well as the perceptions of peer norms. The authors hypothesized that children who engage in bullying behavior may perceive that their peers are engaging in the behavior as well, thus conforming to a social norm. The authors also hypothesized that a misconception of the prevalence of bullying may actually exacerbate the bullying behavior. For the intervention, Perkins et al. (2011) obtained an initial baseline of students' perceptions of bullying. Next, the authors provided the students with feedback of the results of the survey in which conveyed the school's actual positive norms. An example of a norms message was, "most middle school students (9 out of 10) agree that students should always try to be friendly with students who are different from themselves" (Perkins et al., 2011).

Overall, Perkins et al. (2011) found that students' perceptions of the prevalence of bullying as well as peer support for bullying was widely misperceived. Specifically, students overestimated how often bullying occurred at their school and their peers' support for bullying. In addition, there was a positive association between students' perceptions of bullying as a supported and common behavior at their school and engaging in bullying behavior. Post-intervention scores indicated a statistically significant decrease in students' perceptions of bullying, self-reported victimization, and perceived peer support for bullying. Further, there was an increase in students' perceptions of peer willingness to report bullying to a teacher. In other words, it became more socially normative to report bullying behavior.

Also based on the notion that bullying may stem from social influences, Botvin, Mahalic, and Grotpeter (1998) developed a program called "Life Skills Training." As a part of this program, school faculty help students in sixth- through ninth-grade to develop social skills in order to learn how to prevent violence, substance use and abuse, and other high-risk behaviors. The students learn these social strategies by developing personal awareness about their own inter-and intrapersonal responsibilities and objectives.

Interventions aimed at changing the social normative beliefs about bullying, such as the intervention described above, may be effective in reducing bullying. In addition, these interventions also may be effective in making positive interventions (e.g., telling a teacher) a more socially normative behavior among a peer group. These interventions could be less likely to be susceptible to many of the barriers often observed with implementing a manual driven intervention into a school. Specifically, the intervention may not require a third party to train the school administration and teachers on how to implement the intervention and could also be freely available to schools. In addition, the intervention could be easily combined with an existing intervention program.

Although the various aforementioned programs have encompassed different focal points and goals, they all have a commonality in that they are universal interventions. In other words, the majority of the programs have been designed to target all students. However, there are also group interventions that focus on students who have demonstrated a high risk for bullying and/or aggression problems, both as instigators and victims. These group methods can take place in the classroom as a part of small group activities or counseling programs, and can coincide with teacher training groups as well that include support groups for maintaining and extending program activities as programs are implemented in their classrooms or with their students. The most common forms of group interventions are the psychoeducational groups, which are effective in assisting and guiding group members with issues they may have with adjustment, therefore possibly preventing future dysfunction (Home, Stoddard, & Bell, 2007). These psychoeducational groups can also help groups of normally functioning students by teaching fundamental skills in communicating respectfully and with empathy, building relationships with other students in the group, engaging in humor, and empowering each other, all while students practice teaching these skills to each other while minimizing outside discussion and promoting positive exchanges during group (Home, Stoddard, & Bell, 2007.).

Counseling groups are also used to target certain groups of students in the school setting. These groups can target more specific students than the psychoeducational groups, and spend more time addressing particular behaviors that the student(s) have previously demonstrated by examining and developing strategies to eliminate these negative bullying behaviors in the future (Home, Stoddard, & Bell, 2007). These groups typically spend more time on facilitating discussion with group members in order to discover the nature of their problems and allow for time to process emotional and cognitive content in order for the students to develop insight. Instead of teachers leading these counseling groups, typically, mental health professionals will offer guidance over these groups. For both psychoeducation groups and counseling groups, researchers have provided evidence that aggression-reduction focused group counseling may be as effective as individual counseling, which makes these interventions not only effective in reducing bullying behaviors, but also cost-effective (Schectman, 2007).

The various interventions that are available to target bullying allow for schools to select an option that best fits their resources and theoretical orientation. Having multiple options also allow for adults to choose how they want to target bullying, in that they can select to prevent it through policies, educate students through discussions and literature, or appropriately punish to eliminate it. A critical first step in decreasing adolescent bullying is to become aware of the various interventions available and understand the empirical evidence of each intervention's effectiveness in different environments as depicted in scientific literature.

References

Asch, S. E. (1956). Studies of independence and conformity: I. A minority of one against a unanimous majority. *Psychological Monographs: General and Applied,* 70(9).

Beran, T.T., & Li, Q. (2007). The relationship between cyberbullying and school bullying. *Journal of Student Wellbeing,* 1(2), 15–33.

Botvin, G. J., Mihalic, S. F., Grotpeter, J. K., & Elliott, D. S. (1998). Blueprints for Violence Prevention, Book Five: Life Skills Training. *Blueprints for Violence Prevention, Book Five: Life Skills Training.*

Copeland, W. E., & Wolke, D. (2013). Impact of bullying trails both victims, bullies into adulthood. *Brown University Child & Adolescent Behavior Letter,* 29(4), 1-5.

Duffy, A. L. & Nesdale, D. (2009). Peer groups, social identity, and children's bullying behavior. *Social Development,* 18(1), 121-139.

Elsaesser, C. Gorman-Smith, D., & Henry, D. (2013). The role of the school environment in relational aggression and victimization. *Journal of Youth and Adolescence,* 42, 235-249.

Farrington, D. P., & Ttofi, M. M. (2009). School-based programs to reduce bullying and victimization. *Campbell Systematic Reviews,* 6, ii-148.

Horne, A.M., Bortolomucci, C.L., & Newman-Carlson, D. (2003). Bully Busters: A teacher's manual for helping bullies, victims, and bystanders (Grades K-5). Champaign, IL: Research Press.

Home, A. M., Stoddard, J. L., & Bell, C. D. (2007). Group approaches to reducing aggression and bullying in school. *Group Dynamics,* 11(4), 262-271. doi:10.1037/089-2699.11.4.262

Cuypers, K., Kvaloy, K., Bratberg, G., Midthjell, K., Holmen, J., & Holmen, T. J. (2012). Being normal weight but feeling overweight in adolescence may affect weight development into young adulthood: An 11- year follow-up: The HUNT Study, Norway. *Journal of Obesity.* doi: 10.1155/2012/601872

Lee, S., Kim, C., & Kim, D. H. (2013). A meta-analysis of the effect of school-based anti-bullying programs. *Journal of Child Health Care,* 16(1), 1-18.

Paul, S., Smith, P. K., & Blumberg, H. H. (2012). Comparing student perceptions of coping strategies and school interventions in managing bullying and cyberbullying incidents. *Pastoral Care in Education,* 30(2), 127-146.

Pearce, N., Cross, D., Monks, H., Waters, S., & Falconer, S. (2011). Current evidence of best practice in whole-school bullying intervention and its potential to inform cyberbullying interventions. *Australian Journal of Guidance & Counselling,* 21(1), 1-21.

Perkins, H. W., Craig, D. W., & Perkins, J. M. (2011). Using social normal to reduce bullying: A research intervention among adolescents in five middle schools. *Group Processes and Intergroup Relations,* 14(5), 703-722.

Pika, A. (1989). A pure concept of mobbing gives the best results for treatment. *School Psychology International, 10*(2), 95-104. Pika, A. (2002). New developments of the shared concern method. *School Psychology International,* 23(3), 307-326.

Pozzoli, T., Gini, G., & Vieno, A. (2012). The role of individual correlates and class norms in defending and passive bystanding behavior in bullying: A multilevel analysis. *Child Development,* 83(6), 1917-1931.

Rigby, K. (2005). The method of shared concern as an intervention technique to address bullying in schools: An overview and appraisal. *Australian Journal of Guidance & Counselling,* 15(1), 27-34.

Smith, P. K., Pepler, D., & Rigby, K. (2004). Bullying in schools: How successful can interventions be? United Kingdom: Cambridge University Press.

Schechtman, Z. (2007). *Group counseling and group psychotherapy with children and adolescents: Theory, research, and practice*. Mahwah, NJ: Erlbaum.

Snakenborg, J., Van Acker, R., & Gable, R. A. (2011). Cyberbullying: Prevention and intervention to protect our children and youth. *Preventing School Failure,* 55(2), 88-95. doi:10.1080/1045988X.2011.539454

Ttofi, M. M., & Farrington, D. P. (2011). Effectiveness of school-based programs to reduce bullying: A systematic and meta-analytic review. *Journal of Experimental Criminology,* 7, 27-56.

Vreeram, R. C., & Carroll, A. E. (2007). A systematic review of school-based interventions to prevent bullying. *Archives of Pediatrics and Adolescent Medicine,* 161(1), 78-88.

Wong-Lo, M., Bullock, L.M., & Gable, R.A. (2009). Cyberbullying: Facing digital aggressions. Paper presented at the Conference of the Teacher Education Division of the Council of Exceptional Children, Charlotte, NC.

Wurf, G. (2012). High school anti-bullying interventions: An evaluation of curriculum approaches and the method of shared concern in four Hong Kong international schools. *Australian Journal of Guidance and Counselling,* 22(1), 139-149.

In: Handbook on Bullying
Editor: Phoebe Triggs

ISBN: 978-1-63463-023-8

Chapter 5

BULLYING AMONG HEALTH CARE PROVIDERS

Sergey Pisklakov, M.D., Ming Xiong, M.D. and Anuradha Patel, M.D.
Department of Anesthesiology and Perioperative Medicine,
New Jersey Medical School, University of Medicine
and Dentistry of New Jersey, Newark, New Jersey, US

Abstract

Bullying is defined by American Psychological Association as an aggressive behavior which is intended to cause distress or harm and that involves an imbalance of power or strength between the aggressor and the victim. Bullying in the workplace is angering enough people these days to be fueling a nationwide grass-roots legislative effort to force companies to draft and enforce policies aimed at stopping it. Requiring such policies, according to those pushing the legislation, is not an attempt to spawn lawsuits, but an effort to force organizations to deal with the problem. Bullying is blamed for unnecessarily creating high costs of turnover, insurance claims and thwarted productivity. Disruptive behavior has been observed in almost all members of the healthcare team from physicians and nurses to pharmacy, radiology, and laboratory staff members. Physician behavior, however, may have the greatest impact because of the position of authority that doctors hold as members of the healthcare team. A team member may, from fear of intimidation or patronization, withhold valuable or even critical input, such as a medication error or a breakdown in adherence to safety protocols. Hospitals, departments and individual personnel need to develop a higher level of awareness of the problem both in others and in them. Anti-bullying policies should be given a higher profile.

This Bullying is defined by American Psychological Association as an aggressive behavior which is intended to cause distress or harm and that involves an imbalance of power or strength between the aggressor and the victim. A more objective if somewhat wordy definition used by Swedish workers is that bullying emerges when one or several persons over a period of time persistently perceive themselves to be on the receiving end of negative actions from one or several persons in a situation where the one at the receiving end has difficulty in defending him or herself against these actions. This definition incorporates the subjective feelings of the person on the receiving end, even where an individual may have behaved aggressively but with no intention to harm. It puts an onus on each individual to be mindful of the effect of their actions on others. It does not offer protection to those falsely accused of bullying. The main features of this definition are negative behaviors, persistence over time and an imbalance of power (Einharsen et al., 1994). Bullying can be physical, relational, peer sexual harassment and stereotyping. It is a way to gain power (Kozlowska et al., 1997). Bullying in the workplace is angering people these days. It is fueling a nationwide grass-roots legislative effort to force companies to draft and enforce policies aimed at stopping it. Requiring such policies is not an attempt to spawn lawsuits. It is an effort to force organizations to deal with the problem. Bullying is blamed for unnecessarily creating high costs of turnover, insurance claims and thwarted productivity (Rosenstein & O'Daniel, 2005).

In January 2009, a new standard issued by the Joint Commission [formerly JCAHO] went into effect. It requires hospitals to have "a code of conduct that defines acceptable, disruptive, and inappropriate staff behaviors" and for its "leaders [to] create and implement a process for managing disruptive and inappropriate staff behaviors." The rationale for the standard states: "Leaders must address disruptive behavior of individuals working at all levels of the [organization], including management, clinical and administrative staff, licensed independent practitioners, and governing body members." A Joint Commission sentinel alert includes "uncooperative attitudes" and "condescending language or voice intonation and impatience with questions" as disruptive behaviors. The Joint Commission's first-ever alert about the problem is the latest industry effort to address an issue that has challenged the medical community for years (The Joint Commission, 2009). Suggested actions include systems to detect and deter unprofessional behavior; more civil responses to patients and families who witness bad acts; and overall training in "basic business etiquette," including phone skills and people skills for all employees (Joint Commission Sentinel Event Alert, 2008). Administrative response to bullying has been so far ineffective. In some cases no action was taken. This lack of action could lead to serious liabilities since these incidents are not only about bullying, but also sexual harassment and discrimination. Disruptive behavior has been observed in almost all members of the healthcare team-from physicians and nurses to pharmacy, radiology, and laboratory staff members. Physician behavior, however, may have the biggest impact because of the position of power that doctors hold as members of the healthcare team (Quine, 2002). A team member may, from fear of intimidation or patronization, withhold valuable or even critical input, such as a medication error or a breakdown in adherence to safety protocols (Rosenstein, 2005). To ensure good patient care and respect among all healthcare professionals is at the very foundation of the ethics advocated by the American Medical Association. Intimidating, condescending, off-putting, or discouraging behavior by the physician inhibits positive team work. If OR staff works sub optimally because of disruptive behavior by the physician or another team member, overall care quality is compromised and patient safety is threatened. To mitigate these risks, healthcare organizations must re-examine their hospital harassment policies to ensure those policies include specific prohibitions against gender discrimination and harassment. Hospitals also need to create a workplace conduct policy forbidding bullying or harassment regardless of gender. Once policies are in place, comprehensive training courses should be given to all supervisors and physicians. When policies violated, action should be taken.

Bullying is a form of aggression. Physical bullying is obvious in our society. It tends to be the province of children. Adults are more subtle and devious in their approach, and their bullying can take a variety of forms, many of which may not be obvious to a third party. This allows bullies to continue their activities unchecked and enables them to do what they wish (Paice, 2004). The outburst in the OR by a surgeon or anesthesiologist is not uncommon. Misconduct against nurses is common (Uhari, 1994). Bullying and mistreatment during training is also a part of the experience of many doctors, medical students or residents (Quine, 2002). Psychological abuse, gender discrimination, and sexual harassment were prevalent in one study (Stratton, 2005). Nursing staff have been implicated in intimidating and harassing residents by verbal comments (Farrell, 1999; Coverdale, 2005); senior residents have also been implicated (Cohen, 2008; Cook, 1996; Daugherty, 1998). Of course, sometime excessive mentorship can be misinterpreted by trainee as bullying. An individual's personal beliefs and lack of self confidence colors their interpretation of any communication; criticism may be inferred where none was implied. Curt behavior by senior doctors may be interpreted as criticism by juniors even when this was not intended. Where the recipient of certain critical or aggressive behaviors is more junior and therefore constrained in their perceived ability to respond to it, this can be a problem (Moscarello, 1994). A bully tends to be in a position of relative power. This allows him or her to behave towards one or many others in an unacceptable way. This can be as simple as making it impossible for subordinates to progress ups the career ladder by ensuring that they are not given opportunities (Cohen, 2008). Bullies may prevent a subordinate from developing their ideas, and develop them as if they were their own. They may manipulate subordinates to take on unacceptable commitments by playing on their vulnerabilities. The bullies may be perceived as good managers because they get more work done. In the medical world, bullies may avoid taking their fair share of unpleasant tasks in a department. They may do this by offloading some of these tasks onto others who are powerless to protest. If the affected individual does complain, the bully may threaten to activate certain sanctions within their power, to which the victim is vulnerable (Daugherty, 1998). The situation is like that of blackmail. It is not that the victim cannot complain; it is that they perceive themselves as helpless (Cook, 1996; Kozlowska, 1997). Often bullying is an extension of forms of negative behavior frequently seen in the medical world (Carr, 1997). When and where does it cross the line? Is there then an acceptable level of bullying? Awareness of bullying as a problem has increased, and there is evidence that the prevalence is high in medicine. Nevertheless, there is also the possibility that the behavior experienced by some as bullying is perceived by others as normal (Ahmer, 2009; Quinne, 1999, 2002).

People who are accused of bullying fall into two groups. The first group is those who intend to hurt and humiliate their victim, and who choose their victim with a view to getting pleasure from their power over them. This is uncommon. The second group is made up of people who perceive their behavior as reasonable, while the victim perceives it as bullying. When individuals in this latter group are accused of bullying they are often mortified and suffer a major blow to their self-esteem. Problem situations for this second group often relate to a senior/junior interaction. There are several reasons for this. In the past, senior role models may well have shown bullying behaviors. Many senior doctors are focused, dedicated and, at times, obsessional individuals who do not suffer fools gladly. They are often very self-critical. They expect equal levels of self-criticism, dedication and focus from their junior staff. Where the levels of activity they require from trainees are outside the normal range they are likely to be accused of bullying (Paice, 2004; Daugherty, 1998). Another category of bully is the medical manager. Frequently, they have been given little training for the task in hand and the demands of the system are often unrealistic. A proportion of these doctors, under pressure, may resort to any method by which they can achieve results, even if this amount to bullying (Houghton, 2003). Bullying is still part of the organizational culture. For example, even though junior doctors' hours have been agreed, there is, in some specialties, pressure to arrive early and leave late, irrespective of the amount of work to be done. Lastly, even normally amiable senior doctors may behave badly when under personal or professional stress (Johnson, 2009; Roberts, 2009).

One of the reasons is the lack of training for doctors and sometimes other managers in management or leadership skills. They simply may not appreciate that people are different (Daugherty, 1998). Absence self-criticism may exacerbate bullies' reaction to the confrontational situation. Very self-critical people become depressed, while individuals with low levels of self-criticism have problems in relationships with patients and colleagues (Paice, 2004; Daugherty, 1998).

Victims of bullying often believe that a complaint would negatively affect their professional progress, and with an intentional bully this might be the case. Thus, incentives to complain are outweighed by the perceived incentives to keep quiet (Margittai, 1996). This creates a "survival" culture, not too far removed from that of prison or the armed forces. The consequences of bullying are devastating. Bullying is responsible for victims becoming stressed, depressed and intending to leave their jobs. The 2004 study reported that 37% of doctors in training had been bullied in the past year (Uhari, 1994). Although there would appear to be a difference between intentional and unintentional bullying, the initially unintentional violator may gain satisfaction or results from this form of behavior, which will then be reinforced. Intentional bullying is a dysfunctional form of behavior which needs intervention and help (Cohen, 2008). Approaches to unintentional bullying should be both educational and organizational. Work with the individual accused of bullying may need to include psychotherapy to explore the reasons for bullying or aggressive behavior. It should also include work on interpersonal and self-awareness skills so that the bully can explore and adopt alternative ways of behaving (Houghton, 2005). This approach, while emphasizing that bullying is unacceptable, also recognizes that bullying behavior may be understandable and that those using it need help to change (Einharsen, 1994). The organizational culture also needs to change. Many companies have put in place clearly defined written policies to prevent bullying and harassment at work, but the problem persists. Management pressures, which essentially amount to bullying, may compel senior doctors to take on impossible clinical loads or to work in unacceptable facilities. They may in turn adopt bullying behavior with subordinates in response to these pressures. The problem may also persist because, although there is more general awareness of the problem, many victims still do not speak out, for a variety of reasons. One appalling truth is that some of these individuals have such low self-esteem that they do not recognize their treatment as bullying (Kozlowska, 1997; Johnson, 2009).

Hospitals, departments and individual personnel need to develop a higher level of awareness of the problem both in others and in them. Anti-bullying policies should be given a higher profile. This should encourage victims to come forward so that individual bullies can be identified. The unintentional bully will usually, although not always, respond to the strategies outlined above and modify their behavior. They may well respond to personal approaches on the part of the victim. Direct approach of the bully may be counterproductive. The victim should keep a careful record of all behavior they perceive as bullying. It is important to ascertain that what you dealing with are bullying. Once confirmed that you are dealing with bullying, you should approach the bully's line manager or the human resources department. Finally, you could also approach your professional association for advice and support (Houghton, 2004).

We know little about how verbal abuse or bullying is triggered and how it might be prevented (Farrell, 1999). Primary preventive methods include providing educational materials and communication skills training for residents, staff, and educators (Baldwin, 1991). Education on abuse, discrimination, and harassment in the workplace, and how these can be addressed and averted, can also be presented in formal and informal curricula. Such initiatives should promote culture of collegiality and respect for all faculty, staff, and trainees (Quine, 1999). Secondary preventive measures rely on reporting mechanisms. Any occasion of abusive or discriminatory language or behavior needs to be addressed. Measures such as debriefing and supportive counseling should aim to alleviate the psychologically distressing consequences of these behaviors for all recipients and observers. Universal focus on professionalism in medical education and professional behavior of physicians in practice should help us to eradicate this unacceptable behavior (White, 2000).

References

Ahmer, S. et al. (2009). Bullying of trainee psychiatrists in Pakistan: A cross-sectional questionnaire survey. *Acad Psychiatry,* 33, 335-339.http://dx.doi.org/10.1176/appi.ap.33.4.335

Baldwin, D. et al. (1991). Student perceptions of mistreatment and harassment during medical school: A survey of ten US schools. *Western Journal of Medicine,* 155, 140-145.

Carr, M. et al. (1991). A survey of Canadian psychiatric residents regarding resident-educator sexual contact. *American Journal of Psychiatry,* 148, 216-220.

Carr, M. (1997). Comment. *Australian & New Zealand Journal of Psychiatry,* 31, 653-654. http://dx.doi.org/10.3109/00048679709062677

Cohen, J. et al. (2008). The happy docs study: A Canadian Association of Interns and Residents well-being survey examining resident physician health and satisfaction within and outside of residency training in Canada. *BMC Research Notes,* 1, 105. http://dx.doi.org/10.1186/1756-0500-1-105

Cook, D. et al. (1996). Residents' experiences of abuse, discrimination, and sexual harassment during residency training. *Canadian Medical Association Journal,* 15 4, 1657-1665.

Coverdale, J. et al. (2001). A survey of threats and violent acts by patients against training physicians. *Medical Education,* 35, 154-159. http://dx.doi.org/10.1046/j.1365-2923.2001.00767.x

Coverdale, J. et al. (2005). Protecting the safety of medical students and residents. *Academic Psychiatry,* 29, 329-331. http://dx.doi.org/10.1176/appi.ap.29.4.329.

Daugherty, S. et al. (1998). Learning, satisfaction, and mistreatment du- ring medical internship: A national survey of working conditions. *JAMA,* 279, 1194-1199. http://dx.doi.org/10.1001/jama.279.15.1194.

Einharsen, S. et al. (1994). Bullying and its relationship to work and environment quality: An exploratory study. *European Journal of Work and Organisational Psychology,* 4, 381- 404. http://dx.doi.org/10.1080/13594329408410497.

Farrell, G. (1999). Aggression in clinical settings: Nurses' views: A follow-up study. *Journal of Advanced Nursing, 29,* 532-541. http://dx.doi.org/10.1046/j.1365-2648.1999.00920.x.

Hoosen, I., & Callaghan, R. (2004). A survey of workplace bullying of psychiatric trainees in the West Midlands. *Psychiatric Bulletin,* 28, 225-227. http://dx.doi.org/10.1192 /pb.28.6.225.

Houghton, A. (2003). Bullying in medicine. *British Medical Journal,* 326, 12. http://dx.doi.org/10.1136/bmj.326.7393.S125a.

Houghton, A. (2005). Tips on dealing with bullies. *British Medical Journal Career Focus,* 33 0, 201-202.

Huntoon, L. (2004). Abuse of the "disruptive physician" clause. *Journal of the American Physicians and Surgeons, 9,* 68.

Johnson, S. (2009). International perspective on workplace bullying among nurses: A review. *International Nursing Review,* 56, 34- 40. http://dx.doi.org/10.1111/j.1466-7657. 2008.00679.x

Joint Commission (2008). Sentinel event alert—Behaviors that undermine a culture of safety. The Joint Commission (2009). Accreditation requirements. http://www.jointcommission.org/NR/rdonlyres

Kozlowska, K. (1997). Adverse experiences in psychiatric training, part 2. *Australian & New Zealand Journal of Psychiatry,* 31, 641-652. http://dx.doi.org/10.3109/ 00048679709062676

Margittai, K. (1996). Forensic aspects of medical student abuse: A Canadian perspective. *The Bulletin of the American Academy of Psychiatry and the Law,* 24, 377-385.

Moscarello, R. et al. (1994). Differences in abuse reported by female and male Canadian medical students. *Canadian Medical Association Journal,* 150, 357-363.

Paice, E. et al. (2004). Bullying among doctors in training: Cross sectional questionnaire survey. *British Medical Journal,* 329, 658-659. http://dx.doi.org/10.1136 /bmj.38133.502569.AE.

Quine, L. (2002). Workplace bullying in junior doctors: Questionnaire survey. *British Medical Journal,* 324, 878-879. http://dx.doi.org/10.1136/bmj.324.7342.878.

Quine, L. (1999). Workplace bullying in NHS community trust: Staff questionnaire survey. *BMJ,* 318, 228-232. http://dx.doi.org/10.1136/bmj.318.7178.228.

Roberts, S. et al. (2009). The effect of oppressed group behaviors on the culture of the nursing workplace: A review of the evidence and interventions for change. *Journal of Nursing Management,* 10, 1365- 1374.

Rosenstein, A., & O'Daniel, M. (2005). Disruptive behavior and clinical outcomes: Perceptions of nurses and physicians. *The American Journal of Nursing,* 105, 54-64. http://dx.doi.org/10.1097/00000446-200501000-00025.

Stratton, T. et al. (2005). Does students' exposure to gender discrimination and sexual harassment in medical school affect specialty choice and residency program selection? *Academic Medicine,* 80, 400-408. http://dx.doi.org/10.1097/00001888-200504000-00020.

Uhari, M. et al. (1994). Medical student abuse: An international phenomenon. *JAMA,* 271, 1049-1051. http://dx.doi.org/10.1001/jama.271.13.1049.

Vanineveld, C. et al. (1998). Discrimination and abuse in internal medicine residency. *Journal of General Internal Medicine,* 11, 401-405. http://dx.doi.org/10.1007/BF02600186.

White, G. (2000). Sexual harassment during medical training: The perceptions of medical students at a university medical school in Australia. *Medical Education,* 34, 980-986.

In: Handbook on Bullying
Editor: Phoebe Triggs

ISBN: 978-1-63463-023-8

Chapter 6

CYBERBULLYING: BULLYING GONE DIGITAL

Michelle F. Wright[1,*] and William Stanley Pendergrass[2]

[1]Faculty of Social Studies, Masaryk University, Brno, Czech Republic
[2]School of Science, Technology, Engineering and Mathematics,
Department of Information Technology,
American Public University System, West Virginia, US

Abstract

Youths in the 21st century are raised in a digital world where blogs, social networking sites, and instant messaging are part of their everyday life. These youths have been immersed in a digital world for as long as they can remember. As a result of this immersion, youths are at risk for cyberbullying, which has increased in intensity over the years.

Cyberbullying has become a major focus of not only youths, educators, and researchers, but also among the general population, due to high profile cases of cyberbullying victimization involving suicide. This chapter drew on literature utilizing cross-sectional, longitudinal, qualitative, and quantitative research methodologies to describe cyberbullying.

The chapter provided an overview of cyberbullying, including the tools, technologies, and forms, along with the prevalence rates, correlates, and the emotional and behavioral consequences. Also *discussed are the cultural differences in these behaviors, and theoretical underpinnings.* The chapter concluded with recommendations for future research and public policy.

Cyberbullying: Bullying Gone Digital

Millions of children and adolescents utilize electronic technologies (e.g., cell phones, the Internet) everyday, engaging in many different behaviors (Madden, Lenhart, Duggan, Cortesi, and Gasser, 2013). Although their usage of such technologies has many benefits (e.g., fast communication with friends and family, access to an array of rich information), there is also a

---

* E-mail address: michelle.wright@mail.muni.cz; Tel: +420 549 49 5259.

The first author acknowledges the support of the Employment of Best Young Scientists for International Cooperation Empowerment (CZ.1.07/2.3.00/30.0037), co-financed from European Social Fund and the state budget of the Czech Republic.

darker side to youths' electronic interactions: Cyberbullying. An extension of traditional bullying, cyberbullying is a form of bullying which takes place by means of electronic technologies, such as email, instant messaging, Facebook, and text messaging through mobile devices (Cost, 2012; Olweus, 1999). Due to the ability to remain anonymous, the cyber context offers flexibility to cyberbullies, allowing them to harm their potential victims without the constraints and many of the repercussions associated with traditional face-to-face bullying. Cyberbullies can also target the victim or victims quicker, more often, and involve multiple bystanders in the bullying situation. For example, an embarrassing video of a victim or victims can be shared quickly by sending it to multiple recipients, who can also share the video as well.

Drawing on research from a variety of disciplines, such as psychology, education, social work, sociology, and computer science, this chapter is organized into nine sections. These sections include:

- A review of case studies involving cyberbullying victimization is given in the first section.
- Definitions, technologies used, the role of anonymity, and prevalence rates of cyberbullying are described in the second section.
- In the third section, the characteristics and risk factors associated with cyberbullying involvement are discussed.
- The fourth section detailed the relationship between parents and cyberbullying involvement.
- In this section, the roles of peers and school in youths' cyberbullying involvement are explained.
- The sixth section reviews research findings on the psychological and behavioral consequences resulting from cyberbullying involvement.
- Cross-cultural differences in cyberbullying are discussed in the seventh section.
- In the eighth section, two theories, social cognitive theory and online disinhibition effect, are applied to cyberbullying.
- Concluding the chapter is a discussion of future research and public policy recommendations.

Case Studies of Cyberbullying Victimization

At 6 p.m., October 10, 2012, fifteen-year-old Amanda Todd hung herself in her Port Coquitlam, British Columbia, Canada home only five weeks after she posted a gripping video on YouTube which detailed how she was harassed and bullied online for years. The video she posted was entitled, "My Story: Struggling, bullying, suicide and self harm." The video described Amanda's story on a series of flash cards. While she was in 7th Grade, Amanda had an online video conversation with an unknown person. In the course of their conversation, Amanda was asked to flash her naked breasts, which she did. A year later, she was contacted by the person who threatened to post her pictures on the Internet if she didn't provide more naked content. She refused and subsequently had her pictures posted to family and friends alike. She became depressed and anxious, turning to alcohol and drugs in order to cope with this situation. Despite switching schools, the cyberbullying followed her. A Facebook page of her with the picture of her breasts as the profile picture was created. Her schoolmates began to make fun of her, calling her names. She started cutting herself. She moved to yet another school. She made friends but unknowingly began dating a boy who already had a girlfriend. The girlfriend attacked her; the incident was filmed and posted online. Despondent, Amanda tried to kill herself by drinking bleach. She was rushed to the hospital and survived but in the end, the abuse was too much, so she hung herself (Pendergrass and Wright, in press).

On December 9, 2012, sixteen year old Fivay High School student from Hudson, Florida, Jessica Laney, hung herself. Her friends told the authorities that she became suicidal after being cyberbullied and abused through the anonymous Latvian question and answer website "Ask.fm." While Laney's Ask.fm account page, Jessicamarieee1, had its fair share of innocent and friendly comments, there were also a number of posts telling her how fat she was and what a loser she was.

> Classmates of 16-year-old Jessica Laney say she was pretty and bubbly. Still, cruel comments could be found on her Ask.fm webpage. "Nobody even cares about you," reads one anonymous post. "Can you just kill yourself," says another. Close friends Cheyenne Ellsmore and Lisa Arthur say people would post the mean messages anonymously. "You get compliments sometimes but it's those negative comments that bring you down," Ellsmore said. "There's just things you should say and things you shouldn't," said Arthur. "And on Ask.fm, none of that should be said." The girls believe the comments got to be too much for Laney, who took her own life Sunday night. (McVey, 2012)

Rehtaeh Parsons, a seventeen-year-old Cole Harbour District High School student, attempted suicide by hanging on April 4, 2013, in her home in Dartmouth, Nova Scotia, Canada. She did not succeed which led to a coma and brain death. Three days later her family made the decision to take her off life support; she died that day. Back in November of 2011, Rehtaeh was at a small gathering of friends when she was unbeknownst photographed while having sex with (her mother called it rape) one of the boys. After that, the bullying and harassment began unabated. Her mother, Leah Parsons said, "She was never left alone. She had to leave the community. Her friends turned against her. People harassed her. Boys she didn't know started texting her and Facebooking her asking her to have sex with them. It just never stopped" (The Huffington Post, 2013). The family moved to nearby Halifax but the cyberbullying did not stop. Rehtaeh began to suffer from depression and anger, and at one time had to be admitted to a hospital on fears that she would harm herself. After her death, a year-long investigation by the Royal Canadian Mounted Police concluded that there was not enough evidence to charge and convict any of the boys with rape (Pendergrass and Wright, in press).

On September 9, 2013, Rebecca Ann Sedwick, a twelve year old Crystal Lake Middle School student, leaped to her death at a cement factory less than a mile from her home in Lakeland, Florida. She had been the victim of cyberbullying for months. Rebecca had been reported missing about 7 p.m. Monday by her mother after she failed to return home from school that day. After an investigation, two girls were arrested, part of a group of 15 girls who were accused of tormenting Rebecca until she took her own life. The arrests came after one of the two girls tweeted "'Yes IK [I know] I bullied REBECCA nd [sic] she killed her self [sic] but IDGAF [I don't give a fuck]" (Quigley and Gorman, 2013). The torment began after one of the girls began dating a boy whom Rebecca had dated earlier. She eventually turned the other girl, formerly a good friend of Rebecca's, against Rebecca.

> Witnesses told investigators she sent messages to Rebecca, calling her ugly, telling her to "drink bleach and die," and encouraging her to kill herself. Rebecca's computer searches revealed she had searched for ways to commit suicide and asked questions like, "What is overweight for a 13-year-old girl?" One of the Florida girl's screensavers also showed Rebecca with her head resting on a railroad track. Rebecca changed one of her online screen names to "That Dead Girl." Later, she messaged a boy: "I'm jumping." Polk County Sheriff Judd said Rebecca had been "absolutely terrorized" by the other girls. "We can see from what we've been investigating so far that Rebecca wasn't attacking back," Judd said. "She appeared to be beat down. She appeared to have a defeatist attitude. And quite frankly, the entire investigation is exceptionally disturbing". (Quigley et al., 2013)

Even when Rebecca's mother transferred her to another school, the bullying continued online. In December of 2012, Rebecca was hospitalized for three days after cutting her wrists, noting that it was because of bullying.

> "She put on a perfect, happy face. She never told me," said her mother, Tricia Norman. "I never had a clue. I mean, she told me last year when she was being bullied, but not this year, and I have no idea why." Once police checked [Rebecca's] cell phone they discovered that the bullying had not stopped, especially on Kik Messenger, Instagram and Ask.fm. "They would tell her she's ugly, stupid, nobody liked her, go kill herself," Ms. Norman said. (Quigley et al., 2013)

All these recent cases of cyberbullying which led to suicide raise the questions: what actually is cyberbullying, how do we define it, how do we recognize it, how do we protect against it and how do we educate those who we count on to protect youths? With the exponential prevalence of personal contact and communication devices in society nowadays, we cannot afford to ignore the danger of an increasingly interconnected and interdependent societal shift from the days of the schoolyard bully to the now ever-prevalent and unshakable cyberbully. Youth deserve to be protected, parents and teachers deserve to understand the threat, and our society needs to embrace the fact that electronic communication has become important to youths' lives, if not more important, than personal interactions.

What Is Cyberbullying?

Defined as youths' usage of modern technologies to deliberately embarrass or intimate others in a repetitive and hostile manner, cyberbullying, like traditional face-to-face bullying, is also characterized by an imbalance of power between the bully and the victim (Ferdon and Hertz, 2007; Kowalski and Limber, 2007; Topcu, Erdur-Backer, and Aydin, 2008; Wolak, Mitchell, and Finkelhor, 2007; Ybarra, West, and Leaf, 2007). As deliberate behaviors, cyberbullying behaviors are intentionally carried out by perpetrators with malicious intent (Grigg, 2010). When cyberbullying involves repetition, it can mean that the perpetrator targets the victim multiple times and that the humiliating video or nasty text message can be viewed and shared by various bystanders (Vandebosch and Van Cleemput, 2008). As an extension of the traditional face-to-face bullying definition (Olweus, 1999), the definition of cyberbullying adds a technological component. In traditional face-to-face bullying, a bully might punch, kick, or spread a rumor about the victim. Separate from this type of bullying, cyberbullying involves a bully sending unkind text messages and emails, sharing secrets about the victim by posting or sending the secret to someone else, or uploading an embarrassing picture or video of the victim with malicious intent.

There are various examples of cyberbullying behaviors. Some behaviors include making anonymous phone calls, sending abusive emails, theft of identity information or pretending to be someone else, and harassment via instant messenger, social networking sites, and text messages (Wolak et al., 2007; Wright and Li, 2012; Ybarra and Mitchell, 2004). Other cyberbullying behaviors are similar to face-to-face bullying behaviors but they are carried out in the cyber context, including harassment, insults, physical threats, social exclusion, and humiliation (Chisholm, 2006). Extending these behaviors, Rideout and colleagues (2005) also described cyberbullying as encompassing the distribution of explicit videos via various websites, such as social networking sites and online gaming sites. Other forms of cyberbullying behaviors include happy slapping and flaming (Gillepsi, 2006; Smith et al., 2008). In recent research, Arslan et al. (2012) found that the most frequently used technologies to harm others were instant messaging tools and social networking sites (e.g., Facebook, Twitter), which were reported by over half of their sample.

To understand why youths might engage in cyberbullying, some researchers have explained that new technologies allow bullies to hide their identities, which could exacerbate the power differential between the bully and the victim (Wright, 2013; Ybarra et al., 2007). Furthermore, these new technologies allow the bully to engage in repeated and prolonged harassment, while remaining anonymous (Maher, 2004; Wolak et al., 2007; Wright, 2014a; Ybarra and Mitchell, 2004). Therefore, it is not surprising that many youths who engage in cyberbullying choose to remain anonymous while executing their attack (Dehue, Bolman, and Vollink, 2008; Kowalski and Limber, 2007; Wright, 2014a; Ybarra and Mitchell, 2004). The proposal that anonymity is a motivator for cyberbullying is corroborated by research indicating that many cyberbullying victims are often unsure of the identity of the cyberbully (Kowalski and Limber, 2007; Ybarra et al., 2007). The majority of victims, around 80%, in one study were unaware of the identity of the cyberbully (Arslan et al., 2012). The ability to remain anonymous in the cyber context represents an imbalance of power between the victim and the anonymous perpetrator (Vandebosch and Van Cleemput, 2008; Grigg, 2012). Research (e.g., Moore, Nakano, Enomoto, and Suda, 2012) demonstrates that the ability to post anonymously in forums triggers more cyberbullying attacks than less anonymous forums. In recent research, Wright (2013; 2014a) found that feeling more confident with one's ability to remain anonymous in the cyber context was related positively to cyberbullying, especially cyberbullying perpetrated anonymously. Not only is anonymity an issue because it might drive youths toward cyberbullying, but it also intensifies victims' negative feelings, leading to powerlessness (Dooley, Pyzalski, and Cross, 2009; Nocentini, Galmaestra, and Schultze-Krumbholz, 2010; Slonje and Smith, 2008; Vandebosch and Cleemput, 2008; Smith et al., 2008).

Despite the differences in the prevalence rates of cyberbullying, generally due to variations in samples and measurement techniques, understanding how frequently youths are involved in these behaviors is helpful for prevention efforts. One of the earliest studies of cyberbullying in the United States reported that 50% of youths in their sample experienced these behaviors as victims (Wolak et al., 2007). Other studies have found lower rates of cyberbullying involvement in the United States. For example, using a sample of 3,767 middle school students (aged 11-14), Kowalski and Limber (2007) found that 11% had been cyberbullied, 4% had bullied other youths, and 7% were cyberbullies and cyber-victims. Similar estimates concerning the perpetration of cyberbullying were found by Patchin and Hinduja (2006). They found that 29% of their sample reported cyber victimization and that 47% had witnessed cyberbullying. Among youths in Hawaii (N = 677, grades 9-12th), 56.1% reported that they were the victims of cyberbullying (Goebert, Else, Matsu, Chung-Do, and Chang, 2011). In more recent research in the United States, Hinduja and Patchin (2013) found that 4.9% of youths in their sample (N = 4,441, 6-12th grade) had cyberbullied someone in the past 30 days. Utilizing a sample of 1,972 Canadian youths (10th graders), Cappadocia et al. (2013) reported that 2.1% of youths were cyberbullying perpetrators, 1.9% were cyber-victims, and 0.6% were both cyberbullies and cyber-victims. Rates of cyberbullying perpetration and victimization were slightly higher among 399 Canadian youths (grades 8-10th), with 6% reporting that they were perpetrators, 5.8% as victims only, and 5% as cyberbullies and cyber-victims (Bonanno and Hymel, 2013).

Cyberbullying is not a phenomenon linked to only one country, but instead a global concern. Therefore, researchers have directed their attention to cyberbullying involvement in countries, other than the United States and Canada. Drawing on a large Swedish sample (N = 22,544, ages 15-18), Laftman, Modin, and Ostberg, (2013) reported that 5% of their sample were victims of cyberbullying, 4% were perpetrators, and 2% were both cyberbullies and cyber-victims. In a younger sample of 7th through 9th grade Swedish youths, 1.9% were cyber-victims, 2.9% were cyberbullies, and 0.6% were cyberbullies and cyber-victims (Beckman, Hagquist, and Hellstrom, 2012). Similar rates of cyber victimization (6% for Ireland, 6.3% for Belgian, and 4.5% for Australia) were found among Irish (N = 876, ages 12-17; Corcoran, Connolly, and O'Moore, 2012), Belgian (N = 1,042, M age = 15.47; Heirman and Walrave, 2012), and Australian (N = 3,112, grades 6-12th; Campbell, Spears, Slee, Butler, and Kift, 2012) youths. However, rates of cyber victimization were higher (12.5%) among Italian youths (N = 2,326, M age = 13.9 years; Brighi, Guarini, Melotti, Galli, and Genta, 2012). Among German youths (N = 276, ages 13-19 years), 13% were classified as cyberbullies and 11% as cyber-victims (Festl, Scharkow, and Quandt, 2013). In Turkey, estimates of cyberbullying victimization vary from 18% (N= 756, 7th graders; Yilmaz, 2011) to 32% (N= 276, ages 14-18; Erdur-Baker 2010). The rates of being a perpetrator of cyberbullying are 6% (Yilmaz, 2011) to 19% (ages 12-14 year olds; Ayas and Horzum, 2012) among youths in Turkey. In another study, Aricak and colleagues (2008) found that 36% of their sample (N = 269, Turkish secondary school students) were cyberbullies. Although higher than cyber victimization rates from some European countries, but not as high as those in Turkey, Olenik-Shemesh and colleagues (2012) found that 16.5% of their Israeli participants (N = 242, 13-16 years old) were victims of cyberbullying. Lazuras et al. (2013) investigated rates of cyberbullying involvement as witnesses or victims of cyberbullying. Their findings revealed that 32.4% of the sample (N = 355, 13-17 years old) were involved in cyberbullying as victims or bystanders. Cyber victimization (24.9%) rates were comparable among Spanish youths (N = 845, M age = 15.2 years; Gamez-Guadiz, Orue, Smith, and Calvete, 2013).

Research on cyberbullying perpetration and victimization has been slower to develop in Asia. Among Taiwanese (N = 545) youths, 63.4% witnessed cyberbullying, 34.9% were cyberbullied, and 20.4% had cyberbullied others (Huang and Chou, 2010). In Korea, 43% of youths in one sample (N = 3,238, 8th graders) reported that they were involved in cyberbullying either as victims or perpetrators (Jang, Song, and Kim, 2014). Rates of cyberbullying perpetration and victimization were similar in China, with 34.8% of youths admitting that they had cyberbullied someone and 56.9% indicating that they were cyberbullied (N = 1,438 high school students; Zhou, Tang, Tian, Wei, Zhang, and Morrison, 2013). Another study focused on cyberbullying through Facebook among 1,676 13-17 year olds in Singapore (Kwan and Skoric, 2013). Of these youths, 59.4% reported that they experienced victimization through Facebook and 56.9% perpetrated Facebook cyberbullying. In a recent study, Wong and colleagues (2014) found that 13.1% of youths in their sample (N = 1,912, 12-15 year olds) reported cyberbullying perpetration and 12.2% indicated cyber victimization. Considering rates of cyberbullying around the world, there is further need to continue investigating cyberbullying among youths, and understanding risk factors associated with the involvement in these behaviors.

Characteristics of Cyberbullies and Cyber-Victims

Researchers have focused their attention on the risk factors associated with youths' involvement in cyberbullying as perpetrators, victims, and bully-victims. Demographic variables represent the first cluster of risk factors examined in this research. One highly researched risk factor is age. In this research, younger youths were at a greater risk of being cyberbullied, whereas older youths were most frequently the perpetrators of cyberbullying (Ayas and Horzum, 2012). In addition, Williams and Guerra (2007) found that physical forms of bullying and cyberbullying peaked in middle school, but declined in high school. However, age is not a consistent predictor of cyberbullying involvement as Wade and Beran (2011) found that being in the 9th grade increased the risk of cyber victimization and cyberbullying perpetration in comparison to when the youths were in middle school. Like age, gender is also an inconsistent predictor of cyberbullying involvement. Some researchers (Li, 2007; Ybarra et al., 2007) have found that boys were more often the perpetrators of cyberbullying in comparison to girls and that girls experienced cyber victimization more frequently than boys (Hinduja and Patchin, 2007; Kowalski and Limber, 2007). On the other hand, other research has indicated that girls engaged in more cyberbullying perpetration when compared to boys (e.g., Dehue et al., 2008; Pornari and Wood, 2010) and that boys reported higher rates of cyber victimization than girls (e.g., Akbulut, Sahih, and Eristi, 2010; Erdur-Baker, 2010; Huang and Chou, 2010). Yet, other researchers have found no gender differences in cyberbullying involvement (Beran and Li, 2005; Wright and Li, 2013b).

Other frequently researched risk factors include both traditional face-to-face bullying and victimization. Various research studies find significant positive relationships between cyberbullying and traditional face-to-face bullying as well as associations between cyber victimization and victimization by face-to-face bullying (Cappadocia et al., 2013; Mitchell et al., 2007; Steffgen, Kong, Pfetsch, and Melzer, 2011; Fanti, Demetriou, and Hawa, 2012). Face-to-face bullying victimization is also a risk factor for victims and perpetrators of cyberbullying (Wright and Li, 2012). Another risk factor associated with cyberbullying includes frequent Internet use. In particular, higher rates of Internet usage are associated positively with both cyberbullying perpetration and victimization (Aricak et al., 2008; Ybarra and Mitchell, 2004). Cyber-victims report higher rates of chatting, emailing, blogging, gaming, and sending instant messages when compared to non-victims (Smith et al., 2008; Ybarra and Mitchell, 2004). A potential explanation for the relationship between Internet usage and cyberbullying involvement is that the disclosure of personal information worsens online risks, like cyberbullying (Ybarra et al., 2007). Therefore, frequent Internet usage might increase youths' willingness to disclosure personal information online, marking them more vulnerable to victimization. There is research evidence that psychosocial adjustment difficulties are also cyberbullying risk factors. Internalizing problems, such as depressive symptoms, place youths at risk for cyber victimization as such problems might make victims more vulnerable to attacks (Cappadocia et al., 2013; Mitchell et al., 2007; Ybarra and Mitchell, 2004). Externalizing problems, like alcohol use, are related positively to cyberbullying perpetration (Cappadocia et al., 2013). In addition, higher normative beliefs about face-to-face bullying and cyberbullying are linked to cyberbullying perpetration (Ang, Tan, and Mansor, 2010; Burton, Florell, and Wygant, 2013; Wright and Li, 2013a), indicating that cyberbullies view bullying behaviors as normative. Also, lower levels of provictim attitudes (i.e., children's beliefs that bullying is unacceptable, and defending victims is valued) were related to greater cyberbullying (Elledge, Williford, Boulton, DePaolis, Little, and Salmivalli, 2013). Research also indicates that low self-control (Jang et al., 2014), less empathy (Steffgen et al., 2011), and moral disengagement (Lazuras et al., 2013; Robson and Witenberg, 2013) were associated with cyberbullying perpetration. In one study aimed at understanding the longitudinal risk factors associated with cyberbullying involvement, Fanti et al. (2012) found that media violence exposure, and callous and unemotional traits assessed predicted cyberbullying perpetration one year later. However, media violence exposure was the only risk factor associated with cyber victimization. Recent research has also indicated that perceived stress from parents, peers, and academics increases cyberbullying perpetration one year later (Wright, in press). Thus, there are a variety of individual characteristics that make youths vulnerable to cyberbullying involvement. Similarly, youths' relationships with their parents have also been found to be risk factors as well.

Parents' Roles in Their Children's Cyberbullying Involvement

Ample research literature links traditional face-to-face bullying with parental monitoring. In this literature, parents with permissive parenting styles are less likely to acknowledge their children's activities (Marini, Dane, Bosacki, and Ylc-Cura, 2006). Parents of bully-victims frequently utilize an indifferent-uninvolved parenting style, and inconsistently monitor their children's activities (Duncan, 2004). Such findings are important as high levels of parental monitoring are correlated negatively with bullying behaviors (Totura et al., 2009). On the other hand, enmeshed and overprotective family backgrounds are typically associated with victims of bullying (Smith, Madsen, and Moody, 1999). It is hypothesized that such families do not allow their children to develop assertiveness and practice necessary skills for social interactions. The cyber context presents another environment in which parents might decide to monitor their children's activities. In one study, Mason (2008) found that 30% of youths used the Internet for three hours or more daily and that, during the time that they were online, less than 50% reported parental monitoring. In other research, Aoyama and colleagues (2011) revealed that parental mediation and monitoring of their children's online activities were not effective because some parents lack technological skills and many fail to follow-up on the strategies they implemented. Furthermore, many parents report that they are unsure of what their children are up to online and that they are uncertain of how to even discuss the topic of online activities with their children (Rosen, 2007). Rosen also found that many parents set limits on their children's Internet consumption, but many do not actually monitor these limits. Although 93% of parents in one study reported that they set limits on their children's online activities, only 37% of their children reported being given rules from their parents about such activities (McQuade et al., 2009).

Other research has focused on the relationship between family characteristics (e.g., household factors, parenting styles, parental monitoring) and cyberbullying involvement. Findings indicated that poor caregiver monitoring and poor emotional bonds with caregivers were related positively to cyberbullying (Ybarra and Mitchell, 2004). There is no evidence that family income, parental education, and caregiver status (single or married) were associated with cyberbullying perpetration or cyber victimization. However, research does indicate that parental unemployment increases the risk of youths' involvement in cyberbullying as perpetrators and victims (Arslan et al., 2012). Youths with neglectful parents are at greater risk for engaging in and experiencing cyberbullying when compared to non-involved youths (Dehue, Bolman, Vollink, and Pouwelse, 2012). In addition, authoritarian parenting styles were related positively to cyber victimization. The risk of cyber victimization is also increased when parents do not monitor or set rules pertaining to the types of websites their children are allowed to visit (Mesch, 2009; Navarro, Serna, Martinez, and Ruiz-Oliva, 2013). Other research (i.e., Hinduja and Patchin, 2013) suggests that youths who believed that their parents or other adults would punish them for participating in cyberbullying were less likely to engage in such behaviors. These findings indicate the importance of parents' involvement in their youths' online activities.

Peers and Schools Contributions to Cyberbullying

Youths spend most of their time in school until they graduate from high school or college (Parker, Rubin, Erath, Wojslawowicz, and Buskirk, 2005). Therefore, it is not surprising that many studies have revealed that youths' involvement in bullying behaviors is connected to their peers and school environment. In this literature, teachers' perceptions and awareness of cyberbullying vary greatly (Kochenderfer-Ladd and Pelletier, 2008). Cyberbullying presents a complicated consideration for teachers as many educators perceive overt forms of bullying more harshly than they do covert forms, like relational aggression and some forms of cyberbullying (Sahin, 2010). The relationship between cyberbullying and the school is further complicated because many cyberbullying incidences occur off school grounds through electronic technologies, making it difficult for teachers to even be aware of such incidences (Mason, 2008). In addition, many teachers are not trained to properly deal with and recognize such behaviors. Corroborating this proposal, Cassidy and colleagues (2012a) found that some Canadian teachers were unfamiliar with newer technologies, making it difficult for them to deal effectively with cyberbullying. Other research also indicates that Australian teachers were more likely to focus on face-to-face bullying prevention than cyberbullying prevention (Tangen and Campbell, 2010). When teachers were concerned about cyberbullying, this concern rarely translated into policy or programs (Cassidy, Brown, and Jackson, 2012b). Educators must recognize the importance of addressing cyberbullying as the consequences of cyberbullying are felt at school as it impacts the learning process (Shariff and Hoff, 2007). In particular, youths involved in cyberbullying as victims or perpetrators perceived school and teachers less positively than non-involved youths (Bayar and Ucanok, 2012). The fearfulness of classmates who might be perpetrators of cyberbullying can divert youths' attention from academic tasks, reducing learning opportunities (Eden, Heiman, and Olenik-Shemesh, 2013). Furthermore, lower school commitment (Ybarra and Mitchell, 2004) and a negative school climate (Williams and Guerra, 2007) increase cyberbullying perpetration. The literature does indicate the importance of educators for addressing cyberbullying through awareness and prevention. Teachers with confidence in their abilities and a strong commitment to their school are more likely to learn about cyberbullying, boosting their awareness and abilities to effectively manage these behaviors (Eden et al., 2013). However, teachers' motivations for learning about cyberbullying and believing that they can manage cyberbullying decreases from elementary school to middle school. Such results represent a substantial problem as cyberbullying usually increases in the middle school years (Ybarra et al., 2007) and that teachers' ability to intervene at the classroom level is a protective factor associated with cyberbullying (Elledge et al., 2013).

Peers exert a strong influence on youths' behaviors and social norms concerning acceptable and unacceptable behaviors (Miller and Prentice, 1996). Support for such influences was found by Festl and colleagues (2013). In particular, their results revealed that the best predictor of cyberbullying perpetration and victimization were classes with higher rates of cyberbullying incidences. Similarly, youths who believed that their friends engaged in cyberbullying were more likely to perpetrate cyberbullying themselves (Hinduja and Patchin, 2013). Rather than focusing on how peers influence youths' cyberbullying perpetration, other research aims to understand the nature of youths' relationships with their peers. In this research, peer attachment was associated negatively with cyberbullying perpetration and cyber victimization (Burton et al., 2013). Like victimization by face-to-face bullying, cyber victimization is associated with peer rejection after controlling for face-to-face victimization (Wright and Li, 2013b). There is also research evidence which indicates that cyberbullying might be utilized to boost youths' status among their peers. In this research, Wright (2014b) found that higher levels of perceived popularity, a reputational type of popularity in the peer group, increased youths' cyberbullying perpetration six months later.

Psychological and Behavioral Consequences

Various research studies have been conducted on the psychological and behavioral consequences associated with cyberbullying involvement. In this research, cyber-victims reported lower global happiness (i.e., how generally happy they were), school happiness, school satisfaction, family satisfaction, and self-satisfaction (Navarro et al., 2013). In addition, cyber-victims generally felt more anger (Dehue et al., 2008), fear (Beran and Li, 2005), and sadness (Patchin and Hinduja, 2006) when compared to non-involved youths. Cyber-victims also report more emotional and peer problems when compared to cyberbullies. Cyberbullying involvement is also linked to academic difficulties. Results from this research indicated that cyberbullies and cyber-victims both experience problems in school, such as decreased motivation for school, lower academic attainment, and increased school absences (Beale and Hall, 2007; Beran and Li, 2007). Cyberbullies and cyber-victims also report internalizing (e.g., depression, anxiety) and externalizing problems, such as the engagement in aggressive behaviors and the usage of drugs, and alcohol (Arslan et al., 2012; Li, 2007;

Patchin and Hinduja, 2012; Wright, in press; Ybarra et al., 2007). Hinduja and Patchin (2010) proposed that victims of cyberbullying might be at an increased risk of suicide when compared to cyberbullying perpetrators and victims of traditional bullying. Finding partial support for this proposal, Bauman and colleagues (2013) found that perpetrating and experiencing cyberbullying were both related to suicide attempts. However, traditional face-to-face bullying and victimization were stronger predictors of suicidal thoughts, plans, and attempts than cyber victimization, but not cyberbullying perpetration. Although Bauman et al. explain that their results concerning cyberbullies might be a joke perpetrated by their participants, their findings are consistent with Beckman and colleagues (2012) who found that cyberbullies were just as likely as cyber-victims to be at risk for mental health problems. Further supporting the association between cyberbullying perpetration and mental health issues, research (Sourander et al., 2010) results indicated that psychiatric and psychosomatic problems were also associated with cyberbullying involvement.

Other research has focused on the joint effects of traditional bullying and cyberbullying on youths' psychological and behavioral outcomes. In this research, victims of both traditional face-to-face bullying and cyberbullying reported more internalizing problems when compared to youths who experienced only one type of victimization (Gradinger, Strohmeier, and Spiel, 2009; Perren, Dooley, Shaw, and Cross, 2010). Much of the research focused on the psychological and behavioral consequences associated with cyberbullying involvement do not account for traditional face-to-face bullying and victimization. Such considerations are important as there are considerable associations among cyberbullying and face-to-face bullying involvement (Williams and Guerra, 2007; Wright and Li, 2013b). Research indicates that cyberbullying perpetration and cyber victimization are both related to depressive symptoms and suicidal ideation after including face-to-face bullying and victimization in the same model (Bonanno et al., 2013). Utilizing a similar design, Brighi and colleagues (2012) found no support for an association between cyber victimization and loneliness or self-esteem.

Cross-Cultural Research on Cyberbullying

Considering that there is increasing evidence that cyberbullying is a global phenomenon, more attention has been given to cross-cultural investigations of youths' involvement in these behaviors. Much of the research focused on cross-cultural differences in cyberbullying perpetration and victimization classify countries according to an independent self-construal (i.e., viewing the self as separate from the social context and emphasizing autonomy) or an interdependent self-construal (i.e., viewing themselves within the broader social context; Singelis, 1994). Generally, people from Western countries, like the United States, Canada, and England, are primed and reinforced for behaving according to an independent self-construal, whereas people from Eastern countries, such as China, Korea, and Japan, are primed and reinforced for behaving consistently with an interdependent self-construal. The available research indicates that such differences in self-construal affect a variety of social behaviors, including bullying. Independent and interdependent self-construals have been applied to explain cyberbullying behaviors. In one study, Barlett and colleagues (2014) found that participants from the United States self-reported greater levels of cyberbullying than Japanese participants, and that these relationships were moderated by positive attitudes toward cyberbullying. In particular, such associations were stronger among U.S. participants when compared to Japanese participants. Aoyama and colleagues (2011) also found that Japanese high school students reported less cyberbullying than U.S. high school students. Japanese youths also engaged in less cyberbullying behaviors in comparison to Austrian youths (Strohmeier, Aoyama, Gradinger, and Toda, 2013). Similar patterns were found among Chinese and Canadian youths (Li, 2008). Canadian youths self-reported more cyberbullying and knew someone who had been cyberbullied more often than Chinese youths. There were no cultural differences found concerning cyber victimization. However, in another sample, Li (2006) found that Chinese youths were more likely to be cyber-victims when compared to Canadian youths. Further delineating cyberbullying according to the proactive (to obtain a goal) and reactive (response to provocation) classifications, Shapka and Law (2013) found that East Asian youths from Canada engaged in cyberbullying for proactive reasons, whereas Canadian youths did so for reactive reasons. Cross-cultural gender differences in cyberbullying have also been found. In particular, Italian males engaged in more cyberbullying when compared to Spanish and English males (Genta et al., 2012). Additional research is still needed to understand differences in cyberbullying involvement across the world, especially in South America, Africa, and India.

Theoretical Underpinnings

In this section, two theories, the social cognitive theory and the online disinhibition effect, will be discussed, along with their applications to cyberbullying. Within the social cognitive theory framework, researchers propose that adolescents model the behaviors of their parents and/or friends (Duncan, 2004; Hinduja and Patchin, 2008; Mouttapa, Valente, Gallaher, Rohrbach, and Unger, 2004). Olweus (1993) applied the social cognitive theory to explain youths' aggressive behaviors. In his explanation, Olweus proposed that the effects of the model are stronger when the observer has a positive evaluation of the model, such as perceiving the model as tough or fearless. Perceiving the model's aggressive behaviors as positive makes these acts less inhibited for the observer, especially if the model is rewarded for the aggressive actions. Usually the reward involves the bullies' victory over the victim. Barlett and Gentile (2012) elaborated on the social cognitive theory by applying this theory to youths' involvement in cyberbullying. Through observations of successful cyberbullying incidences, many youths learn that cyberbullying is an appropriate aggressive action. The unique features of the cyber context also aid in the social learning behind cyberbullying. That is, cyberbullies learn that they might experience little or no immediate consequences for their behaviors and that they can further increase their ability to not get caught engaging in cyberbullying if they remain anonymous, which they are better able to do in the cyber context (Vandebosch and Van Cleemput, 2008). There is research evidence that being positively reinforced for cyberbullying contributes to youths' positive attitudes toward these behaviors (Barlett and Gentile, 2012). Such positive attitudes relate to later engagement in cyberbullying (Wright and Li, 2013a).

Distinct from the social cognitive theory, which focuses on successful cyberbullying shaping positive attitudes toward these behaviors, the online disinhibition effect proposes that people in cyberspace might not behave in similar ways as they would in real life (Suler, 2004). A core tenant to this theory is that the online environment allows people to loosen or abandon their typical social restrictions and inhibitions that are present in normal face-to-face interactions (Mason, 2008). There is a variety of research demonstrating that people do behave more bluntly when communicating via various electronic technologies. In this early research, McKenna and Bargh (2000) found that there were more misunderstandings, greater hostility, and aggressive behaviors in computer-mediated communication when compared to face-to-face communication. The online environment also removes the ability to see emotional reactions, which might prevent people from modulating their own behavior as they are not able to witness the consequences of their actions (Kowalski et al., 2008). When it comes to cyberbullying, the cyberbully may not witness cyber-victims' reactions, or experience social disapproval and punishment (Willard, 2007). Over time, cyberbullies' behaviors might become more disinhibited, especially when they receive positive reinforcement, fail to recognize the consequences of their behaviors, and lose control of the typical inhibitions present in face-to-face interactions (Hinduja and Patchin, 2009; Wright, 2014a). Another core component of the online disinhibition effect is deindividuation (Joinson, 1998). Deindividuation occurs when people are not accountable for their actions, and anonymity might further reduce accountability. Anonymity in the cyber context, along with the online disinhibition effect, allows youths to distinguish their actions from the real world and their identity, making it easier for them to harm others electronically (Wright, 2014a).

Recommendations

Based on the extensive research reviewed in this chapter, there are a few noticeable gaps in the literature which should be addressed by future research. One recommendation is for research to follow-up investigating the concept of anonymity as applied to cyberbullying. Youths can also engage in anonymous traditional face-to-face bullying, such as anonymously slipping a nasty note in a peer's locker. Therefore, future research should aim to understand more about the differences in youths' conceptualizations of anonymous acts both online and offline, and which factors might contribute to their decision to choose anonymous cyberbullying versus anonymous traditional face-to-face bullying. Similarly, this research should also examine the differences in non-anonymous cyberbullying versus anonymous cyberbullying through social applications, like Ask.fm, or Yik Yak. There is also a need to conduct more longitudinal designs which assess both traditional face-to-face bullying and cyberbullying from early childhood into late adolescents. Such investigations are important as many studies conducted on cyberbullying do not account for previous levels of traditional face-to-face bullying, despite the perpetration and victimization of these behaviors being highly correlated (Wright and Li, 2013a; Ybarra et al., 2007). It is also important for this research to assess children in early elementary school since children are beginning to utilize electronic technologies at a younger age (Madden et al., 2013), which places them at risk for cyberbullying, given the positive correlation between these behaviors and Internet usage (Ybarra et al., 2007).

Cyberbullying is not a concern only for researchers, educators, and youths themselves, but also for our communities. Educational curriculum should include information about cyberbullying, digital literacy, and citizenship as well as positive uses of electronic technologies (Cassidy et al., 2012b). Curriculum should also focus on empathy, self-esteem, and social skills. Schools should also aim to improve school climate through learning students' names, recognizing and rewarding good behavior, and staying technologically savvy (Hinduja and Patchin, 2012). The code of conduct at the school should also address appropriate technology usage and all adults in the school should advocate and enforce these policies.

Parents serve an important role in addressing cyberbullying. Although parents should "join forces with educators," they also need to gain an awareness of the technological environment, and an understanding of the behaviors their children might engage in through that environment (Cassidy et al., 2012a). Parents are also important models for appropriate online behavior. As indicated in the first section of this chapter, many cases of cyberbullying suicide took parents completely by surprise. Therefore, parents should engage in open communication about appropriate technology usage, including discussing with their children the amount of time that they should spend online and the ways they should act in this environment.

It might be difficult to understand how cyberbullying is also a community-problem; in our communities, many of us are bystanders. If we notice someone who needs help, we should help them, instead of expecting others to do it. Helping others models appropriate behaviors for the whole community. Cyberbullying legislation has also been slower to develop in some areas of the world. Such legislation has been helpful for addressing cyberbullying outside of the school (Cassidy et al., 2012b). Cassidy and colleagues note that cyberbullying laws should be part of the solution, but that it is not the whole solution. They advocate for the reformulation of cyberbullying laws which further core social values. Electronic communication has become the standard means of communication for youths as well as adults. As such, many forms of social interactions and social communications have transferred to this medium, including cyberbullying. Attacks in cyberspace are just as powerful as face-to-face attacks, sometimes even more so, because of the persistence of the attack. Society needs to recognize this threat and deal with it as a powerful menace, which can affect everyone. Cyberbullying is not going away. It will remain with us for as long as we interact through this interconnected electronic society.

References

Akbulut, Y., Sahin, T. L., and Eristi, B. (2010). Cyberbullying victimization among Turkish online social utility members. *Educational Technology and Society*, 13, 192-201.

Ang, R. P., Kit-Aun, T., and Mansor, A. T. (2010). Normative beliefs about aggression as a mediator of narcissistic exploitativeness and cyberbullying. *Journal of Interpersonal Violence*, 26, 2619-2634.

Aoyama, I., Barnard-Brak, L., and Talbert, T. L. (2011). Cyberbullying among high school students: Cluster analysis of sex and age differences and the level of parental monitoring. *International Journal of Cyber Behavior, Psychology and Learning*, 1, 1-11.

Aoyama, I., Utsumi, S., and Hasegawa, M. (2011). Cyberbullying in Japan: Cases, government reports, adolescent relational aggression and parental monitoring roles. In Q. Li, D. Cross, and P. K. Smith (Eds.), Bullying in the global playground: Research from an international perspective. Oxford, UK: Wiley-Blackwell.

Aricak, T., Siyahhan, S., Uzunhasanoglu, A., Saribeyoglu, S., Ciplak, S., Yilmaz, N., and Memmedov, C. (2008). Cyberbullying among Turkish adolescents. *CyberPsychology and Behavior*, 11, 253-261.

Arslan, S., Savaser, S., Hallett, V., and Balci, S. (2012). Cyberbullying among primary school students in Turkey: Self-reported prevalence and associations with home and school life. *CyberPsychology, Behavior, and Social Networking*, 15, 527-533.

Ayas, T., and Horzum, M. B. (2010). Cyberbullg / victim scale development study. Retreived from: http://www.akademikbakis.org

Barlett, C. P., and Gentile, D. A. (2012). Long-term psychological predictors of cyber-bullying in late adolescence. *Psychology of Popular Media Culture*, 2, 123-135.

Barlett, C. P., Gentile, D. A., Anderson, C. A., Suzuki, K., Sakamoto, A., Yamaoka, A., and Katsura, R. (2013). Cross-cultural differences in cyberbullying behavior: A short-term longitudinal study. *Journal of Cross-Cultural Psychology*, 45, 300-313.

Bauman, S., Toomey, R. B., and Walker, J. L. (2013). Associations among bullying, cyberbullying, and suicide in high school students. *Journal of Adolescence*, 36, 341-350.

Bayar, Y., and Ucanok, Z. (2012). School social climate and generalized peer perception in traditional and cyberbullying status. *Educational Sciences: Theory and Practice*, 12, 2352-2358.

Beale, A. V., and Hall, K. R. (2007). Cyberbullying: What school administrators (and parents) can do. *Clearing House*, 81, 8-12.

Beckman, L., Hagquist, C., and Hellstrom, L. (2012). Does the association with psychosomatic health problems differ between cyberbullying and traditional bullying? *Emotional and Behavioural Difficulties*, 17, 421-434.

Beran, T., and Li, Q. (2005). Cyber-harassment: A new method for an old behavior. *Journal of Educational Computing Research,* 32, 265-277.

Beran, T., and Li, Q. (2007). The relationship between cyberbullying and school bullying. *Journal of Student Wellbeing*, 1, 15-33.

Bonanno, R. A., and Hymel, S. (2013). Cyber bullying and internalizing difficulties: Above and beyond the impact of traditional forms of bullying. *Journal of Youth and Adolescence*, 42, 685-697.

Brighi, A., Guarini, A., Melotti, G., Galli, S., and Genta, M. L. (2012). Predictors of victimisation across direct bullying, indirect bullying and cyberbullying. *Emotional and Behavioural Difficulties,* 17, 375-388.

Burton, K. A., Florell, D., and Wygant, D. B. (2013). The role of peer attachment and normative beliefs about aggression on traditional bullying and cyberbullying. *Psychology in the Schools,* 50, 103-114.

Campbell, M., Spears, B., Slee, P. H., Butler, D., and Kift, S. (2012). Victims' perceptions of traditional and cyberbullying, and the psychosocial correlates of their victimisation. *Emotional and Behavioural Difficulties*, 17, 389-401.

Cappadocia, M. C., Craig, W. M., and Pepler, D. (2013). Cyberbullying: Prevalence, stability and risk factors during adolescence. *Canadian Journal of School Psychology*, 28, 171-192.

Cassidy, W., Brown, K., and Jackson, M. (2012a). "Making kind cool": Parents' suggestions for preventing cyber bullying and fostering cyber kindness. *Journal of Educational Computing Research,* 46, 415-436.

Cassidy, W., Brown, K., and Jackson, M. (2012b). "Under the radar": Educators and cyberbullying in schools. *School Psychology International*, 33, 520-532.

Chisholm, J. F. (2006). Cyberspace violence against girls and adolescent females. *Annals of the New York Academy of Sciences,* 1087, 74-89.

Corcoran, L., Connolly, I., and O'Moore, M. (2012). Cyberbullying in Irish schools: An investigation of personality and self-concept. *The Irish Journal of Psychology*, 33, 153-165.

Cost. (2012). COST ACTION IS0801 cyberbullying: Coping with negative and enhancing positive uses of new technologies, in relationships in educational settings. Retrieved from: https://sites.google.com/site/costis0801/

Dehue, F., Bolman, C., and Vollink, T. (2008). Cyberbullying: Youngsters' experiences and parental perception. *CyberPscyhology and Behavior*, 11, 217-223.

Dehue, F., Bolman, C., Vollink, T., and Pouwelse, M. (2012). Cyberbullying and traditional bullying in relation to adolescents' perceptions of parenting. *Journal of CyberTherapy and Rehabilitation,* 5, 25-34.

Dooley, J. J., Pyzalski, J., and Cross, D. (2009). Cyberbullying versus face-to-face bullying. *Journal of Psychology*, 217, 182-188.

Duncan, D. R. (2004). The impact of family relationships on school bullies and victims. In D. L. Espelage and S. M. Swearer (Eds.), Bullying in American schools (pp. 277-244). London: Lawrence Erlbaum Associates.

Eden, S., Heiman, T., and Olenik-Shemesh, D. (2013). Teachers' perceptions, beliefs and concerns about cyberbullying. *British Journal of Educational Technology*, 44, 1036-1052.

Elledge, L. C., Williford, A., Boulton, A. J., DePaolis, K. J., Little, T. D., and Salmivalli, C. (2013). Individual and contextual predictors of cyberbullying: The influence of children's provictim attitudes and teachers' ability to intervene. *Journal of Youth and Adolescence,* 42, 698-710.

Erdur-Baker, O. (2010). Cyberbullying and its correlation to traditional bullying, gender and frequent and risky usage of internet-mediated communication tools. *New Media and Society,* 12, 109-125.

Fanti, K. A., Demetriou, A. G., and Hawa, V. V. (2012). A longitudinal study of cyberbullying: Examining risk and protective factors. *European Journal of Developmental Psychology,* 8, 168-181.

Ferdon, C. D., and Hertz, M. F. (2007). Electronic media, violence, and adolescents. An emerging public health problem. *Journal of Adolescent Health*, 41, 1-5.

Festl, R., Schwarkow, M., and Quandt, T. (2013). Peer influence, internet use and cyberbullying: A comparison of different context effects among German adolescents. *Journal of Children and Media*, 7, 446-462.

Gamez-Guadix, M., Orue, I., Smith, P. K., and Calvete, E. (2013). Longitudinal and reciprocal relations of cyberbullying with depression, substance use, and problematic internet use among adolescents. *Journal of Adolescent Health*, 53, 446-452.

Genta, M. L., Smith, P. K., Ortega, R., Brighi, A., Guarini, A., Thompson, F., Tippett, N., Mora-Merchan, J., and Calmaestra, J. (2011). Comparative aspects of cyberbullying in Italy, England, and Spain: Findings from a DAPHNE project. In Q. Li, D. Cross, and P. K. Smith (Eds.), Bullying in the global playground: Research from an international perspective. Oxford, UK: Wiley-Blackwell.

Gillespie, A. A. (2006). Cyber-bullying and harassment of teenagers: The legal response. *Journal of Social Welfare and Family Law*, 28, 123-136.

Goebert, D., Else, I., Matsu, C., Chung-Do, J., and Chang, J. Y. (2011). The impact of cyberbullying on substance use and mental health in a multiethnic sample. *Maternal Child Health Journal,* 15, 1282-1286.

Gradinger, P., Strohmeier, D., and Spiel, C. (2009). Traditional bullying and cyberbullying. *Journal of Psychology*, 217, 205-213.

Grigg, D. W. (2010). Cyber-aggression: Definition and concept of cyberbullying. *Australian Journal of Guidance and Counseling,* 20, 143-156.

Grigg, D. W. (2012). Definitional constructs of cyberbullying and cyber aggression from a triagnulatory overview: A preliminary study into elements. *Journal of Aggression, Conflict, and Peace Research,* 4, 202-215.

Heirman, W., and Walrave, M. (2012). Predicting adolescent perpetration in cyberbullying: An application of the theory of planned behavior. *Psicothema,* 24, 614-620.

Hinduja, S., and Patchin, J. W. (2007). Offline consequences of online victimization. *Journal of School Violence,* 6, 89-112.

Hinduja, S., and Patchin, J. W. (2008). Cyberbullying: An exploratory analysis of factors related to offending and victimization. *Deviant Behavior*, 29, 129-156.

Hinduja, S., and Patchin, J. W. (2010). Bullying, cyberbullying, and suicide. *Archives of Suicide Research,* 14, 206-221.

Hinduja, S., and Patchin, J. W. (2012). Cyberbullying: Neither and epidemic nor a rarity. *European Journal of Developmental Psychology*, 9, 539-543.

Hinduja, S., and Patchin, J. W. (2013). Social influences on cyberbullying behaviors among middle and high school students. *Journal of Youth and Adolescence*, 42, 711-722.

Huang, Y., and Chou, C. (2010). An analysis of multiple factors of cyberbullying among junior high school students in Taiwan. *Computers in Human Behavior*, 26, 1581-1590.

The Huffington Post. (2013). Rehtaeh Parsons, Canadian girl, dies after suicide attempt; parents allege she was raped by 4 boys. The Huffington Post. Retrieved from http://www.huffingtonpost.com/2013/04/09/rehtaeh-parsons-girl-dies-suicide-rape-canada_n_3045033.html

Jang, H., Song, J., and Kim, R. (2014). Does the offline bully-victimization influence cyberbullying behavior among youths? Application of general strain theory. *Computers in Human behavior*, 31, 85-93.

Joinson, A. (1998). Causes and implications of behavior on the Internet. In J. Gackenbach (Ed.), Psychology and the Internet: Intrapersonal, interpersonal, and transpersonal implications (pp. 43-60). San Diego, CA: Academic Press.

Kochenderfer-Ladd, B., and Pelletier, M. (2008). Teachers' views and beliefs about bullying: Influences on classroom management strategies and students' coping with peer victimization. *Journal of School Psychology*, 46, 431-453.

Kowalski, R. M., and Limber, S. P. (2007). Electronic bullying among middle school students. *Journal of Adolescent Health*, 41, 22-30.

Laftman, S. B., Modin, B., and Ostberg, V. (2013). Cyberbullying and subjective health: A large-scale study of students in Stockholm, Sweden. *Children and Youth Services Review,* 35, 112-119.

Lazuras, L., Barkoukis, V., Ourda, D., and Tsorbatzoudis, H. (2013). A process model of cyberbullying in adolescence. *Computers in Human Behavior*, 29, 881-887.

Li, Q. (2007). Bullying in the new playground: Research into cyberbullying and cybervictimization. *Australian Journal of Educational Technology*, 23, 435-454.

Li, Q. (2008). A cross-cultural comparison of adolescents' experience related to cyberbullying. *Educational Research*, 50, 223-234.

Madden, M., Lenhart, A., Duggan, M., Cortesi, S., and Gasser, U. (2013). Teens and technology 2013. Retrieved from: http://www.pewinternet.org/2013/03/13/teens-and-technology-2013/

Maher, D. (208). Cyber-bullying an ethnographic case study of one Australian upper primary school class. *Youth Studies Australia*, 27, 50-57.

Marini, Z., Dane, A., Bosacki, S., and Ylc-Cura, Y. (2006). Direct and indirect bully-victims: Differential psychosocial risk factors associated with adolescents involved in bullying and victimization. *Aggressive Behavior*, 32, 551-569.

Mason, K. (2008). Cyberbullying: A preliminary assessment for school personnel. *Psychology in the Schools*, 45, 323-348.

McKenna, K. Y. A., and Bargh, J. A. (2000). Plan 9 from cyberspace: The implications of the internet for personality and social psychology. *Personality and Social Psychology Review,* 4, 57-75.

McQuade, C. S., Colt, P. J., and Meyer, B. N. (2009). Cyber bullying: Protecting kids and adults from online bullies. Westport: Praeger.

McVey, C. (2012). Friends blame cyber-bullying for student's suicide. Bay News 9. Retrieved from http://www.baynews9.com/content/news/baynews9/news/article.html/content/news/articles/bn9/2012/12/11/friends_blame_cyberb.html

Mesch, G. S. (2009). Parental mediation, online activities, and cyberbullying. *CyberPsychology and Behavior*, 12, 387-393.

Mitchell, K. J., Ybarra, M., and Finkelhor, D. (2007). The relative importance of online victimization in understanding depression, delinquency, and substance use. *Child Maltreatment,* 12, 314-324.

Moore, M. J., Nakano, T. N., Enomoto, A., and Suda, T. (2012). Anonymity and roles associated with aggressive posts in an online forum. *Computers in Human Behavior*, 28, 861-867.

Mouttapa, M., Valente, T., Gallaher, P., Rohrbach, L. A., and Unger, J. B. (2004). Social network predictor of bullying and victimization. *Adolescence*, 39, 315-335.

Navarro, R., Serna, C., Martinez, V., and Ruiz-Oliva, R. (2013). The role of Internet use and parental mediation on cyberbullying victimization among Spanish children from rural public schools. *European Journal of Psychology of Education*, 28, 725-745.

Nocentini, A., Calmaestra, J., Schultze-Krumbholz, A., et al. (2010). Cyberbullying: Labels, behaviours and definition in three European countries. *Australian Journal of Guidance and Counselling,* 20, 129-142.

Olenik-Shemesh, D., Heiman, T., and Eden, S. (2012). Cyberbullying victimisation in adolescence: Relationships with loneliness and depressive mood. *Emotional and Behavioural Difficulties,* 17, 361-374.

Olweus, D. (1993). Bullying at school. What we know and what we can do. Malden, MA: Blackwell Publishing.

Olweus, D. (1999). Sweden. In K. Smith, Y. Morita, J. Junger-Tas, D. Olweus, R. Catalano, and P. Slee (Eds.), The nature of school bullying: A cross-national perspective (pp. 7-27). New York, NY: Routledge.

Parker, J., Rubin, K. H., Erath, S., Wojslawowicz, J. C., and Buskirk, A. A. (2006). Peer relationships and developmental psychopathology. In D. Cicchetti and D. Cohen (Eds.), Developmental Psychopathology: Risk Disorder, and Adaptation, Vol. 2. (pp. 419-493). New York: Wiley.

Patchin, J. W., and Hinduja, S. (2006). Bullies move beyond the schoolyard: A preliminary look at cyberbullying. *Youth Violence and Juvenile Justice*, 4, 148-169.

Pendergrass, W. and Wright, M. F. (in press). Cyberbullied to death: an analysis of victims taken from recent events. Issues in Information Systems.

Perren, S., Dooley, J., Shaw, T., and Cross, D. (2010). Bullying in school and cyberspace: Associations with depressive symptoms in Swiss and Australian adolescents. *Child and Adolescent Psychiatry and Mental Health,* 4, 1-10.

Pornari, C. D., and Wood, J. (2010). Peer and cyber aggression in secondary school students: The role of moral disengagement, hostile attribution bias, and outcome expectancies. *Aggressive Behavior*, 36, 81-94.

Quigley, R. and Gorman, R. (2013). 'I did nothing wrong': girl, 13, accused of bullying suicide victim Rebecca Sedwick speaks out after charges were dropped. Daily Mail. Retrieved from http://www.dailymail.co.uk/news/article-2511202/Katelyn-Roman-accused-bullying-Rebecca-Sedwick-did-wrong.html

Rideout, V. J., Roberts, D. F., and Foehr, U. G. (2005). Generation M: Media in the lives of 8-18-year-olds: Executive summary. Menlo Park, CA: Henry J. Kaiser Family Foundation.

Robson, C., and Witenberg, R. T. (2013). The influence of moral disengagement, morally based self-esteem, age, and gender on traditional bullying and cyberbullying. *Journal of School Violence,* 12, 211-231.

Rosen, L. D. (2007). Me, Myspace, and I: Parenting the Net Generation. New York: Palgrave Macmillan.

Sahin, M. (2010). Teachers' perceptions of bullying in high schools: A Turkish study. *Social Behavior and Personality,* 38, 127-142.

Shapka, J. D., and Law, D. M. (2013). Does one size fit all? Ethnic differences in parenting behaviors and motivations for adolescent engagement in cyberbullying. *Journal of Youth and Adolescence,* 42, 723-738.

Shariff, S., and Hoff, D. L. (2007). Cyber bullying: Clarifying legal boundaries for school supervision in cyberspace. *International Journal of Cyber Criminology*, 1, 76-118.

Singelis, T. M. (1994). The measurement of independent and interdependent self-construals. *Personality and Social Psychology Bulletin*, 20, 580-591.

Slonje, R., and Smith, P. K. (2008). Cyberbullying another main type of bullying? *Scandinavian Journal of Psychology*, 49, 147-154.

Smith, P. K., Madsen, K. C., and Moody, J. C. (1999). What cause the age decline in reports of being bullied at school? Towards a developmental analysis of risks of being bullied. *Educational Research*, 41, 267-285.

Smith, P. K., Mahdavi, J., Carvalho, M., Fisher, S., Russell, S., and Tippett, N. (2008). Cyberbullying: Its nature and impact in secondary school pupils. *Journal of Child Psychology and Psychiatry,* 49, 376-385.

Sourander, A., Brunstein, A., Ikonen, M., Lindroos, J., Luntamo, T., Koskelainen, M., and Ristkari, T., and Helenius, H. (2010). Psychosocial risk factors associated with cyberbullying among adolescents: A population-based study. *Archives of General Psychiatry,* 67, 720-728.

Steffgen, G., Konig, A., Pfetsch, J., and Melzer, A. (2011). Are cyberbullies less empathic? Adolescents' cyberbullying behavior and empathic responsiveness. *CyberPsychology, Behavior, and Social Networking,* 14, 643-648.

Strohmeier, D., Aoyama, I., Gradinger, P., and Toda, Y. (2013). Cybervictimization and cyberaggression in Eastern and Western countries: Challenges of constructing a cross-cultural appropriate scale. In S. Bauman, D. Cross, and J. L. Walker (Eds.), Principles of cyberbullying research: Definitions, measures, and methodology (pp. 202-221). New York: Routledge.

Suler, J. (2004). The online disinhibition effect. *CyberPsychology and Behavior,* 7, 321-326.

Tangen, D., and Campbell, M. (2010). Cyberbullying prevention: One primary school's approach. *Australian Journal of Guidance and Counselling,* 20, 225-234.

Topcu, C., Erdur-Baker, O., and Capa, A. Y. (2008). Examination of cyber-bullying experiences among Turkish students from different school types. *CyberPsychology and Behavior,* 11, 644-648.

Totura, C. M. W., MacKinnon-Lewis, C., Gesten, E. L., Gadd, R., Divine, K. P., Dunham, S., and Kamboukos, D. (2009). Bullying and victimization among boys and girls in middle school: The influence of perceived family and school contexts. *The Journal of Early Adolescence,* 29, 571-609.

Vandebosch, H., and van Cleemput, K. (2008). Defining cyberbullying: A qualitative research into the perceptions of youngsters. *CyberPsychology and Behavior,* 11, 499-503.

Wade, A., and Beran, T. (2011). Cyberbullying: The new era of bullying. *Canadian Journal of School Psychology,* 26, 44-61.

Willard, N. (2007). Cyberbullying and cyber-threats: Responding to the challenge of online social aggression, threats, and distress. Champaign, IL: Research Press.

Williams, K. R., and Guerra, N. G. (2007). Prevalence and predictors of internet bullying. *Journal of Adolescent Health,* 41, S14-S21.

Wolak, J., Mitchell, K., and Finkelhor, D. (2007). Does online harassment constitute bullying? An exploration of online harassment by known peers and online-only contacts. *Journal of Adolescent Health,* 41, 51-58.

Wright, M. F. (2013). The relationship between young adults' beliefs about anonymity and subsequent cyber aggression. *CyberPsychology, Behavior, and Social Networking,* 16, 858-862.

Wright, M. F. (in press). Cyber victimization and perceived stress: Linkages to late adolescents' cyber aggression and psychological functioning. Youth and Society.

Wright, M. F. (2014a). Predictors of anonymous cyber aggression: The role of adolescents' beliefs about anonymity, aggression, and the permanency of digital content. *CyberPsychology, Behavior, and Social Networking,* 17, 431-438.

Wright, M. F. (2014b). Longitudinal investigation of the associations between adolescents' popularity and cyber social behaviors. *Journal of School Violence,* 13, 291-314.

Wright, M. F., and Li, Y. (2012). Kicking the digital dog: A longitudinal investigation of young adults' victimization and cyber-displaced aggression. *CyberPsychology, Behavior, and Social Networking,* 15, 448-454.

Wright, M. F., and Li. Y. (2013a). Normative beliefs about aggression and cyber aggression among young adults: A longitudinal investigation. *Aggressive Behavior,* 39, 161-170.

Wright, M. F., and Li, Y. (2013b). The association between cyber victimization and subsequent cyber aggression: The moderating effect of peer rejection. *Journal of Youth and Adolescence,* 42, 662-674.

Ybarra, M. L., and Mitchell, K. J. (2004). Online aggressor/targets, aggressors, and targets: A comparison of associated youth characteristics. *Journal of Child Psychology and Psychiatry,* 45, 1308-1316.

Ybarra, M. L., Diener-West, M., and Leaf, P. (2007). Examining the overlap in internet harassment and school bullying: Implications for school intervention. *Journal of Adolescent Health,* 1, 42-50.

Zhou, Z., Tang, H., Tian, Y., Wei, H., Zhang, F., and Morrison, C. M. (2013). Cyberbullying and its risk factors among Chinese high school students. *School Psychology International,* 34, 630-647.

In: Handbook on Bullying
Editor: Phoebe Triggs
ISBN: 978-1-63463-023-8

Chapter 7

BULLYING, PERSONAL SELF-REGULATION, RESILIENCE, COPING STRATEGIES AND ENGAGEMENT-BURNOUT: IMPLICATIONS FOR AN INTERVENTION WITH UNIVERSITY STUDENTS

***Jesús de la Fuente, Ph.D.*[1], *Lucía Zapata, Ph.D.*[2], *M. Mariano Vera, Ph.D.*[3], *Mari Carmen González-Torres, Ph.D.*[4] *and Raquel Artuch Garde, Ph.D.*[5]**

[1]Developmental and Educational Psychology, Department of Psychology, University of Almería, Spain
[2]Education & Psychology I+D+I, Spin-Off University of Almería, Spain
[3]Department of Personality, Assessment and Psychological Training, University of Granada, Spain
[4]Educational Psychology, Department of Education, University of Navarra, Spain
[5]Department of Education, University of Navarra, Spain

Abstract

Introduction. Bullying is one of today's biggest problems in Public Health. It occurs very frequently, especially in adolescence, and action is needed to lessen its causes and alleviate its consequences. Research has shown that behavior problems usually interact with other risk and protection factors, as well as with factors of etiological development. The *objective* of this investigation was to establish a hypothetical relationship between *personal self-regulation, resilience, coping strategies* and *engagement-burnout*, which would serve as a foundation for new lines of intervention at university.

Method. A total of 253 university students participated in this research. Assessment questionnaires for *personal self-regulation, coping strategies, resilience* and *positive-negative emotionality* were completed on an anonymous, voluntary basis during class time, at different points during the 2012-2013 academic year. Correlation analyses and structural analysis were performed, using an ex post-facto design.

Results. Results showed significant association relationships between self-regulation and resilience, between resilience and type of coping strategies used to cope with stress, and between resilience and burnout-engagement.

Discussion and conclusions. Greater *personal self-regulation* is significantly associated and interdependent with a greater level of *resilient* behavior, and *resilient behavior* in turn is similarly related to more *problem-focused coping strategies,* and more *engagement behavior* in dealing with stressful situations. The results suggest a line of research for skill-training programs as a means to deal with bullying. This evidence should be applied to intervention programs, both for training in *personal self-regulation,* and for implementing *resilient behaviors* and *coping strategies* with *engagement behavior* for managing this type of stressful situation. Future investigations should explore this line of work, which has not been fully considered to date.

Introduction

Bullying is one of the major problems of Public Health. It occurs frequently and requires attention in order to mitigate its causes and consequences, especially during adolescence (Espelage & Horne, 2007). Research has shown that behavior problems are usually interrelated with other risk and protective factors, as well as with factors of etiological development. Bullying, substance abuse and the increase in a broad range of social problems all point to the need for children and adolescents to develop the skills needed for negotiation and interpersonal relationships (Swearer, Espelage & Napolitano, 2009).

Definition and Scope of the Problem

Olweus (1993) defined it as the situation where one or more students, whether bullies or victims, are repeatedly exposed to negative actions on the part of one or more of their peers. Bullying "is a process of intensification of a conflict (escalation) in which one person is in a position of inferiority and is the victim of systematic negative actions by one or more attackers. Bullying "refers neither to a conflict resulting from an accident or an isolated event, nor a conflict in which the aggressor and the victim have an equal power relationship" (Einarsen et al 2011, p. 15). There are different types of bullying.

1. *Physical and verbal bullying*. Much research has focused on these two types of bullying, including name-calling, pushing and shoving, taking away objects and hitting. A distinction has been made between the motives for and purposes of bullying, as well as between *proactive* and *reactive* bullying.
2. *Relational bullying.* Bullying has generally been defined as behaviors intended to hurt someone else, whether by physical or non-physical means (Berkowitz, 1993). There are different types of non-physical bullying: *Relational* or *social* bullying takes many shapes and has to do with peer relationships, including hurting others through the withdrawal of relations or feelings of acceptance, friendship and inclusion in the group. Rumors and exclusion are used to maintain status between peers (Card, Stucky, Sawalani & Little, 2008). Social bullying has been related to deficient social skills and the increase of psychopathologies (Crick & Zahn-Warler, 2003). In addition, it has been related to a lack of academic engagement, low academic

achievement, conflicts with the teacher and health risk behaviors, such as use of substances (Murray-Close, Ostrov & Crick, 2007). Furthermore, exposure to relational bullying behaviors has a negative impact on the social, emotional and psychological climate of the school, with more feelings of insecurity among the students (Glew, Fan, Katon & Rivara, 2005), a decrease in classroom participation and school avoidance (Buhs, Ladd & Herald, 2006).

3. *Cyberbullying.* Technological systems are not free from relational issues. Bullying in these contexts has been referred to with such names as cyberbullying, e-bullying or digital bullying. As the use of these technologies has grown exponentially among teenagers, there has also been a rise in their misuse.

Academic and Psychological Correlates of Bullying

A recent study (Glew et al., 2005) illustrates the correlation between bullying experiences and low academic achievement. Victims of bullying report negative psychological, emotional and behavioral consequences, as well as poorer school adjustment, with greater levels of depression, avoidance, suicidal ideas and lower self-esteem, than their non-victimized peers. In addition, they report more *internalized problems.* In the long term, problems may become serious, with more *externalized problems* and more probability of psychiatric behaviors. Research that addresses the stability of *bullying* has focused on physical bullying, suggesting that it is a stable trait (Herrenkohl et al., 2009). It has also shown that *victimization* is also relatively stable during childhood (Beran, 2008).

Context of Bullying: Individual, Peer, Family and School-Related

1) Individual characteristics. Certain personal characteristics increase the likelihood of being bullied, such as not fitting into the group, obesity, receiving remedial classes and learning disabilities. Unlike early research (in favor of the girl students), some recent studies minimize the effect of gender on being victimized (Card et al., 2008). There is little research with regard to the role of ethnic groups or religion, but it has been observed that belonging to a minority ethnic group can be a cause of bullying.

There are individual protective factors against bullying. Empathy has a consistent, negative association with bullying, and a consistent, positive association with prosocial skills. This fact is especially important when the bully understands the emotional state of others and wishes to disturb this state. *Anger* and *hostility* have been consistent correlates of bullying, since some studies show anger to be a good predictor of bullying actions. *Impulsiveness* has also appeared to have an important role in victimization and in bullying actions (Espelaje, Bosworth & Simon, 2001). In one study with pre-adolescents, greater use of drugs and alcohol was found in those who practice bullying (Pepler et al, 2002).

2) *Characteristics of peers.* Bullying may be encouraged and sustained by certain characteristics of the peer group, especially by *attitudes* toward following group rules. There are different hypotheses, such as the homophily hypothesis, attraction theory, and dominance theory. Prevention programs must take on systematic assessment and intervention in order to change the rules of peer interaction.

3) *Family characteristics.* With regard to the family context, research has reported that students who practice bullying have authoritarian parents who use physical punishment and show indifference toward their children (Olweus, 1995). Secondary students who were classified as bullies and bully-victims showed significant differences in terms of less social support from their parents, and there is evidence that students with affective maternal experiences showed fewer disruptive relationships and bullying behaviors.

Personal Determining Factors for Coping with Bullying: Personal Self-Regulation and Resilience

Personal Self-Regulation

Personal self-regulation refers to the capacity or ability to control our own thoughts, emotions and actions. Through self-regulation we are able to consciously control the amount that we eat, whether to act on an impulse, our task execution, obsessive thoughts, and even the extent that we allow ourselves to listen to our own emotions. We can therefore affirm that personal self-regulation is a vital process that allows people to behave adequately, carry out tasks properly, and abstain from activities that may be harmful to their own livelihood (Baumeister & Heatherton, 1996). Self-regulation is used in a number of processes including the regulation of emotions, thoughts and actions for physical or behavioral control or restraint (Baumeister, Bratslavsky, Muraven, & Tice, 1998; Vohs et al., 2008).

Different theoretical models have outlined the characteristics of this psychological construct. From a sequential approach, Kanfer (1986) proposed a model within the so-called *open-loop* conception (Bandura, 1986), where self-regulation is conceived as a self-correcting procedure when faced with discrepancies, indications of imminent danger, or conflictive motivational states that activate the system of observation. The present study adopts this conception. Miller and Brown (1991) modify postulates of the Kanfer (1986) model, providing a better explanation for changes in addictions.

If there is a deficit in any of these self-regulation processes, one's behavior regulation will suffer. Within this theoretical framework, Brown (1998) defines self-regulation as a person's ability to "plan, monitor and direct his or her behavior in changing situations" (p.62). In essence, this model adopts the self-regulation postulates of Zimmerman (2002), by defining moments of planning, control and thoughtful evaluation of one's action. Hoyle (2010) also speaks of these discrepancies and of the actions that we carry out in order to obtain our objectives and what we desire. He calls these actions self-regulation, actions that are natural and often are automatic responses of a healthy person in order to cope with the day-to-day discrepancies that are found between one's expectations or desires and one's reality.

Self-regulation as described above has been related mainly to addictive behaviors: gambling, and alcohol and drug use (Brown & Newby-Clark, 2005; Neal & Carey, 2005). This self-regulation takes the qualifier "personal" in order to differentiate it from "academic", and has been studied in both adolescents (de la Fuente, Peralta & Sánchez, 2009; de la Fuente, Trianes, Peralta & Sánchez, 2007) and university students (de la Fuente, Berbén & Martínez, 2006). *Personal self-regulation* is a construct that has been used to a greater extent in the field of health (Brown, 1998; Muraven, Collins, Morsheimer, Shiffman, & Paty, 2005; Muraven, Collins & Nienhaus, 2002). However, after Zimmerman (1998) showed the existence of processes that are common to different domains, experts have begun to show interest in analyzing the self-regulating components that are common to different spheres of life, such as education and work.

Brown, Miller and Lawendowski (1999) constructed the Self-Regulation Questionnaire (SRQ) to measure self-regulation based on their theoretical model. Later, after performing further analyses, they developed an abbreviated version, the *Short Self-Regulation Questionnaire* (SSRQ), which was validated in a Spanish sample by Pichardo, Justicia, Berbén, de la Fuente and Martinez-Vicente (in press). The data show good fit to the structure of seventeen items grouped under four factors (goal setting-planning, perseverance, decision making and learning from mistakes). This instrument has been used mainly in connection with substance abuse, and has been subjected to an examination of its psychometric characteristics on several occasions (Carey, Neal & Colling, 2004; Neal & Carey, 2005). Its use has also been extended beyond substance abuse to address aspects such as psychological well-being, disposition to happiness (Okum, Levy, Karoly & Ruleman, 2009), depression symptoms (Kogan & Brody, 2010) and career adaptability (Creed, Fallon & Hood, 2009), and is in demand in other areas such as education (de la Fuente, Peralta, Sánchez, 2009). However, its possible role as a personal characteristic in the bullying phenomenon has not been established.

Resilience

Spencer et al. (2012) have defined *resilience* as a psychological resistance characteristic (the opposite of vulnerability), especially in extreme situations such as catastrophes and social inequality. The PVEST Model, *Phenomenological Variant of Ecological Systems Theory* (Spencer, 2008) makes several assumptions: Each person has a degree of vulnerability, based on different degrees of protection and of risk; 2) level of engagement in stressful situations refers to the support or possible changes that a person can make within his or her environment. The role of resilience in an individual's social problems, and specifically in bullying situations, has not been precisely established.

Procedural Determining Factors for Coping with Bullying: Coping Strategies

We find ourselves socially at a very complex time, when the word stress appears frequently in day to day life, and has become a familiar concept. When we speak about coping we refer to cognitive and behavioral efforts to manage stress (DeLongis, Holtzman, Puterman, & Lam, 2010). Holroyd and Lazarus (1982) define *coping* as "cognitive and behavioral efforts to master, reduce, or tolerate the internal and/or external demands that are created by the stressful transaction" (p. 843). Lazarus (1991) defines coping as "cognitive and behavioral efforts to manage specific external or internal demands (and conflicts between them) that are appraised as taxing or exceeding the resources of a person" (p. 112).

Coping strategies in the context of Educational Psychology are more related to academic stress and specifically to one of its main stressors, tests (Piemontesi & Heredia, 2009). We consider it of vital importance to examine coping strategies, since all university students must face the external stressor of tests, as well as other stressors. We must also keep in mind that university students are a very specific population, as are the ways that they deal with stress. Hence the importance of introducing this variable in the present research, as mentioned above. Fewer studies have been carried out in this field, but relationships have been found between coping strategies and academic performance (Cohen, Ben-Zur & Rosenfeld, 2008) and student gender (de la Fuente, Cardelle-Elawar, Martínez-Vicente, Zapata & Peralta, 2013). In addition, students' levels of stress have been studied in conjunction with the coping strategies they use (Ticona, Paucar & Llerena, 2010).

Lazarus and Folkman (1986) consider one distinction to be extremely important: the difference between coping that is directed toward handling or altering the problem (*problem-focused coping*), and coping aimed at regulating the emotional response that the problem brings about (*emotion-focused coping*). The importance of the present study stems from the lack of research on coping strategies in conjunction with other variables of Educational Psychology, such as learning approaches, achievement and satisfaction with learning.

Attitudinal Determining Factors for Coping with Bullying: Engagement-Burnout Emotions

While *motivation* has been conceived as a psychological construct, *engagement* has been defined as emotional involvement that accompanies an object or experience of intense interaction. This is created by the dynamics of a situation or the immediate context, and is not very different from the concept of *situational interest* (Hidi & Anderson, 1992). *Engagement* has been conceptualized as a personal trait and as different *states of contextual interaction* (Schunk, Pintrich & Meece, 2008).

According to Shernoff (2012), *engaged students* are those who are absorbed in their scholastic, academic and learning concerns, while *non-engaged students* are bored, distant, separate from and alienated from school. Friedricks, Blumenfeld, and Paris (2004), after observing diverse conceptualizations and measurements of this construct, conclude that *academic engagement* is a multidimensional construct that involves three dimensions: *Cognitive engagement* (an investigation of learning, self-regulation); 2) *behavioral engagement* (positive behaviors, demonstrated effort); 3) *emotional engagement* (interest and not boredom). *Engagement,* as a psychological construct, arises from contributions from the Positive Psychology paradigm, in contrast to the *burnout* construct, a name for emotional fatigue or exhaustion, with loss of control that is produced in situations of ongoing stress. This construct has been studied extensively in different health- and stress-related problems, but it has not been sufficiently related to bullying.

Aims and Hypotheses

Based on the previous research, the *aim* of this investigation was to establish a hypothetical relationship between personal self-regulation and resilience (presage variables), with coping strategies (process variables), and engagement-burnout emotions (product variables), which would serve as a foundation for new lines of intervention in bullying problems at university. Consequently, our hypotheses were:

1. *Personal self-regulation* would be associated positively with *resilience* – where the former is an integral part of the latter – as well as with positive emotionality or *engagement.* It would also be associated negatively with *burnout.*

2. *Resilience* would be associated with greater use of *problem-focused strategies* and with less focus on emotions, thereby contributing to problem resolution in cases of bullying, and not only to avoidance.
3. *Resilience* would show a significant, positive association with the positive emotionality of *engagement,* and a negative association with *burnout.*
4. *Problem-focused coping* strategies would predict positive emotionality, or engagement, while *emotion-focused coping* strategies would predict negative emotionality or burnout.

Method

Participants

A total of 253 students from higher education participated in this research, including current students from the University of Almeria (Spain) and university graduates who were preparing for competitive exams for public employment. The current university students were pursuing degrees in general Psychology or School Psychology (*Psicopedagogía*). The mean age was 23.08 years (SD=4.4).

Instruments

1) *Personal self-regulation* was measured using the *Short Self-Regulation Questionnaire SSRQ* (Miller & Brown, 1991) in its Spanish version, the CAR (De la Fuente, 2003a). It has already been validated in Spanish samples (Pichardo et al, in press), and possesses acceptable validity and reliability values, similar to the English version with 16 items, including such factors as (1) personal goals, (2) perseverance, (3) decision making, and (4) learning from mistakes.

2) The *coping strategies* variable was measured using the *Escala de Estrategias de Coping* (EEC) [Coping Strategies Scale], in its original version (Chorot & Sandín, 1987; Sandin & Chorot, 1993, 2003). A total of 90 items are included where students respond to items on a 4-point likert-type scale ranging from 0 (never use the strategy) to 3 (always use the strategy). The scale possesses acceptable validity and reliability values. It was constructed according to theoretical-rational criteria, considering the Lazarus and Folkman questionnaire (1984) and taking coping assessment studies by Moos and Billings (1982) as a basis. The latter studies make up the theoretical framework, that is, the general dimensions of coping (appraisal-focused, problem-focused and emotion-focused coping), as well as the different categories that belong to these three dimensions. For each dimension in general, more specific subdimensions are identified. Psychometric properties are acceptable. This questionnaire is composed of 13 factors and two dimensions:

Dimension: emotion-focused coping F1. Fantasy distraction; F4. Religious support; F6. Help for action; F8. Preparing for the worst; F9. Venting and emotional isolation; F11. Resigned acceptance;

Dimension: problem-focused coping: F2. Help seeking and family counsel; F3. Actions aimed at the causes; F5. Self-instructions; F10. Positive reappraisal and firmness; F12. Communication of feelings and social support; F13. Seeking alternative reinforcement.

3) *Resilience.* Resilience was assessed using the CD-RISC Scale (Connor & Davison, 2003) in its validated Spanish version. It has adequate reliability and validity values in Spanish samples, with a five-factor structure: F1. Persistence/tenacity and strong sense of self-efficacy (TENACITY); F2. Emotional and cognitive control under pressure. (STRESS); F3. Adaptability/ability to bounce back (CHANGE); F4. Control/meaning. (CONTROL), and F5. Spiritual influence (SPIRITUAL)

4) *Engagement-Burnout.* Engagement burnout was assessed with a validated Spanish version of the *Marlach Burnout Inventory Survey-Utrech Work Engagement Scale for Students* (Shauffeli et al., 2002). This version has shown adequate reliability and construct validity indices in this cross-cultural study.

Procedure

Information from self-reports was collected in the classroom during regular class hours from both types of students. For the university students, data on *Presage* variables (personal self-regulation, resilience, sex, age) was collected during the month of October. Later, in the month of February, students completed the scales measuring *Process* variables (coping strategies). In the months of May-June, engagement-burnout was assessed (*Product* variables).

Design and Data Analyses

The nature of this investigation, in addressing its objectives and hypotheses, adopts a non-experimental ex post-facto design. In terms of data collection, it is a survey investigation using self-reports (questionnaires and scales) and a cross-sectional strategy. Association analysis through Pearson bivariate correlations was used. Analyses were carried out to meet the proposed objectives and test hypotheses using SPSS version 21.00 for Windows. SEM analysis of structural relations was carried out using the AMOS program, v.16.

Results

Personal Self-Regulation and Resilience

Total score on *personal self-regulation* was positively associated with the *Resilience* total (r=.318, p<.001), with high values for *tenacity* (r=.290, p<.001), coping with *stress* (r=.262, p<.001), adaptability to *change* (r=*.128*, p<.01), *control* (r=.221, p<.001) and spirituality (r=.105, p<.05). As for the components of self-regulation, *goals*, *perseverance* and *learning from mistakes* had significant, positive associations with tenacity (max. r=.265, p<.001), with coping with stress (max. r=.299, p<.001) and with control (max. r=.279, p<.001).

Personal Self-Regulation and Engagement-Burnout

Total score on personal self-regulation was positively associated with *engagement* (r=. 369, p<.01), with high values for vigor (r=.350, p<.01), dedication (r=.298, p<.05) and absorption (r=.299, p<.05); and negatively associated with *exhaustion* (r= -.203, p<.05), as well as with lack of effectiveness (r=-.380, p<.01). As for the components of self-regulation, *perseverance* had a significant, positive association with *engagement* (r=.363, p<.01), while *goals* (r=-.299, p<.05) and *decision making* (r=-.302, p<.05) were negatively associated with exhaustion.

Resilience and Coping Strategies

Total *resilience* showed a significant, positive association with problem-focused coping strategies, but not with emotion-focused strategies. The *spirituality* component was associated with use of emotion-focused strategies. The *change* and *control* components were associated with the use of problem-focused strategies. Specifically, the components of *personal competence-tenacity* and *context of stress* were associated with the use of self-instructions, help-seeking, positive reappraisal and firmness, and seeking alternative reinforcement, and negatively associated with emotional venting and resigned acceptance. The *spirituality* component was positively associated with fantasy distraction, religious support and resigned acceptance. Inferential analyses confirmed these differences between the high-medium-low groups in resilience. See Table 1.

Table 1. Relations between coping strategies and resilience

	Tenacity	Stress	Change	Control	Spirituality	Total
F1. Fantasy distraction	.050	.159**	.015	-.044	.190**	.129*
F4. Religious support	.034	.073	-.080	-.032	.383**	.158**
F6. Help for taking action	.136*	.084	.030	.121*	.075	.128*
F7. Reduction of anxiety and avoidance	-.052	-.013	-.066	-.055	.059	.001
F8. Preparing for the worst	.033	.027	.013	-.090	.034	-.013
F9. Emotional venting and isolation	-.153**	-.095	-.244**	-.255**	-.031	-.225**
F11. Resigned acceptance	-.089	.019	-.175**	-.249**	.126*	-.099

Note. *p<.05;**p<.01.

Resilience and Engagement-Burnout

Total score in *resilience* was negatively associated with exhaustion and lack of effectiveness (burnout), and positively associated with vigor (engagement). The most clearly related component of resilience was control, with a significant positive association with vigor, dedication and absorption, and a negative association with exhaustion, cynicism and lack of effectiveness. Similarly, competence-tenacity was positively associated with vigor and negatively with lack of effectiveness.

Table 2. Relations between resilience and engagement-burnout

	Tenacity	Stress	Change	Control	Spirituality	Total
Exhaustion	-.250	.093	.092	-.318*	-.337**	-.363**
Cynicism	-.193	.057	.034	-.341*	-.120	-.244
Lack of effectiveness	-.141**	-.039	-.010	-.403**	-.081	-.346*
Burnout total	-.313*	.055	.23	-.423**	-.248	-.379**
Vigor	.458**	.202	.097	.486**	-.135	.317*
Dedication	.225	-.006	-.067	.489**	.031	.026
Absorption	.197	.235	.049	.296*	-.160	.189
Engagement total	.316*	.156	.019	.482**	-.124	.267

Note.*p<.05;**p<.01.

Coping Strategies and Engagement-Burnout

Total score for *coping strategies* was positively associated with *burnout* (r= .409, p<.01), but not with *engagement.* In complementary fashion, *emotion-focused* and *problem-focused* coping strategies were positively associated with *burnout* (r= .358, p<.01; r= .368, p<.01, respectively).

More specifically, some coping strategies were negatively associated with *engagement,* such as *resigned acceptance* (r= -.419, p<.01), and *emotional venting* (r= -.457, p<.001). However, there were numerous specific associations between *emotion-focused* coping strategies and *burnout*, such as fantasy distraction (r= .300, p<.05), preparing for the worst (r= .536, p<.001), emotional venting (r= .495, p<.001) and resigned acceptance (r= .311, p<.05). There was also a positive association between *problem-focused* strategies and burnout, referring to actions directed at the causes (r= .352, p<.01).

Building a Model of Relations

SEM analyses showed a significant relations model (*Chi-square* = 25,085; Degrees of freedom = 4; p <.001) with acceptable indices (*NFI*= .988; *RFI*= .968; *IFI*= .983; *CFI*= .994; *RMSEA*= .05). This model reveals how *personal self-regulation* (SRQABREV) positively predicts *resilience* (CDRISCTOTAL), as well as *problem-focused strategies* (AFRONTPROBLEMA) and negatively predicts *emotion-focused strategies* (AFRONTEMOCION).

At the same time, the model shows how *burnout* is predicted positively by emotion-focused coping (AFRONTEMOCION) and negatively by problem-focused coping (AFRONTPROBLEMA), while *engagement* is predicted positively by *resilience* (CDRISCTOTAL) and by problem-focused coping. See Figure 1.

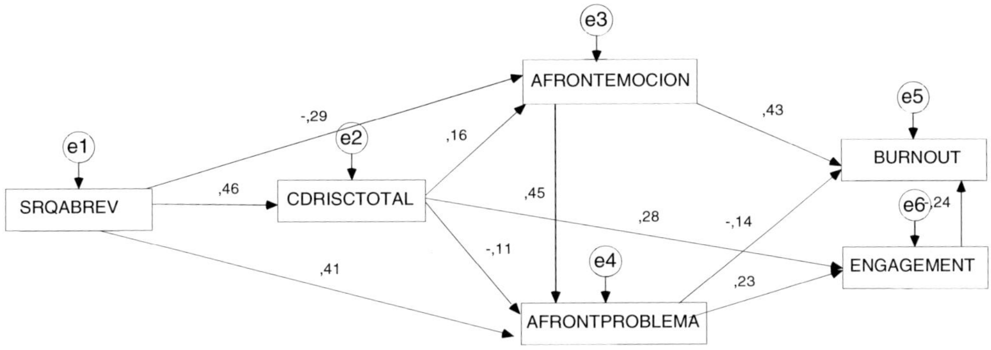

Figure 1. Structural model of relationships between self-regulation, resilience, coping strategies and engagement-burnout.

Discussion

Prior research on *personal self-regulation* has provided evidence of its association with other constructs, such as learning approaches, coping strategies (de la Fuente & Cardelle-Elawar, 2011) and self-regulated learning (Zapata, 2013). Results from the present research are complementary, establishing a consistent connection between these motivational presage variables (personal regulation and resilience), process variables (coping strategies) and product variables (positive vs. negative emotionality), based on the 3P Model by Biggs (2001). In overall terms, they provide empirical support for the hypothesized relationships, helping us understand the role played by the presage variables in the process variables, and the role of both presage and process variables in positive vs. negative emotionality while learning at university. This would mean that, according to one's level of personal self-regulation and resilience, different coping strategies would be used, and these would ultimately produce an experience of psychological well-being and positive emotionality, or alternatively, some level of burnout or negative emotionality.

The results are important because they show how each component of *resilience* is differentially associated with a specific use of *coping strategies*. The common denominator of the resilience components is their positive association with strategies of *self-instructions, positive reappraisal and firmness,* and their negative association with *emotional venting* and *isolation.* There are implications for theoretical relationships between the constructs, as well as for psychological intervention with university students in stressful contexts, particularly in bullying situations.

Prior research has shown the relationship between emotions and attention, memory and problem-solving processes (Clore & Huntsinger, 2009). The direct effect of emotions on performance, especially in the case of test anxiety, has also been evaluated. The cognitive-motivational model by Pekrun (2006, 2009) offers evidence for this relationship, according to the different proposed categories of emotions. Traditionally, *positive emotions* have been considered maladaptive, because they would provoke unrealistic assessments of the situation, for example, about the likelihood of failure. However, a *positive emotional state* has been found to act as an undergirding for activation of positive emotions that lead to engagement in academic performance. For example, a positive correlation has been found between enjoyment of learning and performance on achievement tests (Pekrun, 1992), as well as between positive emotions and students' engagement and achievement (Linnenbrik, 2007).

Additionally, the use of *emotion-focused* strategies for coping with stress is associated with negative emotionality or *burnout,* while use of problem-focused strategies is not. In short, these results reconfirm the need to study *positive emotionality* (engagement) vs. *negative emotionality* (burnout) as an essential element that interacts with motivational and cognitive processes in stressful situations.

Conclusion, Limitations and Implications

The evidence offered here presents psychological mechanisms that are of interest in the study of bullying, but have not been sufficiently examined to date. If personal variables are indeed mediators of stress and stressful experiences, students' level of *personal self-regulation* and of *resilience* when exposed to bullying situations ought to be analyzed – and if appropriate, developed through training -- since these levels predict different use of coping strategies and result in different emotionality. Also, further research and therapeutic interest should be taken for the adjustment of *coping strategies* used in bullying situations. These coping strategies can prove to be essential tools or skills for managing these situations, for maintaining an adequate state of mental health, as has been seen in prior evidence (Hauge, Skogstad, & Einarsen, 2007). Finally, the emotional state of *engagement* or *burnout* can be considered an important correlate for evaluating the psychological impact that bullying may be making on academic achievement.

Therefore, despite the *limitations* of this investigation, with respect to the number of participants and the representativeness of our sample, the results found here alert us to the importance of evaluating levels of personal self-regulation, coping strategies, resilience and engagement-burnout that may be present in cases of bullying.

The *implications* of these results also refer to the importance these variables in understanding the individual characteristics of university students, and for taking steps to specifically train skills for managing academic stress in association with bullying or other stressful personal interactions (Giorgi, 2010; Giorgi et al, 2013). Specifically, these results are important because training in *resilience and coping strategies* can help university students become better adapted in stressful contexts and use more problem-focused strategies. It is a fact that the bullying phenomenon is a health problem, but this fact is mediated by psychological tools available to the person subjected to a bullying situation, thus increasing his or her capacity for taking action (Hoel, Faragher, & Cooper, 2004).

Acknowledgment

R & D Project ref. EDU2011-24805 (2012-2014). MICINN (Spain) and FEDER Fund (UE).

References

Bandura, A. (1986). *Social foundations of thought and action: a social cognitive theory*. Englewood Cliffs, NJ: Prentice- Hall.

Baumeister, R. F., Bratslavsky, E., Muraven, M., & Tice, D. M. (1998). Ego depletion: Is the active self a limited resource? *Journal of Personality and Social Psychology*, 74, 1252–1265.

Baumeister, R. F., & Heatherton, T. F. (1996). Self-regulation failure: An overview. *Psychological Inquiry*, 7, 1–15.

Beran, T.N. (2008). Consequences of being bullied at school. In D. Pepler & W. Craig (Eds.), *Understanding and addressing buylling: An international perspective* (pp. 44-66). Bloomington, IN: AuthorHouse.

Berkowitz, L. (1993). *Aggression: Its causes, consequences, and control*. Philadelphia, PA: Tempe University Press.

Biggs, J. (2001). *Teaching for Quality Learning at University* (3rd Ed.). Buckingham: Open University Press.

Brown, J. M. (1998). Self-regulation and the addictive behaviours. En W. R. Miller y N. Heather (Eds.), *Treating Addictive Behaviors* (2nd ed.) (pp. 61-73). New York: Plenum Press.

Brown, J.M., Miller, W.R., & Lawendowski, L.A. (1999). The self-regulation questionnaire. In: VandeCreek, L, Jackson, TL. (Eds.). *Innovations in clinical practice: A sourcebook*. (vol. 17, pp. 281–292). Sarasota, FL: *Professional Resource Press/Professional Resource* Exchange.

Brown, A., & Newby-Clark, I.R. (2005). Self-regulation and problem gambling. Final report submitted to the Ontario Problem Gambling Research Centre. Accessed February 21, 2013: http:// www.austgamingcouncil.org.au/images/pdf/eLibrary/2009.pdf

Card, N.A., Stucky, B.D., Sawalani, G.M., & Litlle, T.D. (2008). Direct and indirect aggression during childhood and adolescence: A meta-analytic review of gender differences, intercorrelations, and relations to maladjustment. *Child Development*, 79, 1185-1229.

Carey, K.B., Neal, D.J., & Collins, S.E. (2004). A Psychometric analysis of self-regulation questionnaire. *Addictive Behaviours*, 29, 253-260.

Chorot, P., & Sandín, B. (1987). *Escalas de Estrategias de Coping*. [Scales of Coping strategies]. Madrid: UNED.

Clore, G.L., & Huntsinger, J.R. (2009). How the objet of affect guides its impact. *Emotional Review*, 1, 39, 54.

Cohen, M., Ben-Zur, H., & Rosenfeld, M. J. (2008). Sense of coherence, coping strategies, and test anxiety as predictor of test performance among college students. *International Journal of Stress Management*, 15(3), 289-303.

Connor, D., & Davison, R. (2003). The Connor-Davison Resilience Scale, CD-RISC. *Depression and Anxiety* 18, 76–82.

Creed, P.A., Fallon, T., & Hood, M. (2009). The relationship between career adaptability person and situation variables, and career concerns in young adult. *Journal of Vocational Behavior*, 74, 219-229.

Crick, N.R., & Zahn-Waxler, C. (2003). The development of psychopathology in females and males: Current progress and future challenges. *Development and Psychopathology*, 15, 719-742.

De la Fuente, J. (2003). Cuestionario de Autorregulación personal (CAR). [Personal self-regulation questionnaire (SRQ)]. Unpublished manuscript.

De la Fuente, J., Berbén, A.B.G., & Martínez, J.M. (2006). La autorregulación personal de los estudiantes universitarios. [Personal self-regulation of university students.] In J.L. Benítez, A.B.G. Berbén, F. Justicia, & J. De la Fuente (Eds.), *La universidad ante el reto del Espacio Europeo de Educación Superior: investigaciones recientes* (pp. 68-88). Madrid: EOS.

De la Fuente, J., & Cardelle-Elawar, M. (2011). Personal Self-Regulation and Copyng Style in University Students. In L.B., and R.A. Nichelson (Eds.), *Psychology of Individual Differences* (pp. 171-182). New York: Nova Science Publishers, Inc.

De la Fuente, J., Cardelle-Elawar, M., Martínez-Vicente, J.M., Zapata, L., & Peralta, F.J. (2013). Gender as a determining factor in the coping strategies and resilience of university students. In R. Haumann and G. Zimmer (Eds), *Handbook of Academic Performance* (pp. 205-217). New York: Nova Science Publishers, Inc.

De la Fuente, J., Peralta, F.J., & Sánchez, M.D. (2009). Autorregulación personal y la percepción de los comportamientos escolares desadaptativos. [Personal self-regulation and the perception of disadaptive school behaviors.] *Psicothema,* 21(4), 548-554.

De la Fuente, J., Trianes, M.V., Peralta, F.J., & Sánchez, M.D. (2007). Autorregulación personal y comportamientos de inadaptación sociopersonal y escolar. [Personal self-regulation and disadaptive socio-personal and school behaviors]. Presented at the *I Congreso Internacional de Violencia Escolar (Bullying)*. November: Almería.

DeLongis, A., Holtzman, S., Puterman, E., & Lam, M. (2010). Dyadic Coping: Support from the spouse in times of stress. In J. Davila, & K. Sullivan (Eds.), *Social Support Processes in Intimate Relationships* (pp. 151-174). New York: Oxford Press.

Einarsen, S., Hoel, H., Zapf, D., & Cooper, C. L. (2011). The concept of bullying at work: The European tradition. In S. Einarsen, H. Hoel, D. Zapf, & C. L. Cooper (Eds.), *Bullying and emotional abuse in the workplace. International Perspectives in Research and Practice* (pp. 3-30). London: CRC Press.

Espelaje, D.L., Bosworth, K., & Simon, T.R. (2001). Short-term stability and prospective correlates of bullying in middle-school students: An examination of potential demographic, psychological, and environmental influences. *Violence and Victims*, 16, 411-426.

Espelage, D.L., & Horne, M.K. (2007). Dating violence & sexual harassment across the bullying-victim continuum among middle and high scholl students. *Journal of Youth & Adolescence,* 36(6), 799-811.

Friedricks, J.A., Blumenfeld, P.C., & Paris, A. H. (2004). School engagement: Potential of the concept, state of the evidence. *Review of Educational Research*, 74, 59-109.

Glew, G.M., Fan, M., Katon, W, Rivara, F.P., & Kernic, M.A. (2005). Bullying psychosocial adjustment, and academic performance in elementary school. *Archives of Pediatrics & Adolescent Medicine,* 159, 1026-1031.

Giorgi, G. (2010). Workplace bullying partially mediates the climate health relationship. *Journal of Managerial Psychology*, 25, 727-740.

Giorgi G., Ando M, Arenas A., Shoss K.M., & Leon-Perez J.M. (2013). Exploring personal and organizational determinants of workplace bullying and its prevalence in a Japanese sample. *Psychology of Violence,* 2, 185-197.

Hauge, L. J., Skogstad, A., and Einarsen, S. (2007). Relationships between stressful work environments and bullying: Results of a large representative study. *Work & Stress*, 21, 220-242.

Herrenkohl, T.I., Catalano, R.F., Hemphill, S.A., & Toumboutou, J.W. (2009). Longitudinal examination of physical and relational aggression as precursors to later problem behavior in adolescents. *Violence and Victims*, 24, 3-19.

Hidi, S., & Anderson, M. (1992). Situational interest and its impact on reading and expository writing. In A. Renninger, S. Hid, & A. Krapp (Eds.), *The role of interest in on learning and development* (pp. 215-238). Hillsdale, NJ: Erlbaum.

Hobfoll, S.E., & Schröeder, K.E.E. (2001). Distinguishing between passive and active prosocial coping: Bridging inner-city women's mental health and AIDS risk behavior. *Journal of Social and Personal Relationships*, 18, 201-217.

Hoel, H., Faragher, B., & Cooper, C. L. (2004). Bullying is detrimental to health, but all bullying behaviours are not necessarily equally damaging. *British Journal of Guidance & Counselling,* 33, 367-387.

Holroyd, K.A., & Lazarus, R.S. (1982). Stress, coping, and somatic adaptation. In L. Goldberger & S. Breznitz (Eds.), *Handbook of stress: Theoretical and clinical aspect* (pp. 124-140). New York: Free Press.

Hoyle, R.H. (2010). *Handbook of Personality and self-regulations*. Oxford: Wiley.

Kanfer, F.J. (1986). Implications of a self-regulation model therapy for treatment of addictive behaviours. In W.R. Miller & N. Heather (Eds.), *Treating addictive behaviours: Process of Change* (pp. 121-138). New York: Plenum Press.

Kogan, S.M., & Bordy, G.H. (2009). Linking parenting and informal mentor processes to depressive symptoms among rural African American Young adult men. *Cultural Diversity and Ethnic Minority Psychology,* 16(3), 299-306.

Lazarus, R. S. (1991). *Emotion & Adaptation*. New York: Oxford University Press.

Lazarus, R.S., & Folkman, S. (1984). *Stress, appraisal, and coping*. New York, NY: Springer.

Lazarus, R.S., & Folkman, S. (1986). *Estrés y procesos cognitivos.* [*Stress and cognitive process*]. Barcelona: Ediciones Martínez Roca, S.A.

Linnenbrik, E.A. (2007). The role of affect in student learning: A multidimensional approach to considering the interaction of affect, motivation, and engagement. In P. A. Schurtz & R. Perrun (Eds.), *Emotion in education* (pp. 107-124). San Diego, CA: Academic Press.

Miller, W.R., & Brown, J.M (1991). Self-regulation as a conceptual basis for the prevention and treatment of addictive behaviours. In N. Heather, W.R. Miller, & J. Greely (Eds.), *Self-control and the addictive behaviours* (pp.3-79). Sydney: Maxwell Macmillan.

Moos, R.H., & Billings, A.G. (1982). Conceptualizing and measuring coping resources and processes. In L. Goldberger, & S. Breznitz (Eds.), *Handbook of stress: Theoretical and clinical aspects* (pp.212-230). New York: Free Press.

Muraven, M., Collins, R. L., Morsheimer, E. T., Shiffman, S., & Paty, J. A. (2005). The morning after: Limit violations and the self-regulation of alcohol consumption. *Psychology of Addictive Behaviors*, 19(3), 253–262.

Muraven, M., Collins, R. L., & Nienhaus, K. (2002). Self-control and alcohol restraint: An initial application of the self-control strength model. *Psychology of Addictive Behaviors*, 16, 113-120.

Murray-Close, D., Ostrov, J.M., & Crick, N. R. (2007). A short-term longitudinal study of growth of relational aggression during middle childhood: Associations with gender, friendship intimacy, and internalizing problems. *Development and Psychopathology*, 19, 187-203.

Neal, D.J., & Carey, K.B. (2005). A follow-up psychometric analysis of the Self-Regulation Questionnaire. *Psychology of Addictive Behaviors*, 19(4), 414–422.

Okun, M.A, Levy, R., Karoly, P., & Ruehlman, L. (2009). Dispositional happiness and college student GPA: Unpacking a null relation. *Journal of Research in Personality*, 43, 711-715.

Olweus, D. (1993). Bullying/victim problems among school-children: Long-term consequences and an effective intervention program. In S. Hodgins (Ed.). *Mental disorder and crime* (pp. 317-349). Thousand Oasks, CA: Sage.

Olweus, D. (1995). Bullying or peer abuse at school: Intervention and prevention and preventive. In G. Davies & S. Lloyd-Bostock (Eds.), *Psychology, law, and criminal justice: International developments in research and practice* (pp. 248-266). Oxford, England: Walter De Gruyter.

Pekrun, R. (1992). The impact of emotions on learning and achievement. Towards a theory of cognitive motivational mediators. *Applied Psychology*, 41, 359-376.

Pekrun, R. (2006). The control-value theory of achievement emotions: Assumptions, corollaries, and implications for educational research and practice. *Educational Psychology Review*, 18, 315-341.

Pekrun, R. (2009). Global and local perspectives on human affect: implications of the control-value theory of achievement emotions. In M. Wosnitza, S.A. Karabenick, A. Eflides, & P Nenninger (Eds.), *Contemporary motivational research: From global to local perspectives* (pp. 97-115). Toronto, Ontario, Canada: Hogrefe.

Pepler, D.J., Craig, W.M., Connolly, J., & Henderson, K. (2002). Bullying, sexual harassment, dating violence, and substance use among adolescents. In C. Wekerle & A. M. Wall (Eds.), *The violence and addiction equation: Theoretical and clinical issues in substance abuse and relationships violence* (pp. 153-168). New York, NY: Brunner-Rutledge.

Pichardo, M.C., Justicia, F., García-Berbén, A.B., De la Fuente, J., & Martínez-Vicente, J.M. (in press). Psychometric Analysis of the Self-Regulation Questionnarie (SRQ) at Spanish Universities. *The Spanish Journal of Psychology.*

Piemontesi, S.E., & Heredia, D.E. (2009). Afrontamiento ante exámenes: Desarrollo de los principales modelos teóricos para su definición y medición. [Coping with exams: development of the main theoretical models for its definition and measurement.] *Anales de Psicología*, 25(1), 102-111.

Sandín, B. (1995). El estrés [Stress]. In A. Belloch, B. Sandín, and F. Ramos (Eds.). *Manual de psicopatología,* Vol. 2 (pp. 3-52). Madrid: McGraw-Hill.

Sandín, B., & Chorot, P. (2003). Cuestionario de Afrontamiento del Estrés (CAE): desarrollo y validación preliminar. [Questionnaire on Coping with Stress: Preliminary development and validation.] *Revista de Psicopatología y Psicología Clínica*, 8(1), 39-54.

Schunk, D.H., Pintrich, P.R., & Meece, J.J. (2008). Motivation in education: Theory, research, and applications (3ed.). *Upper Saddle River*, NJ: Merrill Prentice Hall.

Shaufeli, W.R., Martínez, I.S., Marqués, A., Salanova, S., & Bakker, A.B. (2002). Burnout and engagement in university students. A Cross-National Study. *Journal of Cross-Cultural Psychology*, 33(5), 464-481.

Shernoff, D. (2012). Engagement and positive youth development: Creating optimal learning environments. In K.R. Harris, S. Graham, & T. Urdan (Eds.), *APA Educational Psychology Handbook* (vol. 2, pp. 195-220). Washington: American Psychological Association.

Spencer, M.B. (2008). Phenomenology and ecological systems theory: Development of diverse groups. In W. Damon & R. Lerner (Eds.), *Child and adolescent development: An advanced course* (pp. 696-740). New York, NY: Wiley.

Spencer, M.B., Dupree, D., Tinsley, B., McGee, E.O., Hall, J., Fegley, S.G., & Elmore, T. E. (2012). Resistance and resiliency in a color-conscious society: implications for learning and teaching. In K.R. Harris, S. Graham, & T. Urdan (Eds.), *APA Educational Psychology Handbook* (vol. 1, pp. 461-494). Washington, DC.

Swearer, S.M., Espelage, D.L., & Napolitano, S.A. (2009). Bullying prevention and intervention: *Realistic strategies for schools*. New York, NY: Guilford Press.

Ticona, S.B., Paucar, G., & Llerena, G. (2010). Stress level and coping strategies in nursing students at the UNSA Faculty. *Revista electrónica cuatrimestral de Enfermería*, 9(2), 1-8.

Vohs, K. D., Schmeichel, B. J., Nelson, N. M., Baumeister, R. F., Twenge, J. M., & Tice D. M. (2008). Making choices impairs subsequent self-control: A limited resource account of decision making, self-regulation, and active initiative. *Journal of Personality and Social Psychology*, 94, 883–898.

Zapata, L. (2013). *Personal Self-Regulation, Learning Approach and Coping Strategies in university teaching learning process with stress*. Doctoral Dissertation unpublisher. Almería: University of Almería.

Zimmerman, B.J. (1998). Developing self-fulfilling cycles of academic regulation: An analysis of exemplary instructional model. In D.H. Schunk & B.J. Zimmerman (Ed.), *Self-regulated learning: From teaching to self-reflective practice* (pp. 1-19). New York: Guilford.

Zimmerman, B.J. (2002). Becoming a self-regulated learner: an overview. *Theory into practice,* 41 (2), 64-70.

In: Handbook on Bullying
Editor: Phoebe Triggs

ISBN: 978-1-63463-023-8

Chapter 8

BULLYING AND MORAL REASONING: THE INFLUENCE OF LIFE VALUES AND CULTURE ON ITALIAN TEENAGERS' SELF-ASSERTION

Antonella Brighi**, *Giovanna Gianesini and Giannino Melotti
Department of Education, University of Bologna, Italy

Abstract

In the last 15 years literature on bullying has emphasized the role of systemic processes in aggressive interactions, as well as the interplay of cognitive and emotional mechanisms leading to antisocial behaviors. Indeed, as adolescents interact with a varied social world, their development entails the formation of different but systematic types or domains of social reasoning. Social situations require a balancing and coordination of different social, individual and moral considerations related to features of the context. In this chapter, we suggest a broader view of moral reasoning trough the investigation of individual, culturally influenced, *life values*. In our non-representative sample of 801 Italian students the prevalence students who witnessed episodes of school bullying was around 75% and the most common type was direct, either verbal (offending, teasing, threating) or physical aggression. Participating roles in bullying were coded into uninvolved (neutral) bystanders (56.8%), victims (37.1%) and bully/bully-victims (6.1%). Moreover, when we examined the relation between aggression and life values, our results evidenced, in addition to a general individualistic tendency for personal success, richness, and ambition; some values specifically pertained to adolescent bullies, as evidenced by little consideration for others' needs and desires, low respect of societal norms and little importance attributed to honesty. Bullies' self-assertion tendencies appeared even stronger in female than in males. These values may be supported by expectations of positive outcomes from the bullying behavior openly expressed by the peers' group (Brighi & Genta, 2010, Brighi et al., 2007) or perceived by the bullies. Only by taking into consideration the interplay between personal goals, life and cultural values a fuller theoretical understanding of peer aggression can be reached. Integrative models are thus needed to investigate both *moral cognition* and *moral affect* in children in relation to their participant roles in different forms of bullying (Arsenio & Lemerise, 2004; Malti & Latzko, 2010).

---

* E-mail address Antonella.brighi@unibo.it

Introduction

Bullying has been originally defined as an aggressive behavior characterized by repetitiveness and imbalance of power between the perpetrator and the victim. It may take different forms, be either direct (physical or verbal) or indirect (isolation, rumors, humiliation etc) and take place in a physical social context (traditional bullying) and/or virtual (cyberbullying) environment. Although cyberbullying may sometimes be an extension of traditional bullying, some of its peculiar features suggest that it may have a very distinct causal pathway (Brighi et al., 2012). Bullying is indeed a social and relational process, involving children as bullies, victims, and bystanders, who can act as assistant or reinforcer of the bully as well as outsider or defender of the victim (Salmivalli, 1999). Indirect bullying is exquisitely relational and refers to harm within relationships caused by covert or subtle manipulative behavior, including isolation and social exclusion, threatening to stop talking (the ''silent treatment''), or spreading gossip and rumors (Perren et al., 2012). Evidences show that it may create just as much or more damage than physical aggression among youth. As bullying is directed toward a specific victim, the roles of both targeted individuals and perpetrators are important in fully understand the phenomenon (Thornberg & Jundert, 2013). Gini (2005) found that while victims showed difficulties in social cognition tasks, bullies showed moral disengagement mechanisms, whereas defenders showed higher levels of moral sensitivity. His study especially evidenced the importance of social cognitive competencies in "*the complex circle of behaviors, attitudes and expectations* (p. 26) upon which bullying is based and the relevance of fine-grained classifications of bullying roles. A more recent study by Pornari and Wood (2010) showed that moral disengagement in both traditional peer aggression and cyber bullying is consistently associated with lower levels of moral emotions like guilt and shame and higher levels of emotions like pride or indifference respectively. While the concept of moral disengagement seems to account for the behavior of bullies and their lack of sense of guilt toward victims, it does not seem to explain differences among victims and control children. Finally, Perren & Gutzwiller-Helfenfinger (2012) have hypothesized cyberbullies to have stronger deficits in morality than traditional bullies only. Despite the evidence of the existence of mediating processes between the moral and the social domains in adolescence, a great deal of research has mainly focused on teens' goal preference rather than on the more complex and general understanding of how moral values shared in the social context influence social goals and aggressive/antisocial behavioral choices. Bullying cannot be understood without considering the cognitive mediators (Arsenio & Lemerise, 2004; Guerra, Nucci & Huesmann, 1994) and moral issues involved in fairness, others' welfare, and refraining from harming others for personal gain (Turiel, 1998, Arsenio & Lemerise, 2001; 2004). Proactive bullying, in particular, could be associated with individualistic and instrumental moral orientation (Bergeron & Schneider, 2005), as suggested also by Menesini, Nocentini & Camodeca (2013). Their study investigated the mediating role of personal values and moral disengagement (bully, victim, and bystander) in traditional and cyberbullying. Traditional bullying was assessed by means of a self-report measures, while a Portrait Values Questionnaire was used to assess 10 values in four dimensions according to the value system model by Schwartz (1992). Results showed that self-enhancement and self-trascendence moderately predicted cyber and traditional bullying respectively, while immoral and disengaged behaviors predicted both. Indirect effect showed that self-enhancement and openness to change predicted both form of bullying through immoral behavior.

Moral Reasoning

Morality (including avoidance of victimization and aggression) and *autonomy* (involving individual goals) are often viewed as being in contrast, which is not necessarily true in social conflicts where a legitimate concern for the self is weighted with moral considerations, personal goals, projects and hobbies (Killen & Nucci, 1995). The pursuit of instrumental goals, per se, is not necessarily conductive of proactive aggression. To investigate how behavioral choices are associated to personal and social goals can have many important implications in addressing in which way proactive aggressive and non-aggressive teens differ on relational dimensions and moral development. Crick & Dodge (1996) fund, in fact, that proactive aggression is associated more with instrumental ("I want this") than relational ("I want to be his friend") goals, although such a sharp contrast between the two seem too simplistic (Arsenio & Lemerise, 2001). According to Bandura's theory, internal mechanisms of self-regulation act as mediators between behavior and internal moral norms and moral emotions such as shame, feeling of guilt, self-blaming, keep the balance between our behaviors and our internalized moral norms and values. Gibbs' (2003) theory of ''social-moral'' reasoning accepts Kolberg's (1984) idea of individuals progressing from more egocentric attributions to forms of reasoning becoming more complex and abstract over time, but places a greater emphasis on the role of social perspective-taking and empathy. What seems particularly fruitful to our goal, is Gibbs's (1993, 1995, 2003) examination of the association between the process of moral reasoning, the content of social cognition, and general cognitive development, specifically those types of cognitive distortions that may contribute to the persistence of immature moral reasoning beyond childhood.

The first and primary cognitive distortion, typical of young children, is the egocentric bias, whereby attitudes and values place the individuals' own concerns as central. Moral reasoning at the lower stages (i.e. immature reasoning) is underpinned by an egocentric bias, with limited social perspective taking and an emphasis on one's own needs and desires ahead of those of other people. A range of secondary distortions supports the egocentric bias (Gibbs, 1993, 2003) and weakens inhibitions to participate in bullying. Among them are relevant *assuming the worst*, or holding a hostile attributional bias (i.e. the tendency to interpret ambiguous events as being hostile), *blaming others* for their own actions, *mislabeling of one's behavior* and *minimization of consequences* to minimize feelings of guilt and regret.

The persistence of a pronounced egocentric bias and the inability to take other people's perspective beyond childhood, along with the accompanying moral developmental delay, can lead to a greater likelihood of aggressive and harmful behavior toward others (Gibbs, 1993). Different studies have confirmed among antisocial and aggressive youths the presence of serve-serving cognitive distortions (e.g. Barriga & Gibbs, 1996; Liau, Barriga, & Gibbs, 1998; Palmer & Hollin, 2000; Slaby & Guerra, 1988) and of a complex belief systems that enable justification of aggression (Vorrath & Brendtro). As such, aggression can be seen to result from a delay in moral development, hypothesized as a mechanism of "disengagement of moral control" (Palmer, 2003a).

Moral Disengagement

The relationship between moral disengagement and aggressive behavior, which is mediated by a reduction of feelings of guilty, pro-social behavior and cognitive evaluations has already been investigated by some researchers (Bandura, et al., 1996) especially among adolescents. Specifically, Menesini, Fonzi and Vannucci (1999) examined the disengagement of moral control in association with different participating roles in bullying (bully, victims and control) and found that bullying boys (age 6 to 14) were more prone to use dehumanization toward victims, compared to control and victim groups. An interesting study by Menesini et al. (2003) analyzed the role of moral emotions and reasoning in groups of children belonging to different participant roles in bullying (bullies, victims and outsiders) and to different cultural contexts. Children, faced with an imaginary bullying scenario, were asked to take on the bully role and were interviewed about their feelings. Moral emotions such as *guilt* and *shame*, (considered as indexes of moral responsibility), and those such as *indifference* and *pride,* (considered as attitude of moral disengagement), were investigated across the three participant roles. Bullies, compared to victims and outsiders, showed significant higher level of disengagement emotions, and showed egocentric reasoning. The study also reported cross-cultural differences attributable to a widespread culture where organized crime is almost accepted as a normal event and can easily support mechanisms of moral disengagement in young children (Menesini et al. 2003). Their results highlighted the link between socio-cultural context and individual moral reasoning and values; moreover, they evidenced how individual moral reasoning and moral emotions may be flexible and may account for different and varied aspect of the social world in which individuals are embedded. Heterogeneity and variability in social judgments and behaviors pertain to given cultures and to different individual members of that culture.

Cultural Values

Values are generally defined as principles, critical and important normative assumptions that underlie morality for individuals in relationships with others (Kurtines & Gewirtz, 1995). They are the affective component of morality and represent the implicitly or explicitly shared abstract ideas about what is good, right, and desirable in a society (Williams, 1970). Individual values and priorities are a product both of shared culture and of a unique personal experience and personality differences (Schwartz, 1999); they represent the guiding principles in life, which stir our emotions and allow us to create internal meaning. Shared cultural values, on the other hand, represent the way in which societal institutions (e.g. family, education, political and religious system) express their priorities, goals and their mode of operation. In other words, personal values (e.g. success, freedom, social order, and tradition) are the vocabulary of socially approved goals used to motivate action and to express and justify the chosen solution.

From the perspective of cross-cultural psychology, the social and cultural context is the key factor affecting the moral development of individuals and the kind of reasoning that individuals from different cultures bring to the moral discourse. The individual moral development refers to how one develops skills in understanding, managing and adhering to the moral expectations of his/her culture (Shweder, 1990; Stigler, Shweder & Herdt, 1990).

Cross-cultural studies have indicated the importance of culture in determining moral reasoning (Mizuno, 1999; Iwasa, 1992; Miller, 1988) and showed the existence of cultural variability in justice morality (Keller, et al., 1998; Edwards, 1994; Harkness, Edwards & Super, 1981; Miller et al. 1990). In the attempt to set the ground for a socio-cultural theory of altruism and aggression, Staub (1994) argued that: "In order to understand how altruism or aggression comes about, we must consider both how people select the aims of their behavior from a multiplicity of aims, and what determines whether they actually pursue the aims they selected… (p. 139)". Some researchers (Robarchek & Robarchek, 1998; Fry, 1998, Howell & Willis, 1989) have speculated that observed differences in aggression may be attributable to disparities in world views, values and belief systems. Both violent and peaceful social interactions could be understood through the sensitive and detailed explication of the values and meanings that embody and shape the behavior in different social settings (Howell & Willis, 1989). Altruistic and aggressive behaviors are multi-determined by individual characteristics, different influences and circumstances which usually join in (Staub, 1994). In studying aggression, researchers have often neglected to acknowledge the crucial relation between culture and moral reasoning. Consequently, the scientific literature on the extent to which the relationship between personal characteristic such as value orientations influences either pro-social or aggressive behavior is limited. Cross-national variability in social behaviors, including aggression and bullying, has often been attributed *post hoc* to "culture", without a clear theoretical framework and operationalization. Many authors have tried to replace "culture" with more specific, explanatory, variables (Hofstede, 1980; Schwartz, 1990). Hofstede (1980) classified culture along four dimensions: 1) Individualism *vs* Collectivism, which describes the emphasis placed on individual needs, ambition and success versus the well-being of the group, 2) Power Distance, which refers to the degree of difformity according to which societies accept the unequal distribution of power in institutions and organizations, 3) Uncertainty Avoidance, which refers to the extent to which rules, norms and rituals that provide stability and predictability are valued, and 4) Masculinity *vs* Femininity, which identifies the set of "masculine" goals, such as success, assertiveness, heroism and advancement, *versus* the "feminine" ones, focused on interpersonal relationships, modesty, nurturance and interpersonal harmony (Hofstede, 1980). Building on Hofstede's work (1980), Schwartz (1994) has proposed the dimensions of *Conservatism* (family security, social order, obedience, respect for tradition) *versus Intellectual and Affective Autonomy* (creativity, broad-mindedness, varied life, pleasure) and *Hierarchy and Mastery* (social power, ambition, wealth) *versus Egalitarian commitment and Harmony* (social justice, equality, unity with nature). Bond (1991) introduced an additional set of values derived from Chinese culture (*Integration, Human-Heartedness, Moral Discipline and Confucian Work dynamism*) in order to avoid the Western culture bias, which further confirmed the robustness of the dimensions cross-culturally.

Recent research has started using the cultural values (e.g., individualism and collectivism) at the national level to explain differences in peer aggression (Bergeron and Schneider, 2005; Forbes et al., 2009). According to Bergeron and Schneider (2005) cross-national differences in aggression could be predicted from values differences at the national cultural-level. Cultures wherein a high value is placed on individual needs and desires, getting ahead and promoting one's own interest regardless of those of others, would be more accepting of aggressive behavior than cultures in which an emphasis is placed on group goals, taking care of the collectivity, and fitting in harmoniously with the environment. Bergeron and Schneider (ibid.) reported that each of the three national values classification systems proposed by Hofstede (1980, 1983), Bond (1991) and Schwartz (1994) was found to predict differences in aggression. Aggression scores were positively related to *Individualistic* values and negatively to *Collectivistic* values. Contrary to the expectations, Schwartz's dimension of *Affective-Autonomy* was not associated to aggression, and *Intellectual-Autonomy* was negatively related to level of aggression. Aggression scores were higher, on the contrary, in cultures where *Mastery* was a high value priority. These results taken together suggest that a generic orientation for individualism, as valued in some societies, may be not directly associated with higher level of aggression, "but rather the need to master and control the environment and the importance of getting ahead through self-assertion are linked to aggression" (ibid, p. 131). The research on cultural value orientation may explain how culture may influence the general attitude toward aggression, but a further level of analysis calls for the investigation of intracultural variations of cultural values, which may contribute to our understanding of explaining factors for individual differences in aggression within a particular culture. Multiple cultural values (e.g., individualism and collectivism) in fact, may coexist within societies and can be simultaneously endorsed by individuals as well as different culturally heterogeneous groups may be present in the same nation (Li et al., 2010).

Aims

In this study we aimed at investigating how individual life values varies in subgroup of students who are differently involved into covert and over bullying.

Based on the forgoing review of the literature and key concepts, we hypothesized that adolescents' endorsement of egalitarian orientation would be negatively related to their overt and relational aggression; conversely, adolescents' endorsement of individualism would be positively related to these aggression outcomes.

Methodology

Sample

Our sample of 801 middle school students (43.8% males, n= 351 and 54.3% females, n= 435, 15 missing; age range 10-15, M=12, SD=1.54) was recruited at two different schools with no specific bullying prevention program nor clear anti/bullying policies. The participating schools were selected from residential neighboroughs with a low rate of immigration and were located in the Italian region of Tuscany and Emilia Romagna. Students belonged to intact middle socio-economic families where the majority of fathers held a high school degree (22.3%) or a college degree (18.4%) with significant gender differences (for mothers 24.7%, 19.9% respectively).

Instruments

An anonymous self-report bullying questionnaire (Darbo, Buccoliero & Costantini, 2003) was administered to students by trained researchers during regular school hours, after parents' consent. Participation was voluntary, after parental written consent, with no reward nor incentive. Questions intended to assess the incidence of bullying in middle school, its type, students participating roles, where it occurs, adults' response and students' attitudes toward it. Below we give a more detailed description of the sections that will be considered in this study.

Peer Relationships at School And Perceived Attitude Toward Bullying

A questionnaire's section investigated the quality of peer relationship at school, wherein students were asked to evaluate the quality of their relationships with classmates and schoolmates on a 5 point Likert scale (from "very bad" to "good"), to report which moment of the school day they preferred to share with them (5 mutually exclusive items) and whether they were ever left alone by them (5 mutually exclusive items). In order to assess the presence of a peer attitude toward bullying in the school we also asked students to report their perception of their schoolmates' general reactions to bullying episodes, choosing two possible answers among 6 items devised to evidence a pro-bully perceived attitude or a pro-victim perceived attitude. Moreover, they were asked about their willingness to disclose what generally happens in school to classmates or friends outside.

Relationship with Adults in and Outside School

In order to evaluate students' relationship with adults we asked students to report the quality of their relationships with teachers in school (on a four point Likert scale from "very bad" to "good") and to report adults' general reaction to bullying in school, choosing only one answer among 5 possible items (yes or no response) *("Adults in my school are not aware of what happens"; "they pretend nothing is happening"; "they're not present when it happens"; "they intervene to help who is victimized"; "they laugh and they have fun of us").*

Moreover students were asked how much they were satisfied about their parents involvements in the school life, choosing their responses on a four-point Likert scale (from "not at all satisfied" to "very satisfied").

Life Values

The Life Values Questionnaire was composed of 12 items pertaining to life values, placed on a three point Likert scale (from "not important/very little important" to "very important"), in order to explore at the intra-individual level the three main culturally based value classification systems suggested by the work of Hofstede, Schwartz and Bond (see previous section).

The Life Values Questionnaire asked students to evaluate how important were for their life values such as Honesty, Order and respect of rules, Respect of others, Equity of possibilities for everybody, Freedom of thought, Solidarity, Justice, Tolerance for opinions and behaviors different from their own, Success, Wealth (Richness), Freedom to do what one wants, Self-realization.

Life Values Questionnaire yielded a good reliability of .86 Alpha, and the 12 items were further classified into three factors by a Confirmative Factor Analysis (see below), in order to obtain individual measures of life values orientation.

Analysis

First, we present descriptive results for all variables of interest, grouped in relationship with peers at school, relationship with adults in and out school, bullying, participating roles (bystanders, bullies and victims) and life values. Second, we describe our value classification system obtained by factor analysis on the 12 life values. Finally, we discuss the results of multivariate analysis examining gender differences and the relationship between bullying participating roles, life values and culturally based value classification systems.

Relationship with Peers at School

Descriptive analysis showed a positive relationship with classmates, (M=4.39, SD=.82, range 1-5) and schoolmates (M=3.94, SD=.89, range 1-5). No significant differences were reported by gender.

However, more than half of our sample (51.9%, n=416) spent no time with class peers if not during *Class time* (28.8%, n=226), confirmed by only a small percentage sharing their *free time* (10.6%, n=85) with classmates outside school walls. Similarly, few students reported (18.8%, n=88) being left alone during school time by schoolmates either at recession (10.6%), during class time (3.7%), on the way to and from school (3.2%), or always (1.7%), while the majority was spending time together with classmates (79.2%, n=634).

Concerning the perceived attitude of their schoolmates toward bullying, a multiple response set was created including the six dichotomous items; the percentages among the total number of responses were analyzed. Students responses showed a tendency to do nothing when seeing bullying episodes (28%), or showing pro-bullies attitudes (25.9%, isolating the victim from the group and supporting actively the bully), while 33.6% of the responses reported answers which were pro-victim oriented (i.e isolating the bully from the group and giving help to the victim); a 13.1% reported to be scared from seeing the bullying episodes.

Results also showed that students felt comfortable in disclosing and discussing school matters within the school (84%, n=673), mostly with a trusted friend at school (59.4%, n=476) or with their classmates (38.8%, n=311).

Relationship with Adults in and Outside School

To evaluate students' perception of the quality of relationship with significant adults (teachers and parents) an Anova was run (satisfaction by Gender) among the responses to the four point Likert scale pertaining students' relationship with teachers. Results showed quite a positive relationship with teachers at school (M=3.07, SD=.77, range 1-4) with higher values for females than for males (Males M=2.99; Females M=3.13, F=6.36, 1 df; $p<.01$).

To assess the presence of supporting adults at school, we asked students to report adults' general reaction to bullying in school. Students reported that 47.3% (n=379) of adults involved in a bullying episode did actively intervene in defense of the victim while 30.3% (n=243) stated that adults were not present at the time of the incident and 10.7% reported adults to be either inattentive (n=87) or pretending nothing was happening (8%, n=64). A small percentage (1.2%) reported that adults in school were laughing when they witnessed Students in our sample seemed open to disclose within school walls (YES responses 84%, n=673); a multiple response analysis on the 5 items concerning whom they were talking to about school issues showed that students relied, as expected for adolescents, on the peer support system (50.3 % relied on a trusted peer, a 33% on classmates), but they were very reluctant in disclosing and discussing school matters with a trusted teacher (8.6%), teachers in general (5.6%) or school personnel (2.2%). Similarly, outside the school, students were less likely to disclose school matters with adults, neither their parents (32.6%) nor any other relative (12.5%) or adult figure in their lives (3.2%), while trusted friends were the reference persons (51.8%).

For what concerns parents' involvements in the school life, an Anova analysis was run by Gender on the scores of the 4-point Likert scale (from "1=not at all satisfied" to 4="very satisfied"), measuring the students' satisfaction of parental involvement. Beside a quite positive evaluation (, M=3.41, SD=1.32, range 1-4), no significant differences between genders emerged. Moreover, we asked students to what extent their parents were able to understand their feelings on a 4-point Likert scale (from "not at all" to "very much"). The majority of them reported having a quite emphatic and emotional connected relationship with their parents (M=3.02, SD=1.70), with no significant differences between genders.

Bullying at School

To assess the prevalence of the bulling phenomenon we asked students to report the presence of bullies in their school, their type (group or individual) and gender. Moreover, we asked what type of aggression they were actually perpetrating, where it was usually taking place and if they were somehow personally involved (as bystander, bully or victim). Results evidences a pervasiveness of school bullying ("*According to you, does someone in your school behaves as a bully?*": YES 75.9%, n=608). A multiple response tabulation on the total of responses to the categories of bullying (more than one choice on a 10 items scale) shows that bullying is characterized by teasing (23.1%), offensive language (20%), malicious jokes (12.9%), physical aggression (11.8%), threats (10.5%), group exclusion (7.8% n=206), stealing (minor 7.6% and major 4.5%) and extortion (1.4%).

A Chi Square analysis was performed on bullying type by Gender, showing females to report more indirect and relational bullying (*teasing*: Pearson Chi Sq. 4.02, 1 df., p<.04; *group exclusion*: Pearson Chi Sq. 8.77, 1 df., p<.003) while males were more sensitive to physical and verbal aggression (*Physical aggression:* Pearson Chi Sq. 3.75, 1 df., p<.05; *stealing*: Pearson Chi Sq. 4.82, 1 df., p<.02; *threats*: Pearson Chi Sq. 31.33, 1 df., p<.000).

Bullying was reported to be perpetrated more often by a group (60%, n=481) of males (75.3%, n=603) or mixed (19.6%, n=157), and much less frequently by one individual alone (22.2%, n=178) or two (14.4%, n=115) or by females (1.3%, n=12). Predominantly bullying took place on school premises, like the corridor (38%, n=304) and the classroom (37.1%, n=297). More rarely, bullying was reported to occur in *bathrooms* (14.7%, n=118), *on the way from and to school* (14.4%, n=114), or *courtyard* (9.1%, n=73).

In terms of direct and personal involvements, in a multiple choice question, students identified themselves as Bystander (84.5%, n=671), Victim (40.8%, n=327) and Bully (6.3%, n=50). Data clearly evidenced an overlap between roles indicating the majority of students as witnesses or victims. Recoding bullying participating roles into three mutually exclusive variables we obtained a very high percentage of uninvolved (neutral) bystanders (56.8% n=455), followed by victims (37.1% n=297) and bully | bully-victims (6.1% n=49). A Chi Square analysis showed that males are more represented in the bully/bully-victims group (4.1% of males vs 1.9% of females) and in the victim group (19% vs 18.3%), compared to females who are mostly neutral bystanders (females 35.1% vs 21.6% males) (Pearson Chi Square 22.70, p<.000).

Life Values

All 12 life values items proposed were evaluated by participants on a 3-point Likert scale ("not important", "important" and "very important"). Results indicated that in the whole sample, for all variables but *success* (M=1.76, SD=.83) and *wealth* (M=1.59, SD=.79), the mean values were above 2.5, indicating they were considered quite important with *respect* ranking as the most important (M=2.62, SD=.78) followed by *freedom* (M=2.60, SD=.77) *and honesty* (M=2.56, SD=.78). A one way ANOVA within subjects was run to compare males and female life values responses. Gender difference were significant for 7 over 12 values.

Table 1. Life Values Items by Gender, Anova

	Sex	N	Mean	Std. Dev.	D.f	F	Sig.
Success	Males	351	1.91	.868	1	19.843	.000
	Females	434	1.65	.743			
Freedom of doing what one wants	Males	351	2.16	.892	1	2.642	.104
	Females	435	2.26	.804			
Justice	Males	351	2.46	.867	1	.292	.589
	Females	435	2.49	.824			
Solidarity	Males	351	2.18	.896	1	3.155	.076
	Females	435	2.29	.879			
Order and respect of rules	Males	351	2.23	.878	1	5.782	.016
	Females	435	2.37	.726			
Equality	Males	351	2.32	.927	1	13.534	.000
	Females	435	2.54	.750			
Tolerance	Males	351	1.97	.886	1	12.251	.000
	Females	435	2.18	.833			
Self-realization	Males	351	2.25	.860	1	3.451	.064
	Females	435	2.35	.782			
Freedom of thought	Males	351	2.55	.830	1	3.435	.064
	Females	435	2.65	.694			
Honesty	Males	351	2.46	.860	1	11.554	.001
	Females	435	2.65	.708			
Wealth	Males	351	1.69	.858	1	8.913	.003
	Females	435	1.52	.732			
Respect of others	Males	351	2.55	.843	1	5.939	.015
	Females	435	2.69	.712			

Females scored higher on values as *Order and Respect of Rules*, (Female M=2.37; Males M=2.23, 1 df, F=5.78, p<.01), *Equality* (Female M=2.54; Males M=2.32, 1 df, F=13.53, p<.000), *Tolerance* (Female M= 2.18; Male M= 1.97; 1 df, F=12.25, p<.000), *Honesty* (Female M= 2,65; Male M= 2,46; 1 df, F=11.55, p<.001) and *Respect of others* (Female M= 2.69; Male M= 2.55; 1 df, F=5.93, p<.015). Males score significantly higher than females on values such as *Wealth* (Male M=1.69, Female M=1.52, 1 df, F=8.91, p<.003) and *Success* (Male M=1.91, Female M=1.65, 1 df, F=19.84, p<.000) (see tab. 1).

Factor Analysis for Value Classification Systems

Moreover, a Principal Component Analysis was run, entering as variables the 12 value items: *Success, Honesty, Order and Respect of Rules, Respect of Others, Equity, Freedom of Thought, Solidarity, Justice, Tolerance, Freedom to do what one wants, Wealth, Self-realization*. Three components were extracted with Varimax Rotation, which explained 63% of the variance. The first component was named "*Conservativism Orientation*", as it was saturated by the values: Honesty, Order and respect of Rules, Respect of Others, Equality, Freedom of Thought; this component explained the 43% of variance (Eigen Value 5.06); the second component was called "*Egalitarian Orientation*" and included the values of Solidarity, Justice and Tolerance; this second component explained the 13.11% of variance (Eigen Value 1.57). The third component was named "*Individualistic orientation*", and was composed by values as Success, Wealth, Freedom to do what one's want, Self-realization (see tab. 2). It explained the 6.8% of variance (Eigen Value .82). The standardized factor scores for each component were used for further analysis.

Table 2. Principal Component Analysis on Life Values

	Life Values Orientations Components		
	Conservativism	**Egalitarian**	**Individualistic**
	Eigen Value 5.06 (42.21%)	**Eigen Value 1.57 (13.11%)**	**Eigen Value 0.82 (6.8%)**
Success	.054	.049	.780
Freedom of doing what one wants	-.025	.538	.549
Justice	.351	.701	.196
Solidarity	.264	.714	-.001
Order and Respect of Rules	.791	.166	.037
Equality	.625	.453	.011
Tolerance	.373	.650	.056
Self-realization	.321	.401	.511
Freedom of thought	.600	.432	.338
Honesty	.823	.184	.130
Wealth	.087	-.014	.779
Respect of others	.763	.297	.090

Extraction Method: Principal Component Analysis. ; Varimax Rotation with Kaiser Normalization.

T-Test for Gender Differences

An independent T-test Gender by standardized Factor scores on the three Value Orientations (*Conservativism, Egalitarian, Individualistic*) evidenced significant gender differences: boys scored significantly lower on *Conservativsm* and *Egalitarian* orientation, but significantly higher than girls on *Individualistic* orientation (*Conservativism*: Males M= -.11; F= .09; Student *t* -2.94, p.<003; *Egalitarian*: Males M= -.11, F=.11; Student *t* –3.16, p<.002; *Individualistic*: Males M=.15 , F= -.11; Student *t* -2.94, p.<000). Italian adolescent girls seem to rely more on the "feminine" extreme of this dimension, giving more importance to interpersonal relationship, harmony and nurturance (see tab. 3) than boys do.

Table 3. Value orientations by gender

	Gender	*n*	*M*	*SD*	*T*	*df*	Sig. (2-tailed)
Conservativism Orientation	M	351	-.11	1.08	-2.94	783	.003
	F	434	.09	.90			
Egalitarian Orientation	M	351	-.11	.95	-3.16	783	.002
	F	434	.11	1.01			
Individualistic Orientation	M	351	.15	1.10	-3.71	783	.000
	F	434	-.11	.88			

ANOVA for bullying roles x Value Orientation

We further explored how value orientation and aggression could be linked by running Anova analysis for each component by the three participant roles, recoded as "neutral and bystanders"(NE); "bullies and bully-victims" (BBV) and "victims" (V). We found significant differences among the role-groups across all the three components (Conservatism F 12.99, p. =.00; Egalitarian F 3.08, p.= .046; Individualistic F 6.54, p.= .001, d.f.=2). (see tab.4)

Table 4. Value orientations by Bullying participant roles Anova

Value orientation	Roles	n	M	SD	Min	Max.	F	Sig.
Conservativism Orientation	Bystander	454	.085	.89	-3.03	1.61	12.99 (2 df)	.000
	Bully or Bully-Victim	49	-.66	1.21	-3.03	1.48		
	Victims	297	-.02	1.07	-3.99	1.76		
	Total	800	.00	1.00	-3.99	1.76		
Egalitarian Orientation	Bystander	454	.06	.95	-2.76	2.15	3.08 (2 df)	.046
	Bully or Bully-Victim	49	-.23	1.13	-2.25	1.98		
	Victims	297	-.06	1.04	-3.01	2.00		
	Total	800	.00	1.00	-3.01	2.15		
Individualistic Orientation	Bystander	454	.00	.93	-2.89	2.45	6.63 (2 df)	.001
	Bully or Bully-Victim	49	.46	1.23	-2.32	2.66		
	Victims	297	-.08	1.03	-2.86	2.33		
	Total	800	.00	1.00	-2.89	2.66		

The post-hoc analysis (LSD) revealed the Bully and Bully-Victim profile (BBV) to be significantly different from other roles on all the values components: Bullies and Bully-Victims scored lower than Bystanders and Victims on *Conservatism* and lower for *Egalitarian* orientation compared to bystander subjects only; on the contrary, Bullies and Bully-Victims scored higher on *Individualistic* orientation compared to bystanders and to Victims; (see Table 3).

ANOVA for Gender x Value Orientation X Bullying Roles

Finally, running an ANOVA on *Conservativism* by Sex and by Roles we tested whether the reported differences among values orientations were due to gender distribution in the bullies- and bully-victims group (BBV). No gender effect was found while the interaction Role by Sex was significant. The difference was due to BBV females that scored lower than BBV males on *Conservativism* (BBV Females M=-.91;BBV Males M=-.43). The *Egalitarian orientation*, when entered into the Anova analysis with Roles and Sex, was significant only for the general effect, but not for the separate variables nor their interaction (Egalitarian Orientation by Sex By Roles, 5 d.f., F 3.56, p=.003; Sex (1 d.f.) F 1.53, n.s; Role (2 d.f.) 1.78, n.s.; Sex by Role (2 d.f.) F 1.89, n.s.). The comparison among means showed that males NE (Bystanders) scored lower than females NE, but no differences due to gender were fund for bully-victims group (BBV) and Victims (V). The *Individualistic* orientation confirmed what we examined above (Individualistic by Sex by Role, (5 d.f.), F 6.78, p = .000; Sex (1 d.f.) F.063, pn.s.; Role (2 d.f.) F 8.69, p = .000; Sex by Role F 3.53, p=.030) with males scoring higher than females, and significant differences for Gender, Role and their interaction (Gender by Role). BBV were significantly higher than NE and V, but surprisingly BBV females reported higher means than BBV males. This seems to suggest that girls who are involved in active bullying have an individualistic orientation which encompasses the cultural "milieau".

Conclusion

Bullying is a social interaction that requires complex relationship solutions at the peer and adult level. Classmate friends and peers who do intervene in bullying make a real difference (Farrington & Ttofi, 2009) as peer relationships are crucial both for the bully who looks to maintain or acquire social status and for the child who looks to cope with and end victimization. Classroom and school climate, school organizational environments and social infrastructure can send a message to all students that bullying conflicts with the basic values of respect and tolerance. Adults are also responsible for ensuring that disclosing bullying, inside and outside school, will lead to a positive outcome and for providing extensive, dynamic, and ongoing support to youth. They can redirect bullies leadership potential from the negative strategies of peer aggression to positive leadership skills and opportunities by teaching them how to relate to others positively, be effective in achieving social goals, and use power in a positive manner. Social skills clearly play an important role in bullying. In our study, bullies belong to two coexisting social worlds: *marginalization* and *connection* (Farmer et al.. 2010). Socially marginalized, unpopular bullies fight against a social system that keeps them on the periphery and lack peer social support, whereas socially connected bullies are socially skilled and competent, peer networked and integrated. Socially connected bullies tend to be proactive and goal-directed in their aggression (Card & Hodges, 2008) and they target children who are likely *not* be defended (Veenstra et al., 2010). Socially marginalized, rejected-aggressive bullies who often are also victims, predominantly act aggressively, impulsively, in reaction to provocation, or in the attempt to gain status that generally eludes them (Pellegrini et al., 2010). In our study, proactive bullies were mostly represented.

They seem to belong to that group of socially competent subjects, using their skills to their advantage, but seem to lack the empathy to integrate such information into their interactions. This manipulation of social relationships requires verbal, cognitive and social skills (Crick & Dodge, 1999) and the ability to identify successfully the social and emotional weaknesses of the targeted victims (Arsenio & Lemerise, 2001). This form of social aggression "may lie in the values of the bully rather than in the accuracy of the cognition (Sutton, Smith, P. K., & Swettenham, 1999, p. 122). The empathic styles, moral and cultural values and emotions of bullies and victims may substantially differ. We have explored in our study the normative area (i.e., moral values, norms, standards, and beliefs) as we consider it also important to in attempts to explain the moral side of bullying. Shared cultural values, in fact, are the basis for specific norms that tell people what is appropriate in various situations within a society and help shaping the contingencies to which people must adapt in the institutions in which they spend their time. They represent the way in which societal institutions (e.g. family, education, political and religious system function) express their priorities, goals and their mode of operation. Our study primary supports the claim that proactive bullying is associated with an individualistic and instrumental orientation: personal success and richness drive bullies, while more social and altruistic values characterizes victims and neutral bystanders. This pattern remains stable, despite the gender influence: female bullies, in fact, report having higher scores on Individualistic orientation, contrary to the cultural expectations, which sees females as more prone to socially oriented values. These results highlight the importance of considering the dimensions of moral orientation and life values in the bullying process.

Our results also confirmed gender differences in moral values, which could as well be attributed to specific cultural orientations and norms. Gender differences were significant, with females indicating more social and altruistic values than males, preferring success and personal achievement. Italy, according to Hofstede (1980), ranked among the countries with the highest scores in the dimension of "Masculinity", corresponding to the value placed on material success, assertiveness, heroism and advancement. This probably could be attributed to a widespread *familialism* (the male breadwinner being the primarily responsible for the wellbeing of all family members) of Italian national culture (Gianesini, 2013). Especially in Italy, where the subsidiary principle and its familistic policies are central, conservative gender-specific division of labor within the family exists and female employment depends on care responsibilities rather than job opportunities and individual qualifications.

Our research, questionnaire-based, differs from other studies on moral reasoning where the primary emphasis was on response evaluation as we broadened the view of moral orientation by including "life values", which are culturally influenced. Some issues need to be addressed here.

The ideological orientations of societies shape the form of moral justifications, sanction detrimental practices and greatly influence who is casted into devalued groups. Cultural and social-structural practices create conditions, which could be conducive to moral disengagement and favor its disinhibitory power. Some of the moral disengagement practices, such as diffusion and displacement of responsibility, are built into the organizational and authority structures of societal systems, and this is especially true for Italy (Gianesini, 2013). A pyramidal hierarchy and an impersonal bureaucracy but with great individualism characterize Italian society (Hofstede, 1980) where the displacement of responsibility derives from very early stage of socialization, which establishes the diffusion of the everybody's and nobody's responsibility notion. It is also true, however, that people are both producers as well as products of social systems. Within a society, individuals may have somewhat a different set of subjective values and, more or less, adapt to the prevailing cultural ideology or have a different subjective interpretation of it. In order to explain the link between cultural values and aggression, is therefore particularly relevant to account for subjective culture and individual measures of cultural variability. Further analyses is needed to improve the measures for individual life values and to explore more in detail the link between moral, social and cultural domains. Different levels of analyses and multiple longitudinal data are necessary to fully understand the interaction of these variables and address bullying in a "comprehensive treatment package". To prevent or contrast the bullying phenomenon, issues related to families and parenting style, social information processing, cognitive distortions, emotion regulation and moral reasoning altogether must be properly addressed, including the affective and motivational side of aggression, to help individuals develop more socially appropriate and competent ways of pursuing their goals in the social context.

References

Arsenio, W. F., & Lemerise, E. A. (2001). Varieties of Childhood bullying: Values, emotion processes, and social competence. *Social Development*, 10, 1, 59-73.

Arsenio, W. F., & Lemerise, E. A. (2004). Aggression and moral development: integrating social information processing and moral domains models. *Child Development*, Vol. 75, n. 4, pp. 987-1002.

Bandura A. (1986). *Social foundations of thought and action: A social cognitive theory*. Englewood Cliffs, NJ: Prentice Hall.

Bandura, A. (1991). Social cognitive theory of moral thought and action. In W. Kurtines & J. Gewirtz (Eds.), *Handbook of moral behavior and development* (Vol. 1), pp. 45-103. Hillsdale, NJ: Erlbaum.

Bandura, A., Barbaranelli, C., Caprara, G.V., Pastorelli, C. (1996). Mechanism of moral disengagement in the exercise of moral agency. *Journal of Personality and Social Psychology*, 71, 364-374

Bandura, A., V. Caprara, C. Barbaranelli, C. Pastorelli & C. Regalia. (2001). "Sociocognitive self- regulatory mechanisms governing transgressive behavior." *Journal of Personality and Social Psychology,* 80: 125-135.

Barriga, A. Q., & Gibbs, J. C. (1996). Measuring cognitive distortion in antisocial youth: development and preliminary validation of the "How I think questionnaire". *Aggressive Behavior*, 22, 333-343.

Bauman, S., & Del Rio, A. (2006). Preservice teachers' responses to bullying scenarios: Comparing physical, verbal, and relational bullying. *Journal of Educational Psychology,* 98(1), 219–231.

Bergeron, N., & Schneider, B. (2005). Explaining cross-national differences in peer directed aggression: A quantitative study. *Aggressive Behavior*. 31, 116-137. Bond, M. H. (1986). *The psychology of the Chinese people*. New York: Oxford University Press.

Berk, L. (2008b). Emotional and social development in adolescence. In M. Misiaszek & J. Ashkenaz (Eds.), *Infants, children, and adolescents* (pp. 597-635). Upper Saddle River, NJ: Pearson Education, Inc.

Bond, M. H. (1991). Chinese values and health: A cross-cultural examination. *Psychology and Health: An International Journal*, 5, 137-152.

Brighi A., Genta M.L. (2010). Bullying: un fenomeno immoral. In: R. Ortega-Ruiz (ed), *Agresividad Injustificada, "Bullying" Y Violencia Escolar*. p. 105-128, Madrid, Alianza Editorial, ISBN: 9788420654614.

Brighi A., Guarini A., Melotti G., Galli S., Genta M. L. (2012). Predictors of victimisation across direct bullying, indirect bullying and cyberbullying. *Emotional and Behavioural Difficulties* 17(3-4),375-388.

Brighi, A., Genta, M. L., Guidi, C., D'Agnese, S. (2007). *Moral orientation, bullying roles and gender differences in italian adolescents*. Paper presented at the 13th European Conference on Developmental Psychology, Jena, 21-25 August 2007 (www.esdp2007de).

Buccoliero E., Darbo, M. , Costantini A., (2003). Piccoli bulli crescono: le scuole superiori. In M.L. Genta (Ed.). Il Bullismo. pp. 115-122, Roma, Carocci.

Caprara, G. V., Pastorelli, C., Bandura, A. (1995). La misura del disimpegno morale in età evolutiva, *Età Evolutiva*, 54, pp. 18-29.

Card, N. A., & Hodges, E. V. E. (2008). Peer victimization among schoolchildren: Correlations, causes, consequences, and considerations in assessment and intervention. *School Psychology Quarterly,* 23, 451–461.

Choi, Yoon G. (Eds). *Individualism and Collectivism: Theory, method and applications*. California, Sage Publications, pp. 41-51.

Crick, N. R., & Dodge, K.A. (1996). Social information processing mechanisms in reactive and proactive aggression. *Child Development*, 67, pp. 993-1002.

Crick, N. R., & Dodge, K.A. (1999). "Superiority" is in the eye of the beholder: A commentary on Sutton, Smith and Swettenham. *Social Development*, 8, 128-131.

Darbo M., Buccoliero, E., & Costantini A. (2001). Piccoli bulli crescono: le scuole superiori. In M.L. Genta (Ed.), *Il bullismo*. Roma Carocci, pp. 115-131.

Debra J. & Pepler D. J. (1998). Observations of Bullying in the Classroom. *The Journal of Educational Research,* 92(2).

DeLara, E. W.(2012). Why Adolescents Don't Disclose Incidents of Bullying and Harassment *Journal of School Violence*, 11(4), 288-305.

Dijkstra, J. K., Lindenberg, S. M., & Veenstra, R. (2008). Beyond the classroom norm. *Journal of Abnormal Child Psychology,* 36, 1289–1299.

Edwards, C. (1994). Cross-cultural research on Kohlberg's stages: The basis for consensus. In B. Puka (Ed.), *Moral development. A compendium* (Vol. 5). New York: Garland.

Erdley C. A., & Asher, S.R. (1996). Children's social goals and self-efficacy perceptions as influences on their responses to ambiguous provocation. *Child Development*, 67, 1329-1344.

Farmer, T. W., Petrin, R. A., Robertson, D. L., Fraser, M. W., Hall, C. M., Day, S. H., & Dadisman, K. (2010). Peer relations of bullies, bully-victims, and victims: The two social worlds of bullying in second-grade classrooms. *Elementary School Journal,* 110, 364–392.

Farrington, D. P., & Ttofi, M. M. (2009). School-based programs to reduce bullying and victimization. *Campbell Systematic Reviews*, 6.

Forbes G, Zhang X, Doroszewicz K, Haas K. (2009). Relationships between individualism-collectivism, gender, and direct or indirect aggression: A study in China, Poland, and the US. *Aggressive Behavior*, 35:24–30.

Fry, D. (1998). Anthropological perspectives on aggression: sex differences and cultural variation. *Aggressive Behavior*, 24, 81-95.

Gianesini G. (2013). Family patterns of change in Italy. Constraints and opportunities for social policies and interventions. In Robila M. (Ed). *Handbook of Family Policies across the Globe*. New York: Springer.

Gibbs, J. C. (1993). Moral cognitive intervention. In A.P. Goldstein & C.R. Huff (Eds.), *The gang intervention handbook* (159-185). Champaigne, Il: Research Press.

Gibbs, J. C. (1995). The cognitive-developmental perspective. In W.M. Kurtines, & J.L. Gewirtz, (1995). *Moral development: An introduction* (pp.29-48). Boston: Allyson and Bacon.

Gibbs, J. C. (2003). *Moral development and reality: beyond the theories of Kohlberg and Hoffman*. Thousand Oaks, CA: Sage.

Gini G. (2005). Social cognition and moral cognition in bullying: what's wrong? *Aggressive Behavior,* 32(6), 528-539.

Guerra, N. G., Nucci, L., & Huesmann, L. R., (1994). Moral cognition and childhood aggression. In L.R. Huesmann (Ed.). *Aggressive Behavior: current perspectives*. (15-33), New York, Plenum Press.

Harkness, S., Edwards, C.P., & Super, C.M. (1981). Social roles and moral reasoning: A case study in a rural African community. *Developmental Psychology*, 17(5), 595-603.

Hofstede, G. (1980). *Culture's consequences: International differences in work related values*. Beverly Hills, CA: Sage.

Hofstede, G., (1983), Dimensions of national cultures in fifty countries and three regions. In G.B Deregowsky., S. Dziurawiec, R.C. Annis (Eds). *Explications in cross-cultural Psychology*. The Netherlands, Swets and Zeitlinger BV, pp. 335-355.

Howell S., & Willis, R. (1989). *Societies at peace: Anthropological Perspectives*. New York, Routledge.

Hsi-Sheng Wei (2009). Instrumental or Emotional Aggression: Testing Models of Bullying, Victimization, and Psychological Maladjustment among Taiwanese Seventh-Graders *Social Work Research* , 33 (4): 231-242.

Hymel, S., Schonert-Reichl, K. A., Bonanno, R. A., Vaillancourt, T., & Henderson, N. R. (2010). Bullying and morality: Understanding how good kids can behave badly. In S. R. Jimerson, S. M. Swearer, & D. Espelage (Eds.), *The handbook of school bullying: An international perspective* (pp. 101-118). New York, NY: Routledge.

Iwasa, N. (1992). Postconventional reasoning and moral education in Japan. *Journal of Moral Education,* 21 (1), 3-16.

Keller, M., Edelstein, W., Fang, F-X., & Fang, G. (1998). Reasoning about responsibilities and obligations in close relationships: A comparison across two cultures. *Developmental Psychology*, 34(4), 731-741

Killen, M., & Nucci, L. (1995). Morality, Autonomy, and the social conflict. In M. Killen & D. Hart (Eds.), *Morality in everyday life: Developmental perspectives*. Cambridge, England, Cambridge University Press, pp. 52-86.

Kohlberg, L. (1984). *Essays on moral development: The psychology of moral development*. Vol. 2. San Francisco: Harper & Row.

Kohlberg, L. (1984). *Essays on moral development*: Vol II. *The psychology of moral development*. San Francisco: Harper & Row.

Kurtines, W.M. & Gewirtz, J.L. (1995). *Moral development: An introduction*. Boston: Allyson and Bacon .

Li Y., Wang, M. Wang, C., & Shi, J., (2010). Individualism, Collectivism, and Chinese Adolescents' Aggression: Intracultural Variations, *Aggressive Behavior* Vol. 36, pages 187–194 (2010) DOI: 10.1002/ab.20341.

Liau, A. K., Barriga, A. Q., Gibbs, J. C. (1998). Relations between self-serving cognitive distortions and overt versus covert antisocial behavior in adolescents. *Aggressive Behavior*, 24: 335-346.

Little, T. D., Jones, S. M., Henrich, C. C., & Hawley, P. H. (2003). Disentangling the ''whys'' from the ''whats'' of aggressive behavior. *International Journal of Behavior Development,* 27, 122–133.

Malti, T., & Latzko, B. (2010), Children's moral emotions and moral cognition: Towards an integrative perspective. *New Directions for Child and Adolescent Development,* (129), 1-10.

Menesini E., Nocentini A.,Camodeca M. (2013). Morality, values, traditional bullying, and cyberbullying in adolescence. *British Journal of Developmental Psychology* 311:1-14. doi: 10.1111/j.2044-835X.2011.02066.x.

Menesini, E., Fonzi, A., Vannucci, E., (1999). Il disimpegno morale: la legittimazione del comportamento prepotente. In A. Fonzi, (Ed.). *Il gioco crudele. Studi e ricerche sui correlati psicologici del bullismo.* Firenze, Giunti, pp. 39-53.

Menesini, E., Sanchez, V., Fonzi, A., Ortega, R., Costabile, A., Lo Feudo, G. (2003). Moral emotions and bullying: a cross-national comparison of differences between bullies, victims and outsiders. *Aggressive Behavior*, 29, pp. 515-530.

Miller, J. G. (1988). Bridging the content–structure dichotomy: Culture and the self. In M. H. Bond (Ed.), *The cross-cultural challenge to social psychology* (pp. 266–281). Beverly Hills, CA: Sage.

Miller, J. G., Bersoff, D. M., & Harwood, R. L. (1990). Perceptions of social responsibilities in India and in the United States: Moral imperatives or personal decisions? *Journal of Personality and Social Psychology*, 58, 33–47.

Mishna, F. & Alaggia, R. (2005). Weighing the risks: A child's decision to disclose peer victimization. Children & Schools, 27(4), 217-227

Mizuno, S. (1999). Psychosocial development and moral development: An exploratory comparison of adolescents in Japan and America. *Psychological Reports*, 84, 51-62.

Okonkwo, R. (1997). Moral development and culture in Kohlberg's theory: A Nigerian (Igbo) evidence. IFE *Psychologia: An International Journal*, 5(2), 117-128.

Palmer, E. J. (2003 a). An overview of the relationship between moral reasoning and offending. *Australian Psychologist*, 38, 165-174.

Palmer, E. J. (2003 b). *Offending behaviour: moral reasoning, criminal conduct and the rehabilitation of offenders*. Cullompton, Uk: William Publishing.

Palmer, E. J., & Hollin, C. R., (2000). The inter-relations of sociomoral reasoning, perceptions of own parenting, attributions of intent with self-reported delinquency. *Legal and Criminological Psychology*, 5, 201-218.

Pellegrini, A. D., Long, J. D., Solberg, D., Roseth, C., DuPuis, D., Bohn, C., & Hickey, M. (2010). Bullying and social status during school transitions. In S. R. Jimerson, S. M. Swearer, & D. L. Espelage (Eds.), *Handbook of bullying in schools: An international perspective*(pp. 199–210). New York: Routledge.

Pepler, D., Craig, W., & O'Connell, P. (2010). Peer processes in bullying. In S. R. Jimerson, S. M. Swearer, & D. L. Espelage (Eds.), *Handbook of bullying in schools: An international perspective*(pp. 469–479). New York: Routledge.

Perren & Gutzwiller-Helfenfinger (2012). Cyberbullying and traditional bullying in adolescence:Differential roles of moral disengagement, moral emotions, and moral values. *European Journal of Developmental Psychology,* 9 (2), 195-209.

Perren, S., Gutzwiller-Helfenfinger E., Malti T. & Humel S. (2012). Moral reasoning and emotion attributions of adolescent bullying, victims, and bully-victims, *British Journal of Developmental Psychology,* 30 (4), 511-530.

Pornari, C. D., & Wood, J. (2010). Peer and cyber aggression in secondary school students: The role of moral disengagement, hostile attribution bias, and outcome expectancies. *Aggressive Behavior,* 36(2), 81-94.

Robarchek, C.A, & Robarchek, C. J. (1998). Reciprocities and realities: World views, peacefulness and violence among Semai and Waroani. *Aggressive Behavior*, 24, 123-133.

Rodkin, P. C., & Berger, C. (2008). Who bullies whom? Social status asymmetries by victim gender.*International Journal of Behavioral Development,* 32, 473–485.

Rodkin, P. C., & Roisman, G. I. (2010). Antecedents and correlates of the popular-aggressive phenomenon in elementary school.*Child Development,* 81, 837–850.

Salmivalli, C. (1999). Participant role approach to school bullying: Implications for intervention. *Journal of Adolescence,* 22, 453–459.

Salmivalli, C., Kärnä, A., & Poskiparta, E. (2010). From peer putdowns to peer support: A theoretical model and how it translated into a national anti-bullying program. In S. R. Jimerson, S. M. Swearer, & D. L. Espelage (Eds.), *Handbook of bullying in schools: An international perspective* (pp. 441–454). New York: Routledge.

Schwartz, S. H. (1990). Individualism-collectivism: Critique and proposed refinements. *Journal of Cross-cultural Psychology*, 21, 139-157.

Schwartz, S. H. (1994). Beyond individualism/collectivism: New cultural dimensions of values. In Kim U., Triandis H.C., Kagitcibasi C., Choi S.C., Yoon G. (Eds).*Individualism and Collectivism: Theory, method and applications*. California, Sage Publications, pp. 85-119.

Schwartz, S. H. (1999). A theory of cultural values and some implications for work. *Applied Psychology: An international review*. 48, 23-47.

Schwartz, S. H., & Bilsky, W. (1990). Toward a theory of the universal content and structure of values: Extensions and cross-cultural replications. *Journal of Personality and Social Psychology*, *58*, 878–891.

Shweder, R. A. (1990). Cultural psychology: What is it? In J. W. Stigler, R. A. Shweder, & G. Herdt (Eds.), *Cultural psychology: Essays on comparative human development* (pp. 1–46). Cambridge, England: Cambridge University Press.

Slaby, R. G., & Guerra, N. G. (1988). Cognitive mediators of aggression in adolescent offenders: 1. *Assessment. Developmental Psychology*, 24, 580-588.

Staub, E. (1994). A Conception of the Determinants and Development of Altruism and Aggression: Motives, the Self, and the Environment. In B. Puka (ed.), *Reaching Out: Caring, Altruism, and Prosocial Behavior*. New York: Garland Publishing, 11-39.

Stigler, J. W., Shweder, R. A., & Herdt, G. (Eds.). (1990). *Cultural psychology: Essays on comparative human development*. Cambridge, England: Cambridge University Press.

Sutton, J., Smith, P. K., & Swettenham, J. (1999). Bullying and Theory of mind. A critique of the "Social skills deficit" view of antisocial behaviour. *Social Development*, 8, 117-127.

Tangney, J. P., Stuewig, J., & Mashek, D. J. (2007). Moral emotions and moral behavior. P*sychology,* 58(1), 345-372.

Thornberg R. & Jungert T. (2013). Bystander behavior in bullying situations: basic moral sensitivity, moral disengagement and defender self-efficacy, *Journal of Adolescence,* (36), 3, 475-483.

Thornberg, R., & Jungert, T. (2014). School bullying and the mechanisms of moral disengagement. *Aggressive Behavior,* 40, 99-108.

Turiel, E. (1983). *The development of social knowledge: Morality and convention.* Cambridge, MA: Cambridge University Press.

Turiel, E. (1998). The development of morality. In W. Damon (series ed.) & Elsemberg (vol. ed.), *Handbook of Child Psychology*, 5th Ed. Vol. 3: *Social Emotional and Personality Development,* pp. 863-932, New York, Wiley.

Veenstra, R., Lindenberg, S., Munniksma, A., & Dijkstra, J. K. (2010). The complex relation between bullying, victimization, acceptance, and rejection.*Child Development,* 81, 480–486.

Vorrath, H. & Brendtro, L. K. (1985). *Positive peer culture* (2nd Ed.). Hawthorne, NY: Aldine Publishing.

Williams, R. (1970). *American Society: A sociological interpretation* (3rd ed.). New York, Knopf.

Wright, J.C. & Bartsch, K. (2008). Portraits of early moral sensibility in two children's everyday conversations. *Merrill-Palmer Quarterly,* 54(1), 56-85.

In: Handbook on Bullying
Editor: Phoebe Triggs

ISBN: 978-1-63463-023-8

Chapter 9

CYBERBULLYING AND STUDENTS' ENGAGEMENT IN SCHOOL: A LITERATURE REVIEW

Feliciano H. Veiga[1], Fernanda García[2], Ana Tomás Almeida[3], Suzana Nunes Caldeira[4] and Diana Galvão[1]

[1]Institute of Education, University of Lisbon, Portugal
[2]University of Valencia, Spain
[3]University of Minho, Portugal
[4]University of Azores, Portugal

Abstract

Background: Cyberbullying refers to an indirect and covert form of aggression, carried out through the use of new technologies, and exhibiting distinct features from those found present in traditional bullying, and has been acquiring its own space of analyses and research; still, it maintains an inevitable proximity with the second, namely, the negative impact on the victim, both the person and the student, with consequences on academic performance, among other aspects.

Purpose: This piece reviews some of the most relevant studies on cyberbullying, its assessment and relation with personal (self-esteem, age, sex, ethnicity and type of aggression) and contextual (family, school context and peer group) variables, as well as with several aspect related to academic context, particularly, students' engagement in school and academic success. Considering the expected link between bullying and cyberbullying, some studies on the first form of aggression were included in this review, as they may be considered a theoretical referential in this subject.

Conclusions: Cyberbullying is a recent and important phenomenon, linked to the inclusion of new technologies in daily life. There are, however, some gaps in research carried out on this issue, which presents different features from those that characterize traditional bullying. Similarly to bullying, studies suggest that cyberbullying presents negative impact both on students and academic success. Students' engagement in school plays an import role in the occurrence of aggression-victimization behaviors and appears to be a valorous strategy in cyberbullying prevention.

Keywords: cyberbullying, students' engagement in school, personal variables, contextual variables, academic performance

Introduction

Cyberbullying appeared in the literature to identify an indirect form of aggression, which occurs through the use of new technologies (Ortega-Ruiz & Núñez, 2012), and currently occupies its own ground of analyses and investigation. Research has been establishing a link between the determinants and effects of in person bullying and cyberbullying (Almeida, Caurcel, & Machado, 2006; MacGriezel, Finger, Bodkin-Andrews, Craven, & Yeung, 2012; Jose, Kljakovic, Scheib, & Notter, 2011; Low & Espelage, 2012); cyberbullying exhibits particular features, when compared to traditional bullying behaviors, still, it is likewise a disturbing element with impact on academic success.

Data on wellbeing during childhood, published in the *Innocenti Report Cards* (as cited in Quental &Veiga, 2010) indicated that 40% of the children surveyed in Switzerland, Austria and Portugal, were victims of bullying, stressing Pereira's findings (2008): a considerable increase in situations of aggression and victimization in Portuguese schools, where one in each five children indicated being continuously victimized by their peers.

This article reviews the most relevant studies on cyberbullying and its relation with several aspects associated with academic context, focusing, particularly, the relationship between cyberbullying and students' engagement in school, a construct which has been in the center of discussions about school institutions and their students. Specific studies about bullying, that may contribute to the understanding of cyberbullying, are also presented, and may work as theoretical referential or add suggestions for empirical research.

Cyberbullying: Conceptualization and Assessment

Cyberbullying and, more traditionally, bullying in school context, constitute occurrences that have called the attention of the educational community, due to their adverse effects on the participants, either individual (self-esteem, self-concept) or scholar – achievement and behavior (Caldeira & Veiga, 2011). The adoption of the expression *bullying* to refer the perpetration, by a *bully,* of hostile behaviors toward a *victim*, intentionally and continuously throughout time, and, often, witnessed by active or passive bystanders, is due to Olweus (1994).

Peer aggression may take several forms, direct — physical, including kicking and beating, and verbal, like calling offensive names —, indirect such as exclusion from groups or, more recently, virtual, through the internet (blogs, emails, websites) or other means of communication like the telephone. The virtual mean stands out not only by for how it occurs, requiring the use of new technologies, but also because of the change in the witnesses' role.

Both cyberbullying and bullying encompass a series of behaviors likely to negatively affect the student exposed to those types of aggression (Caldeira & Veiga, 2011; Veiga, 2007, 2012), as well as the other participants. Vanderbilt and Augustyn (2010) suggest that bullies and witnesses are marked by the effects of the aggression, nevertheless, must be considered as participants in the occurrence.

Santos and Veiga (2012) observed a superiority of verbal aggressions, compared with the other forms. Holfeld and Grabe (2012) found that only 64% of the victims report the incidents (primarily to their parents and peers), being the percentage lower, 60%, in the case of witnesses.

The assessment of this type of aggression relies on some instruments that have been developed for specific studies, although literature suggests that the need to study the relation between bullying and cyberbullying validates the use of instruments allied to the first type of aggression.

There may be found some studies where specific instruments, directed toward cyberbullying, were created for that purpose (Griezel, Craven, Yeung, & Finger, 2008; Heirman & Walrave, 2012; Stewart, Drescher, Maack, Ebesutani, & Young, 2014), being that, many of them were adapted from pre-existant instruments, applied in bullying assessment. Most of the instruments are self-report questionnaires, answered by the students, using Liker-type scales; the items focus is, frequently, students' perception about cyberbullying (*Cyberbullying Scale* - Stewart, Drescher, Maack, Ebesutani, & Young, 2014), and their own experiences (*Cyberbullying Student Survey* - Li, 2010). Some questionnaires present specific forms, for the cyber-victims and the cyber-bullies (*Cyberbullying Scale - CBS,* Topçu, 2008). Projective methods are also found, like in the study carried out by Gomez-Garibello, Shariff, McConnell and Talwar (2012). Other studies attend to the teachers' perceptions, for example, the one by Li (2008), using the *Teachers' Perceptions about Cyberbullying Questionnaire.*

Given their relevance and psychometric qualities, validity and reliability, some assessment instruments are presented:

Safe Schools Survey (Ontario Ministry of Education). Included cyberbullying in its 2nd edition (2004), being composed by 11 items, distributed by eight sections: students' perceptions, inclusion, incidents relating to victimization, incidents relating to perpetration, responses to bullying, reporting bullying, use of technology, and general comments.

Cyberbullying Student Survey (Li, 2010). Consists of four parts: demographic data, students' behaviors and beliefs related to cyberbullying, and students' opinions about online behaviors in general.

Revised Adolescent Peer Relations Instrument – Bully and Target (Griezel, Craven, Yeung, & Finger, 2008). Composed by 61 itens, responses in a 6-point likert-type scale (from 1, never, to 6, everyday).

Teachers' Perceptions about Cyberbullying Questionnaire (Li, 2008). Questionnaire based on the work of Siu (2004) — Teachers' Attitude about Bullying Questionnaire – composed by 26 items, focusing on teachers' perceptions about cyberbullying (from 1, totally disagree, to 5, totally agree).

Griezel et al. (2008) point out some limitations in cyberbullying assessment: little is known about the structure of the cyberbullying construct implying that the instruments applied are not specifically designed for it; using one or two items for the assessment of multidimensional constructs; weaknesses in the research carried out include the sample size, the psychometric fragility of the instruments and even the theoretical approaches.

Violence in school context — and particularly *bullying*, in both its traditional and the most recent cyberbullying form — has been investigated in relation to a number of factors, intrinsic to the student and contextual. Some studies on the relation between individual and contextual variables and the occurrence of cyberbullying are introduced.

Cyberbullying and Personal Variables

Studies on the relation between cyberbullying and personal variables, such as self-esteem, sex, ethnicity and type of aggression are presented.

The relationship between cyberbullying experiences and *self-esteem* was studied by Patchin and Hinduja (2010), with 1963 middle school students, and a moderately significant relation was found between bullying experiences and self-esteem. Those students with cyberbullying experiences (both as a victim and as a bully), showed lower self-esteem, when compared with their peers with little or none experience with that type of aggression.

Several studies found that aggressive behaviors tend to decrease with *age* and as students' progress in schooling, indicating a greater fragility of younger students (Olweus, 1994; Santos & Veiga, 2012). The prevalence of aggressions in school context justifies serious reflection and investing in intervention procedures. Jose et al. (2011) studied adolescents aged between 11 and 16 years, in the context of the *Youth Connectedness Project* (YCP), carried out in New Zeeland, and found that the occurrence of aggressions (either in person or virtual) remains stable during two years. Holfeld and Grabe (2012) studied middle school students' cyberbullying experiences, and concluded that one in each five students had been bullied in the last year. These authors express the variability found in the literature on the prevalence of cyberbullying, what seems due to methodological and sampling differences: a review by Patchin and Hinduja (2010) found a variation between 5,5% and 72% (mean of 24,4%) in the prevalence of cyberbullying. Still, according to these authors, this type of occurrence is significant and tends to increase all over the world. Research also indicates that bullies tend to preserve such attitudes as adults, and their children, frequently, also become bullies. This seems also true concerning to victims (O'Connel, Peppler, & Craig, 1999).

Differences according to *sex* appear contradictory, in research; some authors found differences in cyberbullying in favor of boys, either bullies or victims (Wang, Iannotti, & Nasel, 2009); other found a superiority in favor of girls (Holfeld & Grabe, 2012 – as victims, bullies or witnesses); further others, found no differences between sexes (Williams & Guerra, 2007). Boys showed a higher probability to act as bullies, while girls to be victims, concerning to cyberbullying (Wang, Iannotti, & Nasel, 2009). Differences according to sex were also found by Arslan, Sevim, Hallett and Balci (2012), with a higher prevalence of boys acting as bullies. In the sample, 27% of respondents indicated having been bullied; 16% appeared as bullies; and 15% were both victim and bully. Zhou, Tang, Wei, Zhang and Morrison (2013) also found a higher probability of boys to be involved in cyberbullying occurrences, either as bullies or victims.

Considering *ethnicity,* a study by Wang, Iannotti and Nasel (2009 found a higher association of Afro-American adolescents to bullying behaviors (physical, verbal and virtual), and a smaller association with victimization. Low and Espelage (2012) investigated the differences between non-physical bullying and cyberbullying, according to ethnicity (and considering individual and family predictors), in adolescents from 5th to 7th grade, considering three different moments separated from each other by six months. In general, data suggests a higher prevalence of cyberbullying among Afro-American adolescents, in comparison with white students. In a study with 518 Canadian adolescents of either East Asian or European descent, of both sexes, aged between 12 and 18 years (7th-12th grades). Shapka and Law (2013) analyzed the differences in cyberbullying using a self-report questionnaire. Data was subjected to regression analyses and suggested that East Asian adolescents were less likely to be involved in cyberbullying; East Asian adolescents were more likely to participate in cyber-aggressions for proactive (instrumental) than reactive (as a response to provocation) reasons, and the opposite was true for European descent adolescents. The superiority of proactive reasons, in East Asian adolescents, was significantly higher in males, compared tofemales. The authors confirm the correspondence of such results with the ones found in literature, and highlight the cultural impact on the drives underlying cyberbullying behaviors.

Attending to the *types of aggression,* in a study carried out by Santos and Veiga (2012), boys presented higher values in physical and verbal victimization, while girls showed higher scores in the social dimension of victimization, similarly to what was found by Olweus (1994), Craig (1998), Beane (2006), or Wang, Iannotti and Nasel (2009). In a study on cyberbullying behaviors, Feldman (2012) found that in adolescents who were simultaneously victims and bullies, the involvement in these type of behaviors was related to poorer psychosocial functioning and relations, compared to students who were solely victims or bullies, or were not involved in these type of behaviors.

Cyberbullying and Contextual Variables

Some studies on the relation between cyberbullying and environmental variables are introduced, such as family, school context and peer group.

Family has arisen as a study context, in seeking for predictors for the occurrence of aggression behaviors. Studies on direct bullying suggest a relation between these type of behavior and conflicting or severe parental styles (Baldry & Farrington, 2000; Bowes et al., 2009; Olweus, 1994), as well as low parental monitoring (Vanderbilt & Augustyn, 2010; Veiga, 2007, 2012a). Family rules (too rigid or absent) appear associated with aggressive behaviors (Caldeira & Veiga, 2011; Smith & Sharp, 1998; Vanderbilt & Augustyn, 2010; Veiga, 2012a). In a study carried out by Low and Espelage (2012), family monitoring appeared related to high levels of cyberbullying at wave 3, though the use of substances, in white females. Non-physical bullying was related to high family violence and low parental monitoring, explained by hostility (in boys and white race subjects) and depressive symptoms (Afro-American boys). Wang, Iannotti and Nasel (2009) found that cyberbullying (similarly to bullying, physical, verbal, and relational), was also related to low parental support. Shapka and Law (2013) also attended to the relation between cyberbullying and parental behaviors (parental control, behavioral boundaries definition; parental solicitation, knowledge obtained from the children; children's disclosure, knowledge obtained from the children's spontaneous sharing) in East Asian and European descents youth. They found that high levels of parental control and low levels of parental solicitation were associated with low involvement in cyberbullying behaviors in East Asian participants, when compared to their European peers.

The belief that bullying behaviors could be punished by significant adults appeared related to non-participation in this type of actions, in a study by Hinduja and Patchin, (2013) with adolescents from 6th to 12th grades

Considering the variable *school context,* Stauffer, Heath, Coyes and Ferrin (2012) studied teachers' perception about the effects of cyberbullying on students, as well as the most effective strategies to address this type of aggression. Approximately ¼ of the teacher indicated cyberbullying would have a small long-lasting negative impact on students, and less than half were in favor of formal prevention programs development. Teachers pointed out a few strategies for being more effective in responding to cyberbullying: increasing parental involvement, alerting students about the consequences for cyberbullying, and increasing effective consequences for cyberbullying occurrences.

Peer group assumes particular importance during adolescence. Some authors have confirmed the link between the adolescent's' behavior and the one exhibited by his peers (Bray, Adams, Getz, & McQueen, 2003), which turned out present concerning cyberbullying behaviors, in a study carried out by Shapka and Law (2013). The amount of friends was associated with more bullying behaviors and lower victimization (verbal, relational, physical), result not found in cyberbullying, in a study developed by Wang, Iannotti and Nasel (2009).

Engagement in School and Cyberbullying

Students' engagement in school – SES is a concept that, in the context of intervention in cyberbullying, has been presenting a protective role (Low & Espelage, 2012; Mehta, Cornell, Fan, & Gregory, 2013; Shapka & Law, 2013; Veiga, 2012a; Zhou et al., 2013). SES may be characterized as a multidimensional construct, which encompasses students' thoughts, feelings and behaviours (Fredericks, Blumenfeld, & Paris, 2004; Furlong et al., 2003), or as the experience of centripetal connection of the student to the school (Veiga, 2012, 2013), including four components – cognitive, behavioural, emotional and agentic.

Researches discussed in the literature have found a relation between this concept and peer victimization (Seeley, Tombari, Bennet, & Dunkle, 2009; Wilson, 2004). Engagement has been addressed as a predictor of several behaviors (better grades, less behavior problems) and is likely to be influenced by numerous variables, both personal and contextual. These types of relations are presented.

Wang, Nansel and Iannotti (2011) emphasize that — if bullying carries a body of *personal* (for example anxiety, aggression, hyperactivity and behavior problems) and *schoolar effects* – some effects may be superior in the case of cyberbullying, such as depression and task disengagement. A study carried out by Arslan et al. (2012) found an association between exposure to cyberbullying (either as victim or bully) and low levels of *school satisfaction* and *academic achievement*, in 372 students from 2nd to 4th grades.

Studies on bullying, as the following, may lead to posing hypothesis about what may occur in cyberbullying situations (Low & Espelage, 2012; Shapka & Law, 2013; Veiga, 2012; Zhou et al., 2013). A study conducted by Bayar and Uçanok (2012), with 1263 high school students (mean age: 14,9), concluded that those students who were not implied in aggression situations showed more positive perceptions of their school and teachers, when compared with aggressive peers.

Mehta et al. (2013) analyzed students' engagement in terms of commitment to school (affective and cognitive dimensions) and participation (behavioral dimension), in order to investigate whether students' perceptions about bullying climate in school were associated with low levels of engagement. The author used a sample of 7058 9th grade students, from Virgínia schools, 50% male. The results indicated that those students who perceive school as a place where bullying often occurs, are less engaged, affectively and cognitively, compared to those who perceive less bullying situations. As for the relation between bullying perception and participation, there were no statistically significant results; however, the authors indicate that students who perceive a bullying climate show less participation in extracurricular activities. With regard to contextual variables, the authors noted that school size stands as a predictor of students' cognitive and affective engagement, result not found regarding behavioral engagement. This study concludes that those schools with more bullying situations reflect lower levels of students' engagement.

Various studies highlight that negative experiences related to peers — such as bullying (Battin-Pearson, Newcomb, Abbott, Hill, Catalano, & Hawkins, 2000; Ma, Phelps, Lerner, & Lerner, 2009), rejection (Buhs, 2005), or the lack of friends (Wentzel, Barry, & Caldwell, 2004) — increase the probability of school disengagement, conducting to school dropout and to the connection with disruptive peers (Battin-Pearson et al., 2000).

Other studies (Low & Espelage, 2012; Shapka & Law, 2013; Veiga, 2012; Zhou et al., 2013) have analyzed, more particularly, the relations between engagement in school variables and bullying. Hirschfield and Gasper (2011) found that affective and behavioral engagement predicts a decrease in *delinquency*, both in school context and overall. Wilson (2004), using a sample of 2.327 middle school students, found that sense of belonging is inversely related to *victimization*. Li and Lerner (2011) analyzed the effects of school engagement (behavioral and emotional) on school grades and *risk behaviors* (delinquency and substance use), and found that high levels of emotional and behavioral engagement were predictors of a minor risk of delinquent behaviors and substance use, being positively associated with better performances and less symptoms of depression.

Seeley et al. (2009), with a sample of 860 6th grade students, found a significant negative association between *victimization* and affective and cognitive engagement, contrary to cognitive engagement; the authors suggest that aggression victims are behaviorally and emotionally affected. Results also showed that engagement is a moderator variable of the impact of victimization on school attendance. Intervention Programs addressing victimization are suggested, and should include the promotion of students' engagement which, in turn, will support the increase in school attendance and academic success.

Conclusion

Cyberbullying, a type of covert aggression consumed through the use of new technologies, presents particular features and consequences (Low & Espelage, 2012; Shapka & Law, 2013; Veiga, 2012; Zhou et al., 2013). Cyberbullying appears related to low engagement in school and negative academic performance, besides its psychological impact, relating to low self-esteem. Hinduja and Patchin (2013) suggest the influence of social factors, such as family, school and peer group, on bullying behaviors, and propose intervention measures like implementing peer mentoring programs, at school, and parental monitoring, at home.

Although a negative *school climate* does not mean an increase in aggression situations, between students, Wilson (2004) highlights that the links experienced by the student, at school, may be among the aspects which better contribute to predict aggression and victimization, either in its direct or indirect form, through new technologies. Even though individual and family factors may be in the basis of cyberbullying, its continuity seems related to school context (Santos & Veiga, 2012). Teacher-student relationship, school organization, and the forms how aggression situations are managed, stand out as factors affecting the students' behavior (Caldeira & Veiga, 2011), suggesting the need to structure a school environment oriented toward prevention and intervention in this type of situations. Literature (Shapka & Law, 2013; Veiga, 2012; Zhou et al., 2013) suggests several lines of action, such as the promotion of a safe environment, involving parents and teacher, and clarifying with the students' their conduct regarding cyberbullying behaviors.

Positive relations with *peers*, during adolescence, appear in the literature as relating to an increase in academic motivation (Furrer & Skinner, 2003), self-esteem (Furrer & Skinner, 2003; Keefe & Berndt, 1996), and academic performance (Veiga, 2012), aspects likely to be affected by the occurrence of direct (bullying) and indirect (cyberbullying) aggression experiences. Disengagement from school may act as a response to negative behaviors from peers, such as victimization and exclusion (Almeida, Lisboa, & Caurcel, 2007; Buhs, 2005; Veiga, 2012), with impact on engagement through time (Li et al., 2011; Simmons-Morton & Chen, 2009).

When considering the *prevention* of cyberbullying, family involvement appears emphasized (Shapka & Law, 2013; Veiga, 2012; Zhou et al., 2013), since aggressions occur by means of internet or mobile phones use, and parental supervision may be crucial. Students' disengagement assumes a relevant role in aggression-victimization behaviors and, therefore, the triggering of strategies pointing students' engagement in school is an important contribution to cyberbullying prevention.

Note

This chapter is a product of the project PTDC/CPE-CED/114362/2009 - Envolvimento dos Alunos na escola: Diferenciação e Promoção/Students' Engagment in School: Differentiation and Promotion, financed by National funding, through the Fundação para a Ciência e Tecnologia (FCT). Correspondence related to this paper should be sent to the lead researcher: Professor Feliciano H. Veiga, Instituto de Educação, Universidade de Lisboa, Alameda da Universidade, 1649-013 Lisboa. E-mail: fhveiga@ie.ul.pt

References

Almeida, A., Caurcel, M. J., & Machado, J. (2006). Perceived characteristics of victims according to their victimized and nonvictimized peers. *Electronical Journal of Research in Educational Psychology*, 9(4), 371-396.

Almeida, A., Lisboa, C., & Caurcel, M. (2007). Por qué ocurren los malos tratos? Explicaciones causales de adolescentes portugueses y brasileños. *Inter American Journal of Psychology*, 41(2), 107-118.

Arslan, S., Sevim, S., Hallett, V., & Balci, S. (2012). Cyberbullying among primary school students in Turkey: self-reported prevalence and associations with home and school life. *Cyberpsychology, Behavior,and Social Networking*, 15(10), 527-533.

Baldry, A. C., & Farrington, D. P. (2000). Bullies and delinquents: personal characteristics and parental styles. *Journal of Community & Applied Social Psychology*, 10, 17–31.

Battin-Pearson, S., Newcomb, M. D., Abbott, R. D., Hill, K. G., Catalano, R. F., & Hawkins, J. D. (2000). Predictors of early high school dropout: A test of five theories. *Journal of Educational Psychology*, 92, 568-582.

Bayar, Y., & Uçanok, Z. (2012). School social climate and generalized peer perception in traditional and cyberbullying status. *Educational Sciences: Theory & Practice*, 12(4), 2352-2358.

Beane, A. L. (2006). *A sala de aula sem bullying: mais de 100 sugestões e estratégias para professores*. Porto: Porto Editora.

Bowes, L., Arseneault, L., Maughan, B., Taylor, A., Caspi, A., & Moffitt, T. E. (2009). School, neighborhood, and family factors are associated with children's bullying involvement: A nationally representative longitudinal study. *Journal of the American Academy of Child & Adolescent Psychiatry*, 48, 545–553.

Bray, J., Adams G., Getz J., & McQueen, A. (2003). Individuation, peers and adolescent alcohol use: A latent growth analysis. *Journal of Consulting and Clinical Psychology*, 71, 553-564.

Buhs, E. (2005). Peer rejection, negative peer treatment, and school adjustment: self-concept and classroom engagement as mediating processes. *Journal of School Psychology*, 43, 407–424.

Caldeira, S., &Veiga, F. H. (2011). Introdução à intervençãoemsituações de indisciplina. In S. Caldeira & F. H. Veiga (orgs.). *Intervir em situações de indisciplina,violência e conflito* (09-13). Lisboa: Fim de Século.

Craig, W. (1998). The relationship among bullying, victimization, depression, anxiety, and aggression in elementary school children. *Personality and Individual Differences*, 24(1), 123-130.

Feldman, M. (2012). *Cyberbullying in High School: associated individual and contextual factors of involvement* (unpublished PHD Thesis), University of South Florida, USA.

Fredricks, J., Blumenfeld, P., & Paris, A. (2004). School engagement: potential of the concept, state of the evidence. *Review of Educational Research Spring*, 74(1), 59-109.

Furlong, M. J., Whipple, A. D., St. Jean, G., Simental, J., Soliz, A., & Punthuna, S. (2003). Multiple contexts of school engagement: Moving toward a unifying framework for educational research and practice. *California School Psychologist*, 8, 99-114.

Furrer, C., & Skinner, E. (2003). Sense of relatedness as a factor in children's academic engagement and performance. *Journal of Educational Psychology*, *95*, 148 – 162.

Gomez-Garibello, C., Shariff, S., McConnell, M., & Talwar, V. (2012). Adolescents' evaluation of cyberbullying events. *Alberta Journal of Educational Research*, 58(3),474-47.

Griezel, L., Craven, R., Yeung, A., & Finger, L. (2008, December). *The Development of a Multi-dimensional Measure of Cyber Bullying*. Paper presented at the Australian Association for Research in Education, Brisbane, Australia.

Heirman, W., & Walrave, M. (2012). Predicting adolescent perpetration in cyberbullying: An application of the theory of planned behavior. *Psicothema*, 24(4), 614-620.

Hinduja, S., & Patchin, J. (2013). Social Influences on Cyberbullying Behaviors among Middle and High School Students. *Journal of Youth and Adolescence*, 42, 711–722.

Hirschfield, P., & Gasper, J. (2010). The relationship between school engagement and delinquency in late childhood and early adolescence. *Journal of Youth and Adolescence*, 40, 3–22.

Holfeld, B., & Grabe, M. (2012). Middle School Student's Perceptions and Responses to Cyberbullying. *Journal of Educational Computing Research*, 46(4), 395-413.

Jose, P., Kljakovic, M., Scheib, E., & Notter, O. (2011). *Journal of Research on Adolescence*, 22(2), 301–309.

Keefe, K., & Berndt, T. (1996). Relations of friendship quality to self-esteem in early adolescence. *Journal of Early Adolescence*, 16(1), 110-130.

Li, Q. (2008). Cyberbullying in schools: An examination of preservice teachers' perception. *Canadian Journal of Learning and Technology*, 34(2), 75-90.

Li, Q. (2010). Cyberbullying in high schools: A study of students' behaviours and beliefs about 53 this new phenomenon. *Journal of Aggression, Maltreatment, & Trauma,* 19(4), 372-392.

Li, Y., & Lerner, R. (2011). Trajectories of school engagement during adolescence: implications for grades, depression, delinquency, and substance use. *Developmental Psychology, 47(1),* 233–247.

Li, Y., Lynch, A., Kalvin, C., Liu, J., & Lerner, R. (2011). Peer relationships as a context for the development of school engagement during early adolescence. *International Journal of Behavioral Development,* 35(4), 329–342.

Low, S., & Espelage, D. (2012). Differentiating cyberbullying perpetration from non-physical bullying: commonalities across race, individual, and family predictors. *Psychology of Violence*, 3(1), 39–52.

Ma, L., Phelps, E., Lerner, J. V., & Lerner, R. M. (2009). Pathways to academic competence for adolescents who bully and who are bullied: Findings from the 4-H Study of Positive Youth Development. *The Journal of Early Adolescence*, 29, 862–897.

MacGriezel, L., Finger, R., & Bodkin-Andrews, H. (2012). The joint development of traditional bullying and victimization with cyberbullying and victimization in adolescence. *Journal of Educational Research*, 105(6), 442-455.

Mehta B. S., Cornell, D., Fan, X,, & Gregory, A. (2013). Bullying climate and school engagement in ninth-grade students. *Journal of School Health*, 83(1), 45-52.

O'Connell, P., Pepler, D., & Craig, W. (1999). Peer involvement in bullying: insights and challenges for intervention. *Journal of Adolescence*, 22, 437±452.

Olweus, D. (1994). *Bullying at School, What we know and what we can do*. Oxford: Blackwell Publishers.

Ortega-Ruiz, R., & Núñez, J. (2012).Bullying and cyberbullying: Research and intervention at school and social contexts. *Psicothema*, 24(4), 603-607.

Patchin, J., & Hinduja, S. (2010). Cyberbullying and Self-Esteem. *Journal of School Health*, 80(12), 614-621.

Pereira, B. O. (2008). *Para umaescolasemviolência: Estudo e prevenção das práticas agressivas entre crianças* (1st ed.). Lisboa: Fundação Calouste Gulbenkian & FCT.

Quental, C., & Veiga, F. (2010). Maltrato entre alunos do ensinobásico: Análise em função do rendimento e da disrupção escolar. *Atas do XVII Colóquio AFIRSE: A escola e o mundo do trabalho*, Lisboa, Portugal.

Santos, E., & Veiga, F. H. (2012). Comportamentos de VitimizaçãonaEscola. In L. Almeida, B. Silva & A. Franco. *Livro de Atas do II Seminário Internacional Contributos da Psicologia em Contextos Educativos* (1661-1669), Universidade do Minho, Braga, Portugal.

Seeley, K., Tombari, M. L., Bennett, L. J., & Dunkle, J. B. (2009). Peer Victimization in Schools: A Set of Quantitative and Qualitative Studies of the Connections Among Peer Victimization, School Engagement, Truancy, School Achievement, and Other Outcomes. *National Center for School Engagement*, 1, 13-46.

Shapka, J., & Law, D. (2013). Does one size fit all? Ethnic differences in parenting behaviors and motivations for adolescent engagement in cyberbullying. *Journal of Youth Adolescence*, 42, 723–738.

Simons-Morton, B., & Chen, R. (2009). Peer and Parent Influences on School Engagement among Early Adolescents. *Youth & Society*, 41(1), 3-25.

Siu, C. (2004). Pre-service teachers' attitudes about school bullying: A new perspective. University of Calgary, Calgary.

Smith, P., & Sharp, S. (1998). *School Bullying.* London: Routledge.

Stauffer, S., Heath, M., Coyne, S., & Ferrin, S. (2012). High school teachers' perceptions of cyberbullying prevention and intervention strategies. *Psychology in Schools*, 49(4), 353-367.

Stewart, R., Drescher, C., Maack, D., Ebesutani, C., & Young, J. (2014). The Development and Psychometric Investigation of the Cyberbullying Scale. *Journal of Interpersonal Violence*, 29(12), 2218-2238.

Topçu, Ç. (2008) *The Relationship of Cyberbullying to Empathy, Gender, Traditional Bullying Internet Use and Adult Monitoring* (unpublished Masters Thesis). School of Social Sciences of Middle East Technical University, Ankara.

Vanderbilt, D., & Augustyn, M. (2010). *Pediatrics and Child Heath, Symposium: Special Needs*. Elsevier.

Veiga, F. H. (2007). *Indisciplina e Violência na Escola: Práticas Comunicacionais para Professores e Pais* (3rd edition, revised and expanded). Coimbra: Almedina. URL: http://www.almedina.net/catalog/product_info.php?products_id=4649

Veiga, F. H. (2012). *Transgressão e Autoconceito dos Jovens na Escola* (3rd edition, revised and expanded). Lisboa: Editora Fim de Século. URL: http://www.wook.pt/ficha/transgressao-e-autoconceito-dos-jovens-na-escola/a/id/12640875

Veiga, F. H. (2013). Envolvimento dos alunos na escola: Elaboração de uma nova escala de avaliação. *International Journal of Developmental and Educational Psychology*, 1(1), 441-449. URL: http://hdl.handle.net/10451/10032

Veiga, F. H. (Org.) (2013). *Psicologia da Educação: Teoria, Investigação e Aplicação — Envolvimento dos Alunos na Escola*. Lisboa: Climepsi Editora. URL: http://hdl.handle.net/10451/10133

Wang, J., Iannotti, R. J., & Nansel, T. R. (2009). School bullying among US adolescents: Physical, verbal, relational, and cyber. *Journal of Adolescent Health*, 45, 368 –375.

Wang, J., Nansel, T., & Iannotti, R. (2011). Cyber and traditional bullying: differential association with depression. *Journal of Adolescent Health*, 48(4), 415-7.

Wentzel, K. R., McNamara-Barry, C. M., & Caldwell, K. A. (2004). Friendships in middle school: Influences on motivation and school adjustment. *Journal of Educational Psychology*, 96, 195–203.

Williams, K. R. & Guerra, N. G. (2007). Prevalence and predictors of internet bullying. *Journal of Adolescent Health*, 41, S14 –S21.

Wilson, D. (2004). The interface of school climate and school connectedness and relationships with aggression and victimization. *Journal of School Health*, 74(7), 293-299.

Zhou, Z., Tang, H., Wei, H., Zhang, F., & Morrison, M. (2013). Cyberbullying and its risk factors among Chinese high school students. *School Psychology International*, 34(6), 630-647.

In: Handbook on Bullying
Editor: Phoebe Triggs

ISBN: 978-1-63463-023-8

Chapter 10

MODULATING VARIABLES OF VIOLENT BEHAVIOR OF AGGRESSIVE VICTIMS OF BULLYING

Isabel Cuadrado-Gordillo [*] ***and Inmaculada Fernández-Antelo***
University of Extremadura, Badajoz, Spain

Abstract

Previous research has revealed the existence of a transfer from bullying to cyberbullying of the roles of aggressor and victim. However, the interaction of physical and cyber environments in adolescents not only fosters this transfer or co-occurrence but also accentuates the adoption of more complex roles such as that of aggressive-victim. This profile, simply defined in traditional bullying situations, takes on new dimensions with the many combinations that arise from the co-existence of the phenomena of bullying and cyberbullying.

The aim of the present chapter is to contribute to knowledge of the aggressive-victim profile in the different categories resulting from physical and cyberspace bullying situations. To this end, we considered two questions to answer. The first was to ask what is the actual prevalence of the aggressive-victim in the various forms that this role might be found in the context of bullying and cyberbullying, and then to analyse the behaviours that it involves. The second concerns the variability of these manifestations according to the mode and frequency of the abuses suffered in the two contexts: physical and cyberspace. To answer these questions by presenting the results of research with 1648 Spanish adolescents (aged from 12 to 16 years).

The most relevant contributions of the chapter reside in the identification of variables that modulate the type of abuse that the different categories of aggressive-victims commit against their peers. Gender, mode and frequency of the abuses suffered by aggressive victims are the three variables that influence in the type of violent behavior that they manifest. Also, the results show the victims of aggression in physical or virtual environments tend to use the same context to in turn abuse their peers.

[*] E-mail address: cuadrado@unex.es (Corresponding author)

Introduction

The continuous advances in ICTs, the availability and accessibility of much of the population, especially adolescents, to these resources, as well as the rapid development of a networked society parallel to the presential one, mean that one can expect there to arise quite novel scenarios of action that will impose their own specific rhythms and norms of interaction. To the mechanisms used in physical contexts, one must add those used to relate specifically with others in networked (virtual or cyber) environments. This co-existence of physical and cyberspace scenarios has generated new questions about the processes of victimization and aggression that adolescents experience in them, and about the co-occurrence of the two phenomena (Bonano & Hymel, 2013). Traditional forms of bullying now coexist with modes of aggression that use the resources of the Internet, and that come under the term of "cyberbullying". There is particularly great interest and uncertainty in determining the scope and implications of the co-existence of the two phenomena – bullying and cyberbullying – amongst youngsters.

Bullying and Cyberbullying: Dependent or Independent Constructs?

The scientific community seems to have reached a consensus on the conceptualization of bullying, understanding it to be an aggressive behaviour that is repeated over time and that is manifest in a physically, psychologically, or socially stronger person who intends to hurt another who is considered weaker (Olweus, 1993). From this definition, three identification criteria are extracted that distinguish the aggressive behaviours specific to bullying situations: the intention to cause physical, psychological, or social harm to another person; repetition of the aggressive behaviour; and an imbalance of power in favour of the aggressor. However, recently, with the emergence of new forms of aggression, the analysis of special and exceptional situations, the consideration of new characteristics and contextual and personal situations, among other factors, imperative compliance with these three criteria is being called into question.

Guerin and Hennessey (2002), for instance, do not believe that intentionality can be considered a defining characteristic of bullying, but rather that an aggressive situation that causes harm can be categorized as bullying, regardless of whether or not there is an intent to harm the victim. Moreover, one can ask in what way the intent of the perpetrator is to be determined.

Similar questions arise about the repetition criterion. Olweus (1993) argues that a single aggressive behaviour could be considered a manifestation of bullying in certain circumstances. However, even today, 20 year later, there has been no specification as to what those circumstances might be. For other authors, an isolated aggression can be catalogued as bullying if the negative effects it has on the victim go on for a long time (Arora, 1996).

Finally, reflections on the criterion of a power imbalance have focused on who should confirm the existence of the abuse of power -- whether the aggressor or the victim -- and on whether such an imbalance must really exist or it is enough for it to be perceived. In this latter aspect, while it has been argued that, indeed, the imbalance of power does not have to be real but that it is enough that the victim perceives it as such for it to be considered an episode of bullying (Tattum, 1997), Smith, del Barrio, and Tokunaga (2013) note the difficulty faced by researchers to correctly assess the perception that victims construct around the abuse of power. There are also questions about how to quantify any imbalance of power -- whether it should be in the form of a dichotomous scheme expressed in absolute terms (yes or no) or in relative terms covering a greater range (Cook, Williams, Guerra, Kim, & Sadek, 2010).

The discrepancies found concerning the conceptualization of bullying are multiplied even further when it comes to delimiting and defining the phenomenon of cyberbullying. Indeed, this is a concept that is still under construction and that is arousing increasing interest and is the subject of continuous debate among researchers (Law, Shapka, Domene, & Gagné, 2012). While some authors consider cyberbullying to be an indirect form of bullying which needs technological resources for its execution (Slonje & Smith, 2008; Werner, Bumpus, & Rock, 2010), others argue that bullying and cyberbullying are two quite different concepts that have their own characteristics that define and differentiate them (Casas, Del Rey, & Ortega, 2013). The characteristics or criteria attributed to cyberbullying, and which enable it to be differentiated from other aggressive acts carried out between peers with the use of technological and cyber resources include: intent to harm (Kowalski, Limber, & Agatston, 2008), repetition (Slonje, Smith, & Frisén, 2013), imbalance of power (Vandebosch & Van Cleemput, 2008), anonymity (Mishna, Saini, & Solomon, 2009), and publicity (Patchin & Hinduja, 2010). The application of these criteria would allow cyberbullying to be defined as acts of abuse, intimidation, and unjustified aggression that one or more persons carry out against one or more others with the use of technological and cyber resources to enhance the diffusion of the aggression, the repeated re-living of the harm that was done, and the feeling of helplessness.

However, compliance of the concept with these criteria is also the subject of major controversies. Regarding the criterion of the intention to harm, its detection in the cyber context involves difficulties related to the absence of face-to-face communication, the ignorance in many cases of the identity of the aggressor, and the aggressor's ignorance of the consequences their actions cause to others (Menesini & Nocentini, 2009). In the case of the repetition of aggressive behaviour, Slonje et al. (2013) note that repetition does not necessarily imply a succession of violent acts from the same aggressor. They understand that a single abuse can be experienced by the victim on numerous occasions due to the permanent and public nature of virtual communications.

The imbalance of power criterion applied to the cyberbullying phenomenon takes on new dimensions that are not related to the physical, emotional, or psychological superiority of the aggressor, but to an asymmetry in the mastery of ICT skills (Slonje et al., 2013). Moreover, although the anonymity or ignorance of the identity of the aggressor is considered a specific criterion of cyberbullying (Nocentini et al., 2010), there are studies which show that most of the victims recognize their cyber aggressors, and identify them with peers belonging to their own school, their own neighbourhood, or their own immediate environment (Slonje et al., 2013). Finally, the publicity criterion, understood as the open and uncontrolled dissemination of aggressive behaviour, despite having a more widely extended presence in acts of cyberbullying (Patchin & Hinduja, 2010), should not necessarily be considered an essential characteristic defining and delimiting an act of cyberbullying, although its relevance in reflecting the seriousness of the aggression has to be recognized (Nocentini et al., 2010).

Modes of Bullying and Cyberbullying

The differences that exist in how cyberbullying is conceptualized are equally present in determining the forms in which it manifests itself. This is different from the case of studies of traditional bullying, in which there seems to be a consensus on the classification of its forms (Olweus, 1993), with five major categories (social exclusion, physical abuse, threats, sexual harassment, and verbal aggressions), which are in turn subdivided into direct and indirect manifestations. In studies addressing the phenomenon of cyberbullying, one finds significant variations in the categories described, with three types of classification being applied: the technological resources used in the aggression; the action instigating the aggression; and the direct or indirect nature of the abuse.

Regarding the technological resources used to cyberbully others, the advances in ICTs have contributed to a progressive diversification that requires continual updating. Some researchers bin the various resources used into two major categories: the Internet, and mobile telephony (Brighi, Guarini, & Genta, 2009). The former include such actions as sending and receiving e-mails, on-line chats, sharing audiovisual material, being part of a virtual community, etc. But the arrival and rapid spread of smartphones combines these two types of action into one resource, so that the above classification requires some kind of redrafting to match current reality. Other studies establish a more specific classification, considering from seven (Smith et al., 2008) to nine (Patchin & Hinduja, 2010) types of media, including phone calls, text messages, sending photos and videos, e-mails, on-line chat, instant messaging, and websites such as those of social networks. Subsequently, network games have also been included in the list (Tippett & Kwak, 2012). Kowalski et al. (2012) follow this classification but add some subdivisions of the website block. They do not, however, consider that these constitute modes of cyberbullying, but rather simple communication channels that facilitate the perpetration of bullying.

When the classification criterion applied is the action instigating the abuse, Willard (2007) formulated seven modalities of cyberbullying that were subsequently expanded to eight (Kowalski et al., 2008): electronic insults, harassment, denigration, supplanted identity, blackmailing and deceitful cajoling, exclusion, and happy slapping (physical aggression of a person which is recorded on the mobile phone and the posted on the Web). Taking the essence of this classification criterion as referent, Nocentini et al. (2010) put forward four categories of cyberbullying behaviour: verbal (spoken or written), visual, supplanted identity, and exclusion. They admit, however, that this classification can not be considered universal, and would vary depending on the country to which it is to be applied. While in Spain these four categories are accepted as forms of cyberbullying, in Italy only two of them are recognized (verbal and visual), and in Germany supplanted identity is excluded as being considered a criminal act (Menesini et al., 2012).

The diversity of categories is reduced to a dichotomy when the classification criterion is related to the private or public nature of the bullying. The resulting modes are grouped under the terms of direct or indirect, respectively. The direct cyberbullying mode refers to cyber-attacks perpetrated against the victim without any public disclosure of them. Only the victim receives the messages, telephone calls, audiovisual material, etc. In contrast, indirect cyberbullying involves either the use of others to harass the victim in cyberspace, or disseminating materials, comments, or messages over the network making the attack public to an unknown number of people. In the case of using accomplices, it may be that they are not even aware that they are being used or manipulated to inflict pain on others.

Transfer of Roles between Physical and Cyber Scenarios: New Types of Aggressive-Victims

The co-existence of physical and virtual contexts in today's society of readily available information and knowledge has led to many studies being conducted on adolescents' ability to adapt to these new situations, integrating the two types of scenario and interacting with them practically simultaneously (Laghi, 2013; Mishna et al., 2009; Valkenburg, 2011). In this line, Subrahmanyam, Smahel, and Greenfield (2006) detected a high level of agreement between the behaviour that adolescents manifest in their off-line and on-line lives, with the behaviours presented in cyber environments showing a continuity with or being a mirror of those in physical environments. They therefore understand cyberbullying to be an extension of bullying. Studies examining the co-occurrence of bullying and cyberbullying confirm this relationship between the behaviours that adolescents' manifest in the two types of scenario, and note the transfer of roles from the physical to the virtual context (Kowalski et al., 2012; Pearce, Cross, Monks, Waters, & Falconer, 2011). This implies that adolescents who have been victims or aggressors of bullying will also be so in the cyber environment. Specifically, Juvonen and Gross (2008) find an interval of between 60% and 80% for the coincidence of roles in situations of bullying and cyberbullying in adolescents, and Olweus (2012) finds this figure to reach more than 90%.

In recent years, some studies have shown that many of the cyberbullies previously played the role of aggressor in traditional bullying. Ybarra and Mitchell (2004) found 3% of the victims of bullying to also be victims of cyberbullying. Smith et al. (2008) report a much greater prevalence, with 14.1% having the victim's role in both physical and cyber contexts. Juvonen and Gross (2008) found 85% had experienced at least one episode of bullying and one episode of cyberbullying in the previous 12 months. However, their study reveals neither whether the roles of victim and cybervictim overlapped nor which came first.

Subsequent studies also present conflicting data. For example, Hemphill et al. (2012) found that few youngsters (7.3%) are involved simultaneously in situations of traditional and cyber bullying. This is in line with the finding of Gradinger, Strohmeier and Spiel (2009) that there was co-occurrence of these two roles in 6.2% of adolescents. In contrast, Olweus (2012) reports that very few youngsters have a purely cybervictim or cyberaggressor role. Instead there is a very strong overlap of roles between the physical and the virtual contexts. In particular, 88% who had felt themselves victims of at least one situation of bullying in the past two months had also suffered episodes of cyberbullying. This co-occurrence of roles has served as a guide for some cyberbullying prevention measures by considering the role played previously in bullying situations as a predictive factor.

The relationship between these two phenomena has also been studied in the reverse sense, with some authors noting a low likelihood of first experiencing episodes of cyberbullying and subsequently being involved in bullying situations (Del Rey, Elipe, & Ortega-Ruiz, 2012; Hemphill et al., 2012).

The study of the co-existence of bullying and cyberbullying has not been limited to the analysis of the coincidence of the dual roles, such as would be the case with a traditional bully becoming a cyberbully, or with the victim of traditional bullying becoming the victim of cyberbullying. There is less empirical evidence about the other more complex situations which can arise and which pose new questions. The study of the co-occurrence of bullying and cyberbullying has yielded new data which require variations in the definition of other roles such as that of the aggressive-victim. For instance, Sabella, Patchin, and Hinduja (2013) argue that the victims of bullying can take on a different role in cyberspace and become cyberbullies. Those authors understand that since these children can not retaliate presentially in the classroom, they use technological means by way of compensation. Del Rey et al. (2012) reinforce this association of roles in showing that victimization in physical contexts can help to predict cyber abuse. However, Hemphill et al. (2012) suggest that the role of cyberaggressive-victims can only be understood as something temporary and that cyberaggressive behaviour can not be predicted from the experiences of victimization in traditional bullying. These authors argue rather for the establishment of a new category of cyber aggressive-victim and note that the victims in cyberbullying episodes show, at least in part, a tendency to manifest cyberaggressive behaviour.

This co-existence of roles has also been studied by Li (2007), but in a different direction. That author analyses the likelihood that those playing the different roles in traditional bullying situations can become cybervictims. Among her conclusions is that there is a high probability that both victims and aggressors of bullying will become cybervictims.

In connection with the transfer of the role of the aggressive-victim of bullying to cyber scenarios, Smith et al. (2008) note that there the observations have not been of any stability of roles between the two contexts, but rather of a shift towards the figure of the cyberbully. These discrepancies in the various investigations reported in the literature, and the unexplored relationships concerning the co-existence of the phenomena of bullying and cyberbullying in other roles such as the aggressive-victim, point to the need for new studies aimed at achieving a more comprehensive view of the reality of teenagers' lives that will contribute to enhancing the effectiveness of prevention and intervention measures.

Gender Differences

The adoption of one or another role as a function of gender, and the influence of this variable on the manifestation of different types of aggressive behaviour, have been extensively studied in bullying situations (Smith, Cowie, Olafson, & Liefooghe, 2002). For the case of aggressive-victims of bullying, Cuadrado and Fernández (2009) confirm a trend towards the predominance of the prevalence of boys over girls, although they state that when the frequency of the aggression is 'sometimes', the trend inverts, and more girl aggressive-victims are detected than boys. The opposite is the case when the frequency increases to 'always'. Moreover, those authors note that the modality of bullying suffered changes the ratio between boys and girls who play that role, with there being detected more girls when the aggression is related to indirect verbal abuse (spreading false rumours) and more boys when there is direct physical aggression, threats, verbal abuse, or social isolation.

However, the results of studies on the influence of the gender variable on the roles involved in cyberbullying have often been contradictory. While some studies conclude that there are no significant gender differences in the roles taken (aggressor or victim) in cyberbullying among adolescents (Livingstone, Haddon, Görzig, & Ólafsson, 2011), others do find such gender differences, although they recognize that these differences are complex (Tokunaga, 2010). In this regard, it is noted that girls are more likely to participate as cybervictims and boys as cyberbullies (Salmivalli & Poyhonen, 2012). Li (2006), while finding no gender differences in the prevalence of cybervictims, states that the number of cyberbullies is twice as high in boys than in girls. In contrast, Rivers and Noret (2010) find that, regardless of the role played, girls are more involved than boys in cyberbullying situations. Other work has nuanced these differences by indicating that the greater participation of girls is generally associated with indirect relational cyber-harassment through text messages or phone calls (Smith, 2012). While Monks, Robinson, & Worlidge (2012) find no significant association between gender and cybervictims, they find such an association between gender and cyberbullies, with the prevalence of girls being higher than that of boys in the use of a wide range of modes of cyberbullying.

The disparity and contradictions in the results, as well as the lack of studies which address the differences of gender in roles such as that of aggressive-victim in its various manifestations that originate from the co-occurrence of the phenomena of bullying and cyberbullying, highlight the need to undertake further research to clarify the situation and provide a solid basis for the design of new prevention and intervention programs addressing violence among adolescents.

Analysis of Violent Behavior of Aggressive-Victims: An Empirical Study

Previous research has revealed the existence of a transfer from bullying to cyberbullying of the roles of aggressor and victim. However, the interaction of physical and cyber environments in adolescents not only fosters this transfer or co-occurrence but also accentuates the adoption of more complex roles such as that of aggressive-victim. This profile, simply defined in traditional bullying situations, takes on new dimensions with the many combinations that arise from the co-existence of the phenomena of bullying and cyberbullying. The few studies that have been published on this issue have not been able to provide conclusive data allowing one to gain a clear vision of these new and varied forms of bullying that teenagers face, and thereby better match bullying prevention and intervention measures to today's reality.

In the present chapter, we try to contribute to knowledge of the aggressive-victim profile in the different categories resulting from physical and cyberspace bullying situations. To this end, we considered two questions to answer. The first was to ask what is the actual prevalence of the aggressive-victim in the various forms that this role might be found in the context of bullying and cyberbullying, and then to analyse the behaviours that it involves. The second concerns the variability of these manifestations according to the gender, mode and frequency of the abuses suffered in the two contexts: physical and cyberspace. To answer these questions by presenting the results of research carried out in Extremadura (Spain), involving 1648 adolescents (48.9 % girls; SD = .5) with ages between 12 and 16 years (M = 14.1, SD = 1.3). The instrument used for data acquisition was a revised version of the questionnaire applied by Cuadrado and Fernández (2009) to identify and define the profile of the aggressive-victim of bullying. The modifications made to this questionnaire consisted of the insertion of two new categories that corresponded to the phenomenon of cyberbullying: cybervictimization and cyberbullying itself. Thus, the final version of the questionnaire consisted of four categories: victimization, bullying, cybervictimization, and cyberbullying. The first two (corresponding to traditional bullying) comprise behaviour related to six modes of aggression: exclusion, verbal aggression, direct physical aggression, indirect physical aggression, threats, and sexual harassment. The last two (corresponding to cyberbullying) comprise behaviour related to four modes of cyberaggression (Nocentini et al., 2010): written-verbal aggression, visual aggression, impersonation, and exclusion. The response options to all the items were presented on a 4-point Likert scale indicating the frequency of the attack suffered or perpetrated in the preceding two months: 1 – never; 2 – once or twice; 3 – once a week; and 4 – various times a week.

Continuity vs. Discontinuity between Physical and Cyber Contexts as a Key Element in the Identification and Classification of Aggressive-Victims

Depending on the type of bullying suffered and the means used for its perpetration, the role of victim acquires a twofold dimension: victim (when the abuse corresponds to traditional modes of bullying and is manifested in presential, classroom contexts), and cybervictims (when the abuse is experienced through the Internet, or by electronic or telephony devices). Similarly, the role of aggressor also has this twofold dimensionality: bullies (in traditional bullying) and cyberbullies (when ICTs are used to perpetrate the abuse). The combination of these dimensions yields four profiles of adolescents who are themselves bullied and then turn to bullying others of their peers: aggressive-victims (166 boys, 123 girls), cyberaggressive-victims (93 boys, 59 girls), aggressive-cybervictims (37 boys, 30 girls), and cyberaggressive-cybervictims (30 boys, 23 girls).

The values of Pearson's correlation coefficient and the level of significance found for these four types of aggressive-victim indicate that their presence in the school context is neither random nor extraordinary: aggressive-victims (.485**), cyberaggressive-victims (.502**), aggressive-cybervictims (.280*), and cyberaggressive-cybervictims (.637**).

The composition of these four modes corresponds to pure profiles. However, the results revealed the existence of a group of 89 participants who did not strictly fall in to any single one of these categories. These were aggressive-victims who were being bullied in both the physical and the virtual contexts, and who in turn, rather than adopting a specific pattern of perpetrating aggression, combined different modes of bullying and cyberbullying to hurt their victims. In the present study, we have excluded this group of adolescents from the analysis since they present behavioural patterns shared with members of the four "pure" aggressive-victim types.

Modulating Variables of Violent Behavior of Aggressive Victims

The results reveal the existence of three variables that modulate the type of abuse that the different categories of aggressive-victims commit against their peers: the type of aggression suffered, gender of the victim and the frequency of the abuse suffered. Then we analyses the profile of different categories of aggressive-victims depending of each of these modular variables.

Abuse Suffered as a Determinant of the Type of Aggression Committed

The analysis of the synergy established between the modes of bullying suffered and perpetrated shows significant differences depending on the category of aggressive-victims.

Aggressive-Victims of Traditional Bullying

The results show that, regardless of the type of abuse suffered, the type of aggression they usually perpetrate against their peers is that of a verbal character (insults, name-calling, and spreading false rumours), followed by indirect physical (hiding, breaking, or stealing personal items). They also show that sexual harassment is just a residual behaviour among the totality of manifestations of violence. Even in those cases, however, there was no significant relationship between the types of bullying suffered and perpetrated (Table 1).

Table 1. Correlations between abuses suffered and perpetrated by aggressive-victims

Bullying perpetrated Bullying suffered	Exclusion	Verbal	Indirect physical	Direct physical	Threats	Sexual harassment
Exclusion	.207	.502**	.538**	.291	.163	.027
Verbal	.157	.421*	.476*	.202	-.108	.098
Indirect physical	.235	.605**	.647**	.606**	.664**	.049
Direct physical	.347*	.754**	.275	.868**	.623**	.103
Threats	.170	.597**	.546**	.363*	.121	-.058
Sexual harassment	.239	.591**	.360*	.149	.695**	.156

* p<.05, ** p<.01.

However, there are a certain mimicry of the type of bullying perpetrated with the type of bullying experienced, whether verbal (.421*), indirect physical (.647**), or direct physical (.868**). Also, those who have been victims of direct physical bullying tend to attack their peers with indirect physical bullying (.606**), or threats (.363*). And those who had suffered indirect physical bullying tended to exclude others (.538**) and to attack with insults (.476*), indirect physical bullying (.647**), threats (.546**) y sexual harassment (.360*).

Cyberaggressive-Victims

The cyber abuse that the cyberaggressive-victims mostly commit are verbal (spoken or written) and visual, independently of the aggression suffered (Table 2). The results also show that supplanted identity is a behaviour that is often used by those who suffer intimidating threats from their peers (.367*). Similarly, exclusion from forums and virtual spaces tends to be behaviour adopted by those who have suffered isolation in physical contexts (.618**). Also, they show an inclination to disseminate compromising or ridiculing audiovisual material of other classmates and to send messages via telephone or the Internet (.543**), or to make threatening telephone calls in order to instill fear and cause pain (.369*).

Table 2. Correlations between abuses suffered and perpetrated by cyberaggressive-victims

Cyberbullying perpetrated Bullying suffered	Written-Verbal	Visual	Impersonation	Exclusion
Exclusion	.369*	.543**	.333	.618**
Verbal	.257	.259	-.101	.176
Indirect physical	.565**	.490*	-.111	.385*
Direct physical	.283	.579**	.117	-.078
Threats	.580**	.588**	.367*	.254
Sexual harassment	.462*	.756**	.673**	.302

* p<.05; ** p<.01.

The cyberaggressive-victims who suffer indirect physical bullying tend to commit cyber-attacks via telephone calls, on-line chats, or text messages (.565**). Those who suffer threats and sexual harassment also show a very similar pattern of aggressive behaviour, with cyberbullying transmitted visually or verbally, or supplanting the identity of others to commit misdemeanours or to ridicule the victim in front of the rest of their companions (Table 2).

Aggressive-Cybervictims

The analysis of the bullying behaviour perpetrated by aggressive-cybervictims shows only three adolescents who turn to sexual abuse to hurt their peers, and that this manifestation was unrelated to any particular mode of cyberaggression suffered. Also, regardless of the type of bullying suffered, the adolescents in this group attack their peers with insults, name-calling, or spreading rumours (verbal), hiding, breaking, or stealing their personal items (indirect physical abuse), and hitting, kicking, and shoving (direct physical abuse) (Table 3).

Table 3. Correlations between abuses suffered and perpetrated by aggressive-cybervictims

Bullying perpetrated Cyberbullying suffered	Exclusion	Verbal	Indirect physical	Direct physical	Threats	Sexual harassment
Written-Verbal	.332	.706**	.693**	.635**	.324	.112
Visual	.847**	.799**	.429*	.896**	.771**	.056
Impersonation	.235	.605**	.647**	.606**	.664**	-.091
Exclusion	.301	.671**	.466*	.584**	.417*	-.217

* p<.05; ** p<.01.

Those who had suffered abuse consisting of the dissemination of compromising visual or audiovisual material added to their register of aggression in response the modes of social exclusion (.847**) and threats (.771**). This latter mode was also reported by those victims who had had their on-line identity supplanted (.664**) and by those who had been excluded from social networks, forums, on-line chat rooms, or other types of virtual events (.417*).

Cyberaggressive-Cybervictims

With respect to the cyberaggressive-cybervictim group, there was a certain mimicry between the types of bullying suffered and perpetrated except in the case of those who had suffered supplanted identity who responded with other modes of aggression such as sending messages or making anonymous calls (.805**), exclusion (.587*), or dissemination of visual material that threatens the integrity of their victim (.421*). Regardless of the mode of bullying suffered, this group of teenagers used many modes of bullying to attack their peers. This was especially so of those who had been the object of intimidating or harassing messages or telephone calls (Table 4).

Table 4. Correlations between abuses suffered and perpetrated by cyberaggressive-cybervictims

Cyberbullying perpetrated Cyberbullying suffered	Written-Verbal	Visual	Impersonation	Exclusion
Written-Verbal	.702**	.760**	.829**	.675**
Visual	.361	.711**	.445*	.324
Impersonation	.805**	.421*	-.247	.587*
Exclusion	.403*	.279	.126	.789**

* p<.05; ** p<.01.

Variability of Violent Responses of Aggressive-Victims by Gender

The results indicate that boys and girls have different patterns of behavior and react differently to abuse sufferers. Then, we describe the profile that defines of the different categories of aggressive victims based on their gender.

Aggressive-Victims of Traditional Bullying

The differences between boys and girls in the aggressive behaviours that they manifest depend on the abuse they have suffered. Boys who have been verbally and physically abused show a mimetic behaviour when they attack their peers (Table 5). In girls, however, this mimicry is only found in the case of direct physical abuse (.904**).

Table 5. Correlations between abuses suffered and perpetrated by aggressive-victim by gender

Bullying perpetrated Bullying suffered	Exclusion		Verbal		Indirect physical		Direct physical		Threats		Sexual harassment	
	Boys	Girls	Boys	Girls	Boys	Girls	Boys	Girls	Boys	Girls	Boys	Girls
Exclusion	.288	-.162	.587**	.570**	.329	.815**	.244	.529*	.146	.116	.071	.019
Verbal	-.130	.578**	.495**	-.321	.490*	.446*	.257	-.164	.381	-.212	.103	-.071
Indirect physical	.311	-.160	.490*	.741**	.583**	.497*	.475*	.720**	.454*	.903**	.055	.
Direct physical	.539**	-.468	.674**	.755**	.379*	-.184	.819**	.904**	.411*	.883**	.097	.113
Threats	.285	-.381	.691**	.645**	.593**	.362	.300	.220	.232	-.712**	-.064	.009
Sexual harassment	.157	.111	.436*	.671*	.257	.265	-.217	-.184	.638*	.840**	.184	.145

* p<.05; ** p<.01.

Other gender differences indicate that boys who have been victims of direct physical aggressions diversify their own violent behaviour, resorting to exclusion (.539**), threats (.411**), verbal (.674**), and physical (direct and indirect, .819** and .379*) aggression. In contrast, girls tend to abuse their peers through verbal (.755**), direct physical (.904**), and threat (.883**) aggression. When the aggression suffered corresponds to patterns of social exclusion, boys tend to resort to verbal abuse, whereas girls also incorporate into their behaviour direct and indirect physical abuse. Finally, when the adolescents suffer threats, boys abuse their peers verbally (.691**) and with indirect physical aggression (.593**), and girls use verbal abuse (.645**) but not threats (-.712**).

Cyberaggressive-Victims

There is a stronger correlation between the modes of abuse suffered and perpetrated in the case of girls. Boys do not have a well-defined mode of cyberaggressive behaviour, except for the cases in which they are victims of exclusion or threats (Table 6).

Table 6. Correlations between abuses suffered and perpetrated by cyberaggressive-victims by gender

Cyberbullying perpetrated Bullying suffered	Written-Verbal		Visual		Impersonation		Exclusion	
	Boys	Girls	Boys	Girls	Boys	Girls	Boys	Girls
Exclusion	.451*	.508	.616**	.406	.376	.234	.511*	.739**
Verbal	.197	.649**	.193	.545**	.171	.551**	.093	.315
Indirect physical	.371	.711**	.316	.912**	-.250	.217	.261	.488*
Direct physical	.356	.701*	.132	.870**	-.151	.447	-.145	.006
Threats	.645**	.304	.600**	.845**	.441*	.624*	.197	.327
Sexual harassment	.022	.926**	.423	.686*	.412	.603	.334	.420

* p<.05; ** p<.01.

In the case of the boys, visual aggressions can be predicted from previously experienced aggression in physical contexts, e.g., exclusion (.616**) and threats (.600**). Also, when they receive threats, they tend to manifest verbal (spoken or written) aggressive behaviour (.645**). For the girls there are mimicry of the abuse committed with that suffered in the cases of exclusion (.739**) and verbal abuse (.649**). Experiences of being victims of threats, and direct and indirect physical abuse were predictors of visual aggressive behaviours (.845**, .870**, .912**, respectively).

Aggressive-Cybervictims

The results also showed significant gender differences in the synergistic relationship between the modes of abuse suffered and perpetrated. Overall, boys present more diversified aggressive behaviours than girls, except in the cases in which they are victims of impersonation (Table 7). In those situations, girls resort to threats (.586*) and indirect (.716*) and direct (.560*) physical aggression, while boys are inclined to abuse others mainly through social isolation (.554*).

Table 7. Correlations between abuses suffered and perpetrated by aggressive-cybervictim by gender

Bullying perpetrated Cyberbullying suffered	Exclusion		Verbal		Indirect physical		Direct physical		Threats		Sexual harassment	
	Boys	Girls	Boys	Girls	Boys	Girls	Boys	Girls	Boys	Girls	Boys	Girls
Written-Verbal	.337	.125	.604*	-.558	.759**	-.778	.831**	.857*	.590*	.765	.112	.
Visual	.635**	.807*	.790**	.463	.546*	-.271	.700**	.807*	.342	.919**	.097	-.103
Impersonation	.554*	-.226	.524	-.513	.308	.716*	.502	.560*	.287	.586*	.016	.238
Exclusion	.270	.578	.794**	.625	.574*	.802*	.629*	.590	.735*	.829*	-.119	-.308

* p<.05; ** p<.01.

A result that stands out refers to the verbal abuse perpetrated by aggressive-cybervictims. In the case of boys, this behaviour manifests itself when they are victims of verbal (.604*), visual (.790**), or exclusion (.794**) cyberaggression, whereas in girls this behaviour is uncorrelated with any of the modes of cyber abuse suffered (Table 7).

Prediction of aggressive behaviour is more limited in the case of the girls than in that of the boys. Threats are the commonest type of abuse used when the girls had been victims of cyber-exclusion (.829*) or visual aggression (.919**). For the boys, when the abuse suffered is verbal, they tend to attack others through both direct (.831**) and indirect (.759**) physical aggression. When the aggression suffered is visual, the boys' aggressive behaviour tends to consist of insults and spreading false rumours (categorized together under the verbal mode: .790**) or direct physical abuse (.546*). When the abuse suffered is cyber-exclusion, the boys' manifest aggression in the form of threats (.829*).

Cyberaggressive-Cybervictims

The analysis of gender differences shows that, when this group of adolescents suffers impersonation, while boys present no well-defined pattern of cyberaggression (Table 8), girls are strongly inclined to commit verbal (.954**), visual (.764**), or exclusion (.818**) modes of cyber abuse. Also, when the aggression suffered is related to cyber-exclusion, as well as the mimetic behaviour presented by these cyberaggressive-cybervictims, boys also tend to commit verbal abuse (.540*), whereas girls opt for visual abuse (.677*).

Table 8. Correlations between abuses suffered and perpetrated by cyberaggressive-cybervictims by gender

Cyberbullying perpetrated Cyberbullying suffered	Written-Verbal		Visual		Impersonation		Exclusion	
	Boys	Girls	Boys	Girls	Boys	Girls	Boys	Girls
Written-Verbal	.615*	.867**	.520*	.917**	.850**	.748*	.749**	.517
Visual	.332	.463	.727*	.713*	.526	-.316	.302	.420
Impersonation	.504	.954**	.135	.764**	.071	-.460	.394	.818**
Exclusion	.540*	.298	.155	.677*	.192	-.214	.720**	.819**

* p<.05; ** p<.01.

Synergy between Frequency of the Abuse Suffered and the Aggression Perpetrated

In this chapter we present the results of the correspondence between the frequency of the aggressive-victim's being or having been mistreated and the frequency with which they themself attack their peers in each of the categories of victims aggressive analyzed.

Aggressive-Victims of Traditional Bullying

There are a positive correlation between the frequencies of the abuse suffered and the abuse perpetrated. In this regard, about 60% of the aggressive-victims who had been subjected to social exclusion, threats, or verbal or physical aggression had suffered these episodes of bullying with a frequency of 'once or twice' in the preceding 2 months, and had resorted to attacking their peers with this same frequency. Also, more than 20% of the aggressive-victims who had been subjected to social exclusion, or direct and indirect physical or verbal bullying had suffered these episodes 'various times a week', and had resorted to these or other types of bullying with the same frequency. However, this percentage varied in the case of 'various times a week' aggressive-victims of sexual harassment, being 35.2%. The correlation established between the frequencies of bullying suffered and perpetrated indicates that these sexually harassed aggressive-victims 'various times a week' threaten and attack verbally and indirectly physically others of their peers. Similarly, there were 12% of the aggressive-victims who are threatened 'various times a week' and resorted to verbally and physically abusing others with the same frequency.

Finally, analysis of the 'once a week' frequency of bullying revealed that more than 20% of the aggressive-victims suffering sexual or physical (direct and indirect) abuse or threats resorted to perpetrating bullying with this same frequency. Only 10% of the aggressive-victims who suffered verbal abuse or social exclusion stated that they suffered these abuses 'once a week' and attack others with verbal or indirect physical abuse with the same frequency.

Cyberaggressive-Victims

Regarding the relationship between the frequencies of bullying suffered and perpetrated, over 60% of the cyberaggressive-victims who are subjected to situations of exclusion, threats, and verbal bullying suffered these attacks and attacked others 'once or twice' in the preceding two months. About 50% of the cyberaggressive-victims who suffered direct and indirect physical bullying also experienced these situations 'once or twice' and attacked their peers with the same frequency. Only 38% of the sexually harassed cyberaggressive-victims suffered this mode of bullying 'once or twice', and they tended to respond perpetrating written-verbal, visual, and impersonation attacks with the same frequency.

When the frequency of the bullying increases to 'once a week', the results showed that around 20-29% of the cyberaggressive-victims suffering threats, direct and indirect physical bullying, or sexual harassment with this frequency committed attacks against their peers also 'once a week'. In contrast, only 10% of the cyberaggressive-victims who suffered exclusion reported a frequency of 'once a week' and perpetrated attacks with this same frequency in the modes of verbal or visual bullying and supplanted identity.

Finally, the results showed that over 30% of the cyberaggressive-victims who suffered sexual harassment and direct physical bullying experienced and perpetrated these episodes with a frequency of 'various times a week'. Also, about 22% of the cyberaggressive-victims who suffered exclusion and indirect physical bullying experienced these episodes 'various times a week', and perpetrated attacks in the modes of exclusion, written-verbal, and visual bullying with the same frequency. In the case of cyberaggressive-victims who were subjected to presential threats, 10.6% reported suffering these situations 'various times a week', and tended to supplant the identity of others in cyberspace, disseminate compromising audiovisual material, or send intimidating messages with the same frequency.

Aggressive-Cybervictims

The frequency of the bullying suffered greatly influenced how often this group itself bullied. Of the aggressive-cybervictims who suffered bullying related to the dissemination of upsetting, compromising, or insidious visual material, 69.6% had experienced these attacks 'once or twice' in the preceding two months, 21.7% 'once a week', and 8.7% 'various times a week'. The correlation found between the frequencies of bullying suffered and perpetrated indicates that these aggressive-cybervictims tend to bully in physical contexts with the same frequency as that with which they themselves suffer cyber-attacks.

In the case of the aggressive-cybervictims who had suffered supplanted identity abuse, 45.5% had experienced this mode of bullying and themselves bullied other peers 'once or twice' in the preceding two months, 36.4% 'once a week', and 18.1% 'various times a week'. The results were similar for the frequencies of bullying suffered and perpetrated by aggressive-cybervictims who had been subjected to on-line exclusion.

Of the aggressive-cybervictims who had suffered written-verbal cyberbullying, 22.7% had experienced these episodes 'once or twice' in the preceding two months and had perpetrated verbal and physical bullying with the same frequency. Similarly, 45.5% of these aggressive-cybervictims had experienced these episodes 'once a week', and they reported this same frequency of their own bullying attacks. The remaining 31.8% had experienced these episodes 'various times a week', and themselves subjected their peers to bullying in physical contexts with the same frequency.

Cyberaggressive-Cybervictims

Results show that, of the cyberaggressive-cybervictims who suffered bullying related with the dissemination of written messages or telephone calls, 36.7% stated to have experienced these situations 'once or twice' in the preceding two months, another 36.7% 'once a week', and 26.6% 'various times a week' in the preceding two months. The correlation between the frequencies of suffering and perpetrating abuse showed these cyberaggressive-cybervictims to abuse their peers with the same frequency that they themselves suffered written-verbal cyberbullying.

When the type of bullying suffered corresponded to impersonation or exclusion, the percentage of cyberaggressive-cybervictims suffering and perpetrating attacks 'once or twice' in the preceding two months was close to 45%, 'once a week' was around 35%, and 'various times a week' was around 20%.

In the case of cyberaggressive-cybervictims who were victims of visual material disseminated to violate their dignity, 44% of them had experienced these attacks 'once or twice' in the preceding two months and had bullied others in the same way and with the same frequency. Some 28% of this group had experienced these visual attacks 'once a week', and had attacked others with the same frequency by means of visual and impersonation modes of bullying. The same results were obtained for the 'various times a week" frequency of attack.

Discussion

The co-occurrence of bullying and cyberbullying in today's dual society calls for specific intervention measures designed to forestall the emergence of new problems and to slow the increase and diversification of violent forms of behaviour. The modulating variables provided in this chapter, together with the definition of the profiles of the different categories of aggressive-victims, may contribute to a deeper understanding of the processes of victimization and aggression that adolescents experience in both physical and cyber contexts. Such knowledge is considered to be one of the keys in the search for effective anti-bullying and anti-cyberbullying programs since it will allow specific actions to be designed for the particular characteristics of those involved and their prior experiences of victimization or cybervictimization, instead of relying on the myths that have grown around these phenomena or on certain general notions that might explain them (Sabella et al., 2013).

Modulating variables shown in this chapter are summarized in three: type of abuse suffered, gender of the victim and the frequency of the aggression suffered.

A first variable is the type of abuse suffered. In the four categories of aggressive-victims analysed, a certain mimicry is found between the modes of abuse suffered and perpetrated, especially when the aggression suffered corresponds to indirect or verbal aggression. This mimicry has been described in previous studies (Cuadrado & Fernández, 2009), and some authors explain it on the basis of the perceptions that these adolescents have of the potential that the type of abuse they have suffered has to cause pain to their peers (Hughes & Trafimow, 2012). The experience of the harm that a certain mode of abuse has caused them can give rise to false beliefs about the potential of that behaviour to hurt others, without their realizing that the others may not have the same vulnerabilities, and will not, therefore, necessarily suffer the same consequences. In the cases in which this mimicry does not occur, there is a synergistic relationship between exclusion suffered, in either physical or cyber contexts, and primarily verbal and indirect physical aggressive behaviour perpetrated. Schwarzwald, Koslowsky, & Brody-Shamir (2006) explain the tendency towards these modes of aggression by referring to the imbalance of power criterion. The situations of victimization which they had suffered previously caused these adolescents to experience such a strong sense of inferiority that it is difficult for them to confront their peers directly.

A second variable is the gender variable. The relevance of this variable lies not only in the detection and identification of aggressive-victims and their subsequent classification into the four resulting categories (aggressive-victim of traditional bullying, cyberaggressive-victim, aggressive-cybervictim, and cyberaggressive-cybervictim), but also in its mediating role in determining the abusive behaviour they demonstrate against their peers. With respect to identification and classification, there is a stronger correlation in the case of girls towards performing the roles of cyberaggressive-victim and cyberaggressive-cybervictim. Girls give greater importance than boys to the imbalance of power criterion in situations of bullying and cyberbullying, which may in part explain that their aggressive behaviour is preferentially committed in a cyber environment as a result of the anonymity that affords them when they are hurting their peers (Cuadrado, 2012). In the same sense, the tendency of boys towards direct aggressive behaviours, more characteristic of physical than cyber scenarios (Erdur-Baker, 2010), could explain the strength of their correlations in the aggressive-victim and aggressive-cybervictim categories.

The last variable is correspondence between the frequency of the aggressive-victim's being or having been mistreated and the frequency with which they themself attack their peers. In particular, it is found that those who suffer occasional episodes of bullying and cyberbullying, themselves also bully others sporadically. Likewise, those who are constantly being mistreated themselves adopt continual aggressive behaviours.

References

Arora, C. M. J. (1996). Defining bullying: Towards a clearer general understanding and more effective intervention strategies. *School Psychology International,* 17, 317-329.

Bonano, R. A., & Hymel, S. (2013). Cyber Bullying and Internalizing Difficulties: Above and Beyond the Impact of Traditional Forms of Bullying. *Journal of Youth and Adolescence,* 42, 685-697.

Brighi, A., Guarini, A., & Genta, M. L. (2009). Bullying in the digital age. In M. L. Genta, A. Brighi, & A. Guarini (Eds.), *Bullying and cyberbullying in adolescence* (pp. 14–39). Rome: Carocci.

Casas, J. A., Del Rey, R., & Ortega, R. (2013). Bullying and cyberbullying: Convergent and divergent predictor. *Computers in Human Behavior,* 29(3), 580-587.

Cook, C., Williams, K. R., Guerra, N. G., Kim, T., & Sadek, S. (2010). Predictors of childhood bullying and victimization: A meta-analytic review. *School Psychology Quarterly,* 25, 65-83.

Cuadrado, I. (2012). Género y rol: variables que modifican la percepción del maltrato entre iguales. *Revista Mexicana de Psicología,* 29(2), 136-146.

Cuadrado, I., & Fernández, I. (2009). Are violent behaviours residual actions of aggressive-victims in schools? Predominance and prediction. *Infancia y Aprendizaje,* 32(4), 531-551.

Del Rey, R., Elipe, P., & Ortega-Ruiz, R. (2012). Bullying and cyberbullying: Overlapping and predictive value of the co-occurrence. *Psicothema,* 24(4), 608–613.

Erdur-Baker, O. (2010). Cyberbullying and its correlation to traditional bullying, gender and frequent and risky usage of internet-mediated communication tools. *New Media & Society,* 12(1), 109-125.

Gradinger, P., Strohmeier, D., & Spiel, C. (2009). Traditional bullying and cyberbullying identification of risk groups for adjustment problems. *Zeitschrift für Psychologie/Journal of Psychology,* 217(4), 205–213.

Guerin, S., & Hannessey, E. (2002). Pupils' definitions of bullying. *European Journal of Psychology of Education,* XVII(3), 249-261.

Hemphill, S., Kotevski, A., Tollit, M., Smith, R., Herrenkohl, T., Toumbourou, J., & Catalano, R. F. (2012). Longitudinal predictors of cyber and traditional bullying perpetration in Australian secondary school students. *Journal of Adolescent Health,* 51(1), 59–65.

Hughes, J. S., & Trafimow, D. (2012). Inferences about caracter and motive influence intentionality attributions about side effects. *British Journal of Social Psychology,* 51, 661-673.

Juvoven, J., & Gross, E. F. (2008). Extending the school grounds? - Bullying experiences in cyberspace. *Journal of School Health,* 78(9), 496–505.

Kowalski, R. M., Morgan, C. A., & Limber, S. P. (2012). Traditional bullying as a potential warning sign of cyberbullying. *School Psychology International,* 33(5), 505–519.

Kowalski, R., Limber, S., & Agatston, P. (2008). *Cyber bullying: Bullying in the digital age.* Victoria: Blackwell Publishing.

Law, D., Shapka, J., Domene, J. F., & Gagné, M. H. (2012). Are cyberbullies really bullies? An investigation of reactive and proactive online aggression. *Computers in Human Behavior,* 28(2), 664-672.

Li, Q. (2006). Cyberbullying in schools: A research of gender differences. *School Psychology International,* 27(2), 157–170.

Li, Q. (2007). New bottle but old wine: A research of cyberbullying in schools. *Computers in Human Behavior,* 23(4), 1777–1791.

Livingstone, S., Haddon, L., Görzig, A., & Ólafsson, K. (2011). *Risks and safety on the internet: The perspective of European children. Full findings.* LSE, London: EU Kids Online.

Menesini, E., & Nocentini A. (2009). Cyberbullying definition and measurement: some critical considerations. *Zeitschrift fur Psychologie/Journal of Psychology,* 217, 230–232.

Menesini, E., Nocentini, A., Palladino, B. E., Frisén, A., Berne, S., Ortega-Ruiz, R., et al. (2012). Cyberbullying Definition Among Adolescents: A Comparison Across Six European Countries. *Cyberpsychology, Behavior, and Social Networking,* 15(9), 455-463.

Mishna, F., Saini, M., & Solomon, S. (2009). Ongoing and online: Children and youth's perceptions of cyber bullying. *Children and Youth Services Review,* 31(12), 1222-1228.

Monks, C. P., Robinson, S., & Worlidge, P. (2012). The emergence of cyberbullying: A survey of primary school pupils' perceptions and experiences. *School Psychology International,* 33(5), 477-491.

Nocentini, A. Calmaestra, J., Schultze-Krumbholz, A., Scheithauer, H., Ortega, R., & Menesini, E. (2010). Cyberbullying: labels, behaviours and definition in three European countries. *Australian Journal of Guidance and Counselling,* 20(2), 129–142.

Olweus, D. (1993). *Bullying at school: What we know and what we can do*. Oxford: Blackwells.

Olweus, D. (2012). Cyber bullying: an overrated phenemenon? *European Journal of Developmental Psychology,* 9, 520-538.

Patchin, J. W., & Hinduja, S. (2010). Changes in adolescent online social networking behaviors from 2006 to 2009. *Computers and Human Behavior,* 26, 1818-1821.

Pearce, N., Cross, D., Monks, H., Waters, S., & Falconer, S. (2011). Current evidence of best practice in whole-school bullying intervention and its potential to inform cyberbullying interventions. *Australian Journal of Guidance and Counselling,* 21(1), 1-21.

Rivers, I., & Noret, N. (2010). Findings from a five-year study of text and email bullying. *British Educational Research Journal,* 36(4), 643–671.

Sabella, R. A., Patchin, J. W., & Hinduja, S. (2013). Cyberbullying myths and realities. *Computers in Human Behavior,* 29(6), 2703-2711.

Salmivalli, C., & Pöyhönen, V. (2012). Cyberbullying in Finland. In Q. Li, D. Cross, & P. K. Smith (Eds.), *Cyberbullying in the global playground: Research from international perspectives* (pp. 57-72). West Sussex: Wiley-Blackwell.

Schwarzwald, J., Koslowsky, M., & Brody-Shamir, S. (2006). Factors related to perceived power usage in schools. *British Journal of Educational Psychology,* 76(3), 445-462

Slonje, R. Smith, P. K., & Frisén, A. (2013). The nature of cyberbullying, and strategies for prevention. *Computers in Human Behavior,* 29(1), 26-32.

Slonje, R., & Smith, P. K. (2008). Cyberbullying: another main type of bullying? *Scandinavian Journal of Psychology,* 49(2), 147–154.

Smith, P. K. (2012). Cyberbullying and cyber aggression. In S. R. Jimerson, A. B. Nickerson, M. J. Mayer, & M. J. Furlong (Eds.), *Handbook of school violence and school safety: International research and practice* (2nd ed.) (pp. 93-103). New York, NY: Routledge.

Smith, P. K., Cowie, H., Olafson, R., & Liefooghe, A. (2002). Definitions of bullying: A comparison of terms used, and age and gender differences, in a fourteen-country international comparison. *Child Development,* 73(4), 1119-1133.

Smith, P. K., del Barrio, C., & Tokunaga, R. S. (2013). Definitions of bullying and cyberbullying: How useful are the terms? In S. Bauman, D. Cross, & J. Walker (Eds.), *Principles of cyberbullying research: Definitions, measures and methodology* (pp. 26–45). New York: Routledge/Taylor & Francis.

Smith, P. K., Mahdavi, J., Carvalho, M., Fisher, S., Russell, S., & Tippett, N. (2008). Cyberbullying: Its nature and impact in secondary school pupils. *The Journal of Child Psychology and Psychiatry,* 49, 376–385.

Subrahmanyam, K., Smahel, D., & Greenfield, P. (2006). Connecting developmental constructions to the internet: identity presentation and sexual exploration in online teen chat rooms. *Developmental Psychology,* 42(3), 395-406.

Tattum, D. (1997). A Whole-Response: From Crisis Management to Prevention. *Irish Journal of Psychology,* 18(2), 221-232.

Tippett, N., & Kwak, K. (2012). Cyberbullying in South Korea. In Q. Li, D. Cross, & P. K. Smith (Eds.), *Cyberbullying in the global playground: Research from international perspectives* (pp. 202–219). Chichester, England: Wiley-Blackwell.

Tokunaga, R. S. (2010). Following you home from school: A critical review and synthesis of research on cyberbullying victimization. *Computers in Human Behavior,* 26, 277–287

Vandebosch, H., & Van Cleemput, K. (2008). Defining cyberbullying: A qualitative research into the perceptions of youngsters. *CyberPsychology & Behavior,* 11, 499–503.

Werner, N. E., Bumpus, M. F., & Rock, D. (2010). Involvement in internet aggression during early adolescence. *Journal of Youth and Adolescence,* 39(6), 607–619.

Willard, E. N. (2007). *Cyberbullying and cyberthreats: responding to the challange of online social aggression, threats, and distress.* Illinois: Malloy, Inc.

Ybarra, M. L., & Mitchell, K. J. (2004). Online aggressors/targets, aggressors, and targets: A comparison of associated youth characteristics. *Journal of Child Psychology and Psychiatry,* 45, 1308–1316.

In: Handbook on Bullying
Editor: Phoebe Triggs
ISBN: 978-1-63463-023-8

Chapter 11

SCHOOL AND PEER CONTEXTS OF BULLYING

Michelle F. Wright*
Faculty of Social Studies, Masaryk University, Brno, Czech Republic

Abstract

This chapter synthesized recent research on bullying and victimization in educational settings. The chapter drew on literature related to the impact of the school context, particularly school climate and school characteristics, on youths' involvement in bullying, as victims and perpetrators. This section of the chapter discussed studies on the effect of school size, class size, racial and ethnic minority composition, and school location on school bullying. School climate was also examined, specifically teachers' attitudes and students' perceptions of teachers' attitudes, and how such climates relate to school bullying. At the end of this section, school-based preventive intervention programs are described, highlighting the effective components of these programs. The second part of this chapter focused on peers' roles in school bullying. It also covered bystanders, peer clustering, peer ecology, and peer status, and how these impact school bullying involvement. This section concludes with the effectiveness of peer-based preventive intervention programs. The final section of the chapter provided recommendations for schools, parents, and youths. The research shared in this chapter utilized cross-sectional, longitudinal, qualitative, and quantitative research methodologies. It also incorporated research across multiple disciplines, including psychology, sociology, education, social work, and anthropology. The research featured is also international to provide a broad overview of school bullying across the world.

Bullying is a global problem, reported in multiple countries throughout the world. The literature on this topic has been evolving over the last 25 years. This research has provided an important framework for understanding the nature, extent, causes, and consequences of bullying. Usually perpetrated in group settings, bullying is likely to occur in schools. Much of the attention given to school bullying by the public has been the result of school shootings. Although school shootings are rare, a hypothesis to explain these shootings is that such events are perpetrated by youths in retaliation for experiencing school bullying. The April 20th, 1999 Columbine High School shooting perpetrated by Eric Harris and Dylan Klebold brought

* E-mail address: michelle.wright@mail.muni.cz; Tel: +420 549 49 5259; Address: Faculty of Social Studies, Masaryk University, Brno, the Czech Republic 60200.

greater awareness of school bullying. To understand their motivations for the shooting, interviews were conducted among their group of friends, and findings revealed that this group was frequently bullied, though other schoolmates indicated that Eric and Dylan were also bullies. Research partially supports the victimization and retaliation hypothesis. For instance, Nansel and colleagues (2003) utilized a nationally representative sample of 6th through 10th graders in the United States to understand the relationship between bullying and more serious violence. Their results indicated that more serious behaviors, like fighting or carrying a weapon to school, were strongly related to both bullying perpetration and victimization. Since 1999 other school shootings have occurred, along with many high profile cases of school bullying victims committing suicide, bringing additional awareness to this topic. Some of this awareness has resulted in bullying programs on school campuses and television commercials dedicated to how youths can prevent school bullying.

Although the 1999 Columbine school shooting has brought more awareness to the problem of school bullying, the systematic study of school bullying began in the 1970s. Olweus's 1973 book, *Aggression in the Schools: Bullies and Whipping Boys*, triggered research on school bullying in Scandinavian countries. When the book was translated into English in 1978, research on school bullying in other countries began to burgeon. No more than 10 years after the English-language translation was available, a European conference was held on school bullying and Olweus launched a preventive intervention campaign aimed at preventing bullying in Norway among primary and secondary school youths. Shortly after this time, in the early 1990s, northwestern European countries, like England, Wales, and Scotland, launched preventive intervention programs, modeled after Olweus's program in Norway. Research and awareness at this time was also sparked outside of Europe in Canada, the United States, Australia, and New Zealand. Despite being a bit slower to develop, there is also a focus on school bullying in Asia, and work is currently underway in Africa and South America. Taken together, it appears that global efforts are being undertaken to eliminate school bullying.

Ample research attention has been given to the relationship between school bullying and the individual-level correlates of bullies and victims. However, it is important to also understand the effect of schools and peers on youths' involvement in school bullying. This chapter draws on interdisciplinary research from psychology, social work, education, sociology, and anthropology to describe the role of schools and peers in school bullying. There are two parts of this chapter:

(1) One part focuses on the role of schools. This part begins with an overview of the literature revealing the relationship of school characteristics and school climate to youths' involvement in school bullying. In the next section, school-based preventive intervention programs are described.
(2) The second part of the chapter focuses on peers. The next two sections of the chapter describe how peers' characteristics influence school bullying and the role of the bystander. The next section describes preventive intervention programs. The chapter concludes with recommendations for schools, parents, and youths.

The School Environment

School Characteristics

Although more research attention has been given to individual-level characteristics associated with school bullying, some studies have highlighted the importance of investigating school-level predictors (Gottfredson, 2001). Schools possess various characteristics that might be protective factors or risk factors that are related to youths' bullying involvement as perpetrators and victims. Some characteristics investigated in the literature include grade level differences, size of student enrollment, class size, teacher-student ratio, racial and ethnic composition, and school location. In this literature, researchers are concerned with whether the location and timing of school bullying can predict when youths will be involved in these behaviors.

Grade level and age are influential predictors of school bullying. Hanish and Guerra (2004) found that school bullying increased with age in primary school, but these behaviors declined as youths got older and reached the later years of secondary school (Rigby, 1996). However, when youths continue to be bullies and victims in secondary school, their rates of bullying and victimization are more stable and permanent over time (Hanish & Guerra, 2000; 2004). Therefore, it has been suggested that older bullies target victims more discerningly and repetitively than younger bullies. In addition, the transition from primary school to secondary school might account for such findings as youths begin attending a new school, which is usually larger. While school bullying decreases with age, it is also at its peak at the beginning of the high school years (Parada, 2000; Pellegrini, 2004). Many of these studies do not distinguish between the different types of school bullying, including physical forms, verbal forms, and social forms. Delineating bullying behaviors according to these forms, Griezel and colleagues (2012) found that younger youths were likely to perpetrate physical bullying when compared to older youths. Other research suggests that relational forms of bullying increase with age as physical forms of bullying are replaced by these more subtle and complex forms of school bullying (Losel & Bliesner, 1999). Similarly, using a Turkish sample of 12-17 year olds, Sirvanli-Orzen (2006) found that relational victimization decreased by age in girls and that experiencing teasing decreased by age for boys. Marees and Petermann (2010) also found negative correlations between age and victimization.

Research findings on the association of school size and class size on school bullying are inconsistent. Some studies have not found any relationship between the involvement in bullying as victims or bullies and school size or class size (Khoury-Kassabri, Benbenishty, & Astor, 2005; Mellor, 1999; Olweus, 1991; Wei, Williams, Chen, & Chang, 2010; Whitney & Smith, 1993). On the other hand, other studies have found that school bullying problems were greater at larger schools and in larger classes (Leung & Ferris, 2008; Stephenson & Smith, 1989). In contrast, O'Moore's and colleagues' (1997), Ma's (2002), and Klein's and Cornell's (2010) findings revealed that, although larger schools had more disciplinary problems, rates of school bullying were lower at these schools. Somewhat supporting these results, Wolke and colleagues (2001) found that smaller schools and classes increased school bullying in English schools but not German classes. Blatchford's and colleagues' (2003) results also revealed that smaller classes had higher incidences of school bullying. There have been some explanations (e.g., larger schools have more and better resources) proposed for why school size and class size might contribute to school bullying, although a detailed description of such theories and research is outside the scope of this chapter (see Klein & Cornell, 2010 for review).

Racial and ethnic composition of schools has little effect on school bullying frequencies. In this literature, most studies have found that racial and ethnic make-up of schools has no effect on school bullying (Boulton, 1995; Junger, 1990; Lumeng, Forrest, Appugliese, Kaciroti, Corwyn, & Bradley, 2010; Moran, Smith, Thompson, & Whitney, 1993; Nguy & Hunt, 2004; Siann, Gallaghan, Glissow, & Rawson, 1994; Whitney & Smith, 1993). However, some researchers (Vervoort, Scholte, & Overbeek, 2010; Wolke et al., 2001) have found relationships between these variables, but the associations were weak.

Like research on the effects of racial and ethnic minority composition, class size, and school size on school bullying, conclusions regarding the association between school location and these behaviors are also mixed. In some of these studies, researchers (e.g., Mellor, 1999; Olweus, 1991) have found no relationship between urban location or socioeconomic status and bullying, whereas others (e.g., Stephenson & Smith, 1989; Whitney & Smith, 1993; Wolke et al., 2001) have found greater amounts of bullying in inner-city, and low socioeconomic areas. Researchers have also investigated the location within schools and its effect on school bullying. School bullying occurs more frequently in areas with fewer rules, larger areas, minimal adult supervision, where the ratio of students to teachers is high, and on the playground (Collins, McAleavy, & Adamson, 2004; Craig, Pepler, & Atlas, 2000; Frost, 1991; Mellor, 1990; Smith & Shu, 2000; Whitney & Smith, 1993; Wolke et al., 2001). Youths are also likely to be bullied in the hallway, the bathroom, and the classroom (Bradshaw, Sawyer, & O'Brennan, 2007; Collins et al., 2004; Espelage & Asidao, 2001; Fite, Williford, Cooley, DePaolis, Rubens, S. L., & Vernberg, 2013; Vaillancourt et al., 2010). The school bus is also another location in which youths report being bullied (Allen, Young, Ashbaker, Heaton, & Parkinson, 2003; deLara, 2008; Raskauskas, 2005).

School Climate

Defined as the quality of schools' social environment, school climate, "the inner workings of the school," includes the social organization of the school, the social relationships between teachers and students, and the cultural system or norms and values in the school (Cohen, McCabe, Michell, & Pickeral, 2009; Ma, Stewin, & Mah, 2001). School climate is an important school-related variable to investigate because it relates to general school disorder (Gottfredson, Gottfredson, Payne, & Gottfredsom, 2005). Positive school climate includes schools that are considered safe, consistent with rules and policies, have high parental involvement, supportive student-teacher interactions, are engaging, collaborative, and respectful (Kasen, Berenson, Cohen, & Johnson, 2004; Ma, 2002; National School Climate Council, 2007; Reis, Trockel, & Mulhall, 2007). Such a climate boosts positive peer interactions, reduces peer rejection, and improves psychosocial development (Loukas & Murphy, 2007). When school climate is positive, the school environment also includes less school bullying and victimization (Nansel et al., 2001; Gottfredson et al., 2005; Welsh, 2000). Therefore, positive school climate has a major role in decreasing the likelihood of perpetrating school bullying (Bandyopadhyay, Cornell, & Konold, 2009; Klein, Cornell, & Konold, 2012).

Poor school climate relates to less concern regarding bullying-related attitudes among teachers and students (Whitney & Smith, 1993). When teachers are less tolerant of school bullying, they are more likely to discuss these behaviors with students, easily recognize bullying behaviors, and more often intervene, with each of these relating to less school bullying. Furthermore, teachers, who are better able to label bullying behaviors and articulate problems with bullying found in their school, show greater concern for controlling and preventing school bullying (Stephenson & Smith, 1991). School climate might also affect youths' perceptions of their schools' ability to handle bullying. Such a proposal is corroborated by research evidence indicating that youths who reported lower school climate felt that teachers were uninterested in stopping school bullying (Rigby, 1996; Harris, Petrie, & Willoughby, 2002). Measuring different types of multiple school climate variables, Harel-Fisch and colleagues (2011) found that the student-teacher relationship was one of the strongest predictors of school bullying perpetration. Taken together, the research on school characteristics and school climates has led researchers to develop a number of preventive intervention programs, which have been implemented within the school environment and tested for effectiveness.

School-Based Preventive Intervention Programs

Many school-based preventive intervention programs focus on the entire school. These "whole-school approaches" are designed to reduce or eliminate school bullying (Farrington, 1993). The primary objectives of these programs are to increase the awareness of school bullying from the perspectives of educators, parents, and students by improving school climate. Another aim of these programs is to establish and implement clear anti-bullying policies about the norms and acceptability of school bullying. Ultimately, the whole school is involved in these types of prevention programs. After the program is in place, the whole school aspires to reduce school bullying, improve participation and involvement in the school environment, focus on creating greater collaboration and support, and increase the school communities' bond. Overall, the school becomes more communal, resulting in decreases of all problem behaviors at the school, especially bullying. Research attention has been given to the association between the whole school approach and school bullying, with results indicating that there are reductions in bullying over the years (Arora, 1994; Clarke & Kiselica, 1997; Olweus, 1994). There are many examples of whole-school approaches to preventing bullying, including Bully Proofing Your School and the Bullying Prevention Program, which are described next.

Bully Proofing Your School is a comprehensive program implemented in an effort to improve the school climate of elementary schools through the creation of norms that any type of school bullying is not acceptable (Garrity, Jens, Porter, Sager, & Short-Camilli, 1994; Garrity & Jens, 1997). This program was modeled after Olweus's core intervention program from 1978, and one of its major goals is to create safe and secure school environments. In this program, facilitators provide training and support to school personnel and parents in an effort to ensure that the program is maintained overtime. The whole school works together to develop disciplinary policies concerning school bullying, which emphasize caring and the consequences of bullying behaviors. The nature of bullying and ways to avoid victimization are implemented into classroom curriculum through discussion, role-playing, books, videos, and skits. Once the program is implemented, school personnel, students, and parents develop not only an awareness of bullying but also accountability for creating solutions and confidence in using preventive strategies for reducing school bullying. Garrity and Jens (1997) found that the Bully Proofing Your School program was effective for producing communal school environments that are more caring, and that experience decreases in school bullying and the fear that these behaviors might occur. Working together, these improvements create a more positive school climate. Similarly, Beran and colleagues (2004) found that schools with longer durations of the Bully Proofing Your School program had more positive attitudes toward victims when compared to schools with shorter program durations.

Olweus's (1991; 1994; 1997) Bullying Prevention Program is one of the most researched antibullying programs. This program also aims to improve school climate by emphasizing and creating warm interactions, positive interest, and high levels of involvement from all adults inside and outside of the school. In addition, the Bullying Prevention Program clearly describes unacceptable behaviors, sets firm rules for negative behaviors, and increases monitoring of students in the cafeteria and on the playground. This program aims to increase awareness of school bullying, to provide education about the types of these behaviors, increase adult involvement in the school and outside of the school, develop clear guidelines for rules and consequences for negative behaviors, and to support and protect victims. To implement these objectives, the program includes all adults in order to bring awareness of school bullying and to highlight the importance of their involvement in prevention efforts. Next, school personnel are administered a survey to understand the nature and extent of the problem at a particular school. The whole school is then recruited to oversee the implementation of the program. Classrooms develop antibullying classroom rules and hold frequent meetings on school bullying. The Bullying Prevention Program reduced bullying incidences in 42 Norwegian schools over two years (Olweus, 1994). The program was also effective for reducing vandalism, fighting, stealing, drinking, and truancy. School climate was also improved as well as classroom order, social relationships, and students' attitudes toward school and schoolwork. Recent research (e.g., Jenson, Brisson, Bender, & Williford, 2013; Low, Brown, Smith, & Haggerty, 2014) suggests that the Bullying Prevention Program is still effective for improving school climate and reducing school bullying.

The Effects of Peers

Peers' Characteristics

As an integral part of school climate, youths' attitudes toward school bullying predict the levels of bullying within the school (Boulton, Bucci, & Hawker, 1999). Generally, youths have neutral attitudes toward school bullying or antibullying attitudes, and many have a hard time understanding why children bully others (Boulton & Underwood, 1993; Stevens, Van Oost, & Bourdeaudhuij, 2000). Most youths find school bullying unpleasant, with a smaller percent of students being indifferent to these behaviors (Charach, Pepler, & Ziegler, 1995). Boulton and Flemington (2002) found that more negative attitudes toward school bullying were related to less bullying among English secondary school students. Such relationships were also found among Greek (Boulton, Lanitis, Manoussou, & Lemoni, 1997) and Swedish (Boulton et al., 1999) students. Although many youths hold negative attitudes toward school bullying, their support for the victim decreases with age (Rigby & Slee, 1992).Therefore, it is not surprising that youths rarely intervene when they witness school bullying (Boulton & Underwood, 1993; Charach et al., 1995; Smith & Shu, 2000; Stevens et al., 2000; Whitney & Smith, 1993). Observational studies also support youths' self-reports that they do not intervene in school bullying (Pepler, Craig, & Roberts, 1989). Craig and Pepler (1995) suggest that this lack of intervention might reinforce bullies. Utilizing another observation methodology, Craig and Pepler found support for this hypothesis. Youths reinforced the bullies' behaviors in 81% of bullying episodes. In addition, peers were more respectful and friendly to bullies than to victims, providing support for the peers' alignment with and reinforcement of bullies. Such behaviors might potentially prolong bullying episodes. O'Connell and colleagues (1997) also found that 31% of youths in their sample admitted that if someone they disliked was being bullied they would join in as well. Other characteristics of the peer group affect school bullying and victimization. When peers were isolated and disliked by their peers, they were more likely to perpetrate bullying or be victimized (Fitzpatrick, Dulin, & Piko, 2007; Newman, Holden, & Delville, 2005; Schafer, Korn, Brodbeck, Wolke, & Schultz, 2005; Veenstra, Lindenberg, Oldehinkel, De Winter, Verhulst, & Ormel, 2005; Williams & Guerra, 2007). Affiliation with delinquent peers is also a consistent risk factor associated with bullying behavior (Mouttappa, Valente, Gallaher, Rohrback, & Unger, 2004; Ybarra, Espelage, & Mitchell, 2007).

The function and importance of the peer group changes dramatically in early adolescence (Crockett, Losoff, & Petersen, 1984; Dornbusch, 1989). Therefore, belonging to the peer group becomes a stronger goal for many youths. During this time, peer dominance hierarchies also increase, and many youths become concerned with social status as peer groups become divided and issues of acceptance and popularity become increasingly important (Corsaro & Eder, 1990; Eder, 1985). Eder (1995) found that toughness and aggressiveness were important determinants of status for boys, whereas appearance was central to girls' social status. Therefore, because many adolescents desire to "fit in" with their peers, some researchers (e.g. Pellegrini, Bartini, & Brooks, 1999; Rodkin, Farmer, Pearl, & Van Acker, 2000) have proposed that the pressure to gain peer acceptance and status might increase bullying in order to demonstrate superiority over other students. Support for this proposal was found by Espelage and colleagues (2001). Their findings revealed that adolescents who wanted to "fit in" adopted bullying behaviors, like teasing, in order to gain more power and a higher social standing. Researchers have conceptualized of two related forms of high peer status, perceived popularity (i.e., high peer status characterized by social prestige, social power, and social visibility) and social preference (i.e., peer acceptance or peer liking), which are differentially linked to school bullying (Bukowski, 2011; LaFontana & Cillessen, 2002; Parkhurst & Hopmeyer, 1998). Social preference is related to prosocial behaviors, whereas perceived popularity is associated with physical forms of bullying in childhood and relational forms of bullying in adolescence (Cillessen & Marks, 2011; Cillessen & Mayeux, 2004). There is also research evidence that youths, particularly adolescents, form goals concerning their desired peer statuses (Covington, 2000; Dweck & Leggett, 1988). Due to their desire to be more popular, adolescents develop goal-directed attitudes and behaviors in order to achieve this higher status. Research evidence demonstrates that adolescents with perceived popularity goals were also more likely to perpetrate school bullying, whereas adolescents with social preference goals did not (Li & Wright, 2013; Wright, Li, & Shi, 2014).

Bystanders

Many youths are uninvolved in school bullying, and around 85% witness these behaviors without directly being involved (Charach et al., 1995; Craig & Pepler, 1997; Hawkins, Pepler, & Craig, 2001; O'Connell et al., 1999). Someone who witnesses one child bully another is referred to as a bystander. Like the consequences associated with bullying and victimization, bystanders can also experience anxiety, depression, guilt, and helplessness (Rivers, Poteat, Noret, & Ashurst, 2009). Bystanders serve three different roles during a bullying incident. In the first role, bystanders do not get involved, only watching the bullying incident occur. Although the bystander isn't instigating the situation, the bystander is giving the bully the attention he or she craves. Not intervening, and remaining silent, might give the impression that it is okay for the bully to continue his or her behavior. In addition, bystanders might not intervene because they fear becoming the new target of the bully's attacks. The second role involves the bystander instigating the bully by laughing, cheering, and making comments throughout the bullying situation (Nickerson, Mele, & Princiotta, 2008). They might even join in on the bullying. The last role is when bystanders directly intervene by discouraging the bully, defending the target, or redirecting the situation. Many bystanders get help from their peers by rallying support to stand up against the bully or to tell an adult about the bullying incident. They will also reach out to the victim to let him or her know everything is okay. Between 10% and 20% of youth intervene when they witness school bullying (Salmivalli, Lagerspetz, Bjorkquist, Osterman, & Kaukiainen, 1996). Research evidence also reveals that the presence of bystanders can influence rates of bullying. Felson (1982) found that verbal disputes escalated quicker when bystanders were present, especially bystanders of the same gender. Utilizing an experimental design, Howard, Landau, & Pryor (2014) found that moral disengagement and positive attitudes concerning bullying were greater when youths were exposed to a passive bystander. In the Cyberball task, these youths were also less willing to include the victim in the game. Due to the strong impact of peer support and contributions to school bullying, many peer-based preventive intervention programs have been developed.

Peer-Based Prevention Programs

Lots of attention has been given to the development of peer support interventions which harness youths' potential to tackle school bullying. These programs, like the Students' Welcomers Program and Students' Antibullying Committee, also utilize the whole-school approach to bullying prevention, but focus more attention on the student component. Peer support programs are structured systems used to foster youths' abilities to help reduce school bullying. In primary schools, students who appear lonely are befriended or become buddies with a trained student (Smith & Samarra, 2003). Secondary schools utilize similar schemes but activities typically focus on trained students doing some type of activity with their peers, such as running a lunchtime club, offering support, listening to students' problems, doing group work with a tutor group, or working as mediators to resolve conflicts (Cowie & Wallace, 2000; Fernandez, Villaoslada, & Funes, 2002; Smith & Watson, 2004). Training of the students usually involves learning how to actively listen and respond genuinely and authentically to the needs and feelings of those seeking help. Programs which focus more attention on the peer support system are effective for creating more communal school environments. Findings from one peer support program revealed that school bullying was significantly reduced among 9th graders who had a greater likelihood of being victims (Peterson & Rigby, 1999). Naylor and Cowie (1999) also found that implementing a peer support system had positive impacts on improving the social organization of a school and for reducing school bullying incidences. Follow-up research by Cowie and colleagues (2002) demonstrated that these effects were still observed two years later. Testing the effectiveness of the ChildLine Peer Mentoring System, Smith and Watson (2004) found that youths in this program generally found it helpful in both primary and secondary schools. Other research by Cowie et al. (2008) found that peer support schools helped students feel that their schools were safer, friendlier, and more engaging. These students also worried less about school bullying.

Conclusion & Recommendations

School bullying should not only be a concern for schools, but students, parents, and communities. Research (e.g., Bandyopadhyay et al., 2009; Cohen et al., 2009; Gottfredson et al., 2005; Kasen et al., 2004; Klein et al., 2012; Ma et al., 2001; Reis et al., 2007) demonstrates the effects these individuals have on school climate, which is important for reducing school bullying. Many schools are embracing and implementing the characteristics necessary for positive school climate by increasing their participation and involvement with reducing school bullying as well as establishing supportive and collaborative relationships with students and parents. More research is needed to understand and clarify the relationships of school characteristics and school climate on school bullying. Parents and adults from schools should not only talk about bullying with youths, they should also help youths recognize when situations are actually school bullying versus playful teasing and everyday conflicts (Arora, 1994; Clarke & Kiseica, 1997; Garrity et al., 1994; Olweus, 1997). Each of these considerations is important as they help to empower youths to intervene when they witness school bullying. Such empowerment is helpful for reducing school bullying as peer support systems are accepted as valuable systems for reducing school bullying. Bystanders should be able to recognize when they need to help and how they can help, empathize with the victim, and accept responsibility for intervening (Nickerson et al., 2008; Salmivalli et al., 1996). To support bystanders' abilities to intervene, adults should role-play different bullying situations and provide information about how to help and act. In conclusion, as a community, we must take school bullying seriously and consider it as harmful and unwanted behaviors. Together we must convey that school bullying is wrong and never justified. Everyone should feel safe and never be abused by anyone. Ultimately, "it takes a whole village to raise a child," and such a phrase has application to school bullying as these behaviors are a global concern, warranting everyone to do their part to end them.

Acknowledgment

The author acknowledges the support of the *Employment of Best Young Scientists for International Cooperation Empowerment (CZ.1.07/2.3.00/30.0037), co-financed from European Social Fund and the state budget of the Czech Republic.*

References

Allen, M., Young, E. L., Ashbaker, B. Y., Heaton, E., & Parkinson, M. (2003). Sexual harassment on the school bus: Supporting and preparing bus drivers to respond appropriately. *Journal of School Violence,* 2, 101-108.

Arora, C. M. J. (1994). Is there any point in trying to reduce bullying in secondary schools? *Educational Psychology in Practice,* 10, 155-162.

Bandyopadhyay, S., Cornell, D. G., & Konold, T. R. (2009). Validity of three school climate scales to assess bullying, aggressive attitudes, and help seeking. *School Psychology Review,* 38, 338-355.

Beran, T. N., Tutty, L., & Steinrath, G. (2004). An evaluation of a bullying prevention program for elementary schools. *Canadian Journal of School Psychology,* 19, 99-116.

Blatchford, P., Edmonds, S., & Martin, C. (2003). Class size, pupil attentiveness and peer relations. *British Journal of Educational Psychology,* 73, 15-36.

Boulton, M. J. (1995). Patterns of bully/victim problems in mixed race groups of children. *Social Development,* 4, 277-293.

Boulton, M. J., Bucci, E., & Hawker, D. S. (1999). Swedish and English secondary school pupils' attitudes towards, and conceptions of, bullying: Concurrent links with bully-victim involvement. *Scandinavian Journal of Psychology,* 40, 277-284.

Boulton, M. J., & Underwood, K. (1993). Bully/victim problems among middle school children. *European Education,* 25, 18-38.

Bradshaw, C. P., Sawyer, A. L., & O'Brennan, L. M. (2007). Bullying and peer victimization at school: Perceptual differences between students and school staff. *School Psychology Review,* 36, 361-382.

Bukoski, W. M. (2001). Popularity as a social concept: Meanings and significant. In A. H. N. Cillessen, D. Schwartz, & L. Mayeux (Eds.), *Popularity in the peer system.* New York, NY: Guilford Press.

Charach, A., Pepler, D., & Ziegler, S. (1995). Bullying at school: A Canadian perspective. *Education Canada,* 35, 12-19.

Cillessen, A. H. N., & Marks, P. E. L. (2011). Conceptualizing and measuring popularity. In A. H. N. Cillessen, D. Schwartz, & L. Mayeux (Eds.), *Popularity in the peer system.* New York: Guilford Press.

Cillessen, A. H. N., & Mayeux, L. (2004). From censure to reinforcement: Developmental changes in the association between aggression and social status. Child Development, 75, 147-163.

Clarke, E. A., & Kiselica, M. S. (1997). A systematic counseling approach to the problems of bullying. *Elementary School Guidance, and Counseling,* 31, 310-315.

Cohen, J., McCabe, E. M., Michell, N. M., & Pickeral, T. (2009). School climate: Research, policy, teacher education and practice. *Teachers College Record,* 111, 180-213.

Collins, K., McAleavy, G., & Adamson, G. (2004). Bullying in schools: A Northern Ireland study. *Educational Research,* 46, 55-71.

Corsaro, W. A., & Eder, D. (1990). Children's peer cultures. *Annual Review of Sociology,* 16, 197-220.

Covington, M. V. (2000). Goal theory, motivation, and school achievement: An integrative review. *Annual Review of Psychology,* 51, 171-190.

Cowie, H., Hutson, N., Oztug, O., Myers, C. (2008). The impact of peer support schemes on pupils' perceptions of bullying, aggression and safety at school. *Emotional and Behavioural Difficulties,* 13, 63-71.

Cowie, H., Naylor, P., Talamelli, L., Chauhan, P., & Smith, P. K. (2002). Knowledge, use of an attitudes towards peer support. *Journal of Adolescence,* 25, 453-467.

Cowie, H., & Wallace, P. (2000). *Peer support in action.* London: Sage.

Craig, W., & Pepler, D. (1995). Peer processes in bullying and victimization: An observational study. *Exceptionality Education Canada,* 5, 81-95.

Craig, W. M., Pepler, D., & Atlas, R. (2000). Observations of bullying in the playground and in the classroom. *School Psychology International,* 21, 22-36.

Crockett, L., Losoff, M., & Petersen, A. C. (1984). Perceptions of the peer group and friendship in early adolescence. *Journal of Early adolescence,* 4, 155-181.

deLara, E. W. (2008). Bullying and aggression on the school bus: School bus drivers' observations and suggestions. *Journal of School Violence,* 7, 48-70.

Dornbusch, S. M., (1989). The sociology of adolescence. *Annual Review of Sociology,* 15, 233-259.

Eder, D. (1985). The cycle of popularity. Interpersonal relations among female adolescents. *Sociology of Education,* 58, 154-165.

Eder, D. (1995). *School talk: Gender and adolescence culture.* New Brunswick, NJ: Rutgers University Press.

Espelage, D. L., & Asidao, C. S. (2001). Conversations with middle school students about bullying and victimization: Should we be concerned? *Journal of Emotional Abuse,* 2, 49-62.

Espelage, D. L., Bosworth, K., & Simon, T. S. (2001). Short-term stability and change of bullying in middle school students: An examination of demographic, psychosocial, and environmental correlates. *Violence and Victims,* 16, 411-426.

Farrington, D. P. (1993). Understanding and preventing bullying. In M. Tonry (Ed.), *Crime and justice*, vol. 17. Chicago: The University of Chicago.

Felson, R. B. (1982). Impression management and the escalation of aggression and violence. *Social Psychology Quarterly,* 45, 245-254.

Fernandex, I., Villaoslada, E., & Funes, S. (2002). *Conflicto en else Centro Escolar.* Madrid: Catarata.

Fite, P. J., Williford, A., Cooley, J. L., DePaolis, K., Rubens, S. L., & Vernberg, E. M. (2013). Patterns of victimization locations in elementary school children: Effects of grade level and gender. *Child & Youth Care Forum,* 42, 585-597.

Fitzpatrick, K. M., Dulin, A. J., & Piko, B. F. (2007). Not just pushing and shoving: School bullying among African American adolescents. *Journal of School Health,* 77, 16-22.

Frost, L. (1991). A primary school approach: What can be done about the bully? In M. Elliot (Ed.), *Bullying: A practical guide to coping for schools.* Harlow, UK: Longman.

Garrity, C., & Jens, K. (1997). Bully proofing your school: Creating a positive climate. *Intervention in School and Clinic,* 32, 235-244.

Garrity, C., Jens, K., Porter, W., Sager, N., & Short-Camilli, C. (1994). *Bully proofing your school.* Longmont, CO: Sopris West.

Gottfredson, D. C. (2001). *Delinquency and schools.* New York: Cambridge University.

Griezel, L., Finger, L. R., Bodkin-Adrews, G. H., Craven, R. G., & Yeung, A. S. (2012). Uncovering the structure of and gender and developmental differences in cyber bullying. The *Journal of Educational Research,* 105, 442-455.

Gottfredson, G. D., Gottfredson, D. C., Payne, A. A., & Gottfredson, N. C. (2005). School climate predictors of school disorder: Results from a national study of delinquency prevention in schools. *Journal of Research in Crime and Delinquency,* 42, 412-444.

Hanish, L. D., & Guerra, N. G. (2000). Children who get victimized at school: What is known? What can be done? *Professional School Counseling,* 4, 113-119.

Hanish, L.D., & Guerra, N. G. (2004). Aggressive victims, passive victims, and bullies: Developmental continuity or developmental change? *Merrill-Palmer Quarterly,* 50, 17-38.

Harel-Fisch, Y., Walsh, S. D., Fogel-Grinvald, H., Amitai, G., Pickett, W., Molcho, M., ... Craig, W. (2011). Negative school perceptions and involvement in school bullying: A universal relationship across 40 countries. *Journal of Adolescence,* 34, 639-652.

Hawkins, D., Pepler, D. J., & Craig, W. M. (2001). Naturalistic observations of peer interventions in bullying. *Social Development,* 10, 512-527.

Harris, S., Petrie, G., & Willoughby, W. (2002). Bullying among 9th graders: An exploratory study. *NASSP Bulletin,* 86, 3-14.

Howard, A. M., Landau, S., & Pryor, J. B. (2014). Peer bystanders to bullying: Who wants to play with the victim? *Journal of Abnormal Child Psychology,* 42, 265-276.

Jenson, J. M., Brisson, D., Bender, K. A., & Williford, A. P. (2013). Effects of the Youth Matters prevention program on patterns of bullying and victimization in elementary and middle school. *Social Work Research,* 37, 361-372.

Junger, M. (1990). Intergroup bullying and racial harassment in t he Netherlands. *Sociology and Social Research,* 74, 65-72.

Kasen, S., Berenson, K., Cohen, P., & Johnson, J. G. (2004). The effects of school climate on changes in aggressive and other behaviors related to bullying. In D. L. Espelage & S. M. Swearer (Eds.), *Bullying in American schools: A social-ecological perspective on prevention and intervention* (pp. 187-210). Mahwah, NJ: Erlbaum.

Klein, J., Cornell, D., & Konold, T. (2012). Relationships between bullying, school climate, and student risk behaviors. *School Psychology Quarterly,* 27, 154-169.

Khoury-Kassabri, M., Benbenishty, R., & Astor, R. (2005). The effects of school climate, socioeconomics, and cultural factors on student victimization in Israel. *Social Work Research,* 29, 165-180.

LaFontana, K. M., & Cillessen, A. H. N. (2002). Children's perceptions of popular and unpopular peers: A multimethod assessment. *Developmental Psychology,* 38, 635-647.

Leung, A., & Ferris, J. S. (2008). School size and youth violence. *Journal of Economic Behavior & Organization,* 65, 318-333.

Li, Y., & Wright, M. F. (2013). Adolescents' social status goals: Relationships to social status insecurity, aggression, and prosocial behavior. *Journal of Youth & Adolescence,* 43, 146-160.

Low, S. T., Brown, E. C., Smith, B. H., & Haggerty, K. P. (2014). Engagement matters: Lessons from assessing classroom implementation of Steps to Respect: A Bullying Prevention Program over a one-year period. *Prevention Science,* 15, 165-176.

Lumeng, J. C., Forrest, P., Appugleiese, D. P., Kaciroti, N., Corwyn, R. F., & Bradley, R. H. (2010). Weight status as a predictor of being bullied in third through sixth grades. *Pediatrics,* 125, 1301-1307.

Ma, X. (2002). Bullying in middle school: Individual and school characteristics of victims and offenders. *School Effectiveness and School Improvement,* 13, 63-89.

Ma, X., Stewin, L. L., & Mah, D. L. (2001). Bullying in school: Nature, effects, and remedies. *Research Papers in Education,* 16, 247-270.

Marees, N., & Petermann, F. (2010). Bullying in German primary schools: Gender differences, age trends, and influence of parents' migration and educational backgrounds. *School Psychology International,* 31, 178-198.

Moran, S., Smith, P., Thompson, D., & Whitney, I. (1993). Ethnic differences in experiences in bullying: Asian and White children. *British Journal of Educational Psychology,* 63, 431-440.

Mouttapa, M., Valente, T., Gallaher, P., Rohrbach, L. A., & Unger, J. B. (2004). Social network predictors of bullying and victimization, *Adolescence,* 39, 315-335.

Nansel, T. R., Overpeck, M., Pilla, R. S., Ruan, W. J., Simmons-Morton, B., & Scheidt, P. (2001). Bullying behaviors among US youth: Prevalence and associations with psychosocial adjustment. *Journal of the American Medical Association,* 285, 2094-2100.

National School Climate Council. (2007). The school climate challenge: Narrowing the gap between school climate research and school climate policy, practice guidelines and teacher education policy. Retrieved from: http://www.schoolclimate.org/ about/council.php

Naylor, P., & Cowie, H. (1999). The effectiveness of peer support systems in challenging school bullying: The perspectives and experiences of teachers and pupils. *Journal of Adolescence,* 22, 467-479.

Newman, M. L., Holden, G. W., & Delville, Y. (2005). Isolation and the stress of being bullied. *Journal of Adolescence,* 28, 343-357.

Nguy, L., & Hunt, C. J. (2004). Ethnicity and bullying: A study of Australian high-school students. *Educational and Child Psychology, 21,* 78-94.

Nickerson, A. B., Mele, D., & Princiotta, D. (2008). Attachment and empathy as predictors of roles as defenders or outsiders in bullying interactions. *Journal of School Psychology,* 46, 687-703.

O'Connell, P., Sedigdeilami, F., Pepler, D., Craigt, W., Connolly, J., Atlas, R., Smith, C., & Charach, A. (1997). Prevalence of bullying and victimization among Canadian elementary and middle school children. Poster session presented at the meeting of the Society for Research in Child Devleopment, Washington, D.C.

Olweus, D. (1978). Aggr*ession in the schools: Bullies and whipping boys.* Washington, DC: Wiley.

Olweus, D. (1991). Bully/victim problems among schoolchildren: Basic facts and effects of a school-based intervention program. In D. Pepler & K. Rubin (Eds.), *The development and treatment of childhood aggression*. Hillsdale, NJ: Erlbaum.

Olweus, D. (1994). Bullying at school: Long-term outcomes for the victims and an effective school-based intervention program. In L. R. Huesmann (Ed.), *Aggressive behavior: Current perspectives.* New York: Wiley.

O'Moore, A. M., Kirkham, C., & Smith, M. (1997). Bullying behaviour in Irish schools: A nationwide study. *There Irish Journal of Psychology,* 18, 141-169.

Parada, R. H. (2000). Adolescent peer relations instrument: A theoretical and empirical basis for the measurement of participant roles in bullying and victimisation of adolescence: An interim test manual and a research monogram. Bankstown, Australia: Publication Unit, Self-Concept Enhancement and Learning Facilitation Research Centre, University of Western Sydney.

Pellegrini, A. D. (2004). Bullying during the middle school years. In C. S. Sanders & G. D. Phye (Eds.), *Bullying: Implications for the classroom* (pp. 177-202). Orlando, FL: Academic Press.

Pellegrini, A. D., Bartini, M., & Brooks, F. (1999). School bullies, victims, and aggressive victims. Factors relating to group affiliation and victimization in early adolescence. *Journal of Educational Psychology,* 91, 216-224.

Pepler, D. I., Craig, W. M., Ziegler, S., & Charach, A. (1994). An evaluation of an antibullying intervention in Toronto schools. *Canadian Journal of Community Mental Health,* 13, 95-110.

Peterson, L., & Rigby, K. (1999). Countering bullying at an Australian secondary school with students as helpers. *Journal of Adolescence,* 22, 481-492.

Raskauskas, J. (2005). Bullying on the school bus: A video analysis. *Journal of School Violence,* 4, 93-107.

Reis, J., Trockel, M., & Mulhall, P. (2007). Individual and school predictors of middle school aggression. *Youth & Society,* 38, 322-347.

Rigby, K. (1996). Bullying in schools – and what to do about it. Victoria, Australia: ACER Press.

Rivers, I., Poteat, V. P., Noret, N., & Ashurst, N. (2009). Observing bullying at school: The mental health implications of witness status. *School Psychology Quarterly,* 24, 211-222.

Rodkin, P. C., Farmer, T. W., Pearl, R., & Van Acker, R. (2000). Heterogeneity of popular boys: Antisocial and prosocial configurations. *Developmental Psychology,* 36, 14-24.

Schafer, M., Korn, S., Brodbeck, F. C., Wolke, D., & Schultz, H. (2005). Bullying roles in changing contexts. The stability of victim and bull roles from primary to secondary school. *International Journal of Behavioral Development,* 29, 323-335.

Siann, G., Gallaghan, M., Glissow, R. L., & Rawson, L. (1994). Who gets bullied? The effect of school, gender, and ethnic group. *Educational Research,* 36, 123-134.

Sirvanli-Orzen, D. (2006). The relationship between the adolescents' exposure to peer victimization and their age, parental style and self-image. *Turkish Journal of Psychology,* 58, 77-98.

Smith, P. K., & Samara, M. (2003). Evaluation of the DfES Anti-Bullying Pack. Research Brief No. 7438, 512-514.

Smith, P. K., & Watson, D. (2004). Evaluation of the CHIPS (ChildLine in Partnership with Schools) programme. Research Report RR570. London: DfES.

Smith, P. K., & Shu, S. (2000). What good schools can do about bullying: Findings from a survey in English schools after a decade of research and action. *Childhood,* 7, 193-212.

Stevens, V., Van Oost, P., & Bourdeaudhuij, I. (2000). The effects of an anti-bullying intervention programme on peers' attitudes and behaviors. *Journal of Adolescence,* 23, 21-34.

Vaillancourt, T., Brittain, H., Bennett, L., Arnocky, S., McDougall, P., Hymel, S., Short, K., Sunderani, S., Scott, C., Mackenzie, M., & Cunningham, L. (2010). Places to avoid:

Population-based study of student reports of unsafe and high bullying areas at school. *Canadian Journal of School Psychology,* 25, 40-54.

Vervoort, M. H.M., Scholte, R. H. J., & Overbeek, G. (2010). Bullying and victimization among adolescents: The role of ethnicity and ethnic composition of school class. *Journal of Youth & Adolescence, 39,* 1-11.

Stephenson, P., & Smith, D. (1989). Bullying in the junior school. In D. Tattum & D. Lane (Eds.), *Bullying in schools.* Stoke-on-Strent, UK: Trentham.

Veenstra, R., Lindenberg, S., Oldehinkel, A. J., De Winter, A. F., Verhulst, F. C., & Ormel, J. (2005). Bullying and victimization in elementary schools: A comparison of bullies, victims, bully/victims, and uninvolved preadolescents. *Developmental Psychology,* 41, 672-682.

Wei, H., Williams, J. H., Chen, J., & Chang, H. (2010). The effects of individual characteristics, teacher practice, and school organizational factors on students' bullying: A multilevel analysis of public middle schools in Taiwan. *Children and Youth Services Review,* 32, 137-143.

Whitney, I., & Smith, P. K. (1993). A survey of the nature and extent of bullying in junior/middle and secondary schools. *Education Research,* 35, 3-25.

Williams, K. R., & Guerra, N. G. (2007). Prevalence and predictors of internet bullying. *Journal of Adolescent Health,* 41, S-14-S21.

Wolke, D., Woods, S., Stanford, K., & Schultz, H. (2001). Bullying and victimization of primary school children in England and Germany: Prevalence and school factors. *British Journal of Psychology,* 92, 673-696.

Wright, M. F., Li, Y., & Shi, J. (2014). Chinese adolescents' social status goals: Associations with behaviors and attributions for relational aggression. *Youth & Society,* 46, 566-588.

Ybarra, M. L., Espelage, D. L., & Mitchell, K. J. (2007). The co-occurrence of internet harassment and unwanted sexual solicitation victimization and perpetration: Associations with psychosocial indicators. *Journal of Adolescent Health,* 41, S31-S41.

In: Handbook on Bullying
Editor: Phoebe Triggs

ISBN: 978-1-63463-023-8

Chapter 12

FROM BULLYING TO PANDEMY OF TERRORISM: SYNERGETIC BIO-PSYCHO-SOCIO-SPIRITUAL METHODOLOGY OF MENTAL HEALTH PROTECTION

Pavel Ivanovich Sidorov*

Mental Medicine Institute, Northern State Medical University, Arkhangelsk, Russia

Abstract

The chapter examines special developmental features of the terrorist demoralization syndrome; it discerns terrorism in the classification of destructive social epidemics highlights mechanisms of manipulations with human consciousness in extremist organizations and formulates the characteristics of mental paradigm of national security. It also offers a synergetic bio-psycho-socio-spiritual system for preventive and correctional activities based on the mental medicine methodology.

Keywords: Mental terrorism, syndrome of terrorist demoralization, forms of terrorism, mechanisms of manipulations, spiritual immunity, synergy of defense, mental paradigm of national security

The pandemic of terrorism undermines civilizational fundamentals of the contemporary world. Fear and anxiety, that deform social consciousness, are becoming an everyday reality. Many countries have developed and implemented special technologies to provide special psychological and psychiatric help in case of emergency, disaster, terror, or violence. However, the questions of efficient resource provisions for the early and systematic prevention of destructive social epidemics still remain unsolved.

The chapter aims to present a conceptual and methodological explanation of terrorism and its forms, demonstrate its place in the classification of destructive social epidemics, single out mechanisms of manipulation with human conciseness in extremist organizations, show

* E-mail address: pavelsidorov13@gmail.com; . Address: 163001, Arkhangelsk, Troitsky pr., 51 (Academic at Russian Academy of Sciences, head of Mental medicine institute at Northern State Medical University)

characteristics of the mental paradigm of national security, establish the synergy of effective defense in frames of the mental medicine methods.

1. Synergetic Bio-Psycho-Socio-Spiritual Methodology

1.1. Mental Health Synergetics

Mentality is a worldview that is formed throughout upbringing, education, and life experience in a specific cultural environment. Mentality (from Late Latin *mentalis* "of the mind," from Latin *mens* "mind,") describes notions (like *mind* in English) that have no exact equivalent in Russian. Further research will help to outline scientifically all the main definitions in mental ecology and mental medicine.

"The world health report 2001 - Mental Health: New Understanding, New Hope" (2001) by WHO reveals the decision to support scientific research that would aid a better understanding of the nature of mental health disorders and help to develop effective prevention methods.

Mental health is a state of well-being in which every individual realizes his or her own potential, can cope with the normal stresses of life, can work productively and fruitfully, and is able to make a contribution to her or his community (WHO, 2001). Most importantly, apart from the classic bio-psycho-social trinity this definition includes moral elements of self-fulfilment, resistance to stress, and productive work that are impossible without business communication ethics. The civil and political element in the appeal to "to make a contribution to her or his community" looks even more pretentious.

Mental ecology is a section of human ecology that studies connections in the "environment - society - individual" system alongside factors and resources of mental health.

Using the "Evaluation of health ecology" method we [33] quantified the effects of lifestyle (25%), environment (21%), mentality (20%), healthcare (18%), and genetics (16%) on health. Unlike the four groups of factors determined by the WHO (1992), mentality is categorised separately in our research as it is to a significant extent a behavioural expression of lifestyle (table 1).

The idiosyncrasies of the mental ecology mission lie in its interactive support for civilizational trends (figure 1). Mental health integrates the potential of moral, spiritual, psychiatric, somatic, and social health and is a constructively creative resource of the public consciousness and public health of a nation. The mental ecology mission substantially compliments the basic definition of psychotherapy as an interactive process of psychologically assembling the past, present, and future of a person, a family, a group, and society as a whole in order to achieve a set target [21]. Within synergetic methodology, a concise definition of psychotherapy as a science about adaptive management of mentality of individual and collective consciousness may be presented. Mentality is the matrix of psychotherapeutic influence in the consciousness of the client and patient, predetermining his or her lifestyle and trajectory of his or her destiny.

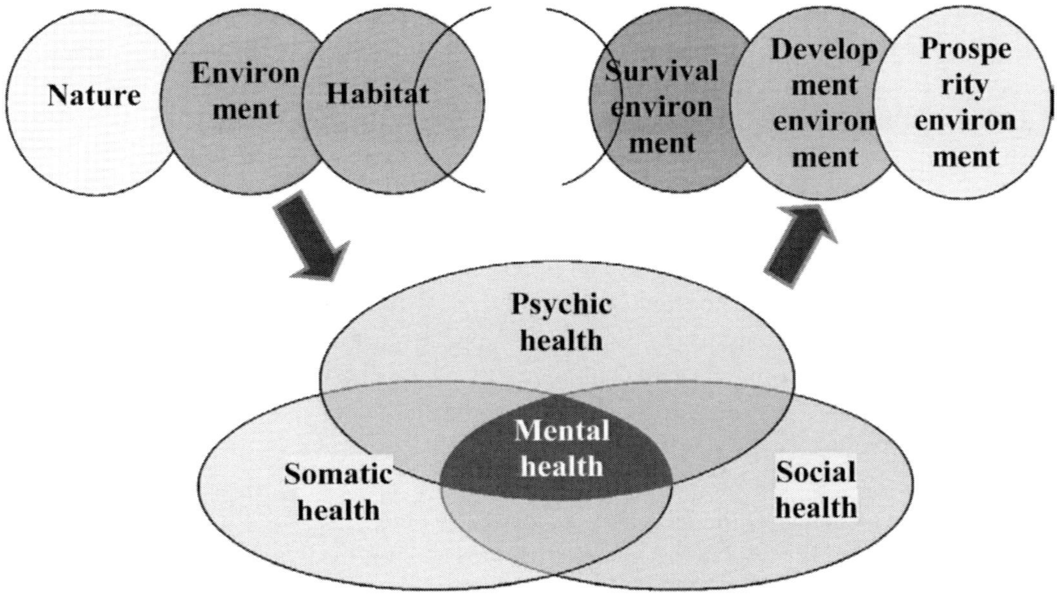

Figure 1. Mission of mental ecology in interactive provision of civilizational trends.

Table 1. Health components (%)

Author, year	FACTORS				
	Lifestyle	Environment	Genetics	Healthcare	Mentality
Lisitsyn Yu.P. (1987)	49–53	17–20	18–20	8–10	-
Alexeev S.V. (1991)	50–52	10–20	18–25	10–20	-
WHO (1992)	50	20	20	10	-
Petlenko V.P. (1996)	40–50	25	20	11	-
Rubtsov A.V. (2005)	50-55	20-25	15-20	10-15	-
Koreneva M.R. (2005)	49-53	17-20	18-22	8-10	-
Sidorov P.I., Novikova I.A. (2008)	25	21	16	18	20

Devaluation of the moral-spiritual paradigm of development became a deep-seated cause of the global crisis and many of the problems in Russian society. Russia has essentially lost its official ideology and its society has lost its spiritual and moral ideals. “More modern” ideals replaced traditional upbringing and education:

- *christian virtues* – general humanitarian values;
- *teaching respect of the elderly and joint labour* – development of a creative egoistic personality;
- *virtue, abstinence, self-restriction* – total permissiveness and satisfaction of personal needs;
- *love and self-sacrifice* – pragmatic self-affirmation psychology;
- *interest in the culture of the motherland* – exceptional interest in foreign languages and foreign traditions.

All of this lead to growing dehumanisation and loss of ethics in the public consciousness, exposing the ineffectiveness of the pseudo-humanistic utopia connected to the idealisation of material values and self-regulating market economy. It is the main argument behind the "Concept for moral-spiritual development and character education of a Russian citizen" published by the Russian Federation Ministry of Education and Science in 2009.

Moral-spiritual education lies in forming:

- *moral feelings* - conscience, duty, faith, responsibility;
- a *moral portrait* - patience, mercy, humility;
- a *moral position* - ability to distinguish good from evil, to express selfless love, readiness to overcome life's difficulties;
- *moral behaviour* - readiness to serve the people and the motherland, obedience, good will.

A polymodal mentality is the target for (or matrix of) moral-spiritual training, education, and psychological and psychotherapeutic influence in the individual and public consciousness. To measure, figuratively speaking, the strength of personality and its potential we [33] developed and patented the "Mental ecology of a personality system" that provides for evaluation of the psycho-, socio-, somato-, and animogenesis of an individual or a group in a screening regime.

Anima, animus (Latin *anima* -soul, *animus* -spirit) are terms that in Ancient Greek culture express the phenomenon of the psyche, act as stages of the evolution of spiritual understanding: anima (soul) is inseparable from its bodily carrier, while animus (spirit) has an autonomous status.

Animogenesis is the term that integrates understanding of soul and spirit and signifies the central quarter in the three-dimensional bio-psycho-social model of mental health's ontogenetic development, filling it with bio-psycho-social-spiritual contents [32]. The major difference between animogenesis and psychogenesis is in unlocking of the content of polymodal mentality.

Synergetics is the new methodological instrument for examining the mental ecology of a person; it is an interdisciplinary science that studies formation and self-organisation. Hermann Haken coined the term "synergetics". It studies systems that consist of multiple parts, components or subsystems that interact in a complex manner.

The main principles of synergetics are its non-linearity, instability, openness, dynamic hierarchy and its observability. Synergetic methodology is based on an integrative approach to studying thermodynamically open dissipative structures far from equilibrium [2].

Dissipative structures are discretionary self-organising systems that dissipate energy, distinguished by their spiral formation in multidimensional space, its trajectory and a stable amplitude have a multifactorial quality and are predetermined by a combination of forces from varying directions and by factors relating to differing bifurcation points.

Dissipative structures form and exist in society and in the biosphere and are intermittently going through self-organisation, following their internal formation logic, they become more complex and degrade throughout their existence.

A strange attractor is an important concept in synergetics – an object in the phase space that almost all the trajectories aim for and upon which they are unstable. An *attractor* is a *fractal* (from

Latin *fractus* - fragmented) characterized by its fractional size and is a region in which trajectories disperse in some directions and attract in others.

A fractal is a self-similar figure made up of parts that are each similar to the whole and has nontrivial structure in all scales.

Fractal dynamics is the transformation of a quantum system from one condition to another via bifurcation, bypassing which, a dissipative structure starts aiming for a new attractor and a new structure, which in clinical psychiatry equates to the development of psychiatric disorders or recovery - depending on which of the attractors (leading to progression or remission of a mental illness) turns out to be more relevant.

Synergetics views the human body as a complex open system with non-linear processes. Its behaviour cannot be called determinate. The change of the system does not follow linear laws because of presence of internal fluctuations [28, 34], that change trajectory of development

When accumulating a large number of fluctuations, exaltation of the system towards internal or external influences grows to such an extent that those variables whose changes have not caused any significant influence on the system, start to affect change. Such points that the system passes (bifurcation points) make it possible to use the mechanism of a local increase in small fluctuations, which will enable change to the behaviour and the trajectory of the system's development in the right direction (figure 2).

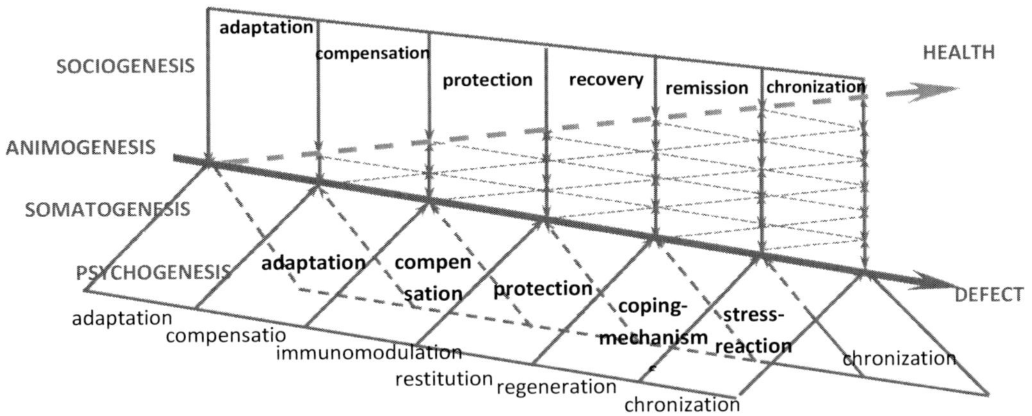

Figure 2. Fractal trajectory of conditions' (illnesses) development and defence mechanisms.

The term developmental "trajectory" of a condition or illness is often used in modern foreign and Russian literature [3]. However, its use by Russian Academy of Medical Sciences member A.B. Smulevich [38] regarding "problems of personality disorder trajectory in the field of minor psychiatry" met reprimands from reviewers because it was deemed a "beautiful" term. From our point of view, the term "trajectory" is completely justified and is borrowed from the synergetic methodology for describing development in multidimensional (at least three-dimensional) space, when traditional "flat dynamics" become incapable of describing the multi-modal relationships and scenarios with multiple options of development within modern evidence-based medicine.

The synergetic concept of ontogenesis that we developed presupposes interplay of equal factors:

- *somatic health* that forms as a result of biogenesis;
- *psychic health* that appears during psychogenesis;
- *social health* that develops in the sociogenesis process.
- *moral-spiritual health* that forms during animogenesis.

The sum of the separate parts of these factors for a certain population provides an estimate of the level of its somatic, mental, social, and moral-spiritual functioning, and uniting these results helps to conduct systematic monitoring of the level of public health and public consciousness of the population under study.

Psycho-somato-social and moral-spiritual health of an individual (and public health) are impossible to imagine in isolation – independent to the effect of external factors, which in turn transform as a result of various influences on them from individuals, influencing the environment. These relationships result in a formation of a complex, nonlinear, unstable, open, self-organising system of a dissipative type that conducts energy exchange and is defined in its development by influence of multidirectional forces.

The synergetic approach can be visualised (figure 3) through the main plains (vectors) of the bio-psycho-social model of ontogenesis: somato-, psycho-, and sociogenesis. Somatogenesis presupposes the development of systems and functions of the organism; psychogenesis is the development of psychic functions; sociogenesis is the development of social roles and relationships. The central part of the intersection and integration of the three vectors forms the fourth and the main aspect – the moral-spiritual aspect of animogenesis, the core of which is a polymodal mentality. The model promotes an interdisciplinary and integrated approach to complex and complicated cause and effect relationships. The synergetic model is multidimensional and nonlinear, unstable and open. The developmental trajectories of the condition or the illness are set and corrected at bifurcation points, achieving spiral-like qualities and multiple possibilities. Nonlinear discretion and fractality replace linear and nososentric dynamics.

The main planes of ontogenesis penetrate each other, forming transit zones and a central zone that contains consciousness, an integral part of mental health, the highest level of self-regulation and reflection of reality that accumulates moral-spiritual potential (figure 4). In the dynamics of ontogenesis the amplitude and rhythm of the main aspects diminish and by the time they fade the person's soul and consciousness become the last relevant factors [32,34].

According to the synergetic concept the development of any disorder has non-linear dynamics, the trajectory of which includes the following fractals: predisposition (family disontogenesis); latent (diathesis); initial (functional disorders); clinical picture; chronicity (forms and types of progress of the illness); outcome. In clinical medicine, a fractal is both progress and condition, uniting temporal and qualitative characteristics of the system and organism.

Synergetic methodology permits the systematic and successive integration of the whole variety of factors and resources of mental ecology in order to promote an optimal level of national health.

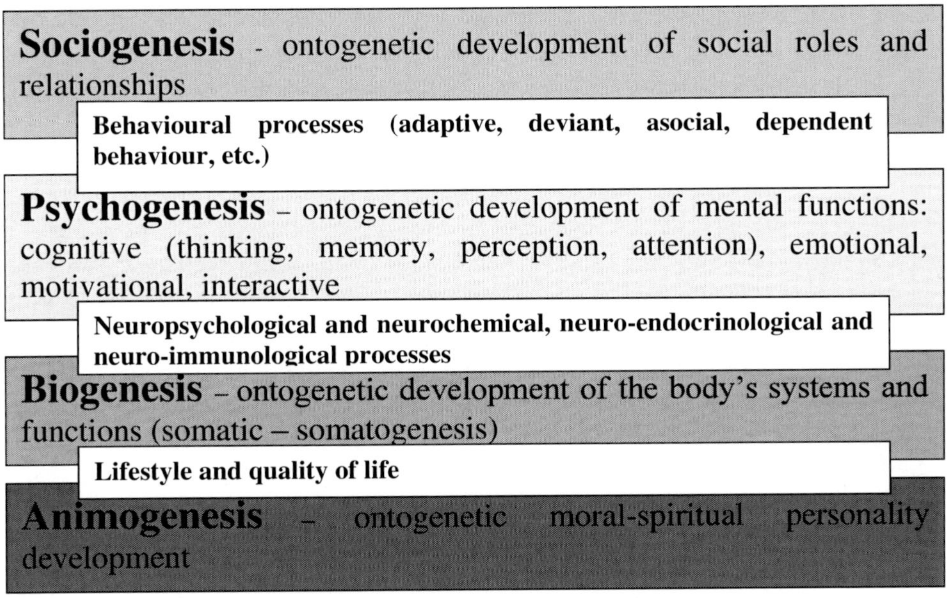

Figure 3. Bio-psycho-socio-spiritual model of ontogenesis.

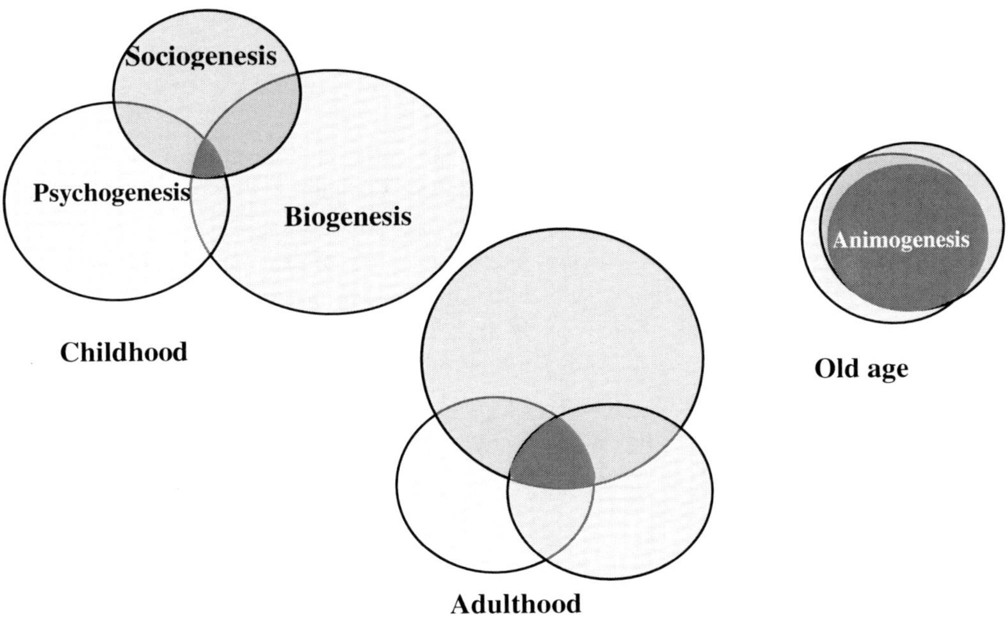

Figure 4. Age dynamics of bio-psycho-socio-spiritual assimilation.

1.2. System Crisis of Psychiatry and Alternative Mental Medicine

The urgency of the problem of the scientific and methodological system crisis in psychiatry, that found itself on the verge of exhausting habitual concepts, often becomes a subject of discussion for experts that propose changing paradigms in psychiatry [28,33] as it appears to be a particular example of a more common difficulty faced by many modern sciences that have reached the end of another cycle of civilisation. The interdisciplinary nature of psychiatry and even more so that of psychotherapy determine the interest of various disciplines in this problem: natural sciences, humanities, technical sciences. It makes the synergetic approach all the more relevant.

Modern system problems in psychiatry are illustrated by the ICD-10 that displays eclecticism, lack of unified stylistic and ideological concepts, and a deficit of new ideas, whereas old concepts no longer measure up to the challenges of the times. These circumstances augmented the contradictory tendencies of modern psychiatry: "globalisation of approaches… and classification criteria" and "the increasing informational excessiveness of various data" [17] that divided psychiatry into a "psychiatry of facts" based on diagnostic standards and a "psychiatry of values" that individualises the approach to the patient [5].

The interdisciplinary quality of psychiatry was engendered by its interaction with other sciences leading to its unique integrity. However, in the ICD-10 the psychiatry's interdisciplinary nature and integrity look like a mechanical union of ideas and different styles, which are often contradictory. Because of this, the problem of terminology became more relevant, highlighting on the one hand the limits of some classical terms, and on the other hand – the artificiality of new definitions. The mechanical and eclectic unity of the two approaches determined the system crisis of the ICD-10 that, along with obvious "successes" contains definitions that seem to be "multiplying the essence without need" [18]

It is notable that countries using the DSM IV diagnostic system, with all of its shortcomings, did not challenge tradition in the face of changing psychiatric treatments and their ethical and legal aspects, by adjusting to the latest ICD, which thus cannot be considered truly "international".

The solution may lie only in establishing new synergetic methodology.

Synergetics permits us to examine mental health and mental illnesses within a single methodology. The same group of professional psychotherapists, psychiatrists, clinical psychologists, and social workers is using the same technologies and is working on both strengthening mental health of clients (who have difficulties in adapting in the absence of a diagnosis) and treating the mental health of the patients. As such mental medicine is built on an interdisciplinary synergetic methodology which unites nosocentric clinical psychiatry and health centric preventive mental health care.

Mental medicine is a science that studies etiopathogenesis and diagnostics along with the clinical picture and treatment of mental disorders, bio-psycho-socio-spiritual resources of personality and societal development, strategies and mechanisms of adaptation and professiogenesis based on a single synergetic methodology. This wording includes the classical definition of psychiatry in all the modes, specified in the mental health definition by WHO (2001), which are the priorities of mental preventology.

Mental preventology is a section of general preventive medicine, a science that studies methods of achieving and maintaining the optimum level of mental health, psycho-hygiene and psycho-prophylactics on a systematic and interdisciplinary synergetic basis.

The main tasks are combining the classical psychiatry's sphere of use with the field of interest of *mental medicine* that apart from mental illnesses studies bio-psycho-socio-spiritual resources of personality development, mechanisms of socialisation and adaptive professiogenesis, and the search for a new health-centric concept that widens the possibilities for de-stigmatisation and the work of experts in donosologic field.

In light of the aforementioned thoughts it seems relevant to compare and combine classical clinical psychiatry and mental preventology against the most important criteria of their content - direction and nature of functioning (table 2) within unified mental medicine.

Table 2. Mental medicine as a unified theory of improving mental health and treatment of mental illnesses

Criteria	Mental medicine	
	Clinical psychiatry	**Mental preventology**
Concept	Nosocentricity	Health-centricity
Strategy	Illness treatment	Prevention of pathology
Aim	Return of mental health	Raising quality of life
Task	Removing symptoms	Preserving functions
Object	Ill person	Healthy person
Focus	Psychiatric disorder	Normal function
Technologies	Treatment, rehabilitation	Preservation, optimisation
Priorities	Clinical	Holistic
Relationships	Paternalism	Partnership
Process	Hospitalisation	Socialisation
Dynamics	Linear	Multidimensional
Ethics	Stigmatisation	De-stigmatisation

This table permits us to compare the direction of mental preventology and clinical psychiatry, outlining their mutual compatibility when solving tasks in strengthening the mental health of the nation. Integration in mental medicine of the traditional psychiatric nosocentricity with the growing health-centric trend of improving mental health became possible via synergetic methodology and interdisciplinary teamwork. This information casts doubt on the concept of viewing the psychiatric disorder as the main and only aim and task of psychiatry. In today's context, diagnostics, treatment, and prophylactics of psychopathology have become a tactical fragment of the common strategy and direction of mental medicine towards preserving and optimising a person's mental health and increasing his or her quality of life. Mental medicine becomes a unified science pertaining to mental health and mental illnesses.

Thus, the more intensive development and research of branches of medicine, both already existing and those that have not been fully formed yet, is a natural and relevant task of modern science – not only from a scientific determinism point of view, but also from the point of view of other methodological approaches, one of them being synergetics as the base for organisationally functional interdisciplinarity, capable of forming a new paradigm of mental medicine. Projecting it on the traditional field of classical psychiatry widens the area of use for specialist knowledge, directing it at situations that do not have a clinical interpretation yet. It demands perfecting of mental health's systematic monitoring technologies that can compliment and transform traditional clinical examination; formalising the prophylactic monitoring activity of specialists (with the appearance of specialities like "preventive medicine", "monitoring and strengthening health"); forming strategies for work on donosological field, screening mental health factors and resources; multiple potentials of trajectories of correctional prophylactic and treatment rehabilitation routes; evaluating the quality of life and social functioning, which in the end secures better results in improving the mental health of the population.

1.3. Anti-Psychiatry

Philosophical discrepancies of the mid-20th century lead to the appearance in 1960s of a movement called *anti-psychiatry* within classical psychiatry that chose existentialism and socially critical philosophy as its foundations. World Psychiatric Association President Mario May (2008) said the following about anti-psychiatry: "Anti-psychiatry is a reality in some countries. Our profession is unique in that it can create its own antibodies."

The period of decline of empires in the post-war era generated anti-system leanings in many spheres of human life. The traditional system of classical psychiatry was subjected to revisionist attempts from its opponents. Supporters of anti-psychiatry were aiming to "discover the truth hidden amongst the drivel," and in the process almost doubting the status of classical psychiatry itself as a medical science, protesting against its claims to qualifying people as mentally ill.

Anti-psychiatrists Ronald Laing, David Cooper, Thomas Szasz and others thought that the decision not to treat patients was right and that their individual and social needs, including those expressed in psychotic motives, had to be satisfied: "Instead of psychiatric hospitals, these processing plants, we need places where people who went further than psychiatrists in their wanderings and consider themselves mentally healthy would have a possibility to go even further in internal time and space and return from there"[19]. Or, as clinical practice demonstrates, never come back.

American sociologist Erving Goffman highlighted the negative sides of *psychiatric total institutions*. In Italy Franco Basaglia, the initiator of de-institutionalisation of psychiatric hospitals became the leader of the anti-psychiatry movement. In the Netherlands Jan Foudraine lead the student movement targeted against professional authority in psychiatric hospitals. Classical psychiatry was accused of having discriminating procedures within its regulations. A movement appeared for banishing psychiatric intervention from the framework of a hospital structure that for almost two hundred years had been seen as treating psychiatric patients in a space isolated from society. In 1965 David Cooper, Ronald Laing and others created the Philadelphia association, aimed at "changing the perception of *mental health and illness of the soul*" [1].

Anti-psychiatry expressed fundamental criticism of the following:

a) illegal use of medical categories and methods regarding social and psychiatric phenomena;
b) conventional nature of nosologic categories in classical psychiatry, their highly provisional nature, dubious medical status;
c) not enough theoretical and clinical reasoning for distribution of these categories into rubrics in classifications;
d) toxicity and side effects of psychotropic medicine;
e) lack of a clearly and legally defined standard of psychiatric norm;
f) use of non-voluntary treatment;

g) ignoring other approaches to the problem of psychiatric disorders;
h) compromising connections of classic psychiatry with pharmaceutical companies;
i) cruel treatment and tight control regarding the mentally ill.

Anti-psychiatry brought to the fore the following problems:

a) existential factors for psychiatric disorders;
b) pathological status of psychiatric disorders
c) place of the mentally ill in society;
d) institutionalisation/ de-institutionalisation of the mentally ill;
e) psychiatric disorders treatment methods;
f) personality suppression and functioning of the institutions of authority;
g) peculiarities of inter-personal interaction;
h) unconscious mechanisms of society's functioning;
i) human rights protection for people with mental illnesses.

Not one of the pioneers of anti-psychiatry developed a complete theoretical system: Laing and Cooper worked with phenomenological and existential concepts based on the theory of pathology of communication inside the family; Basaglia was concerned with politics, ideology and revolutionary social reforms; Szasz's views formed under the influence of Ludwig Binswanger and Freudianism. However, the anti-psychiatry movement influenced classical psychiatry, the nature of work by its institutions, and the quality of help for the mentally ill. Anti-psychiatry brought to light some contradictions of classical psychiatry – its conceptual and philosophic disagreement; known diagnostic arbitrariness that depends on priorities of regional schools and philosophical preferences.

Thanks to the anti-psychiatry movement, starting from the 1960s, new methods and forms of working with the mentally ill became more popular. Therapeutic communities (soterias) appeared and became popular again, but they were a modification of a method used by classical psychiatry in the 19th century (housing patients in peasant families for their full social rehabilitation and labour therapy like in the Belgian town Geel and a number of other European locations); stricter laws were passed that limited the use of non-humane methods of treatment and the regulation of non-voluntary hospitalisation; a more humane view of the mentally ill appeared; social and psychological methods became more common in their treatment and rehabilitation. Perceptions of ethical norms in classical psychiatry formed. The monopoly of the biological approach to psychiatry was broken; psycho-social approaches appeared and became more active.

Anti-psychiatry became the *antithesis* to the *thesis* of classical psychiatry, criticising its important concepts, achievements and theories, doubting its practical implementation and viability. Anti-psychiatry attacked the foundation of nosology and epistemology of classical psychiatry, criticised its lack of satisfactory criteria for diagnostics and the objectivity of its methods; doubted the very medical model of a mental illness accepted by the classical psychiatry, considering the nosological classification arbitrary; criticised methods of therapy ("pharmacotherapy is chains locked from the inside") and prophylactics that did not take into account social conditions; put the psychosocial aspect of the problem instead of the biological one to the foreground, treating psychotherapy as social manipulation and control; protested against obligatory hospitalisation, considering it a measure of segregating the mentally ill bereft of their human rights.

The philosophical ideology of anti-psychiatry was also eclectic and cumulative, combining the philosophical concepts of the sentimental humanism of Jean-Jacques Rousseau, existentialism of Jean-Paul Sartre, and anarchism of Peter Kropotkin. Student riots in Paris in 1968 do not look coincidental in this context: readers of Sartre were prisoners of romantically viewed anarchism and Trotskyism. It was the first example of mental design and strategies, technologies and mechanisms of the future artificial "colour revolutions."

The difference between the authorities' thoughts on the forms of realising the ψ-function and peculiarities of its social use were expressed through psychiatric hospitals and the mentally ill in socialist and capitalist countries. Inside the socialist system, the ψ-function came down to isolating this category of people in conditions where it was easy to conduct monitoring of this cohort. It is the *totalitarian* option of ψ-function implementation. Capitalist socio-economic formation featured the *liberal* option, declaring human rights a priority and regulating psychiatric activity with this point of view in mind.

There was an explosion of popularity and the network distribution of such methods of psycho-correction and psychotherapy as group sessions, family psychotherapy, training, role games, and behaviour modification among others. All of this became the prologue to the modern *Era of Psychotherapy*. Psychotherapy, having achieved the revolutionary breakthrough to the medical donosological field, radically changed the focus of the ψ-mission of the state and society from mental illnesses to mental health. This secured dynamic development of the whole complex of neurosciences and sped up the development of social psychiatry and narcology, leading to the birth in the last decade of mental ecology and mental medicine.

1.4. System Synthesis of Mental Medicine

If before the 20th century it was possible to talk about long-term paradigms in philosophy and science (particularly in classical psychiatry), then now various concepts of philosophical directions that exist simultaneously form a contradictory ontology and a perception of the worldview as unstable.

The world is losing stability and steadiness at the speed of a gallop and it is important to note that this is not simply the perception of "shadows of scientific illusions". Terrorist attacks by suicide-bombers and online hacker attacks easily explode the global public consciousness, demanding principally new approaches to protecting the mental resources of the civilisation. Psychiatric fences and bars in the global and open world became totally anachronistic. Humanity as a whole and each one of us individually are so defenceless that the very realisation of this fact creates ground for social stress disorders.

Acceptance that the former canons of scientific world study turned insolvent became a common topic of polemic statements. Urgent desire for defenceless integration of classification systems in classical psychiatry is today accompanied by "the known futility of the announced methodological approach; its lack of theory; change from nosological to syndrome level of clinical evaluations; bulkiness; inability to reflect cultural variety even when using the descriptive method, and eclecticism because of a lack of theoretical principle" [24].

Materialistic science and philosophy fully humiliate the person and the truth. Almost all empirical theories of the 19th and 20th centuries were refuted by the verdict of history as strained and pretentious exhibits of vain erudition. Despite the significant number of historical, statistical, pseudo-experimental, clinical and other data, not a single unified theory was created. At best, they only restored in a vulgar and more primitive form the generalisations of the previous generations [40].

This problem was formulated by Carl Gustav Jung in relation to classical psychiatry and psychotherapy [11]: "Modern medicine can no longer understand the psyche as part of the body and is thus considering the so-called *psychic factor* more." "Practical loss of empiricism of modern culture is revealed in our growing inability to control humanity and the course of social and cultural processes" [40]. However, it is psychiatry that is the slowest in leaving behind the empirical period of scientific development.

In the context of a globally permanent and paroxysmally progressive crisis that fundamentally relates to the mental paradigm, modern possibilities for perfecting classical psychiatry and anti-psychiatry have almost been exhausted. "We are, seemingly, at the dusk of an era" [20]. But this "...imaginary dying agony is nothing else but sharp pain from the birth of a new form of culture, labour pains, accompanying new creative forces"[40], "a reassuring sign of possible deeper changes of the spiritual disposition"[13].

"The 21st century will become the century of returning to continuity, to all-round understanding of common problems. The key will be technologies of a certain system integration, *system synthesis*"[22], because "the main thing in the study of the living phenomena are not the elements that do not matter by themselves and do not exist, but something else – *synthesis, form, idea*"[14]. "Gradually the understanding that there is *one* humankind with *one* psyche is born and developed ... would also do away with the awkward hypothesis of psychophysical parallelism and afford us an opportunity to construct a new world model closer to the idea of the *unus mundus*" [10]

The crisis of classical sciences in the 20th century generated the use in scientific methodology of *various* interpretative and methodological systems, which lead to the understanding that it is necessary to utilise the *principle of complementarity.* "Being can only be described in part, as the other part remains at any given time unrecognised and unlimited. Life processes cannot be explained based on just the causality principle" [12].

Contradiction unites into a whole the battle and the unity of opposites, and *unity* mutually supposes and *battle* mutually exclude opposite sides. The battle of the thesis of classical psychiatry and the antithesis of anti-psychiatry brought these concepts to unipolar renditions in which both failures and achievements of these areas were subject to relativism from the opposing side. However, the thesis of classical psychiatry that was replaced by the antithesis of anti-psychiatry created conditions both for formation through the complementarity principle of a constructive *synthesis* of these contradicting concepts in mental medicine, promising a qualitatively new level of understanding and interpretation of mental health problems and mental illnesses (table 3).

Internal contradictions of the thesis and antithesis are removed by the synthesis of former ideas, capable of using new philosophical *ideology of synergetics*, called exactly "system synthesis," "synthesis with the developed analysis" (which shows a meaningful combination of former methodological priorities and achievements) as a base for forming a new scientific discipline – *mental medicine.*

Synergetics that uses a complex approach, and has among its most important systematic concepts the complementarity principle, can creatively unite the achievements of classical psychiatry and anti-psychiatry, evading their shortcomings that first of all appear in their methodological relativism that denies the ideological priorities of the opposing side. The appearance of a new holistic philosophy inevitably generates new synthetic methodology, capable of retrieving the practical psychiatric science from the dead end of today's contradictory and irreconcilable concepts: theory will inspire practice. Elements of new practical trends are noticeable in the achievements of psychotherapy, narcology, and social psychiatry, with their more varied forms and methods of work, that fall outside the repertoire of traditional classic psychiatry. Mental medicine, whose polymodal structure is aimed at the *wholesome* holistic approach to mental illnesses, that considers not only nosological categories, but also *potential risks* of their formation can be the new base for implementation of the new synergetic philosophy in the mental health field.

Table 3. System synthesis of mental medicine

№	Criteria	Clinical psychiatry (thesis)	Anti-psychiatry (antithesis)	Mental medicine (synthesis)
	Philosophy	Positivism, neopositivism, scientism	Existentialism	Synergetics
	Concept	Nosocentricity	Existential freedom of personality	Health-centricity
	Priorities	Clinical	Social	Holistic
	Trend	Biological	Socio-psychological	Bio-psycho-socio-moral-spiritual
	Strategy	Treatment of mental illnesses	Individual mentality	Preventive correction and treatment rehabilitation
	Aims	Return of mental health	Implementing individual rights and freedoms	Improving quality of life and mental health levels
	Tasks	Removing the symptoms	Maintaining the subject's right to his or her uniqueness	Preserving functions and mental potential
	Objects	Sick person	Psychiatry as the ψ-functional institution of authority	Healthy person – client-patient
	Focus	Mental disorder	Peculiarities of interpersonal interaction	Normal – changed – unbalanced mentality
	Technologies	Treatment, rehabilitation	Communication	Preservation – optimisation - recovery
	Process	Hospitalisation	Liberalisation	Adaptation – socialisation-humanisation – re-adaptation
	Dynamics	Linear	Counter-linear	Multidimensional
	Relationship	Paternalism	Protectionism	Partnership
	Ethics	Stigmatisation	Presumption of mental uniqueness	De-stigmatisation
	Forms of implementation	Hospital, clinic, care home	Therapeutic communities	Systematic monitoring of mental health

Considering that mental illnesses consume up to 50% of the budget in developed countries' healthcare systems, the central task is the answer to the sacramental question – what is more effective socially and economically, more clinically viable and humane: to preserve the subpopulations with mentality disorders in their changed reality or to bring them to a legitimate reality which they do not accept? Mental medicine provides the answer; it allows the strengthening of mental health in multiple scenarios and the treatment of mental illness. Mental medicine allows us to justify and implement a worthy care path and fate for any patient or client with specific resources of the polymodal mentality in an adequate for him or her multicultural or virtual hospital reality.

The dialectics of history in general and scientific research in particular are made up of the stages of "throwing away the stones" and their "gathering," meaning, respectively, processes of analysis and synthesis. However, in essence, they are just procedural thesis and antithesis, and this dyad demands its own logical conclusion, which must be the third stage – construction of the new Cathedral of Science from the gathered stones. This stage can be called the system synthesis of mental medicine.

2. Terrorism as an Outcome of the Demoralization Syndrome

The terrorist attack in Volgograd (December 2013) and its following media coverage "exploded" Russian public conscience and revealed the existing exhaustiveness of traditional obstructive strategies used to counteract suicidal terrorism.

The experience of other countries demonstrates that one must not respond to terror with terror as it only spurs violence and the spiral of terror unwinds even further. That is why the announced formation of a new antiterrorist unit in the city of Volgograd (07.01.2014) was perceived by terrorists as an official recognition of defeat from Russian authorities and a call for expanding the geography of violence. The serial murders in Stavropol (January 2014) became a continuation of this antiterrorist scenario. Psychologists have spent many years discussing the phenomenon of terrorism and compared it to a flood when antiterrorist measures are an attempt to scoop out water with a teaspoon: "Personally addressed counterterrorism only procreates terrorists" [23].

The escalation of terror and state counterterrorism represents the best way to eliminate countries and peoples. Every day we can find the confirmation of this fact in our "mental TV sewerage", it is present even on family and history channels. Thus, hundreds of millions of TV viewers all over the world enjoy a wonderful TV serial "The Magnificent Century". It draws a bright and convincing picture that shows how the awe of unmotivated death, terrorism and state counterterrorism created the great Ottoman Empire. The same terror, having reached its apogee and worldwide protest reaction (that was caused by the barbarian genocide of Armenians) destroyed the Empire and made it possible for Atatürk to create a secular republic. This republic has recently undergone the difficult times of "Islamic reformation".

Since ancient times terror has been the most archaic way of governing people and societies. In the contemporary technological-virtual world it is acquiring new epidemic features that symbolize the completion of another global civilizational cycle. The point here is that *terror itself has become the universal form of war prosecution,* it has radically changed the concept of warfare and armed forces. There is no front line and there can be no battle line in the contemporary world, that functional and organizational army infrastructure is a thing of the past, it has lost its efficiency with the parity of space military forces.

Ten years ago it was possible to try and compare terrorism and guerrilla warfare, terrorism and revolutionary violence, terrorism and struggle for national liberation. In the past this comparison could be based on the subject's position and on differential diagnostic evaluations. Today there are practically no alternatives – it is more and more obvious that terrorism is becoming a new universal form of war prosecution. In this new quality terrorism demonstrates independent epidemic mechanisms of self-development and has nothing to do with the traditional reasons and factors that used to provoke it in the past. Terrorism is becoming an independent tool for solving political problems: "The future picture of the world is no longer possible without terror and violence" [6].

The notion of civil population is disappearing from our lexicon, and what we have left is *already dead and still alive, everyone is contused by the informational explosion waves brought by the pandemic of terrorism.*

The special feature of the Volgograd tragedy is the fact that, for the first time, Russian mass media stopped spreading explosive informational waves of this attack and damage the public conscience of the country. To intimidate and demoralize a society – is the objective of terrorists, it is not the objective of mass media. Russian leading psychologists have been discussing the necessity of censoring reports on terrorist attacks for 10 years.

It is possible to try and link the tragedies in Volgograd and Stavropol with the preventive intimidation of Russia before the Olympic Games in Sochi. But it is much more important to see and hear another communicative message from terrorists – "Russia is destroying itself", and it happens because more and more frequently (according to Russian mass media) terrorists are of Slavic origin.

Sorrowful information about civilian casualties and the *consequences of yesterday's failed "Volgograd battle"* are known, with the active phase of the antiterrorist war only beginning. It is important to learn the lesson in a timely manner and make adequate conclusions by building a system of effective defense.

Long before becoming suicide bombers terrorists themselves became victims of *mental terrorism* – destructive manipulation with their conscience in extremist camps, gangs, and armies [31]. A as result of this "brain wash" they developed a fanatic belief in their messianic and self-sacrificing role of fighters against the "infidels". The outcome of *terrorist demoralization syndrome* manifests itself in the deranged formation and deranged development of moral feelings, cast of mind, social position, and behavior, which are responsible for personal moral socialization.

The ontogenetic approach forms the foundation of this definition. Derangements in the formation of *primary moral feelings* (conscience, duty, faith and responsibility) are most often predetermined by spiritual and moral deficit as well as by family ambivalence. Such derangements develop even above orthodox and pious backgrounds as well as above patriarchal characters.

During adolescence derangements in moral socialization cause a delay and disharmony in the development of *moral make-up fundamentals* – such as patience, tolerance, mercy, humanism, honor, and dignity. At the same time manipulative characteristics of conscience and susceptibility to nationalistic provocations with xenophobia begin their formations.

Derangements in the formation and development of the *spiritual and moral position,* accumulated in the personality's motivational and mindset complex, manifest themselves by the decreased ability to differentiate between good and evil, friendship and love, amorphous personal position and low level of self-criticism in everything that does not include the categories of "infidels" and "strangers", inability to see life perspectives, pessimistic and catastrophic perceptions of the world, capitulation before encountering difficulties sublimated in sacrificial struggle, inability to realize the value of human life.

As a result of the *terrorist (fanatic, extremist) demoralization syndrome* there appear: a complete loss of the socially accepted moral norms of behavior, demonstrative neglect of traditional concepts concerning what is due and what is unallowable, rejection of any moral duties and moral self-control, inability to act independently and irresponsibility for one's actions, increased suggestibility and dependence, complete devaluation of legal awareness and law-abidance, loss of social and personal identity. All this allows a militant-manipulator to easily "create" new generations of suicidal terrorists. The recruitment of suicide terrorists looks even more tragic and dramatic when it comes to women, aged people, mentally ill and disabled individuals, teenagers and children. On January 08, 2014 the 1st Russian channel reported a story of a 10 year old Afghan girl whose farther and elder brother were forcing the child to become a suicide attacker. It was a miracle that she managed to escape and reach the police station that she was supposed to explode by the order of her relatives. This story reflects the monstrous *family variant of the terrorist demoralization syndrome*, when parents are ready to send children to their death. In this case it is not so important whether they do it for money or fighting for an "idea". Any form of terrorism inevitably destroys and eliminates individual human lives of terrorists as well as the lives of family members who support it. That is why from the psychiatric point of view terrorism represents the most destructive form of the *epidemic suicidal behavior*. To launch and support such destructive social epidemics of suicidal terrorism three conditions are sufficient and must be met [41]: religious culture of martyrdom, decision of a terrorist organization, possibility of compulsory but made to appear as voluntary recruitment of future suicide attackers.

The development of demoralization syndrome has multiple variants in the ethno-cultural environment. It has minimum dependence on the intellectual potential and quality of education. Terrorism, like alcoholism and drug addiction can derive from rich and poor backgrounds. There is no coincidence that the number one and most mythologized terrorist of the world Ben Laden came from a well-educated and wealthy family.

3. Terrorism as Destructive Social Epidemics

Demoralization syndrome – is a moral and psychological foundation of any social epidemic regardless of its form: drug addiction, fanaticism, extremism, terrorism and many others.

Social epidemics– is the appearance (outbreak) of a social decease in a community (or on a given territory) when the rate of this decease exceeds regular expectations. Social epidemics become *destructive*, when they begin to threaten the national security of a country as a whole. This is when the mechanisms of social ailment generation and their extensive and uncontrolled reproduction become active and transform an epidemic into a *pandemic* that can overtake not only countries but also continents [6].

Generalization shows itself in the form of new infringements when more serious and punishable social norms are more and more often violated. Thus hard drinking primarily represents a phenomenon of immoral behavior that breaks ethics rules. It is followed by alcoholism that represents a medical/psychiatric condition which is likely to result in administrative infringements of the law after which some of the patient's rights will be restricted. Sever forms of alcohol abuse or alcohol psychosis are bound to unlawful behavior and criminal responsibility.

Extended reproduction shows itself in a highly latent form of social ailments. At best, every out-patient department for drug addicts has an official record of only 1 alcoholic out of 10. Furthermore, it has an official record of only 1 drug addict out of 30 habitual abusers. The remaining addicts successfully continue their personal destruction together with the destruction of their families. They get new generations involved into the consumption of drugs. The first vacant place is always reserved for youth. We have the same situation with grave crimes and AIDS because only 1 case out of 5 is detected. There exists no accurate statistics or estimation that could reflect the actual spread of tuberculosis, STDs, corruption and prostitution, gambling addiction, extremism and fanaticism as well as many other problems.

The uncontrollability of social epidemics is predetermined by the absence of a mental health monitoring system and the presence of immediate interdepartmental barriers that exist in organizations with preventive and correctional missions as well as in treatment and rehabilitation clinics.

Epidemiological recognition of the threats and challenges posed by terrorism and extremism is not another myth or banal abuse of psychiatric terminology. It is not what happened in the case of trappidomania diagnosis or so the called pathological craving for freedom among American slaves, delirium of reformation, and criminal prosecution of homosexualismin the USSR. Today clinical psychiatry makes diagnoses, which yesterday were viewed as a purely social phenomenon. For example, the Mobbing syndrome evolved from banal "office wars". Today it is a form on non-lethal mental terrorism that destroys the mental health of its "Mobbing targets" and corporate society.

It is of fundamental importance to note the unity and universality of the social epidemic base. Drug and alcohol addictions, crime and violence, extremism and terrorism unite the subpopulations of people "exiled" from the normative social systems [1].

The following [6] groups of conditions initiate the epidemiological spread of terrorism:

1. *formation of the information society*, that indefinitely spreads the potential effect of terrorisms;
2. *vulnerability of the technological environment* that is responsible for human existence, it makes the pinpoint destruction of the technological environment's social, natural, and technological foundations possible;
3. *smearing of the traditional society* with modernization and liberal values: concept of the social contract, ideas that proclaim state authorities responsible before their society, ideas promoting the value of law and human life;
4. *crisis stages of social development* accompanied by the ideas of separatism, religious, ethnic, and ideological conflicts.

Terrorism represents one of the most polymodal types of *destructive social epidemics*, its working classification includes:

1. *Social epidemics of dependent disorders*:
   a) chemical: alcoholism, drug addiction (drug dealing is the financial foundation of terrorism) and others;

b) non-chemical: gambling and others;
c) vicarious, those that fill moral and psychological emptiness: workaholism, sectarianism, radicalism, fanaticism, extremism, mental terrorism and others;
d) electronic: internet and computer (cyber terrorism) and others;
e) changing people's dietary habits: dietmania, manipulative nutraceutics (nutritional supplements) and others;
f) expansive forms of sexual self-assertion: public group exhibitionism, hypercompensatory sex parades and others.

2. *Social epidemics of induced disorders*:
   a) early hysteria-demonic: manarik and emiryachenie (Yakut hysteria), lishinka and kila, ikota and sheva (that require to "draw blood" of the chaki - a sorceress who put an evil curse, in order to regain health) and others;
   b) hysteria-demonic renascence: shamanism, magic, sorcery, pseudo-religious extremism and terrorism and others;
   c) induced nervous-psycho disorders: somatoform, social - stress and others;
3. *Epidemics of social ailments:*
   a) infectious diseases: especially dangerous infections (bio-terrorism), tuberculosis, AIDS and others;
   b) psychic disorders: mobbing-terrorism, social phobias, panic reactions to terrorist attacks and others;
4. *Epidemics of sociopathy*:
   a) suicidal behavior: suicides, suicidal terrorism and others;
   b) organized serial crime: terrorism, corruption and others.

Terrorism is an exceptionally polymorph phenomenon with different types and classes of usable aggressive agents. That is why it is present in all four groups of the suggested classification. Thus, the arsenal of bio-terrorism includes 13 types of viruses, 7 – bacteria, 3 – rickettsiae that cause dangerous infectious diseases, 12 microbial toxins. Long ago special methods of diagnostics and therapy have been developed to counter these threats.

The situation with *mental terrorism* appears to be much more dramatic. This form of terrorism affects mental health together with ideological, spiritual, and moral bases of culture, society, and statehood. Furthermore, it is followed by the stirring of national hatred, depreciation of spiritual and moral values with their ideals, marginalization and criminalization of social consciousness. This is an everyday reality for Russia while it keeps on sinking in the "waterfalls of mental TV sewage". As a result of this phenomenon there developed increased uncertainty about tomorrow and hesitancy about the state, profound sense of anxiety, aggression and emotional instability, suggestibility and trustfulness, distrust to official information with preference given to rumors, decreased criticality [31, 43].

Such peculiarities of the public consciousness are characteristic of emergencies. It turns out that in Russia the sate of emergency, caused by mental terrorism, exists de-facto, but de jure the society is already unable to perceive it adequately. Furthermore, public consciousness and the Russian state itself are undergoing painless destruction under the anesthetization of the «mental TV-sewage». This image has a serious associative and medical interpretation. Psychiatric practice has encountered and described cases of cloacae gas poisoning that lead to the instant death of the cerebral cortex and visualize in the form of profound encephalopathy (hydrogen sulfide intoxication can be in-plant or take place in natural environments: areas of natural gas release, around sulfurous mineral waters, in deep wells and pits, with rotting organic substances that contain sulphur). During my 40 year clinical practice there have been only several cases of such intoxication. For example, when construction workers opened airtight pits half of them died and the remaining half acquired dementia. With this decease they produced the impression of preteens. All this really reminds me of the situation on the Russian television where infantile intonation is being used in order to facilitate the manipulation of human consciousness.

It is the decrease of the stress-resistance threshold by means of the infantile *reverberatory* tuning of public consciousness through electronic mass media that allows exploding the public consciousness with the informational shock waves of any terrorist attack or any kind of emergency. The chain reactions of anxiety and fear are multiplied and doubled. Their cumulative effects are amplified as they provoke different kinds of induced socially stressful and somatoform neuropsychic disorders. Today's mass media policy significantly favors this harmful influence. It relies on the "sinister charm of violence and fear" [7, p. 432] and is guided by the principles like "corpses make our picture more alive" [7, p. 428]. This is how mass media imprints the image of our contemporary society on the public consciousness. It is the society of utter and unpredictable violence. Due to perverted professional ethics and esthetics the media coverage of any terrorist attack or tragedy literally turns into a "satanic necrophilic feast" that creates epidemic waves of induced disorders.

The following classification of social epidemics can is based on their epidemiological scale:

1. social epidemics (all forms);
2. destructive social epidemics (all forms);
3. generalized destructive social epidemics: nationalistic bashing and massacre, "color" revolutions, genocide, civil wars and others;
4. pandemics of destructive social epidemics: drug addiction, terrorism, corruption and others.

The world epidemics of drug addiction and terrorism are closely interconnected. According to the American Drug Enforcement Administration, 39 % of terrorist organizations are associated with drug dealing. The global volume of drug traffic, according to different estimations, makes up from 400 to 1 000 billion dollars every year. There is no coincidence that the former president of Columbia M. Pastrana called drug dealing "the main financier of terrorism and death in the world" [27]. One can easily add here the total corruption that systematically embraces the entire civilized infrastructure and creates premises for *planetary suicide.*

Social epidemics become *generalized* as a significant percentage of the dependent subpopulation (population suffering from dependent personality disorders) gets involved. According to our data, it makes up 30 % of the whole population.

The first generalized social epidemics in Russian history was "Smutnoe vremya" (the Time of Troubles), that ended about 400 years ago. It was accompanied by large scale hysteria-demonic and infectious epidemics, plunder, robberies and demolitions, burning of witches and magicians, appearance of various impostors, summoned and recognized by the corrupt elite. The whole country and its population have remembered this lesson for 300 years and it was only in 1917 when the October revolution demonstrated its blood red results and dramatic scenarios.

The student disturbances in Paris (1968) are an example of a *bloodless color revolution* in the contemporary European history. The organizers of this coup d'etat who overthrew president Charles de Gaulle gave young people a possibility to "let off some fume" on barricades. That protesting youth was sincerely engrossed with the ideas of Sartre and was held captive by the romantic illusions of Anarchism and Trotskyism.

Today the mental design of the technological-virtual world (which is composed of numerous ideas and illusions) quickly changes its arrangement of the public consciousness and it happens as if somebody unnoticed swings his mighty wand to conduct the show. One way or another, the newest generations of "color" revolutions industrialized the strategies, tactics, forms and techniques of destroying traditional, natural, cultural and socioeconomic structures of countries and people for the benefit of the financing party. That is why it is extremely difficult to develop a spiritual immunity to all kinds of social epidemics; the development of such immunity has become one of the major priorities of the state. Spiritual immunity is composed of moral and value-based potential of a personality realizing its unity with countrymen and motherland. Here is no coincidence it is the spiritual culture that happens to be the first target of the contemporary aggressor.

Anomia forms the foundation of any destructive social epidemics, it becomes apparent when fundamental moral values of a system get corrupted. Contradictions typically develop between the announced objectives and the impossibility for the majority of citizens to accomplish them using traditional methods. It results in the personality's isolation from society and depressive disillusionment in life. Anomia favors the spread of permissivity – destabilization and the abolishment of socially accepted prohibitions that are structural and ethical elements of society. In such conditions any person can lose his supporting point and be left without his system of moral values as well as support of traditional public morals. All this creates basic conditions for the recruitment of individuals among the dependant subpopulation and their further participation in different forms of destructive social epidemics. The most tragic form of these epidemics is terrorism.

4. Forms of Terrorism and Mechanisms of Personality Deformation

Terrorism (from Latin *terror*) – is a weapon of mass destruction, that combines direct physical damage of the victims with the significant damage done to the bio-psycho-socio-spiritual resources of a society. The meaningful content of terror is restricted to three characteristics: act of intimidation, request of submission, meaningful content [6, 23, 31].

Generalized psychological portrait of a terrorist [45, 30, 31, 41, 43] most often includes the following characteristics:

- young people around 20 (+/– 5);
- patriarchal or highly religious family culture;
- dominant view about some historic injury of his nation;
- deep emotional connections with his ethnos;
- anxiety about pinched national pride;

- distorted and mythologized views about some historical insulters and need for revenge;
- topical psychological injury, often this injury is caused by the death of relatives in front of the future terrorist;
- early deprivation of parental care and attention;
- deficit of emotional connections during childhood;
- high level of pretentions that showed up since childhood, overrated self-esteem, tendency to fantasize and demand of increased attention;
- as a rule "black sheep", outsider among his peers;
- disposition towards aggression and vandalism;
- often has obvious or hidden physical defects;
- traumatogenic youth with privations, humiliations, bereavement;
- disturbance of moral socialization;
- settlement of conflicts only through violence;
- difficulties with adaptation to social principles and regulations;
- seeking recognition and self-assured;
- prevalence of hysteric explosive traits of personality;
- high level of neurosis and frustration;
- personality disorders with high level of aggression and self-actualization;
- submission of one's individuality to group identity;
- high impulsivity, inclination to immediate actions.

Among the most characteristic *mental peculiarities of terrorists* [45, 15, 30, 31, 41, 43] it is possible to single out the following features:

- displacement of time perception (present includes past);
- archaic and binary picture of the world;
- disappearance of borders between reality and fantasy;
- infantilism and naivety, high suggestibility;
- primitiveness of cognitive styles;
- presence of apocalyptic feelings and fantasies;
- ideas of messianism, unique purport of life and sacrificial service;
- ambivalent sadomasochist position;
- identification with aggressor;
- no receptiveness to counterarguments and dissuasion;
- loss of pragmatism and rationality;
- religious arrangement of ideas promoting struggle and revenge;
- cultivation of conceptions about death and life after death;
- glorification of sacrificial death and the heroic deeds of martyrs;
- absence of fear and repentance;
- derangements in the formation and development of moral feelings (conscience and duty, faith and responsibility), character (patience and tolerance, mercy and humanism, honor and dignity), position (ability to differentiate between good and evil, expression of friendship and love), behavioral ethics and communication;
- predilection for illusory-compensatory way of satisfying one's needs instead of active and creative;

- tendency to quick, final and easy solutions;
- primitive mythologizing and sign-symbolic mediation of one's primary activity with compulsory emphasis made on the list of enemies;
- utmost, terminal and artificial dramatization of the situation;
- loss of tactical prognostication resources and vision of strategic perspectives in life.

Contemporary terrorism is characterized by the galloping tempos of its cruelty growth, usage of newest lethal and non-lethal weapons, cyber and nanotechnologies, expanded reproduction of terrorist movements' quantity, generalization and globalization of their activity scale, high level of organization and professionalism, sacrificial fanaticism and shocking corruption. It is not without reason that long time ago Israeli psychologists came to the conclusion that it is impossible to reconstruct or reform the personality of convicted terrorists. This conclusion might be connected with the fact that quite recently special antiterrorist units all over the world began to liquidate terrorists rather than detain them. However attempts to find corrective methods have not been stopped. Thus, neurobiologists from the Oxford University made an announcement about the development of a pilot technology for treating Islamic fundamentalists. This announcement was made two weeks after a shocking public murder in London when two Nigerians cruelly killed a soldier of the British army (Lee Rigby) [8]. The technology includes both biological methods and psychotherapeutic sanitization of extremist beliefs. Moreover, the scientists have suggested that "radical attitudes" should be classified as psychic disorders! It was revealed that the British security service MI5 had attempted to hire one of those Nigerians six month before the terrifying murder took place. This episode really reminds of the contacts that the Russian special service had established (as reported by the Russian mass media) with one the Volgograd suicide bombers prior to the terrorist action in the city. It means that in the struggle against terrorism one cannot rely solely on special services. They simply cannot have all necessary information to prevent such acts of terrorism. These tragedies have demonstrated that the approach towards terrorism requires a systematic synergetic review. It goes without saying that special operations and systematic monitoring of the information field are absolutely necessary antiterrorist activities, however, fighting against destructive social epidemics of terrorism requires, figuratively speaking, a*dyke of spiritual immunity that is structured by the moral and value-based potential of the population and cemented with the energy of creative and rallied nation.*

It is deeply symbolic that last year the world mass media proclaimed the president of the Russian Federation V.V. Putin a *spiritual leader of humanitarian anti-terror* after the threat of Syria's terrorist annihilation was overturned with the help of Russia. Of course opponents have not forgiven Russia and Putin for that and the tragedies in Volgograd and Stavropol serve as evidence of this fact.

The classification of terrorism forms includes: ideological and religious, political and ecological, chemical and physical, nuclear and biological, psychological and suicidal, spiritual and mental forms. According to its territorial scale terrorism can be classified as corporative (including the syndrome of mobbing-terrorism in "office wars"), municipal (for example in Volgograd), provincial, regional (republics of the Northern Caucasus), federal, international.

We have singled out [31] the following mechanisms of exposing influence on personality in extremist and terrorist organizations. These mechanisms lead to the practically irreversible deformation of one's personality.

1. *Monologue* – unidirectional impact that excludes alternative sources of information.
2. *Mythological* – use of tested mythological schemes that inspire to die for some idea.
3. *Emotional* – compensation of emotional feelings and care that were not received in society.
4. *Collectivism* – use of group forms self- and mutual induction: training "referent group" prepares a suicide terrorist and leads him till the very end.
5. *Counter argumentation* – suggestion of counter arguments to anticipated doubts and contradictions that is done in advance.
6. *Intolerance* – stimulation of suggestibility in the background of psychophysical exhaustion, especially in field conditions and underground.
7. *Selectivity*– recruitment of suicidal terrorist among the most non-adapted and deficient people.
8. *Manipulative* – use of an extensive psycho-technological arsenal of suggestion.
9. *Paranormal* – use of fictional achievements based on supersensory experience.
11. *Controllability* –ensuring total control of personality and his behavior.
10. *Ritualistic*– creation and nailing down of behavioral habits and models of killing and committing a suicide.

Teaching hatred and brainwashing have three objectives:

1. to deny a positive emotional evaluation of the enemy;
2. to cultivate malice and fear (a classical example of it can be found in the novel of D. Orwell "1984" «five-minute periods of hatred»);
3. generation of decisions based on mistaken cognitive conclusions and faulty critical thinking [42].

The model of psychology of hatred developed by Robert Sternberg [42] has three components and the following blocks:

1. Disgust or rejection of closeness with the enemy. Its source can be found in the peculiarities of the subject's personality, his own actions or propaganda.
2. Passion as a measure of emotional energy, connected with the dynamics of hatred, described in the terms of fear emotions, malice and rage.
3. 3. Obligation that consists of two components: cognitive aberration to decrease the value and significance of the hated group of people: individuals who compose it are viewed as not quite human and very often as "subhuman". Its second component is behavioral; it is a decision to struggle, use violence an even die.

Interaction between these three elements allowed the author [42] to single out six types of hatred:

1. Hatred expressed in the form of *disgust* towards a hated group (for example a nation).The subject does not want to have anything in common with them because they, from his point of view, have very little in common with people.
2. *«Furious»*hate is expressed in extreme emotional manifestations of malice and fear and it can lead to violence or attempt to avoid the threat that is (in the view of the hatred subjects) posed by the hostile group.
3. *«Cold»*hate that is characterized by the perception of a hostile group as low and mean.
4. *«Boiling»*hate that combines disgust towards a hated group with the need to illuminate the threat that this group poses.
5. *Hardly restrained* hate is characterized by the feeling of constant disgust and fear; at the same time the hostile group is perceived as a gathering of "supermen".
6. *«Burning hate»*this type of hate is associated with feeling of necessity to physically exterminate the hated enemy. In this case all three elements of hate are present and this type of hate most often becomes the subject of study in frames of terrorism research and studies.

This is how *–through brainwashing and teaching hatred–* the personality of a future suicidal terrorist gets destroyed in order to turn him into a simple "means of transportation". Only the organizers get the greater part of the client's reward. There is nothing personal here. Some action appears on TV screens and a sum of money is transferred to someone's bank account. *A terrorist war* is a business for its organizers and bloody politics for the ordering party.

5. Mental Synergy of Terrorism

The conventional and generalized synergetic concept that demonstrates the development of social epidemics of terrorism is presented in table 1. The illustration to this table shows only the basic markers of this dynamic disorder which has a great polyvalence and multivariance; those markers are connected with the clinical psychopathological and somato-neurologic, socio-psychological, spiritual and moral personal topologies as well as the forms and trajectories of epidemic development.

To make it more convenient for perception, the model of synergetic epidemic is presented in the flat-bed projection even though it is multidimensional, non-linear and unlocked. Its trajectories of development are set and corrected in the points of bifurcation demonstrating multivariance and strombuliform. Non-linear discreteness and fractality have come to replace the nosocentric dynamics with its traditional its stages. Fractal — is a projection onto the wide natural-science field of quantum views. Fractal — is an integral of the dissipative system development that has its inner mechanisms of self-organization, self-development, multivariate trajectories of motion in the multidimensional space. Table 1 demonstrates only the progredient variant of the terrorism epidemic development, it shows four interdependent planes of sociogenesis, psychogenesis, somatogenesis, and animogenesis. The epidemic nature of this disorder and its individual trajectories of development are defined by the unique combination of different bio-psycho-socio-spiritual factors, effectiveness of defense, compensatory and adaptation mechanisms, methods of mental preventology and mental medicine.

Animogenesis (ontogenetic spiritual and moral development of a personality) begins in the fractal of *predisposition — mobbing family* (and/or environment), it is distinguished by *spiritual and moral deficiency* and ambivalence, high frequency of asocial and dependant disorders of parents and close relatives, various forms of violence, harassments, cavils, intimidations, insults, mockery, rudeness, deception, moral pressing and isolation.

Early imposition of the "mobbing target" image on children and adolescents leads to "mobbing sensibilization" of the inner world, formation of perverted and simplified mental models of interpersonal interaction and behavior. This family and millisocial environment have anomic and permissive nature, they are very likely to marginalize and dehumanize the moral values of a personality.

During the *latent fractal of bullying diathesis* defensive and compensatory, spiteful and aggressive protest reactions of behavioral nature develop for self-assertion; they increase the polarization of relationship and isolation.

The formation of primary moral feelings is disturbed: conscience, duty, faith and responsibility.

The deformation of spiritual development shows itself in the form of distorted self-esteem and failure to understand the purport of life, unreadiness to act independently as a full-grown individual, undeveloped moral self-consciousness and moral responsibility.

In the initial fractal of crowding mass outbreaks (mass forms of sadistic aggression and vandalism) a *deformed moral image* becomes fixated through training and behavioral practice in street teenage gangs and groups, various legal and illegal fan movements, radical and extremist movements; it lays the corner stone to the development of the demoralization syndrome. Delay and disharmony of the development of the moral image foundations show themselves as the absence of tolerance, patience, mercy, humanism, honor, dignity, deficiency and disharmony of creative potential in spiritual, figural and productive activities; unreadiness and inability to be professionally and socially labile, inability to maintain continuous development and education; manipulative capability of consciousness, susceptibility to nationalistic provocations; painful emotional stress caused by strangulated national pride and xenophobia; exceptional stereotypical reactions to challenges and difficulties – aggression and vandalism.

In the debut fractal of the social epidemic of terrorism the pro-social spiritual and moral position of personality is lost and the syndrome of terrorist demoralization is formed; at the same time the abilities to differentiate good and evil, friendship and love decrease. An affected personality becomes amorphous and deficient, low self-criticism develops together with the personality's impairment. The vision of life becomes stereotyped with the only purport of life being the struggle for the right and the inability to realize the value of human life. Crowding terrorists are distinguished by the archaic and binary ethical picture of the world that has blurred borders between reality and fantasy. They are fixated on dominant ideas of the nation's historical trauma and perverted mythologized image of the enemy. Crowding terrorists remain prisoners of their obsessions with messianic ideas and believe in a special meaning of life that infers selfless service in the name of justice and historical revenge. They distinguish themselves with easy perception and neglect of multiple adaptation difficulties to social conventions and moral rules, inclination to "solve problems" only with the help of quick and easy solutions based on violence, preference to primitive styles of mental representation, and armed aggression, religious ritual coverage of their struggle for the right, cultivation of heroized ideas about martyr death and redemptive life after death.

The fractal of chronization of the destructive social epidemic of terrorism is characterized by different forms and types of immoral and illegal behavior development; this behavior threatens the national security of a country. The syndrome of terrorist demoralization shows itself as a complete loss of the socially accepted mediated moral behavior that is based on the concepts of good and evil, indebted and unacceptable, demonstrative disregard of any moral duties and rejection of moral self-control, dependence and irresponsibility of personal actions, inability to carry out moral self-evaluation of one's behavior and inability to respect the ethical norms of business communication, loss of personal and social identity, devaluation of legal awareness and law-obedience, avoidance of personal moral choice making as well as any kind of responsibility. The anonymity of cyber-terrorists and facemasks on participants of terroristic civil wars demonstrate it.

The fractal of outcome is characterized by the maximum epidemic level of pandemic, terminal complications and consequences for the society and terrorists. The ethical component of personality's difficult asocial development makes terrorists absolutely insensitive to counterarguments and dissuasion. Together with comorbid and associated disorders it leads to metal defects, results in the loss of pragmatism and rationality, absence of fear and repentance, super- glorification of sacrificial death and heroic martyrdom in the terrorist civil war.

All this allows militant manipulators to "create" new generations of suicidal terrorists easily. *In fact, they are engaged in mental terrorism – individual, distractive and mercenary creation of adherents.* The only difference of mental terrorism from traditional forms of propaganda and agitation is in the population format of the public consciousness, that is "being attacked" by mass media. The growing network interactivity of the global world is making the information front line the primary battlefield in the war against terrorism.

Serial and deadly equifinal terroristic wars develop according to the mechanism of a dependant disorder when only an injurious act of terrorism can provide a psycho-emotional relief and fill a desperate and inescapable existential situation with illusionary meanings. These illusionary meanings are literally covered with the masks of "unknown soldiers".

The development of the terrorist demoralization syndrome is exceptionally multivariate, it is predetermined by the initial ethical topology of personality, ethno-cultural and socio-economic, religious and political factors of the environment. The latter factors are turning into a dehumanized and demoralized *"terroristic world" that is undermining the civilizational foundations of humanity.*

Sociogenesis (ontogenic development of social roles and relations) in the fractal of *predisposition* is characterized by the high frequency of various disorders in the structure and functions of the mobbing family. They substantially predetermine the mental representation of destructive cognitive models of disharmonious interpersonal relations: the cult of strength and aggression, humiliations and insults, social deprivations and isolations, negativism and protest.

Table 4. Fractal dynamics of epidemic development of terrorism

	Prenosological fractals			Nosological fractals		
Vectors of ontogenesis	**Predispositions:** mobbingogenic family and/ or environment	**Latent:** bullyingogenic diathesis	**Initial:** mass crowding	**Debut:** Social epidemic	**Chronizations:** Destructive social epidemic	**Outcome:** Pandemic and terminal complications
Somatogenesis	Hereditary somatic burden	Derangements of neuroprocesses	Somatoform dysfunctions	Somatized disorder	Comorbid psychosomatic illness	Somato-neurological complications and degradation of public health
Psychogenesis	Psychopathological burden	Polymodal psychopatization of personality	Asocial and/or dependent personality outside personal space	Asocial and /or dependent personality disorder	Asocial and/ or dependent personality development	Psychic defect and destruction of public consciousness
Sociogenesis	Derangements of structure and family function	Derangements of personality socialization	Non-pathological dependent and /or asocial behavior	Pathologic dependent and / or asocial behavior	Social decompensation	Social disadaptation and dehumanization of society
Animogenesis	Moral and spiritual family deficiency	Derangements in moral feelings formation	Deformation of moral image	Loss of moral position	Amoral and unlawful behavior	Serial criminality and suicidal terrorism, demoralization of public conciousness

In the latent fractal of bullying diathesis the dispersion and inversion of the "mobbing target" and "mobbing terrorist" take place as a result of the personality's maturation and socialization disorders. These disorders develop in a disharmonious millisocial environment and are later followed by the "bullying terrorist" whose distinctive features are hyper-compensatory cruelty and aggression. Such personalities do not have psychosocial resources for productive self-realization through their professional and educational activities, inside their families and social networks. To a significant extant that is the exact reason why non-pathological dependant behavior develops through compensatory mechanisms. It is characterized by perverted obsessive fantasies that are realized through sadistic and cruel compulsive group tortures of defenseless animals and vulnerable peers, subordination of personal interests to some kind of paraphilia, long fixation of attention and, decreased ability to control, immersion into asocial dependence, dependency and passivity when choosing behavioral strategies and verbal response strategies, self — and mutual induction during *mass outbreaks of crowding terrorism in the initial fractal.*

In the fractal of the social terrorism epidemic debut the reference nucleus of the epidemic hotbed and its leaders display *pathologic dependent and asocial behavior*; it is notable for the episodes when changed conditions of consciousness are present at the moment of psychological and physical dependence realization, irresistibility and compulsivity of the asocial activity, stereotypization of the terroristic lifestyle, cancelation syndrome between delicts and acts of terrorism.

In the chronization fractal a destructive social epidemic of terrorism unfolds, it has different instruments and mechanisms depending on the type and form of terrorism, however, it inevitably leads the participants of an epidemic process to social decompensation and threatens the national security of a country as a whole.

In the outcome fractal a total social disadaptation is formed at liberty; in the case of lifetime imprisonment a forced adaptation to the prison conditions develops. The development of terroristic pandemic is accompanied by and matched with various social markers of the global dehumanization crisis and civilization degradation: famine, unemployment, migration, etc.

Psychogenesis (ontogenic development of mental functions) *in the fractal of predisposition.* To a significant degree psychogenesis is predetermined by the premorbid psychopathological complication of the mobbing family, it is distinguished by non-motivated psycho-emotional instability and communicative deficiency. Children who grow in such families, even those with orthodox and patriarchal backgrounds, experience an acute shortage of emotional connections, and painfully go through the early loss of parental care. Trying to compensate for them they develop an aptitude to fantasize and demand increased attention. Very often an early psychological trauma is related to a glorified martyr death of a relative or another close acquaintance that was witnessed by the future terrorist. This death becomes a matrix of mental representation for tomorrow's terroristic lifestyle and death.

In the latent fractal of bullying diathesis addictive radicals of an early psychopathic disorder and personal deformation are formed and fixated, they show themselves as anticipating malicious and aggressive verbal reactions to all challenges and difficulties; they stereotype aggressive and auto-aggressive styles of behavior, lauch the mechanism of hypercompensatory "asocial hysteria" and polymodal asocial dependant disorder. Such a personality can demonstrate various socially stressful disorders even in the situation when it encounters banal life difficulties. All this speeds up the formation of a primary dependant pattern, that will be able to change its modality later as well as the form of dependence. However, the asocial radical of this dependence will be steadily preserved engrossing the personality's nucleus.

In the initial fractal of crowding terrorism mass outbreaks behavioral realization of previously learned mental schemes and scenarios of asocial self-assertion takes place, this is the only outcome based on the cognitive and cultural personal resources. An asocial and dependant personality demonstrates vivid realistic reminiscences and fantasies glorifying terrorism outside his disorder. It happens above the background of infantilism and suggestibility, openheartedness and sensory spontaneity, curiosity and high searching activity, minimalism and egocentrism, impressionability and impatience, aptitude to taking risks and provoking dangerous situations, generalized aggression and vandalism. This personality gets a chance to overcome the inferiority complex of an individual rejected in his prosocial environment and get rid of the "black sheep" label only in street gangs, extremist and fanatic groups. The extrusion and disactualization of such obsessive reminiscences about one's traumatic youth, that had multiple humiliations and losses, is accompanied by the hyper-compensatory necessity to revenge not only some particular offenders, but the whole cruel and unjust world, revenge for one's nation. This is how the psychological mechanisms of epidemic terrorism generalization demonstrate themselves.

All 10 types of personality disorders, described in ICD 10, can take place among terrorists and extremists. However, the most significant role in launching epidemic processes belongs to mutually reinforcing asocial and dependant disorders with their radicals. They easily create a TV image that shows the unity of people and their leaders. An epidemic develops according to self and mutual induction mechanisms as it adds complications to the existing personality disorder.

Borderline personality disorder — is a severe emotional instability and impulsive aggression, disturbance of interpersonal relations and self-destructing behavior. Prevalence among population 1,5-2 %.

Personality disorder - are deep-rooted styles of behavior and thinking with rigid response reactions in excessively expressed forms. Prevalence 6-18 % [2].

At the time of K. Schneider [7] not only the afflicted person suffered from this disorder, the whole society was affected as well. Today the epidemic spread of extremism and terrorism mobilizes the mechanisms of induction and generalization, it turns them into a global populational mutation, and poses the threat of civilization suicide. Moreover, it is necessary to take into account the fact that up to 30% of the population suffer from various forms of dependences [4], the controlled social switching of their modality can quickly lead to the emergence of social epidemics.

The debut fractal of the social epidemic of terrorism is most often represented by asocial and dependant personality disorders of the epidemic hotbed referent nucleus. It induces the fellow-fighters who make part of the polymodal subpopulation.

Dependant personality disorders are characterized by the deficiency of normative sociality and widening of the asocial manifestation's specter, personality deformation and emotional burnout, inability to make decisions independently outside one's terroristic lifestyle, frequent combinations of schizoid personality features with bad tolerance of loneliness. It facilitates the development of anxious depression, urging an individual to commit excesses, delicts and acts of terrorism that provide a temporary psycho-emotional relief.

The fractal of chronization of the destructive social epidemic of terrorism is represented by multivariate *asocial and dependant personality developments*, terrorism begins to take the leading position in the their constellation and it turns into a dominant dependence. A changing personal and social identity, new cognitive schemes and mental models of business interaction allow moderators to easily find suitable euphemisms ("red brigades", "right sector" and etc.), and complimentary-compensatory labels (commandant, centurion, national guardsman, etc), although, all this is unable to change a developed terroristic nucleus of a paraphilic personality.

In April 2014 all Russian TV channels showed the recording of Alexander M. (one of the leaders of Kiev Maidan) when he expressed his sadistic threats to the deputies of the regional council; in this video he appeared dressed in camouflage and was holding an assault rifle as if it was a phallus like prosthesis. In a different video he experiences a masochistic ecstasy from the strikes of female heels against the head. Undoubtedly, internet screening and TV pictures can let us express only a supposition about sadomasochism or multiple disorders of sexual preferences, that are usually represented by a combination of such paraphilias as fetishism, transvestism and sadomasochism. The producers of tragedy could not allow this militant (who sincerely believed in his messianic role of a fighter) to continue his vivid illustration of this clinical case of parahpilia. This "tele-hero" was doomed to failure from the moment of his TV screen debut. *Terror inside a terroristic community is a law of moral anomia in a legion of assassins*. The classification of paraphilia as a dependant disorder [1], the same refers to mobbing, bullying and crowding [6], makes it possible to *view terrorism as an independent type of polymodal dependant disorder.*

There is no doubt that the participants of mass murders and sexual violence in Odessa's Hatyn, (those that were registered by audio and video devices) will never be found by any international commission.

The weapons of terrorists, besides their direct purposes, serve as a *hypercompensatory attribute that masks*: the inability to make decisions without advice of their senior leaders and financing mentors; readiness to delegate them rights without demur when it comes to making decisions of critical importance; anticipating preparedness to agree with their masters caused by the fear to be rejected (even when knowing that they are wrong); difficulties when starting something independently; readiness of one's own free will to carry out risky and dangerous orders in order to get a reward or appraisal from the principle; bad tolerance of loneliness and readiness to undertake any efforts in order to avoid it; feeling of being drained or being helpless when falling out of one's "national guard"; easy susceptibility and vulnerability to manipulability, enchainment with anxiety and fear to be rejected that pushes to commit new and new delicts and acts of terrorism.

In the outcome fractal one can expect a psychic defect – it differs considerably depending on various forms of terroristic asocial dependencies that range from the syndrome of emotional burn out and destructive professiongenesis with mobbing-, bullying- and crowding –terrorism to the psychoorganic syndrome with traumatic lesion of the brain or chemical dependences.

The escalation of a terroristic civil war inevitably leads to the augmented *destruction of the public consciousness as an integral quality of the nation's mental health.*

Somatogenesis (ontogenic development of somatic functions) refers to the least studied aspects. It is generally accepted that nonspecific hereditary burden (fractal of predisposition), unfavorable intra- perinatal exposures play an important role in it. Different normative psychosomatic reactions can be response reactions to challenges and difficulties; later they transform into functional psychosomatic disorders — organ neuroses (*latent fractal*) and somatoform disorders, they provide a clinical description of an individual with forming "withdrawal syndrome" (*initial fractal*). The severity of possible somatization disorders (*debut fractal*) and comorbid psychomotor disorders is defined by the duration of the "withdrawal syndrome", unwillingness and inability of a deformed personality to attain psycho-emotional relief in frames of his adaptive and prosocial behavior (*chronization fractal*).

All forms of social epidemics are characterized by the absence of parallelism in the expression of mental and somato- neurological, moral and spiritual, social and psychological disorders. While chemical dependences during their somatogenesis result in the evolution of the given disorders and are strongly connected to the toxic agent, the non-chemical ones (as a compensatory variant of development) more often lead to comorbid psychosomatic disorders. The accepted name of this mechanism is somatization of dependence. *In the outcome fractal* one can expect different somato-neurological complications; as for the level of social health – regress and degradation can be expected. The notion of comorbidity is not so much based on traditional views about compatibility of pathologies but on etiopathogenic unity of all dependent behavior forms [3].

Dependency signs may stipulate dangerous aggressive actions in frames of self- and mutual induction of social terrorism epidemics; they become evident with the following classic syndromes:

1) *syndrome of changed reactivity* is represented by a higher rated of delicts and acts of terrorism, growth of multimodal tolerance and sadistic aggressiveness, impoverishment and exhaustion of the out of episode normative sociality;
2) *syndrome of psychic dependence* is represented by an obsessive attraction, mental comfort condition during a deviant and criminal situation, changed and perverted form of emotional experience towards delict or act of terrorism;
3) *syndrome of physical dependence* is represented by a compulsive attraction, composed of physical comfort during a deviant or criminogenic situation; changed and perverted forms of delict and terrorist act manifestation, "withdrawal syndrome".

The syndromes of psychic and physical dependence determine the multi-episodic and compulsory nature of the epidemic generalization with asocial dependent behavior as well as the involuntariness of its appearance and difficulty in overcoming anomalous attraction of the commenced episode. They influence the degree of freedom when it comes to choosing a behavioral pattern. That is how they act as a psychopathologic foundation of possible dangerous serial actions [1]. Unfortunately, "Odessa's Hatyn", is just the beginning…

The growth of tolerance acts as a psychopathological foundation for the increased amount of aggressiveness and autoagression, severity of repeated and serial delicts, acts of terrorism.

The out of episode dynamics of social terrorism epidemic shows itself in the form of growing destructive professiongenesis, emotional burnout and personality deformation, development of associated and comorbid psychosomatic disorders.

It is of principle importance to emphasize, that the *model of "synergetic individual" allows to obtain a unified bio-psycho-socio-spiritual methodology of analysis for all epidemic forms of dependent disorders — ranging from alcoholism and drug abuse to fanaticism and terrorism, it corresponds to the high-priority directions of the mental medicine development [5].*

6. Medical-psycho-socio-spiritual Defence from Destructive Social Epidemics

The synergetic approach, that forms the foundation of mental medicine, presupposes a significant review of medical treatment, rehabilitation and preventive strategies of providing help to the dependent population and changing their ideology. The methodology of traditional socio-therapeutic and psychotherapeutic, socio-psychiatric and addiction relief services must be reviewed as well. Every dependent personality requires constant and interactive sanitization and correction that can only change the vector and modality of dependence.

When treating a dependent personality the main objective is to replace the modality of his dependence and change it from destructive to constructive, from non-adaptive to adaptive, from asocial to prosocial, from autoaggressive to self-preserving. This needs to be done at the earliest stage possible. The preventive strategy for treating dependent subpopulation requires adequate and regular loading of *adaptive socio-psychological and moral-spiritual content.*

On the basis of the synergetic concept of the destructive social epidemics development [11] we have elaborated a program of treatment and rehabilitation with preventive and correctional help. It represents a *unified multidisciplinary protocol that* is being implemented by a brigade of specialists. This program includes four blocks: medical, psychiatric, spiritual and moral, social (see table). These blocks are based on the four main types of ontogenesis planes (sociogenesis, psychogenesis, somatogenesis, and animogenesis) and are interconnected. All together they represent the synergetic methodology of mental medicine [10].

Medical block includes professional help of qualified psychiatrists,, narcologists,, general practitioners and physicians in frames of somatogenesis (ontogenetic development of the organism systems and functions).

Psychological block presupposes professional help of mental health specialists such as psychotherapists, clinical psychologists, psychiatrists in frames of psychogenesis (ontogenetic development of psychic functions).

Social help is provided in frames of sociogenesis (ontogenetic development of social roles and relationships) with the participation of social services (specialists in social work, social workers).

Spiritual and moral block animogenesis (ontogenetic spiritual and moral development of personality) this block is implemented with consultants and experts in ethics, clinical psychologists and general practitioners who know the peculiarities of the patient's family moral climate. Psychotherapeutic, educational and training methods together with the personal growth and coaching techniques block the syndromes of demoralization and destructive professiogenesis. When conflict situations emerge mediation on the basis of ethical committees is administered. Patients and clients get involved into development programs of different social organizations. This is how they consolidate the adaptive strategies of business communication ethics. The same objectives are reached when patients become participants of voluntary and social movements of paraprofessionals. They are needed in the rehabilitation programs for dependent people. Church-going patients may be effectively helped by spiritual mentors– representatives of official confessions.

Table 5. Programme for medico-psycho-socio-spiritual help in social epidemics

	Donosological fractals			Nosological fractals		
Blocks	**Predispositions**	**Latent**	**Initial**	**Detailed clinical finding**	**Chronisation**	**Outcomes**
Medical	Detection of people with hereditary predisposition, including them in the group of risk, early preventive examination	Detection of people with organ neuroses	Diagnostic of somatoform dysfunctions; medicamental and non-medicamental treatment	Detection of comorbid psychiatric diseases, prescribing medical therapy, prevention of complications	Adequate medicinal therapy of psycho-organic stigmatisation and psychosomatic diseases	Treatment for somato-neurological complications
Psychological	Detection of people with psychological load and taking preventive measures with them	Sanitation of psychopathisation of the personality	Detecting the dependent personality beyond personal disorder and correction of disorders	Correction of major personal disorders, psychotherapy.	Psychotherapy and psych-pharmacotherapy of dependent personality disorder	Psychological rehabilitation for psychiatric defect
Social	Detection and correction of violations of family structure and function	Correction of personality socialisation disorders	Correction of non-pathological dependent behaviour	Complex treatment of pathologically-dependent behaviour	Correction of social decompensation	Social rehabilitation
Morally-spiritual	Screening and correction of the family's "moral climate"	Correction of formation and development of moral feelings	Correction of formation and development of moral portrait	Reconstruction of moral positions	Reconstruction of moral behaviour	Morally-spiritual rehabilitation
	Mental preventology			Clinical psychiatry		
	Mental medicine					

Primary preventive measures should be taken in the *predisposition fractal*, where they can be used to determine hereditary and psychological predispositions as well as help with the psycho-psychological, spiritual and moral harmonization of the family relationship.

In the *latent fractal* special measures are taken to detect those individuals who are prone to organ neuroses. Attempts are made to correct the moral socialization of a personality as well as any psychopathic personality traits.

In the *initial fractal* when a non-pathological dependent behavior develops, special medicamental and psychiatric treatments are administered. This treatment prevents the development of dependent behavior and deformation of the moral make-up. In the fractal with *revealed clinical findings* early professional anti-addiction, psychotherapeutic, psychological, social, moral and spiritual help is required.

In the *chronization fractal* adequate medicamental therapy, psychotherapeutic treatment of the dependent disorder, socio-psychological, spiritual and moral corrections of the demoralization syndrome are administered regardless of the demoralization syndrome variant. These procedures are used with the alcohol demoralization syndrome as well as with the terroristic demoralization syndrome.

In those cases when there is a threat of *psychic defect or social dezadaptation* psychological, social, medical, moral and spiritual rehabilitations become necessary. They can be organized on the multidisciplinary basis with the help of the mental health service.

Mental health service – is a synergetic bio-psycho-socio-spiritual Ψ-cluster of society and state. It provides preventive and correctional protection of mental health and medical rehabilitation help for people with mental disorders.

The mental health service methodologically and technologically utilizes the resources of mental medicine, it creates a synergetic foundation that integrates classical clinical psychiatry, mental preventology (see table), makes it possible to organize a *systematic monitoring of mental health* and cardinally increases the efficiency social protection from destructive social epidemics. It is necessary to *reevaluate the mission of the prophylactic medical examination* (that are currently undergoing reforms) and conceptualize the systematic monitoring of the nation's social and mental health, expand the spectrum of its activity from narrow-specialized tactical tasks (infections, customer oriented, and others) *to strategic objectives that would create a social platform of national security.*

V. A. Medvedev [23] singled out the levels of motivation that give birth to terror and arranged them in a regressive sequence. This sequence shows the regression of generic and sociocultural nature and progression of individual personality components: biological (population), historic and cultural (mythological), ethno-psychological, group, individual psychopathology and sociopathy. The mirror reflection of these levels structures *the echelon system of antiterrorist defense.* All contemporary humanitarian counterterrorism models are based on the *systematic spiritual and ideological construction of national security that is founded on the life-forming meanings and moral values.*

The mental paradigm of national security includes: abatement of mental ailments consequences, strengthening of the nation's mental health; reduction of the spread of social destructive epidemics, self-destructive and dependent behavior, decrease of high mortality rates and social violence; lessening of the social stratification, poverty and unemployment; elimination of social vulnerability of seriously ill people and individuals with disabilities; overcoming of anomia and permissivity, deformation of social and individual consciousness, social isolation of an individual; formation of multivariant strategies of adaptive professiogenesis and effective self-management.

All preventive, correctional, therapeutic and rehabilitation measures of the bio-psycho-socio-spiritual programs, administered by the mental health service, must be inspired with the ideology of correction. The pessimistic and disastrous paradigm of world perception needs to be removed and replaced with the constructive life strategy that predetermines adaptive professiogenesis and stable development, prevention of endemic dependent disorders and spiritual immunity to destructive social epidemics.

References

[1] Baillon G. *Introduktion a lantipsychiatrie//* La Nef. 28 annee. № 42. Janvier-mai 1971, p 23.

[2] Barantsev R.G. Баранцев Р.Г. *Synergetics in modern natural sciences* / R.G. Barantsev. Moscow, Editorial URSS, 2009, p 160.

[3] Chernobrovkina T.V. Philosophic problems in biology and medicine: synergetics in addictology. *Addictology*. 2005. №1, pp 14-20.

[4] Demcheva N.K. New clinical-epidemiological and sociometric approaches to evaluating the population's mental health // *S.S. Korsakov neuropatology and psychiatry journal*. 2006. V.106. №6, pp 58-61.

[5] Fulford K. Looking with both eyes open fact and value in psychiatric diagnosis? // *World Psychiatry*. 2005. Vol. 4. №2, pp. 78-86.

[6] Gilinskii Ya. I. Modern terrorism: Who is "at fault" and what is to be done? // Psychology and psychopatology of terrorism. *Humanitatrian strategies of anti-terror*. Saint-Petersburg, 2004, p. 20.

[7] Goodman M. et al. Parental viewpoints of trajectories to borderline personality disorder in femaile offspring. *J Pers Disord* 2010, pp 2004-2016.

[8] Islamskikh radikalov budut lechit' [Islamic radicals will be treated] // *Week's Arguments*. 2013. no. 21(363). Available at: URL: argumenti.ru/talks/n391/259380 (accessed 17 January 2014).

[9] Jung C.G. Complete works. *Psychology of the unconscious*. Moscow, Canon, 1994, p 251.

[10] Jung C.G. Paracelsus the Physician. Complete works in 19 volumes. V. 15. *Phenomenon of spirit in art and science*. Moscow, Renessans. 1992, p 29.

[11] Jung C.G. Modern man in search of a soul. *The Modern Spiritual Problem*. Moscow. Progress-Univers publishing group.1994, p 314.

[12] Jung C.G. *Psychological types*. St Petersburg, Yuventa, Moscow, Progress-Univers publishing group. 1995, p 553, p 716.

[13] Jung C.G. *Flying saucers: A modern myth of things seen in the skies*. C.G. Jung on modern myths. Moscow, Praktika, 1994, pp 55, 171, 173.

[14] Karsavin L.P. *Apologetic essay* // Small compositions. St Petersburg. AO Aleteya. 1994, p 380.

[15] Katkov A. L. *Destructive Social Epidemics*. Saint Petersburg, 2013, 484 p.

[16] Kazakovtsev B.A. *Development of mental health services*. Moscow, GEOTAR-Media, 2009, p 672.

[17] Krasnov V.N., Kokhanov V.P. *Psychiatry of extreme situations.* Moscow. Practical medicine, 2008, p 478.

[18] Krasnov V.N. *Educational programme on depressive disorders in three volumes.* V.1, v.2, v.3 T.1, T.2, T.3"/ - Moscow, Moscow Psychiatry Scientific Research Institute, 2010. V.1 — p 119., v.2 — p 171., v.3 — p 303.

[19] Laing R.D., La Poljtique de l^experience. Essai sur l^alientation et l^oiseau de Paradis. Paris: Stock. 1969, p 88.

[20] Lem S. *Summa technologiae.* Moscow, St Petersburg, AST. 2006, pp 231, 365.

[21] Makarov V.V. Psychotherapy: science, art, craft / *Psychotherapy* 2013. № 1, pp 2-3

[22] Malinetsky G.G., Potapov A.B. *Non-linear dynamics and chaos. The main notions.* Moscow, KomKniga. 2006, p 42.

[23] Medvedev V. A. Terror as foundation of communicative culture of XXI century: from understanding to interpretation // *Psychology and psychopathology of terrorism. Humanitarian strategies of anti-terror.* Saint Petersburg, 2004, pp. 102-130.

[24] Morozov P.V., Ovsyannikov S.A. History of development of scientific bases of psychiatry // *Psychiatry. National manual.* Edited by T.B. Dmitrieva, V.N. Krasnov, N.G. Neznanov, V.Ya. Semke, A.S. Tiganov. Moscow, GEOTAR-Media. 2009, p 58.

[25] Moshchelkov E. N. i dr. Modern terrorism: reasons, essence, principles of building of counter-terrorism humanitarian models. *Modern terrorism and fight against it: social-humanitarian dimensions.* Moscow, 2007, pp. 19-26.

[26] Nazaretyan A. P. *Psychological studies of spiritual-moral problems.* Moscow, 2011, pp. 428, 432.

[27] Neznanov N.G. Medical-psychological aspects of oncology (analysis of the problem and general recommendations). "*Mental disorders in common medicine.* 2009. №1, p 13-16.

[28] Nuller Yu.L. Changing paradigms in psychiatry? *Psychiatry and psychopharmacotherapy.* 2008. v. 9, №5, pp 4-7.

[29] Porter R. *Madness: a brief history* / R. Porter. Moscow, AST-Astrel, 2008, pp 13, 194, 197, 201. 224 p.

[30] Reshetnikov M. M. *Scetches to terrorist psychological portrait* // Psychology and psychopathology of terrorism. Humanitarian strategies of anti-terror. Saint Petersburg, 2004, pp. 341-343.

[31] Sidorov P. I. *Mental terrorism – non-lethal weapon of mass destruction* // Russian journal of psychiatry. 2005, 3, pp. 28-34.

[32] Sidorov P.I. *Narcological preventive medicine:* guide Moscow, MEDpress-inform, 2006, p 720.

[33] Sidorov P.I. *Method of evaluating a person's mental ecology* / P.I. Sidorov, I.A. Novikova // Patent for invention №2347528 registered on 27.02.2009.

[34] Sidorov P.I. *From mental ecology to mental medicine* / Human ecology 2013. № 1, pp 33-38.

[35] Sidorov P. I. *System Synthesis of Mental Medicine* // Human Ecology. 2013, 10, pp. 37-48.

[36] Sidorov P. I. *Movement-Related Brain Potentials* // Human Ecology. 2014, 1, pp. 30-37.

[37] Silverman M. et. al The course of anxiety disorders other than PTSD in patients with borderline personality disorder and axis II comparison subjects: a 10-year foiiow-up study. *J Pers Disord* 2012, pp 804-816.

[38] Smulevich A.B. Mental disorders in clinical practice. Moscoww, MEDpress-inform, 2011, p 720.

[39] Smulevich A.B. For the problem of trajectory of mental personality disorders in the field of minor psychiatry / *Psychiatry and psychopharmacology* 2012.. v.4 № 5, pp 47-49

[40] Sorokin P.A. Crisis of our time // *Man. Civilisation. Society.* Moscow, IPL. 1992, pp 433, 500-502.

[41] Sosin V. A. *Psychology of modern terrorism.* Moscow, 2012, 160 p.

[42] Sternberg R. J. A duplex theory of hate: Development and application to terrorism, massacres, and genocide. *Review of General Psychology*. 2003, 7 (3), pp. 299-328.

[43] Troshin V. D., Pogodina T. G. *Terrorism and nervous-mental disorders: diagnosis, treatment, prevention*. N. Novgorod, 2007, 314 p.

[44] Yastrebov V.S. Economic evaluation of the scale of investment and losses because of mental illnesses: methodology of studying and socially-economic prognosis of consequences. // *Social and clinical psychiatry.* 2009. №4, pp 21-28.

[45] Zinchenko Yu. P., Shilko R. S. Detection of risk groups representing terrorism developmental resources and grounding of principles of anti-terrorist activities on this direction// *Modern terrorism and fight against it: social-humanitarian dimensions.* Moscow, 2007, pp. 36-37.

In: Handbook on Bullying
Editor: Phoebe Triggs

ISBN: 978-1-63463-023-8

Chapter 13

BULLYING AMONG TRAINING SCHOOL MALE ADOLESCENTS AND MALE ADULT PRISONERS: DESCRIPTIVE ANALYSIS

Kristi Kõiv, Ph.D. **[*] *and Liine Maasikas***
Institute of Education, University of Tartu, Estonia

Abstract

The current study aims to address the lack of research exploring differences between male adult prisoners and male juvenile training school students in relation to their bullying behavior.

A training school is a correctional facility that is used for the custody and re-education of juvenile offenders. Training schools are a part of the educational system in Estonia and they are used to prepare incarcerated youth for returning to society. The first sample of this study consists of all 53 male adolescent offenders (13–17 years old with average age 14.7 years) at the only maximum security male juvenile training school in Estonia, and the second sample consists of 105 male adult offenders (21–66 years old with average age 33.1 years) at one of four maximum security male prisons in Estonia.

The present study used a self-reported questionnaire developed by Ireland and Archer (1996) to provide not only a descriptive analysis of the nature and extent of bullying among adolescents in training school and among adults in prison, but also a comparison between two study group to assess the hypothesis that adolescents' bullying would involve a greater proportion of direct forms than adults' would, and that adults' bullying would display a greater proportion of indirect forms than youth' would.

The perceived extent of bullying was higher in prison compared with juvenile training school. Bullying in the juvenile training school was predominately physical (direct) but adult reported a higher frequency of indirect bullying in prison. A particular characteristic of individuals (e.g. vulnerable) was viewed as being predisposed to become a victim of bullying and various reasons (e.g. victims are easy targets) were suggested as to why a person was bullied, but adults in prison were significantly more likely than juveniles in training school to suggest sex offenders, and adolescents more likely than adults the physical weakness of victim. Bullying was seen to occur at locations out of sight of staff but more in living areas in

[*] E-mail address: kristi.koiv@ut.ee; Tel: +3727376474; Address: Salme 1a Tartu, 50103, Estonia. (Corresponding author)

the prison and more at school and private areas in the juvenile training school. More juveniles at training school then prison inmates reported that both they and staff were willing to help the victims of bullying. A relatively higher percentage of inmates in both institutions - prison and training school, admitted to being bullies, victims and bully/victims with on average 2 to 4 bullying incidents in previous week.

Keywords: Bullying, prison, training school, male adolescent and adult inmates

Introduction

Research on bullying in diversity of settings (Monks, Smith, Naylor, Barter, Ireland & Coyne, 2009) has grown rapidly during the last two decades, initially in schools but also in other settings and relationships: between siblings, in children's homes, in prisons, and in the workplace among children, adolescents, and adults. Common trends across contexts include age and sex differences. For example, general trends in prison bullying can in part be understood in terms of the developmental model (Björkqvist, Österman, & Kaukiainen, 1992) whereas younger inmates are more likely to use direct and physical forms of bullying and older inmates more indirect and less physical bullying forms; and with special trends in prison settings. Namely, indirect aggression is used to the same extent (or even more), than direct aggression as and due to its covert nature, it reduces the risk of being caught and of the perpetrator being subjected to any official punishment (Ireland, 1999a).

Main settings of studying bullying are schools (overview: Smith, 2011) and prisons (overview: Ireland, 2011), but bullying in training schools is a setting that interweaves these two abovementioned study areas. Bullying in prison occurs more frequently than among schoolchildren (Ireland 2005). For example, between 15 and 20 per cent of children and adolescents experienced intense and repeated victimization during their school years, which give an example to the extensive range of research on school bullying in whole world (Smith and Brian, 2000; included Estonia: Kõiv, 2009). Nearly two decades there is a scientific interest to the topic of prison bullying with leading role of studies in the United Kingdom (Ireland, 2002a).

Within school context, bullying tends to be defined as specific phenomenon as a subsection of aggressive behavior (intended, repeated attack with power imbalance), whereas in the prison context it is seen within the wider approach indicating that frequency, duration and intent as criteria for defining bullying may be not always applied (Coyne & Monks, 2011; Ireland, 2005a). But other researchers (Edgar, 2005) have argued that repetition is an essential element for behavior to be labeled bullying in prison. Ireland (1999a) has noted that one way in which researchers try to avoid definitional problems in bullying research is to present respondents with a definition of the phenomenon. In addition to the different definitions applied to prison-based studies, a variety of methods have also been used to collect data: interviews, official records, and self-report questionnaires (Ireland, Jarvis, Beck, & Osiowy, 1999), and in this field research has commonly used self-reports to measure the nature and the extent of bullying (included direct measurement of bullying, and measurement of behavior indicative of bullying), which have been found to be more reliable and valid that either staff or peer-reports (Connell and Farrington, 1997).

This chapter compares the nature and extent of bullying by male inmates in two settings – one is juvenile training school and the other is adult male prison. Training schools are correctional facilities that are used for the custody and re-education of juvenile offenders. The primary focus of training schools is to provide care, treatment, education and custody for juveniles committed by the courts and to create programs that will rehabilitate, re-educate and re-socialize juvenile offenders. To keep juvenile offenders from falling behind in their education, the training school offers a full range of academic courses as well as art, sports and music electives, and also vocational training. At the same time, juvenile courts reserve the power of incarcerating the juveniles in this type of correctional institutions (e.g. Milan, 1996). The effectiveness of these schools has been the subject of recent controversy (e.g. Inderbitzin, 2006). The age of trainings school inmates more closely matched samples of juveniles in prison-based research.

Although, the overall interest to prison bullying research has increased covering full remit of the prison population – adults, young offenders, juveniles, men and women, although of these juveniles and women remain the least researched (Ireland, 2005a), with Ireland and Monaghan (2006) stressing the need for more research in juveniles in correctional institutions. The current study aims to assess the lack of research exploring differences between juvenile males in training school and adult males in prisoners in relation to bullying behavior, whereby both facilities were maximum security correctional institutions.

The focus of prison bullying research has been on adult offenders, especially to men (Ireland, 2011), whereby few studies focus on the differences in bullying behavior in prison among 18–20 year old (young offenders) and 14–17 year old (juveniles) offenders.

At one side, research exploring differences between adults and young prisoners self-reported bullying behavior have been restricted to five studies: two of them exploring bullying behavior across sample of male and female inmates (Ireland, 1999a; 1999b), one examining bullying behavior and attachment and emotional loneliness among males (Ireland & Power, 2004); one exploring bullying and psychological health among males and females (Leddy & O'Connell, 2002); and another (Smith, Pendleton, & Mitchell 2005) concentrated to bullying behavior and prison anti-bullying policy experiences among males. Ireland et al. (1999) conducted a brief review studies and reported a high prevalence rate for self-reported bullying and victimization in young offender institutions compared to adult institutions. In prison settings male youth offenders reported more psychological, physical and verbal bullying than adults (Ireland, 1999a, 1999b; Ireland & Power, 2004): adults did demonstrate a preference for indirect aggression, whereas young offenders demonstrated a preference for direct aggression displaying psychical and verbal bullying types towards others.

On the other side, only few studies explored self-reported bullying behavior among juveniles in prison: four studies (Ireland, 2002b, 2005b; Ireland & Archer, 2004, Ireland & Monaghan, 2006) had examined the nature and extent of bullying between young and juvenile male offenders, with focusing on the aggressive traits (Ireland & Archer, 2004), and on the psychological health (Ireland 2005b); one descriptive study explored the perceptions of male adult, young and juvenile prisoners with regards to how bullying was defined (Ireland & Ireland, 2003); and one study compared juvenile, young and adult prisoners within the same dataset (Ireland & Hafiz, 2010).

The prison-based research with regards to adolescents has been descriptive in nature exploring the nature and extent of bullying: Juveniles were found to be more likely to report behaviors indicative of "being bullied physically" than young offenders (Ireland, 2002b; Ireland & Monaghan, 2006), with indicating (Ireland, 2005b; Ireland & Monaghan, 2006) that this extended to psychological, verbal, and overall direct forms of victimization; juveniles were more likely than young offenders to be classified as bully/victims, whereas young offenders were more likely to be classified as not involved than juveniles (Ireland, 2005b; Ireland & Hafiz, 2010), and both juveniles and young offenders reported similar levels of indirect bullying behavior (Ireland, 2002b).

The present study used a self-reported questionnaire to provide a descriptive analysis of the nature and extent of bullying at training school among male adolescents and at prison among male adults, and the aim of the study was to compare the nature and extent of bullying between these two male institutionalized study groups. It was hypothesized that adolescents' bullying at training school would involve a greater proportion of direct forms than adults' would; and that adults' bullying in prison would display a greater proportion of indirect forms than juveniles' would. It is hoped that this will address the lack of research which examines nature and extent of bullying in training school setting for male juvenile delinquents.

Method

Samples

The first sample consists of 105 male adult offenders 21 - 66 years old with average age 33.1 years (SD=9.3) at one of the four maximum security male prisons in Estonia (overall: five prisons and one of them for females). All had been sentenced with an average length of 3.1 years; the combined range of offences included property crimes (43.8%), violent offences (18.9%), drugs offences (11.9%), homicide (9.4%) sex offences (4.6%), criminal damage (3.55%), and other offences (7.9%). 54% were Estonians, 44% Russians and 2% mixed nationality.

The second sample consists of 53 male adolescent offenders (whole sample) 13-17 years old with average age 14.7 years (SD=1.24) at the only maximum security male juvenile training school (the other training school is for girls) in Estonia. All male adolescents at training school had been *incarcerated* with an average length of 1.1 years; the combined range of offences included public order crimes (72.1%), property crimes (36.6%), violent offences (44.2%), drugs offences (49.0%), and other offences (4.5%). 57% were Estonians, 40% Russians and 3% mixed nationality.

The men's maximum security prison was part of the correctional system, whereas the juvenile training school was part of the educational system. Both institutions had no anti-bullying policies.

Instrument

The self-report questionnaire developed by Ireland and Archer (1996) was used to measure the awareness of bullying in the correctional institution, individual involvement in bullying, characteristics of bullies and victims, types of bullying, staff and peers intervention, the prevention of bullying and places in the institution where bullying occurred consisting of close end and open end questions. A definition of bullying was given near the start of the questionnaire. Questions about temporal occurrence of bullying (during day and week) in the institution were added into the questionnaire. Additionally, the extent of bullying was measured using the number of inmates who reported themselves as being involved in bullying behavior.

Pretest and Procedure

After approval was received from the prison and training school institutions' internal review boards, an announcement was made on all of the units in both facilities to participate in the study. Before survey research, the Estonian and Russian version of questionnaire was pre-tested in prison and juvenile correctional facility by the authors. Pre-testing was done on a small sample of respondents (N=16) from the target population. After the pilot test respondents were asked a series of questions regarding the survey as well as the process of data collection during the debriefing session.

Participants were invited to *participate voluntarily* and asked to fill in an anonymous questionnaire without being informed of its nature. *The authors conducted questionnaire surveys* in both correctional institutions. The questionnaire was administered in small groups of two or three, with respondents seated in available rooms, at separate corners, facing away from each other. They were asked individually to read the information preceding the questionnaire including definition of bullying and the explanation of the research. The anonymity of questionnaire was stressed. Each respondent was provided with unmarked sealable envelope in which to place their completed questionnaire. Respondents were asked if they had any difficulties in reading and if so the questionnaire was conducted individually and verbally. All defaced, non-completed questionnaires (total 2.4%) were disregarded and not entered into the analysis.

The results were content analyzed and differences assessed through Chi-square or *t*-tests. The overall percentage of agreement between two raters on the descriptive categories of open-ended questions developed after data collection was 92.3% (these data were unsuitable for analyze).

Results

Extent of Bullying

The perceived extent of bullying, based in the Likert scale of 0 (none) to 7 (a lot) showed a mean of 4.08 among adult prisoners and 2.50 among juvenile delinquents, with prisoners responding a significantly higher value than young offenders (t=4.46, $p<0.001$).

Number of Inmates Seen or Heard in the Past Week Being Bullied

Most of the inmates (77% adults and 62% adolescents) reported having seen an inmate being bullied with highest frequency of inmates was seeing 2 – 4 (59% in both institutions).

More inmates in prison (63%) compared with inmates in juvenile training school (44%) have heard about bullying of inmates in the past week (χ^2=4.1; $p<0.05$) with highest frequency of involving of 2 - 4 inmates.

Bullies, Victims and Bully/Victims

The *self-reported prevalence* rates of *bullying,* victimization, and *bully/victims* in the prison were accordingly: 21%, 18%, and 17%. In the juvenile training school the rate of bullies was 17%, prevalence of victims 13%, and bully/victims 15%. Overall 56% of inmates were involved in bullying behavior in prison versus 45% in juvenile correctional facility (there were no significant differences between rates between two types of correctional facilities).

About half of all bullies reported having 2 to 4 occasions of bullying (among adults 52% and youth 55%), and half of victims reported being a target of bullying 2 to 4 occasions (among adults 54% and youth 57%) during past week. (Henceforward: Subjects offered more than one response across categories.). More than one third (prison: 36%, training school: 40%) of bullies know their victims beforehand, and more than 70% (prison: 71%, training school: 82%) victims know their bully beforehand.

Table 1. Overall ranked responses (%) among male adult prisoners and juveniles in training school to the open-ended question "Why they are bullied?"

Category	Adult prison inmates (N=105)	Juvenile delinquents (N=53)
The victim deserved it	14%	27.6%
Victim is sex offenders	15.8%	0%
Boredom/fun	49.1%	9.3%
Those considered of low physical power	0%	34.6%
Bullying involves all	10.5%	10.9%
Those considered of low intelligence	1.8%	6.9%
Minority/differences/not liking	5.3%	3.4%
No real reason	3.5%	8.2%

Table 2. Overall ranked responses (%) among adult prisoners and juvenile offenders in training school to the open-ended question "Why do they get bullied?"

Category	Adult prison inmates (N=105)	Juvenile delinquents (N=53)
Minority/difference	12.4%	13.7%
Older/younger inmates	8.1%	10.7%
Boredom/fun	36.7%	3.5%
Refusing to comply with bully's demands	12.4%	0%
Isolated/rejected	14.6%	3.6%
Because of their offence	9.2%	0%
Bully wishes to assert power/physical weakness of victim	9.5	67.9%
Victims are easy targets	2.1%	3.6%

Most common reasons given as to why they bullied included "the victim deserved it", but differed in some aspects: adults explain bullying more by boredom and with victims' sex offenders than adolescents (15.8% vs. 0%; χ^2=8.9; p<0.01; 49.1% vs. 10.3%; χ^2=8.3; p<0.01), and adolescents mentioned more often than adults that victims had low physical power

(34.6% vs. 0%; χ^2=9.7; p<0.00), whereby about one tenth of inmates had an attitude, that bullying involves all inmates in the institutions (Table 1).

Reasons offered as to why victims felt they had been bullied included being different/minority and older/younger inmates with more attention to reasons connected to boredom or fun for adults (41.7% vs. 10.3%; χ^2=9.0; p<0.00), to isolation or rejection for adults (14.6% vs. 3.6%; χ^2=5.0; p<0.05), to refusing to comply with bully's demands for prisoners (12.4% vs. 0%; χ^2=5.8; p<0.05), to their offence for prisoners (9.2% vs. 0%; χ^2=4.8; p<0.05), and to physical weakness for adolescents (67.9% vs. 12.5%; χ^2=12.0; p<0.00) in correctional institutions (Table 2).

Who Was Bullied

Adults in prison were significantly more likely than juveniles in training school to suggest sex offenders (χ^2= 12.2; p<0.00), and adolescents more likely than adults the physical weakness (χ^2=12.4; p<0.00) younger inmates (χ^2=5.4; p<0.05), whereby both study groups viewed victims as vulnerable and introvert, as different from others inmates (mentally, socially, nationally) with little connections with peers (subculture) network (Table 3).

Table 3. Overall ranked responses (%) among adult prisoners and juvenile offenders in training school to the open-ended question "What sorts of people get bullied here?"

Category	Adult prison inmates (N=105)	Juvenile delinquents (N=53)
Vulnerable, introverts	21.1%	19.4%
Physically weak	14.5%	40.3%
Young inmates	1.6%	13.9%
Sex offenders	19.1%	0%
Those considered of low intelligence	12.5%	6.9%
Minority/difference	6.3%	1.4%
No effective social skills	2.3%	4.3%
All are bullied	6.6%	6.9%
Non-conformists with criminal subculture	9.4%	6.9%
No social support from other peers	3.1%	2.6%
Problem history	1.2%	0%
Staff is bullying	2.3%	0%

Why Inmates Were Bullied

Men in prison were significantly more likely than male youth in youth institution to offer the category "because of their sex offence", and "boredom"(accordingly: χ^2=6.7, p<0.00; χ^2=4.7, p<0.05), whereas adolescents were significantly more likely to offer "physically or mentally weak" (χ^2=4.9, p<0.05) and the category "victims are easy targets" (χ^2=8.6, p<0.01) and then adults, whereby the last category was most characteristic for both study groups (Table 4).

Table 4. Overall ranked responses (%) among adult prisoners and juvenile offenders in training school to the open-ended question "Why do they get bullied?"

Category	Adult prison inmates (N=105)	Juvenile delinquents (N=53)
Victims are easy targets	31.8%	50.7%
Boredom	11.8%	1.6%
Because of their sex offence	11.4%	0%
Physically or mentally weak	4.1%	14.9%
Bully wishes to assert power	9.8%	8.0%
Non-conformists with criminal subculture	9.5%	13.4%
Isolated or rejected	9.1%	11.9%
Belonging to the lower hierarchy	3.2%	1.5%
Unable to look after themselves	3.2%	1.5%
Younger inmates/old inmates	1.4%	4.5%
Bulled by staff	0.9%	0%

Who Was Bullying

Both groups of inmates generally characterized bullies as whose persons who wish to assert power, but adolescents more likely than adults (χ^2=11.9, p<0.00). Prisoners mentioned more frequently bullying of inmates by staff than juveniles (χ^2=5.5, p<0.05) (Table 5).

Table 5. Overall ranked responses (%) among adult prisoners and juvenile offenders in training school to the open-ended question "What sorts of people bully others here?"

Category	Adult prison inmates (N=105)	Juvenile delinquents (N=53)
Bully wishes to assert power	58.9%	85.8%
Staff is bullying	13.0%	0%
Aggressive/violent	10.3%	8.1%
Low intelligence/education	4.1%	0%
Young/old inmates	4.8%	4.1%
All are bullies	2.7%	2.0%
Boredom	6.2%	0%

Types of Bullying

The main common category of bullying in two types of institutions was mainly verbal bullying (about one third of cases) and also in some degree (less than 3%) sexual bullying, but juvenile offenders were significantly more likely than adults to report gossiping (χ^2=4.1, p<0.05), intimidation (χ^2=13.1, p<0.00), rejecting (χ^2=4.2, p<0.05), and ostracising (χ^2=4.0, p<0.05), whereby juvenile male offenders report more often than men physical assaults (χ^2=23.8, p<0.00) (Table 6).

Table 6. Overall ranked responses (%) among adult prisoners and juvenile offenders in training school to the open-ended question "Describe the type of bullying that takes place in as much detail as possible?"

Category (type of bullying)	Adult prison inmates (N=105)	Juvenile delinquents (N=53)
Verbal (direct)	33.9%	32.9%
Grossiping (indirect)	7.5%	0%
Intimidation (indirect)	20.8%	2.6%
Rejecting (indirect)	9.0%	1.3%
Ostracising (indirect)	6.5%	0%
Physical (direct)	12.9%	56.6%
Sexual (direct)	3.3%	1.3%
Taking things (direct)	6.1%	6.6%

When the categories were conducted into direct and indirect aggression, then adolescents in training school were more likely than adult prisoners to report direct forms of bullying (93.6% vs. 57.1%; χ^2=4.0, p<0.01), and prisoner more likely report indirect forms of bullying than youth inmates (42.9% vs. 6.4%; χ^2=4.0, p<0.01).

A brief description of the names given to specific acts of bullying by: (1) the prison inmates includes words describing forms of verbal, indirect bullying, and also bullying for fun, and (2) the juvenile offenders describing consists forms of physical bullying using their mother tongue and English synonym, whereby both study groups described specific acts of sexual bullying.

Where Bullying Occurs

The main categories arising from the question "Where do they get bullied?" were "anywhere" (in prison: 25.7% and in juvenile training school: 21.5%) and "out of sight of staff" (in prison: 14.1% and in juvenile institution: 15.2%), and in the yard (prison: 5.6% vs. juvenile institution: 5.6%). Differences between two study groups revealed among three categories: prisoners were significantly more likely than juveniles in training school tended to offer category "living quarters" (accordingly: 45.1% vs. 24.1%; χ^2=13.4, p<0.00), and adolescents more frequently than adults reported category "washrooms/toilets" and "classroom" (accordingly: 2.1% vs. 13.7%; χ^2=9.4, p<0.01 and 3.3% vs. 24.1%; χ^2=14.9, p<0.00).

When Bullying Occurs

Answers to the questions "When does bullying occur during the day in the institution?" were as follows: Morning (significant differences between two study groups with more prevalent results among adolescents compared with adults: accordingly 15.1% vs. 6.4%; χ^2=5.3, p<0.01), afternoon (in prison: 32.3% and in juvenile training school: 17.8%), evening (in prison: 38.5% and in training school: 24.7%), and at midnight (more frequently mentioned among adolescents compared with adults: accordingly 2.4% vs. 21.9%; χ^2=15.2, p<0.00).

Research results indicated that more prisoners than juveniles reported that bullying occurring in the institution during all days in the week (79.6% vs. 47.8%; χ^2=8.4, p<0.00) whereas more juvenile offenders mention significantly more likely that bullying occurs in the institution during working days compared with prisoners' opinions (10.2% vs. 29.3%; $\chi^2=7.4$, $p<0.00$).

Interventions with Bullying

The majority of inmates (prison: 56%, training school: 62%) stated that other inmates would try to help when bullying is occurring. Nearly one sixth of adult prisoners and adolescents revealed that when someone of inmates is being bullied they try to calm the situation down (accordingly: prison inmates: 14.9% and juvenile delinquents: 13.1%). Also, juveniles in training school were significantly more likely than inmates in prison to say that they try to help the victim unconditionally (accordingly: 57.9% vs. 17%; $\chi^2=13.6$, $p<0.00$) and reported to the help of adult staff members (accordingly: 23.7% vs. 0%; $\chi^2=8.9$, $p<0.001$). Adult prisoners were significantly more likely than juveniles to reveal that they help conditionally: when the victim is friend (29.8% vs. 5.3%; $\chi^2=4.1$; $p<0.05$), when it is useful for them (21.3& vs. 0%; $\chi^2=7.2$, $p<0.01$) or even support the bully (17% vs. 0%; $\chi^2=4.2$, $p<0.05$).

Reasons given as to why other inmates would not help included "non of their business/not want to get involved" (prison: 45.4% and training school: 28.1%), "fear of retaliation" (prison: 39.4% and training school: 50.0%), "the victim usually deserves it" (prison: 9.1% and training school: 6.3%), and "there are many bystanders of bullying" (prison: 6.0% and training school: 15.6%), whereby no significant differences was found.

Staff Intervention

Juvenile offenders in training school were significantly more likely than inmates in prison to say that staff try to intervene when bullying occurs in correctional institution (87.5% vs. 57.9%; $\chi^2=15.4$, $p<0.00$). Most prison inmates and juvenile delinquents stated that staff would intervene by "placing the bully on report on punishment" (prison: 21.7% and training school: 16.7%), "warning/confronting bully" (prison: 37.7% and training school: 29.6%), and "separating the bully and victim" (prison: 20.3% and juvenile training school: 25.9%). Additionally, inmates in prison revealed more likely than juveniles at training school that staff intervention is ineffective (37.7% vs. 0%; $\chi^2=10.4$, $p<0.00$), and juveniles stated two more possibilities for staff intervention: monitoring and talking to the victim (14.8% vs. 0%; $\chi^2=7.6$, $p<0.00$; 13.0% vs. 0%; $\chi^2=4.2$, $p<0.05$).

Reasons given for why staff would not help included: "unaware of the problem" (significant differences between two groups with more prevalent results among adolescents compared with adult inmates accordingly: 93.8% vs. 34.8%; $\chi^2=11.7$, $p<0.00$), "not bothered/don't care" with frequent answers among prisoners compared with juveniles (45.5% vs. 62.%; $\chi^2=8.8$, $p<0.01$), "indulgent attitude towards bullying" (13.6% vs. 0%), and "can't really do anything to stop it" (7.1% vs. 0%) with prisoners' prevalent answers.

To Whom Would an Inmate Advise a Victim of Bullying to Speak to

The two main choices were "another inmate" (prison: 21.8% and training school: 17.8%) and "prison officer or school teacher" (prison: 22.8% and training school: 18.7%), and "nobody" (prison: 2.1% and juvenile institution: 5.0%). Additionally, adolescents in training school revealed more frequently than adult prisoners that they prefer friends and family members (accordingly: 20.8% vs. 1%; $\chi^2=13.6$, $p<0.00$; 19.8% vs. 5.8%; $\chi^2=10.7$, $p<0.00$) as sources of help about bullying issues, and prisoners tended to prefer more frequently specialists in institution than adolescents in training school (40.3% vs. 18.8%; $\chi^2=11.3$, $p<0.00$).

Intervention into Bullying

Most frequent suggestions for intervention of bullying included "nothing" (prison: 23.9% and training school: 37.7%), "more activities and work" (prison: 30.2% and training school: 20.8%), "victim must be more *assertive" (*prison: 10.6% and training school: 13.2%), remove the bullies (prison: 6.9% and training school: 17%), harsher punishment (prison: 7.4% and training school: 11.3%), and increase staff awareness about bullying (prison: 6.3 % and training school: 4.1%). Adult prisoners were more likely than adolescents to suggest "stop mixing prisoners with violent/sex offence history" (17.7% vs. 0%; $\chi^2=13.2$, $p<0.00$).

Conclusion

This study provides a descriptive analysis and compares bullying behavior in the male adult prison and in the male juvenile training school, whereby both institutions were maximum security facilities. Male adults in prison and male adolescents in training school were surveyed by self-report questionnaire developed by Ireland and Archer (1996) about the extent of bullying, the frequency the respondent had bullied or been bullied, their perception of bullying, possibilities about prevention and intervention of bullying; and time and place where bullying occurred.

The research aims of the present study were to provide a descriptive analysis of the nature and extent of bullying to examine differences between the male adults in prison and the male adolescents in training school.

Differences between male adolescents in training school and male adult prisoners were found in relation to extent of perceived bullying in these correctional institutions: the perceived extent of bullying was higher in prison compared with juvenile training school. Previous studies support this tendency among juvenile prisoners compared with young offenders (Ireland, 2002b) and among adult prisoners (Ireland & Archer, 1996).

Reports of actually seen of bullying incidences was high (higher than reported among adult prisoners: Ireland & Archer, 1996) - more than 60% of adults and adolescents reported in prison and in training school, whereby the prevalence of hearing of bullying incidents was more frequent in prison compared with juvenile training school setting. Thus, the findings confirm that bullying is a widespread problem not only in male prison, but also in male adolescent training school too, and the key question is not whether, but to what degree.

Overall, 56% of adult males in the prison (not involved 54%), and 45% (not involved 55%) adolescent males in the training school classified, when asked directly, as bullies, victims or bully/victims, with on average 2 to 4 victims each in previous week. Also, approximately the same prevalence of bullying behavior was found among juvenile prisoners (Ireland, 2002b; Ireland & Monaghan, 2006; Leddy & O'Connell, 2002). The overall percentage of self-reported bullying behavior in this study was relatively high, with nearly equal proportion of bullies, victims and bully/victims in both male institutions (prison: 21%, 18%, 17%; training school: 17%, 13%, 15% respectively). Previous studies showed that the proportion of prisoners reporting behaviors indicative of ''being bullied'' and of ''bullying others'' were broadly consistent among male young and juvenile offenders (Ireland, 2002b;

Ireland & Archer, 2004; Ireland & Monaghan, 2006) and among male young offenders and adult offenders (Ireland & Power, 2004) with regards to classification into these groups; although there was a trend for a higher proportion of young offenders to be classified as bully/victims than adults (Ireland & Power, 2004), and less proportion of young prisoners to be classified as bully/victims than juveniles in prison (Ireland, 2005b; Ireland & Monaghan, 2006). Regardless of the specific method to classify prisoners into groups bully/victims tending to be the most common and representative of the categories in prison (measured by the behavior indicative of bullying: e. g. Ireland, 2002a; Ireland & Ireland, 2008), in this research direct measurement of bullying was used and differences between proportion of bully/victim category among adult prisoners and juveniles in training school was not revealed.

A particular characteristic of individuals (e.g. vulnerable, introvert) was tended to be viewed as being predisposed to become a victim of bullying among both study groups, as reported previously among adult prisoners (Ireland & Archer, 1996). Additionally, it was revealed that among the male adults in prison, the description of potential victims concurred with reported by Ireland & Archer (1996) and Brookes (1993) featured – sex offenders, but juveniles in training school empathized more frequently the physical weakness of victim and young inmates as victims. Also, Ireland (2002b) revealed that male juveniles were less likely than young offenders in prison to perceive sex offenders as targets for bullying and juveniles were more likely than young offenders to report younger prisoners. The present study confirms these tendencies and specifies it across to settings – male prisoners reported significantly more sex offenders and male juvenile delinquents physically vulnerable and young inmates as potential victims of bullying with general trend for both groups to report victims as vulnerable and introvert characteristics.

Perceptions of causes of victimization included different reasons viewed (1) by juvenile offenders as being predisposed to become victims of bullying as weak (physically or mentally), easy targets and bullies as perpetrators assessing power over victims; and (2) *boredom and particular offence (sex offence) was* behind many incidents of bullying in prison with acknowledgement that bullying may occur as bullying of prison inmates by staff. Thus, juvenile offenders' perceptions about the causes of bullying included the notification of the bullying phenomenon in the area of overt power imbalance, and prisoners perceived the causes of bullying as reflection of specific aspects of lower-stimulation closed prison environment, supporting previous studies (e.g. Ireland & Archer, 1996). As school bullying is defined as subsection of aggressive behavior with repetitiveness and power imbalance (Olweus, 1996), the essence of bullying for juvenile delinquents was analogical for this concept. Additionally, it was revealed that bullying was more probably motivated by boredom in prison than in training school, supporting previous (Spain, 2005) studies among incarcerated youth. Some previous research advocated that bullying in young offenders prison (Spain, 2005) and in juvenile offenders prison (Peterson-Badali, & Koegl, 2002) raveled not only among prisoner, but also between prisoners and staff - bullying of prisoners by staff; and this study support these findings first of all in the male adult prisoners setting.

It was hypothesized that adolescents' bullying at training school would involve a greater proportion of direct forms than adults' would; and that adults' bullying in prison would display a greater proportion of indirect forms than juveniles' would; and these hypotheses were supported.

Overall, the majority of adult prisoners' and juvenile offenders' bullying behavior comprised verbal bullying followed by physical bullying by adolescents in training school and indirect bullying by prisoners. Namely, the types of bullying in prison among men were predominately indirect (gossiping, intimidation, rejection, and ostracizing), corresponding with previous evidence from male prisoners (e.g. Brookes, 1993; Ireland & Archer, 1996; Turner & Ireland, 2010), whereby male juveniles in training school used predominately physical forms of bullying, corresponding with pervious evidence from males in juvenile prisons (Ireland & Monaghan, 2006; Ireland & Hafiz, 2010) and from male young offenders in prison (Ireland, 1999b; Ireland & Power, 2004). The finding that juveniles reported being subjected to more physical bullying than adult offenders is consistent with developmental pathways (Björkqvist, Österman, & Kaukiainen, 1992]) suggesting that younger age groups may indeed use more physical aggression. Indirect aggression, on the other hand, carries a higher chance of being caught and the perpetrator risks retribution (Ireland, 2002a), empathizing the possibility that in a prison setting adult prisoners have come to recognize the value of indirect bullying over direct, and employ it. However, male prisoners used more indirect forms of bullying than juveniles in training school did, and both contingents used also direct verbal forms of bullying, whilst sexual bullying was the least common - a pattern also akin with previous prison research (Connell & Farrington, 1996; McGurk & McDougall, 1986, Ireland, 2005b).

In the adult prison and juvenile training school settings the terms connected with bullying (but not the term bullying) were not culturally sensitive, but tended to reflect the prevalent forms of bullying in the detention facility with holding negative connotations. Ireland and Ireland (2003) also asked young and juvenile male prisoners through a self-report questionnaire about their perceptions of bullying and results indicated that bullying could include predominately direct forms of bullying.

Bullying was seen to occur: (1) at locations throughout the correctional institution – mainly out if sight of staff, but relatively more frequently in living areas in prison and more private areas (e. g. bathrooms) in juvenile training school; and (2) during all days a week and all time of day, but relatively more frequently in the morning and midnight during working days among juvenile delinquents. In previous studies young offenders have mentioned more than juveniles that bullying occurred in their living areas in prison (Ireland, 2002b) and much of bullying happened during evening and meal time, on social period in the evening, and at night in the dormitory in young and adult male prisons (Smith, Pendleton, & Mitchell, 2005).

Male inmates of both correctional institutions in this study reported that both they and staff were willing to help victims of bullying, but relatively more (1) prisoners admit that staffs' help was ineffective; self-help was conditional (helping friends, beneficial support), and they even supported the bully; and (2) juvenile offenders tended to believe that staffs' help was effective: monitoring and talking to the victim, and self-help was unconditional. Also, Spain (2005) examining young offenders' attitudes regarding ways for the establishments to combat bullying in prison showed that the majority of participants revealed staffs' failure for supervision.

Regarding interventions, most training school juveniles and prison inmates reported that staff and inmates would intervene – it is consistent with previous studies (Ireland & Archer, 1996; Ireland, 2002b). The reasons why prisoners and juvenile offenders do not intervene were the same as was revealed previously (Ireland & Archer, 1996) in prison context: Fear, detach, blame of victim, but differentiated concerning with perceived reasons of staff nonintervention – more juveniles revealed that staff is unaware of the bullying problem in the institution than prison inmates, and more prisoners than juveniles had accepting attitude toward bullying or even supported bullies. Researchers (Ireland, 2005c) have reported attention on the motivators and functions underlying prison bullying, pointing out also the role of fear.

Two main choices for which an inmate in prison and juvenile training school would advice a victim of bullying to approach were either peer or prison office/school teacher, whereby prisoners prefer more often specialists in prison and juvenile offenders' friends and family members. The last trends were reveled in previous studies (Ireland, 2002b): Juveniles were more likely than young offenders to advise a victim of bullying to speak to their family, a specialist, and a prison officer.

Regarding the possibility of preventing bullying, the most frequent suggestion, as in previous works (Ireland & Archer, 1996I), was "nothing" illustrating attitude that bullying is part of every day's life in prison and in training school too. Parallel with this pessimistic view, there were also suggestions connected with improvement of social environment of both institutions (activation of inmates, punishment of bullies, and increasing of staffs' awareness about bullying), whereby the only prison settings related suggestion was made concerning with separating violent or sex offenders form other inmates. Additionally, previous studies revealed that the most common piece of advice by young or juvenile offenders in prison with reference to how to combat bullying was action on the part of the young offender being victimized (Spain, 2005; Ireland, 2002b). This highlights the importance of taking into account the specific environment (e. g. training school versus prison; male versus female correctional institution) in which the bullying behavior is taking place before applying prevention and intervention.

Like early studies in the research history in the emerging area of prison bullying (Ireland, 2011) employed measures based on school-based definitions that asked offenders directly about their experiences of bullying, using the term ''bullying'' itself (e.g. Ireland and Archer, 1996), our study is the first one in this area in Estonia. Needless to say that issue of bullying behavior within prison settings has been started now in Estonia and should be continue within adolescent and adult and male and female offenders in prison-based settings as a part of research (Kõiv, 2009) on bullying in diversity settings. Although only descriptive in nature, the present study is the first to offer a valuable insight into bullying behavior that occurs within juvenile training school setting. It demonstrated that, in this setting, bullying is a prevalent phenomenon, which takes various forms and which is worth further investigation. Building on prison-based research among juvenile, young and adult offenders, this paper also highlighted the importance of addressing research across comparison of different age and sex groups to have focus on similar correctional settings. By applying a questionnaire which did use the term bullying, this study has not managed to overcome the methodological difficulties connected with shortcomings leading to possible underestimation of the extent of bullying as mentioned by Ireland (2002b). It is important to note, however, that the current study employed a relatively small sample of adult prisoners and juvenile training school adolescents and thus the conclusions drawn with regard to developmental differences must be done with caution. By examining differences in the nature and extent of male bullying behavior, intervention programs can focus on specific juvenile inmate population in different correctional institutions, included juvenile training schools.

References

Björkqvist, K., Österman, K., & Kaukiainen, A. (1992). The development of direct and indirect aggressive strategies in males and females. In K. Björkqvist & P. Niemela (Eds.), *Of mice and women: Aspects of female aggression* (pp. 51–64). San Diego: Academic Press.

Brookes, M. (1993). Reducing bullying at HMP Ranby. East Midlands, *Psychology Research Report,* No. 8, U.K.

Connell A, & Farrington D. (1997). The reliability and validity of resident, staff and peer reports of bullying in young offender institutions. *Psychology, Crime, and Law,* 3, 287–300.

Coyne, I., & Monks, C. P. (2011). An overview of bullying and abuse across settings. In C. P. Monks & I. Coyne (Eds.), *Bullying in different context* (pp. 231–256). UK: Cambridge University Press.

Edgar, K. (2005). Bullying, victimization and safer prisons. *The Journal of Community and Criminal Justice,* 52(4), 390–400.

Inderbitzin, M. (2006). Lessons from a juvenile training school: Survival and growth. *Journal of Adolescent Research,* 21, 7–26.

Ireland, J. L. (1999a). Bullying behaviors among male and female prisoners: A study of adult and young offenders. *Aggressive Behavior,* 25, 161–178.

Ireland, J.L. (1999b). Provictim attitudes and empathy in relation to bullying behaviour among prisoners. *Legal and Criminological Psychology,* 4, 51–66.

Ireland, J. L. (2002a). *Bullying among prisoners: Evidence, research and intervention strategies*. London and Hove: Brunner-Routledge.

Ireland, J. L. (2002b). Do juveniles bully more than young offenders? A comparison of the perceived and actual bullying behaviour reported by juvenile and young offenders. *Journal of Adolescence,* 25, 155–168.

Ireland, J. L. (2005a). Bullying among prisoners: The need for innovation. In J. L. Ireland (Ed.), *Bullying among prisoners: Innovations in theory and research* (pp. 1–30). Hove: Willan Publishing.

Ireland, J. L., (2005b) Psychological health and bullying behavior among adolescent prisoners: A study of young and juvenile offenders. *Journal of Adolescent Health,* 36, 236–243.

Ireland, J. L., (2005c). Prison bullying and fear: Can fear assist with explanations of victim responses?. In J. L. Ireland (Ed.), *Bullying among prisoners: Innovations in theory and research* (pp. 129–149). Hove: Willan Publishing.

Ireland, J. L. (2011). Bullying in prisons: Bringing research up to date. In C. P. Monks & I. Coyne (Eds.), *Bullying in different context* (pp. 137–156). UK: Cambridge University Press.

Ireland, J. L., & Archer, J. (1996). Descriptive analysis of bullying in male and female adult offenders. *Journal of Community and Applied Social Psychology,* 6, 35–47.

Ireland, J. L., & Archer, J. (2004). Association between measures of aggression and bullying among juvenile and young offenders. *Aggressive Behavior,* 30, 29–42.

Ireland, J. l. & Hafiz, N. (2010). Psychological ill health, social self-esteem and bullying behavior among prisoners: A study of juvenile, young and adult male prisoners. In: K. Österman (Ed.), *Indirect and direct aggression* (pp. 203–213). Peter Lang Pub Inc.

Ireland, J. L., & Ireland, C. A. (2003). How do prisoners define bullying? A study of adult, young and juvenile male offenders. *Legal and Criminological Psychology,* 8, 159–173.

Ireland, J. L., & Ireland, C. L. (2008). Intra-group aggression among prisoners: Frequency of bullying and exploration of victim-perpetrator mutuality. *Aggressive Behavior,* 34, 76–87.

Ireland, J. L., & Monaghan, R. (2006). Behaviors indicative of bullying among young and juvenile male offenders: A study of perpetrator and victim characteristics. *Aggressive Behavior,* 32, 72−180.

Ireland, J.L., & Power, C. L. (2004). Attachment, emotional loneliness and bullying behavior: A study of adult and young offenders. *Aggressive Behavior,* 30, 298–312.

Ireland, J. L., Jarvis, S., Beck, G. and Osiowy, S. (1999). Recent research into bullying in prison. *Forensic Update,* 56, 4–9.

Kõiv, K. (2009). Bullying among Estonian pupils: an overview. Mikk, J.; Veisson, M.; Luik, P. (Eds.), Teenagers in Estonia: Values and behaviour (pp. 103−123). Frankfurt am Main Berlin Bern Bruxelles New York Oxford Wien: Peter Lang Europäischer Verlag der Wissenschaften.

Leddy, J., & O'Connell, M. (2002). The prevalence, nature and psychological correlations of bullying in Irish Prison. *Legal and Criminological Psychology,* 7, 131–140.

McGurk, B. J., & McDougall, C. (1991): The prevention of bullying among incarcerated delinquents. In: P. K. Smith and D. Thompson (Eds.), *Practical approaches to bullying* (pp. 130–140). London: David Fulton.

Milan, M. A. (1996). Working in institutions. In C. R. Hollin, & K. Howells (Eds.), *Clinical approaches to working with young offenders* (pp 85-108). Chichester: John Wiley & Sons.

Monks, C. P., Smith P. K., Naylor, P., Barter C., Ireland, J. L., & Coyne, I. (2009). Bullying in different contexts: Commonalities, differences and the role of theory. *Aggression and Violent Behavior* 14, 146–156.

Olweus, D. (1994). Bullying at school: Basic facts and effects of a school-based intervention programme. *Journal of Child Psychology and Child Psychiatry,* 35, 1171–1190.

Peterson-Badali, M., & Koegl, C. J. (2002) Juvenile experiences of incarceration: The role of correctional staff in peer violence, *Journal of Crime Justice,* 30, 41–49.

Smith, P. K. (2011). Bullying in schools: Thirty years of research. In C. P. Monks & I. Coyne (Eds.), *Bullying in different context* (pp. 36–60). UK: Cambridge University Press.

Smith, P. K., & Brain. P. (2000). Bullying in schools: Lessons from two decades of research. *Aggressive Behaviour,* 26, 1–9.

Smith, P. K., Pendleton, E., & Mitchell, H. (2005). Bullying and anti-bullying policies: A young offender institution and an adult prison. In J. L. Ireland (Ed.), Bullying among prisoners: Innovations in theory and research (pp. 109–125). UK: Willian Publishing.

Spain, A. (2005). Bullying among young offenders: Findings from a qualitative study. In J. L. Ireland (Ed.*), Bullying among prisoners: Innovations in theory and research* (pp. 62-83). UK: Willian Publishing.

Turner, P., & Ireland, J. L. (2010). Do personality characteristics and beliefs predict intra-group bullying between prisoners? *Aggressive Behavior,* 36, 261–270.

In: Handbook on Bullying
Editor: Phoebe Triggs

ISBN: 978-1-63463-023-8

Chapter 14

CYBERBULLYING VALIDATION

***Vinita Nahar*[*] *Xue Li*[†] *and Chaoyi Pang*[‡]**
School of Information Technology and Electrical Engineering
The University of Queensland, Australia
The Australian E-Health Research Center, CSIRO, Australia

Abstract

Cyberbullying is widely recognised as a serious social menace which affects millions of people around the world, especially teenagers and adolescents. In this Chapter, we present the results of an online survey, which is conducted to understand and differentiate between real cyberbullying and cyberbullying-like instances in user-generated content. We study the subtle differences between the motives of the sender of messages similar to cyberbullying, and how messages are perceived by the recipient. In particular, we investigate forms, prevalence, and key indicators of cyberbullying within written contents. Firstly three variants of cyberbullying are introduced, namely: 'direct', 'indirect' and 'misinterpreted' forms of cyberbullying, based on the involvement of the recipient in these types of cyberbullying. Then we validate the key indicators which make written contents becomes cyberbullying, based on users' online experiences and the frequency with which they received and/or sent cyberbullying messages.

The findings reveal that: i) For direct cyberbullying, 'presence of loud language' and 'teasing - repeated comments or messages that may upset someone' are the main indicators in social networks. ii) For indirect cyberbullying, 'bullied or picked on by someone indirectly, as a third person, while online', 'been talked about online in ways that make you feel uncomfortable or upset', and 'been mentioned in a message to someone else in a way that is mocking or otherwise makes you feel uncomfortable or upset' are the main indicators. iii) For misinterpreted form of cyberbullying, 'bullied or picked on a friend or relative while online', 'been talked about online by a friend or relative, in ways that make you feel uncomfortable or upset' and 'been mentioned in a message to a friend or relative in a way that is mocking or otherwise makes you feel uncomfortable or upset' are the main indicators. These results are discussed in the light of the relatively limited cyberbullying detection research undertaken to date.

[*]E-mail address: v.nahar@uq.edu.au
[†]E-mail address: xueli@itee.uq.edu.au
[‡]E-mail address: Chaoyi.Pang@csiro.au

Keywords: cyberbullying; victimization; prevalence; social networks; cyberbullying indicators

1. Introduction

This study is driven by an urgent need for the early detection of cyberbullying activities in social networks. Recently, a public row broke out when seemingly private messages of an Indian Union minister were published on his Twitter feed, which resulted in tragic suicide of his wife. He is a former U.N. diplomat, a prolific author, and one of the most active users of the microblogging site in government, whose Twitter account shows more than 2 million followers. In another case, an Australian top model committed suicide on 21 February, 2014 because of cyberbullying. Therefore, more generalised opinion of online community's who either experienced or were involved in cyberbullying needs further investigation.

Cyberbullying is defined as "an act of posting cruel or harmful material to others or engaging in other forms of social aggression using the Internet or other communication technologies" [23]. Though cyberbullying is a common phenomenon among adolescents and children, breakthrough advancements in information and web-based technologies, such as social networking sites, straddle age groups, where non-physical aggression is often observed among different age group users. Research conducted in various countries, including Serbia, the UK, the USA, Korea, Turkey, Italy, and Australia clearly indicate that nearly 90% of school-aged students access the Internet at home, with over 50% reporting daily use [3, 24, 26], which they use to interact in cyber space. Teachers and administrators have recognized student's use of information and communication technology, particularly in their social interaction via the expanding use of electronic communication in school classrooms [2, 9]. World-wide, studies reveal that most school-aged students now own a mobile phone and this increases with age [3]. An empirical study conducted by Aricak (2009) in the Turkish environment reveals the fact that ease of maintaining anonymity in cyberspace is one of the most significant causes of cyberbullying [1]. He also found that males are more likely than females to validate that they would engage in cyberbullying in the future. Furthermore, this study also suggests that cyberbullying is not limited to children and adolescents, but extends to adults as well.

The very act of a bullying activity is harmful in some way or the other and its implication are so dangerous that it may destroy the precious lives of youths when they fail to cope with the unbearable pressure of insulting or humiliating messages, especially on the Internet, where the potential audience of cyberbullying is limitless [8]. In such settings, it is beneficial to have an automatic system which can monitor such harmful messages and alert users of its repetitive occurrence. This will help to maintain a safe and healthy online environment for all users and confirms there is a need for detection software.

In the view of the facts that: (i) Young people have seized the Internet as both an option and a means for socializing [23] such as Social Networking sites; (ii) There is increasing evidence of the existence of cyberbullying, including situations where the outcome has been suicide; (iii) Bullying in cyberspace is a difficult occurrence for parents or guardians to monitor young children/students' actions [16]; (iv) Young people (especially teenagers) are reluctant to tell adults about incidents where they are being bullied, whether in real life or cyberspace. In addition, only a few participants use appropriate means to prevent incidents of online bullying [6]. This chapter aims to study the online user's comprehension of the existence and frequency of cyberbullying. The study is based on the frequency of received and sent messages under varying conditions, including participation in direct, indirect and the misinterpreted forms of cyberbullying. In addition, this study explores the cyberbullying indicators in user-generated content that can be utilised for the detection of cyberbullying on Social Networks (SNs) [4, 5, 7, 10, 17, 18, 25, 15, 12, 13, 11, 14].

Though cyberbullying is a problem that gets a lot of attention from a Social Science point of view, less attention has been paid to it from an automatic detection angle. A number of definitions of cyberbullying, revealing the principal characteristics of cyberbullying are: an imbalance of power, repetitive patterns, intentional hurt, and where a victim is unable to defend him or herself.

To differentiate between cyberbullying and cyber teasing requires understanding the subjective difference between the way a message is intended in relation to how it is perceived. As a result, automatic detection becomes an important research challenge. The aim of this study is to establish a number of rules that can be included in cyberbullying detection tools. Rules will be established based on the frequency of potentially offending messages and the patterns of communication between online users taking part in harassing /cruel or threatening/unpleasant messaging. In this chapter, we examine a number of indicators in user-generated content which identify the online content as apparently of a bullying nature. We look at the frequency of offensive or hurtful messages being sent and received as a basis to predict the communication pattern of intentionally hurtful acts.

Based on the above-mentioned literature, previous compiled research into the characteristics of cyberbullying, and profiles of cyber bullies; this chapter will take the following into account:

First, the demographic characteristics (gender, age and religion) of the Internet users, who have involved or experienced cyberbullying will be studied. Second, indicators of direct cyberbullying and the frequency where users see themselves engaged as a bully, or a victim, of a direct form of cyberbullying will be included in the analysis. Third, indicators of indirect cyberbullying and the user's engagement based on the frequency in indirect cyberbullying will be examined. Forth, indicators of misinterpreted form of bullying, and the frequency of the misinterpreted form of bullying (cyberbullying-like posts or messages between close friends or people in close a relationship) will be explored.

2. Methodology

2.1. Participants and Settings

The study focuses on obtaining feedback on the nature and prevalence of cyberbullying from the Internet users of different age groups and genders, based on the frequency of offensive posts received. Consequently, in this study, an anonymous online survey via SurveyMonkey was conducted through Social Media websites (Twitter and Facebook). A link to the questionnaire was distributed on Social Networks including Twitter and Facebook, and participants were randomly invited to complete it.

Voluntary participants included but were not limited to students/staff/members of the University of Queensland (UQ) community. Students, academics and research peers were also approached to fill out the online questionnaire. Although not specifically targeted, people from communities outside of the UQ have also participated. As a strategy to obtain informed consent, it was requested that people under 18 years seek the permission from a parent or guardian before participating in the survey. Prior to the research being conducted, the study had been cleared in accordance with the ethical review processes of the University of Queensland, Australia.

2.2. Procedure

To closely investigate the amount of cyberbullying and cyber harassment, we chose groups in various age ranges (12-17 years, 18-21 years, 22-25 years, 25-30 years) and grouped users above 30 years as a single entity. In addition, we made the assumption that these Internet users had Social Network accounts on Twitter and Facebook. The questionnaire was separated into five parts:

Part A: Relating to demographic factors;
Part B: Relating to direct cyberbullying;
Part C: Relating to indirect cyberbullying;
Part D: Relating to misinterpreted form of cyberbullying;
Part E: General questions about cyberbullying.

The pilot survey was carried out by interviewing a few UQ students and academics. After this, modifications were made based on the feedback and the revised questionnaire was posted on the SurveyMonkey website.

A filter question (Have you experienced or been involved in cyberbullying?) was used to filter out participants who have never been involved in, nor experienced cyberbullying. To determine the best indicators of direct, indirect and misinterpreted forms of cyberbullying; the definitions of these types of cyberbullying were provided explicitly. Additionally, indicators were prepared for each type of cyberbullying independently.

Respondents were asked to respond to each question regarding what constitutes cyberbullying, and the number of times they have experienced or been involved in any of the three types of cyberbullying. The statistical analysis of all the data was done by computing the Cronbach's alpha, the Spearman's Correlation Coefficient, Linear Regression Analysis and the Coefficient of determination using SPSS. Significance was calculated both 5% and 1% levels.

2.2.1. Demographic Factors

Participants were asked for their age, gender and religious background in order to study their profile, which constitutes Part A of the questionnaire.

Cyberbullying is defined as "an aggressive, intentional act carried out by a group or individual, using electronic forms of contact, repeatedly and over time against a victim who cannot easily defend him or herself" [19]. After giving this definition, four indicators - 'appearance of bad words in messages such as insults, e.g. *fool*, or crude words, e.g. *bitch*', 'direct use of bad words to describe someone, e.g. *You are a fool*', 'presence of loud language, foul words, names written in capital letters making it obvious in a message, e.g. *You FOOL!!*', and 'teasing' - repeated comments or messages that may upset someone, were examined to measure what constitutes cyberbullying on the Likert six-point scale from 'Strongly agree' (scale level - 5)' to 'Not applicable' (scale level - 0). Another Likert six-point scale from 'Every day' (scale level - 5) to 'Never' (scale level - 0) was constructed to measure their experiences and involvement with cyberbullying in Part B of the questionnaire. The participants were asked how frequently they had been involved in cyberbullying as a victim or as a bully by explaining their experience using eleven indicators.

For the bully, the indicators included: 'bullied or picked on someone online', 'sent or posted offensive message to others', 'sent or posted a secret message to someone and that person was upset about this', 'sent a message online, which mocked the receiver or otherwise upset them' and 'sent an offensive message online to a friend or relative'. For victims, indicators included: 'been bullied or picked on by someone, or a group, online', 'received offensive message from others', 'been frightened to go online', 'received a message that you did not want others to see', 'received a message online, which mocked you or otherwise upset you' and 'received an offensive message online from a friend or relative'.

2.2.2. Indirect Cyberbullying

In Part C of the questionnaire, a model for 'indirect cyberbullying' was created. The definition of indirect bullying was defined as 'the presence of bad words in a message in association with the third person pronoun (i.e. 'he', 'she' etc.) e.g. *He is a fool*'. Then, to measure participants' experience with indirect cyberbullying, they were asked how often they had experienced or been involved with indirect cyberbullying, using the Likert six-point scale from the 'Every day' (scale level - 5) basis to the 'Never' (scale level - 0).

Another Likert six-point scale from 'Every day' (scale level - 5) to 'No cyberbullying' (scale level - 0) was developed to measure their engagement as a victim or as a bully in indirect cyberbullying, based on the five points scale. The indicators for the bully are: 'talked about others, in ways that would make them feel uncomfortable or upset', and 'mentioned someone in a message to a third party in a way that was mocking or otherwise makes them feel uncomfortable or upset'. For the victim, indicators include: 'bullied or picked on by someone indirectly, as a third person, while online', 'been talked about online in ways that make you feel uncomfortable or upset' and 'been mentioned in a message to someone else in a way that is mocking or otherwise makes you feel uncomfortable or upset.

2.2.3. Misinterpreted Form of Cyberbullying

The fourth model (Part D) is defined as a 'misinterpreted form' of cyberbullying, which is introduced in the questionnaire to understand the difference between cyberbullying and cyber-teasing. A misinterpreted form of cyberbullying is defined as "the harassing or rude behaviour that appears between close friends or in close relationships". Close friends may often use coarse or rude language without intending to hurt/insult/upset each another, for example simply cracking a joke may sometimes be seen as an insult. To measure misinterpreted form of cyberbullying and bullying behaviour, instances within close relationships and friendships were carefully examined. Two questions similar to those used for indirect cyberbullying were constructed on the same scale. In addition, to understand the reaction of the receiver of bullying-like message online, a new question is added. Respondents indicated their reaction through multiple-choice options: 'took it seriously and replied with a bullying message', 'took it seriously and never replied', 'didn't take it seriously and replied in a normal way', 'didn't take it seriously and ignored it' and 'other - please specify'.

Another Likert six-point scale from 'Every day' (scale level - 5) to 'No cyberbullying' (scale level - 0) is developed to measure their engagement as a victim or as a bully in misinterpreted form of cyberbullying, based on the five points scale. The indicators for misinterpreted form of cyberbullying are: 'talked about a friend or relative, in ways that would make them feel uncomfortable or upset', and 'mentioned by a friend or relative in a message in a way that was mocking or otherwise makes them feel uncomfortable or upset'. While for the victim, indicators include: 'bullied or picked up by a friend or relative, while online', 'been talked about online by a friend or relative, in ways that make you feel uncomfortable or upset', and 'mentioned by a friend or relative in a message in a way that was mocking or otherwise makes them feel uncomfortable or upset'.

2.2.4. General Questions about Cyberbullying

In Part E, three multiple-choice questions were developed regarding the general questions about cyberbullying, such as main sources of cyberbullying, motives of cyberbullying, and participants' reactions to cyberbullying messages. A question to measure the level of severity of cyberbullying based on the percentage of cyberbullying was developed. Four severity levels were defined including 'Severe', 'Moderate', 'Normal', and 'Non-bullying'. Participants were also asked to provide five unusual bullying words they have encountered for the first time.

3. Results and Discussions

This study into cyberbullying among Internet users explored the phenomenon of cyberbullying from the perspective of identification of the indicators of cyberbullying in user-generated content. In this study, the prevalence of cyberbullying is investigated only from the respondents who have experienced or been involved in cyberbullying.

3.1. Demographic Details

Figure 1 shows the percentage distribution of participants based on gender. Of those who took part in the study, a total of 53.4% female, 42.7% male, and 3.9% of respondents did not mention their gender. We can note that the female participation is slightly higher than males. Nevertheless, the study was consistent to obtain almost equal opinions of male and female online users of their cyberbullying experiences.

The age is divided into five groups: 12-17 years, 18-21 years, 22-25 years, 26-30 years and 30 years plus. As shown in Figure 2, out of the total participants, 27.3% belong to the age group 12-17 years, which is the highest percentage, followed by 24.1% users aged over 30 years, 19.0% of 18-21 years group, 16.8% people of 26-30 years, 11.9% users fall in to the 22-25 years of age group and 1% of users didn't reveal their age. For our study, we can also conclude that people over 30 years are almost equal in number that those who

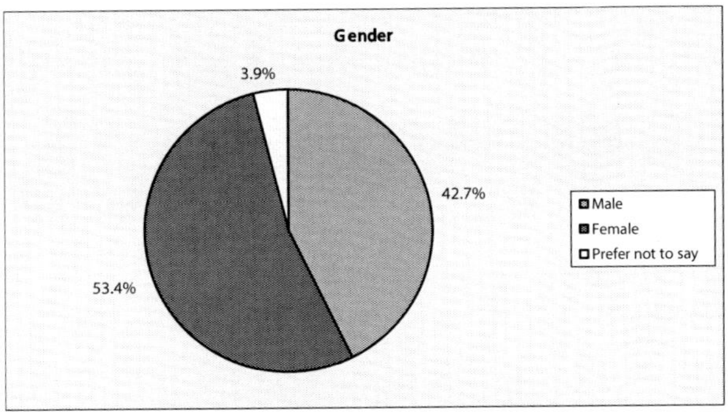

Figure 1. Victim and Predator Identification graph.

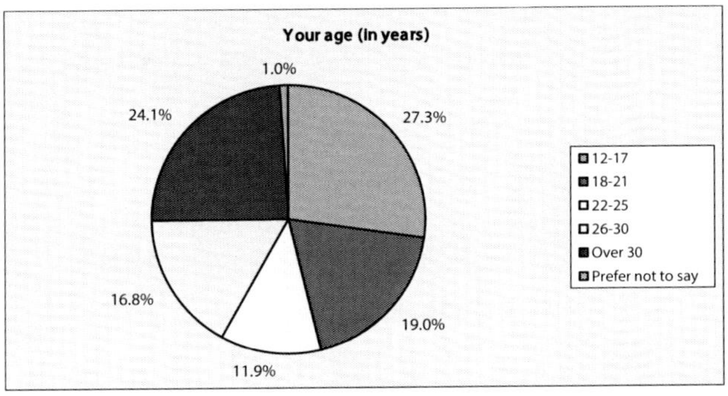

Figure 2. Victim and Predator Identification graph.

are between 12-17 years old. This shows that not only teenagers and young children are users on social networking sites, but elder group of people are also frequent users of these websites. This is in line with our intuition that with the proliferation of social networks, people of all ages are being affected by online bullying and abuse.

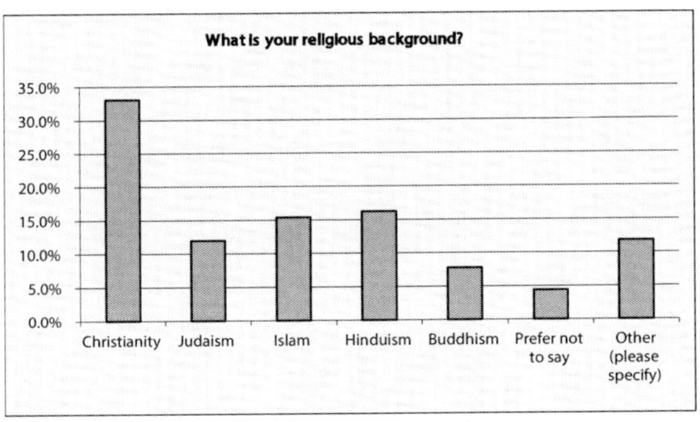

Figure 3. Victim and Predator Identification graph.

Figure 3 illustrates the religious background of the respondents. The highest number of participants were Christians, which was 33.1%, followed by Hindu with 16.2% participations, then Islamists (15.4%), Jews (12.0%) and Buddhists (7.8%) in decreasing order. Also, 4.4% of users preferred not to reveal their religion and 11.8% said 'other'. In our cyberbullying validation instrument, which is a questionnaire, a *filter question "Have you experienced or been involved in cyberbullying?"* was employed to filter out participants who have never been involved in or experienced any form of cyberbullying.

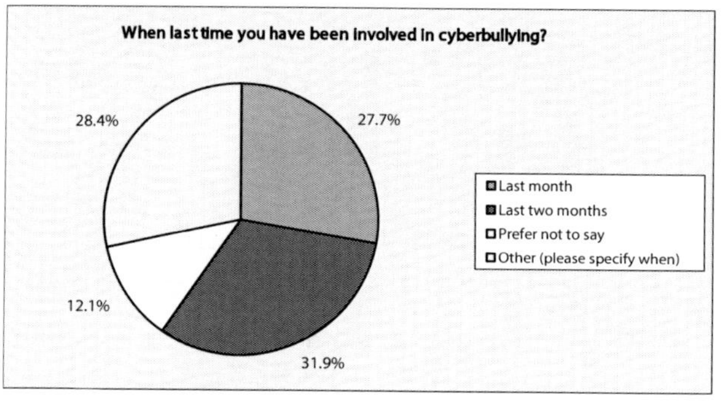

Figure 4. Victim and Predator Identification graph.

As described in Figure 4, of the total users who actually experienced or who have been involved in cyberbullying, 27.7% of respondents agreed that it happened to them in the previous month, while 31.9% said they encountered it within the previous two months. 28.4% people selected 'other', which shows that it happened to them earlier in their lifetime as some respondents shared their previous school-time experience of cyberbullying, while 12.1% who responded chose not to answer the question.

A total of 422 Internet users comprising 175 males, 219 females, 16 respondents who did not reveal their gender, and 12 respondents who skipped this question, participated in the study. The internal reliability of all the indicators of the questionnaire and experience or involvement in cyberbullying was calculated using Cronbach's alpha. The overall alpha coefficient is 0.952 (range if one item deleted, from 0.947 to 0.962), which suggests an excellent reliability.

3.1.1. Gender and Age Groups (Q2 & Q3)

As shown in Figure 5, the majority of males belong to the age groups 12-17 years (39.3%), 18-21 years (73.1%) as well as over 30 years (38.4%). Similarly, the majority of females belong to 22-25 years (70.8%), 12-17 years (53.6%) and over 30 years (54.5%).

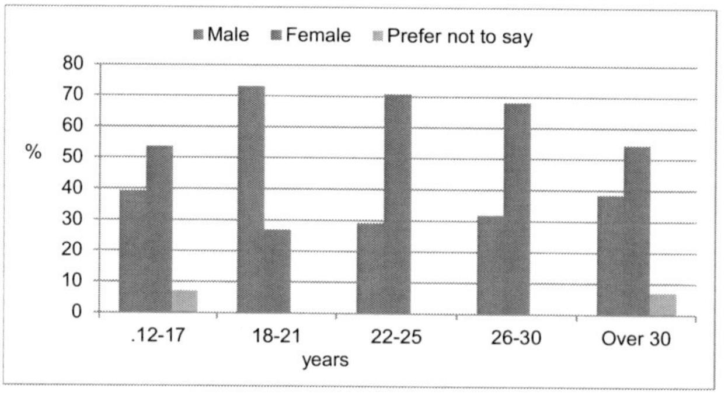

Figure 5. Victim and Predator Identification graph.

Table 1. Correlation between involvement or experience of cyberbullying, and age groups (Q3 & Q6)

Correlations		
		Have you experienced or involved in cyberbullying?
Have you experienced or involved in cyberbullying?	Pearson Correlation	1
	Sig. (2-tailed)	
	N	408
Your age (in years)	Pearson Correlation	-.107*
	Sig. (2-tailed)	0.031
	N	408

*Correlation is significant at the 0.05 level (2-tailed)

Table 2. Recent involvement in cyberbullying based on age groups

Indicators	**Age (years)**				
	12-17	**18-21**	**22-25**	**26-30**	**Over 30**
Last month	**52.4%**	23.1%	23.5%	8.3%	16.7%
Last two months	23.8%	**61.5%**	**41.2%**	**41.7%**	6.7%
Prefer not to say	9.5%	3.8%	11.8%	20.8%	16.7%

**Correlation is significant at the 0.01 level (2-tailed)

3.1.2. Age Groups and Involvement or Experience of Cyberbullying (Q3 & Q6)

As shown in Table 1, the correlation coefficient between experience or involvement in cyberbullying and age groups is significant at the 0.05 level (2-tailed), which shows a strong relationship existed between these two variables as teenagers are more vulnerable to cyberbullying.

3.1.3. Age Groups and Frequency of Experience or Involvement in Cyberbullying (Q3 & Q7)

Table 3 shows that during the last month, teenagers were most frequently involved in cyberbullying or targeted by cyberbullies (52.4%), compared to other groups. The frequency of the involvement of people of other age groups is lower in the previous month compared to the previous two months. Also, we can observe that the frequency of the involvement decreases as age increases. It shows that teenagers are the most involved group, whereas the least involved people are over 30 years old. We can see that involvement in cyberbullying activity is decreasing with the age, and there is an immediate need to spread awareness among teens.

Table 3. Recent involvement in cyberbullying based on age groups

Indicators	Age (years)				
	12-17	**18-21**	**22-25**	**26-30**	**Over 30**
Last month	**52.4%**	23.1%	23.5%	8.3%	16.7%
Last two months	23.8%	**61.5%**	**41.2%**	**41.7%**	6.7%
Prefer not to say	9.5%	3.8%	11.8%	20.8%	16.7%

**Correlation is significant at the 0.01 level (2-tailed)

Table 4. Correlation between involvement or experience of cyberbullying and frequency of cyberbullying (Q6&Q7)

Correlations		
		Have you experienced or involved in cyberbullying?
Have you experienced or involved in cyberbullying?	**Pearson Correlation**	1
	Sig. (2-tailed)	
	N	408
When last time you have been experienced or involved in cyberbullying?	**Pearson Correlation**	0.333*
	Sig. (2-tailed)	0.000
	N	267

**Correlation is significant at the 0.01 level (2-tailed)

As shown in Table 4, the correlation coefficient between experience or involvement of cyberbullying and last time involvement in cyberbullying is highly significant at the 0.01 level (2-tailed), which shows a strong relationship existed between these two variables.

3.2. Direct Cyberbullying

The internal reliability of the four indicators of Q8 and the eleven indicators of Q9 and experience or involvement of cyberbullying (Q6) is calculated by using Cronbach's alpha. The overall alpha coefficient is 0.953 (range if one item deleted, from 0.958 to 0.946), suggesting excellent reliability.

3.2.1. Involvement or Experience of Cyberbullying and Indicators of Direct Cyberbullying (Q6 & Q8)

Participants were asked what constitutes direct cyberbullying, by providing the list of four indicators: 'appearance of bad words in messages', 'direct use of bad words to describe someone', 'presence of loud language' and 'teasing - repeated comments or messages that may upset someone'. In addition, five options from 'strongly agree' (scale level - 5) to 'not applicable' (scale level - 0) were given in the questionnaire. The 'strongly agree' indicators (at scale level - 5) proving to be most common were the 'teasing - repeated comments or messages that may upset someone' (56.8%) and 'presence of loud language' (48.7%). Furthermore, 'direct use of bad words to describe someone' (63.2%) and 'appearance of bad words in messages' (51.3%) were the most frequent 'agree' items (at scale level - 4). It is important to note that none of the respondents answered 'Not applicable' for any of these four items, while less than 2% of the respondents marked the occurrences of these indicators as 'strongly disagree' as a sign of cyberbullying. This demonstrates that the four given points are good indicators to identifying online bullying content. Nevertheless, the 'presence of loud (capitalised) language' and 'teasing' are more prominent than the 'appearance of bad words' and the 'direct use of bad words' to describe the constitution of cyberbullying. The detailed table is given in Appendix II.

Table 5. Involvement or experience of cyberbullying and indicators of direct cyberbullying (Q6 & Q8)

S. No.	Indicators	Percent	Mean	Standard Deviation	R	R^2	Adjusted R^2
a.	Appearance of bad words in message, such as insults (e.g. 'fool'), or crude words (e.g. 'bitch').	51.3 (Agree)	3.848	0.986	0.247**	0.061	0.056
b.	Direct use of bad words to describe someone, e.g.: 'you are a fool'.	63.2 (Agree)	3.968	0.776	0.183*	0.034	0.028
c.	Presence of loud language - bad words/ name written in capital letters to making it obvious in a message. e.g.: 'you FOOL!!'	48.7 (Strongly agree)	4.225	0.938	0.357**	**0.127**	0.123
d.	Teasing - repeated comments or messages that may upset someone.	56.8 (Strongly agree)	4.494	0.649	0.331**	**0.109**	0.105

N=422

**Correlation is significant at the 0.01 level (2-tailed)

*Correlation is significant at the 0.05 level (2-tailed)

The experience and involvement in cyberbullying is a dichotomous variable coded 1 if the respondent answered 'Yes', 2 if a respondent answered 'No'. As shown in Table 7, the correlation coefficient between experience and involvement of cyberbullying, and for all the indicators of direct cyberbullying, is highly significant at the 0.01 level (2-tailed), which shows a strong relationship existed. However, linear regression analysis between the dependent variable (experiences of or involvement in cyberbullying) and independent variables (as given in Table 7 from serial letters 'a' to 'k') suggests that the coefficients of determination (R^2), between involvement in or experience of cyberbullying and 'had been bullied or picked on by someone or a group online', 'had received an offensive message', 'received a message online, which mocked you or otherwise upset you', 'they received an offensive online message from a friend or relative', and 'they felt frightened to go online', is 46.1%, 38.0%, 37.4%, 33.9%, and 32.3% respectively. This means these independent variables accounted for 46.1%, 38.0%, 37.4%, 33.9%, and 32.3% of the total variation of the dependent variable i.e. involvement in or experience of cyberbullying. These five independent variables are the main indicators of direct cyberbullying based on frequency, whereas the R^2 between involvement or experience of cyberbullying and all the eleven indicators of Q9 is 48.8%, as shown in Table 8.

The experience and involvement in cyberbullying is a dichotomous variable coded 1 if the respondent answered 'Yes', 2 if a respondent answered 'No'. As shown in Table 5, the correlation coefficient between experience of, or involvement in cyberbullying, and the 'appearance of bad words in messages, such as insults', 'presence of loud language' and 'teasing' is 'highly significant' at the 0.01 level (2-tailed), which shows a strong relationship existed. Whereas, significant for 'direct use of bad words to describe someone' at the 0.05 level (2-tailed). However, linear regression analysis between the dependent variable (experience of or involvement in cyberbullying) and independent variables (as given in Table 5 from serial letters 'a' to 'd') suggests that the coefficients of determination (R^2) between involvement in or experience of cyberbullying, and 'Presence of loud language' and 'Teasing' are 12.7% and 10.9% respectively. This means these independent variables accounted for 12.7% and 10.9% of the total variation in the dependent variable i.e. involvement in or experience of cyberbullying. These two independent variables are the main indicators of direct cyberbullying, whereas the R^2 between involvement or experience of cyberbullying and all the four indicators of Q8 is 15.6% as shown in Table 6.

3.2.2. Involvement or Experience of Direct Cyberbullying and Its Frequency (Q6 & Q9)

Given the list of eleven cyberbullying examples, participants were asked the frequency on a scale from 'Every day' to 'Never' by which they have been bullied or have bullied others. The majority of participants agreed on the 'A few times' option as they 'had received an offensive message' (41.0%), 'they had received a message online which mocked or upset them' (40.4%), 'had received a message that they did not want others to see' (39.9%), 'had been bullied or picked on by someone or a group online' (37.0%), 'they felt frighted to go online' (35.4%), and 'they received an offensive online message from a friend or relative' (34.8%). Furthermore, the majority of the respondents (43.8%) said that they never sent a message online which mocked the receiver or otherwise upset them. The detailed table is

Table 6. Regression (stepwise) analysis, model summary (Q6 & Q8)

	Coefficients[a]					
S. No.	**Model**	**Unstandardised Coefficients**		**Standardised Coefficients**	**t**	**Sig.**
		B	**Std. Error**	**Beta**		
	(Constant)	-0.540	0.258		-2.095	0.038
a.	Appearance of bad words in message, such as insults (e.g. 'fool'), or crude words (e.g. 'bitch').	0.060	0.047	0.120	1.271	0.205
b.	Direct use of bad words to describe someone, e.g.: 'you are a fool'.	-0.067	0.060	-0.106	-1.118	0.265
c.	Presence of loud language - bad words/ name written in capital letters to making it obvious in a message. e.g.: 'you FOOL!!'	0.122	0.057	0.232	2.124	0.035*
d.	Teasing - repeated comments or messages that may upset someone.	0.146	0.067	0.192	2.170	0.031*
	R	**R^2**	**Adjusted R^2**	**d.f.1**	**d.f.2**	**Significance F**
	0.395^a	0.156	0.137	4	183	0.000**
	a. Dependent Variable: Have you experienced or been involved in cyberbullying?					

**Significant at $p \leq 0.01$
*Significant at $p \leq 0.05$

given in Appendix III.

On one hand, around 50% people said that they have received cyberbullying messages, while on the other hand fewer than 10% of people accepted that they have ever sent bullying messages. This opens up a new direction of research to discover if people are ignoring the fact they are bullying others; or if they have done it unknowingly. Here we can see that there is a huge gap between intentional cyberbullying and unintentional cyberbullying. Nevertheless, whatever the case is, around 50.0% of people accepted that they felt bad on receiving a message of an apparently cyberbullying nature.

3.3. Indirect Cyberbullying

The internal reliability of Q10 and the five indicators of Q11 and experience of or involvement in cyberbullying (Q6) is calculated by using Cronbach's alpha. The overall alpha

Table 7. Involvement or experience of direct cyberbullying and its frequency (Q6 & Q9)

S. No.	Indicators	Percent	Mean	Standard Deviation	R	R^2	Adjusted R^2
a.	You have been bullied or picked up by someone or a group online.	37.0 (A few times)	1.434	1.388	0.679**	**0.461**	0.458
b.	You have bullied or picked up someone online.	48.7 (Never), 23.5 (Once/ twice)	0.952	1.174	0.549**	0.302	0.298
c.	You have received offensive message from others.	41.0 (A few times)	1.617	1.317	0.617**	**0.380**	0.377
d.	You have sent or post offensive message to others.	48.7 (Never), 26.2 (Once/ twice)	0.904	1.113	0.495**	0.245	0.240
e.	You have been frightened to go online.	35.4 (A few times)	1.201	1.353	0.569**	**0.323**	0.320
f.	You have received a message that you did not want others to see.	39.9 (A few times)	1.436	1.254	0.539**	0.290	0.286
g.	You have sent or posted a secrete message of someone's and that person is upset about this.	53.5 (Never), 14.4 (A few times)	0.866	1.163	0.485**	0.235	0.231
h.	You have sent a message online, which mocked the receiver or otherwise upset them.	43.8 (Never), 28.1 (Once/ twice)	0.995	1.120	0.476**	0.226	0.222
i.	You have received a message online, which mocked you or otherwise upset you.	40.4 (A few times)	1.447	1.259	0.611**	**0.374**	0.370
j.	You have sent an offensive message online to a friend or relative.	50.5 (Never), 16.1 (A few times)	0.914	1.164	0.465**	0.216	0.212
k.	You have received an offensive message online from a friend or relative.	34.8 (A few times)	1.342	1.364	0.582**	**0.339**	0.335

N=422
**Correlation is significant at the 0.01 level (2-tailed)
*Correlation is significant at the 0.05 level (2-tailed)

coefficient is 0.940 (range if one item deleted, from 0.922 to 0.951), suggesting excellent reliability. Given a model for 'Indirect cyberbullying', which includes a series of indirect cyberbullying examples, respondents were asked the frequency by which they had been involved in or experienced indirect cyberbullying on the scale of 'Every day' to 'No cyber-bullying'. The majority of people accepted that 'A few times' they have 'been talked about online, in ways that make you feel uncomfortable or upset' (39.2%), 'been mentioned in a message to someone else in a way that is mocking or otherwise makes you feel uncomfortable or upset' (38.8%), and 'bullied or picked up by someone indirectly, as a third person, while online' (35.4%). These three items are identified as the most common examples for the involvement in indirect cyberbullying activities. In addition, nearly the same percentage of respondents said that they have not bullied others in any of these ways. This also suggests that the majority of victims of indirect cyberbullying did not indirectly cyberbully others.

Table 8. Regression (stepwise) analysis, model summary (Q6 & Q9)

	Coefficients[a]					
S. No.	**Model**	**Unstandardised Coefficients**		**Standardised Coefficients**	**t**	**Sig.**
		B	**Std. Error**	**Beta**		
	(Constant)	0.220	0.046		4.793	0.000
a.	You have been bullied or picked up by someone or a group online.	0.231	0.066	0.641	3.517	0.001**
b.	You have bullied or picked up someone online.	-0.017	0.061	-0.041	-0.281	0.779
c.	You have received offensive message from others.	0.016	0.051	0.043	0.324	0.746
d.	You have sent or post offensive message to others.	0.022	0.075	0.049	0.288	0.774
e.	You have been frightened to go online.	0.041	0.050	0.110	0.814	0.417
f.	You have received a message that you did not want others to see.	-0.040	0.041	-0.101	-0.970	0.333
g.	You have sent or posted a secrete message of someone's and that person is upset about this.	-0.118	0.065	-0.276	-1.813	0.072
h.	You have sent a message online, which mocked the receiver or otherwise upset them.	-0.041	0.068	-0.093	-0.602	0.548
i.	You have received a message online, which mocked you or otherwise upset you.	0.105	0.062	0.263	1.692	0.093

Table 8. Continued

	Coefficients[a]					
S. No.	**Model**	**Unstandardised Coefficients**		**Standardised Coefficients**	**t**	**Sig.**
		B	**Std. Error**	**Beta**		
j.	You have sent an offensive message online to a friend or relative.	0.028	0.066	0.067	0.430	0.668
k.	You have received an offensive message online from a friend or relative.	-0.001	0.056	-0.003	-0.018	0.985
	R	**R²**	**Adjusted R²**	**d.f.1**	**d.f.2**	**Significance F**
	0.698[a]	0.488	0.454	11	170	0.000**
	a. Dependent Variable: Have you experienced or been involved in cyberbullying?					

N=422

**Significant at $p \leq 0.01$

*Significant at $p \leq 0.05$

These findings are in line with the direct versus indirect measurement of cyberbullying [6], where indirect measures includes the experience of youngsters with traditional bullying, and their Information and Communication Technology's (ICTs) use was measured in order to situate cyberbullying within these youngsters' lives. Their findings suggested that 61.9% of respondents had been victims, 52.5% had been perpetrators, and 76.3% had been bystanders to at least one POP (potentially offensive Internet and mobile phone practice). The detailed table is given in Appendix IV.

The experience and involvement in cyberbullying is a dichotomous variable coded 1 if the respondent answered 'Yes', 2 if a respondent answered 'No'. As shown in Table 9, the correlation coefficient between experience of or involvement in cyberbullying and all the indicators of indirect cyberbullying is highly significant at the 0.01 level (2-tailed), which shows a strong relationship existed. However, linear regression analysis between the dependent variable (experience of or involvement in cyberbullying) and independent variables (as given in Table 9 from serial letters 'a' to 'e') suggests that the coefficients of determination (R^2), between involvement or experience of cyberbullying and 'been mentioned in a message to someone else in a way that is mocking or otherwise makes you feel uncomfortable or upset', 'bullied or picked on by someone indirectly, as a third person, while online', and 'been talked about online, in ways that make you feel uncomfortable or upset', is 40.6%, 38.7%, and 37.6% respectively. This means these independent variables accounted for 40.6%, 38.7%, and 37.6% of the total variation in the dependent variables i.e. involvement or experience of cyberbullying. These three independent variables are the main examples of indirect cyberbullying based on frequency, whereas the R^2 between involvement in or experience of cyberbullying and all the five indicators of Q11 is 45.4%, as shown in Table 10.

Table 9. Involvement or experience of indirect cyberbullying and its frequency (Q6 & Q11)

S. No.	Indicators	Percent	Mean	Standard Deviation	R	R^2	Adju-sted R^2
a.	You have been bullied or picked up by someone indirectly, as a third person, while online.	35.4 (A few times)	1.284	0.452	0.622**	**0.387**	0.384
b.	You have been talked about online, in ways that make you feel uncomfortable or upset.	39.2 (A few times)	1.382	1.406	0.613**	**0.376**	0.373
c.	You have talked about others, in ways that make them feel uncomfortable or upset.	13.6 (A few times)	1.455	1.237	0.454**	**0.206**	0.201
d.	You have been mentioned in a message to someone else in a way that is mocking or otherwise makes you feel uncomfortable or upset.	38.8 (A few times)	1.084	1.224	0.638**	**0.406**	0.403
e.	You have mentioned someone in a message to a third party in a way that is mocking or otherwise makes them feel uncomfortable or upset.	32.6 (Once/ twice)	1.421	1.238	0.465**	**0.217**	0.212

N=422

**Correlation is significant at the 0.01 level (2-tailed)

*Correlation is significant at the 0.05 level (2-tailed)

3.4. Misinterpreted Form of Cyberbullying

The internal reliability of Q12 and the five indicators of Q13, and experience of or involvement in cyberbullying (Q6) is calculated by using Cronbach's alpha. The overall alpha coefficient is 0.927 (range if one item deleted, from 0.903 to 0.933), suggesting excellent

Table 10. Regression (stepwise) analysis, model summary (Q10 & Q11)

	Coefficients[a]					
S. No.	Model	Unstandardised Coefficients		Standardised Coefficients	t	Sig.
		B	Std. Error	Beta		
	(Constant)	0.243	0.043		5.624	0.000
a.	You have bullied or picked up by someone indirectly, as a third person, while online.	0.155	0.041	0.439	3.803	0.000**
b.	You have been talked about online, in ways that make you feel uncomfortable or upset.	0.054	0.059	0.136	0.919	0.359
c.	You have talked about others, in ways that make them feel uncomfortable or upset.	-0.092	0.062	-0.224	-1.472	0.143
d.	You have been mentioned in a message to someone else in a way that is mocking or otherwise makes you feel uncomfortable or upset.	0.122	0.065	0.305	1.870	0.063
e.	You have mentioned someone in a message to a third party in a way that is mocking or otherwise makes them feel uncomfortable or upset.	0.003	0.069	0.008	0.051	0.960
	R	**R^2**	**Adjusted R^2**	**d.f.1**	**d.f.2**	**Significance F**
	0.674[a]	0.454	0.438	5	169	0.000**
	a. Dependent Variable: Have you experienced or been involved in cyberbullying?					

**Significant at $p \leq 0.01$

*Significant at $p \leq 0.05$

Table 11. Involvement or experience of misinterpreted form of cyberbullying and its frequency (Q6 & Q13)

S. No.	Indicators	Percent	Mean	Standard Deviation	R	R^2	Adjusted R^2
a.	You have been bullied or picked up by a friend or relative, while online.	38.2 (No cyber-bully-ing), 33.1 (A few times)	1.241	1.116	0.659**	**0.434**	0.431
b.	You have been talked about online by a friend or relative, in ways that make you feel uncomfortable or upset.	36.4 (A few times)	1.369	1.044	0.650**	**0.422**	0.419
c.	You have talked about a friend or relative, in ways that would make them feel uncomfortable or upset.	37.3 (Once/ twice), 36.2(No cyber-bully-ing),	0.904	0.788	0.534**	0.285	0.281
d.	You have been mentioned in a message to a friend or relative in a way that is mocking or otherwise makes you feel uncomfortable or upset.	34.8(A few times), 28.7 (No cyber-bullying)	1.365	1.055	0.660**	**0.436**	0.433
e.	You have mentioned by a friend or relative in a message in a way that was mocking or otherwise makes them feel uncomfortable or upset.	36.5 (Once/ twice), 36.5 (No cyber-bullying)	0.904	0.793	0.496**	**0.246**	0.242

N=422

**Correlation is significant at the 0.01 level (2-tailed)

*Correlation is significant at the 0.05 level (2-tailed)

reliability.

A list of five items and the frequency scale from 'Every day' to 'No cyberbullying' were given for the 'misinterpreted form' of cyberbullying model. Participants were asked the frequency by which they had been involved in or experienced misinterpreted form of cyberbullying on the scale of 'Every day' to 'No cyberbullying'. Of the total, 38.2%, 37.3%, and 36.5% respondents opted 'No cyberbullying' for the 'bullied or picked up by a friend or relative, while online', 'talked about a friend or relative, in ways that would make them feel uncomfortable or upset', and 'mentioned by a friend or relative in a message in a way that was mocking or otherwise makes them feel uncomfortable or upset', respectively. The majority of people accepted that 'A few times' they have 'been talked about online by a friend or relative, in ways that make you feel uncomfortable or upset.' (36.9%), and 'been mentioned in a message to a friend or relative in a way that is mocking or otherwise makes you feel uncomfortable or upset.' (34.8%), and 'bullied or picked up by a friend or relative, while online' (33.1%). These three items are identified as the most common examples for the involvement in misinterpreted form of cyberbullying activities. In addition, nearly the same percentage of respondents said that they have not bullied others in any of these ways. This also suggests that the majority of victims of misinterpreted form of bullying did not bully others in the same way. The detailed table is given in Appendix V.

The experience of and involvement in cyberbullying is a dichotomous variable coded 1 if the respondent answered 'Yes', 2 if a respondent answered 'No'. As shown in Table 11, the correlation coefficient between experience of or involvement in cyberbullying and all the indicators of misinterpreted form of cyberbullying is highly significant at the 0.01 level (2-tailed), which shows a strong relationship existed. However, linear regression analysis between dependent variables (experience of or involvement in cyberbullying) and independent variables (as given in Table 5.10 from serial letters 'a' to 'e) suggests that the coefficient of determination (R^2), between involvement in or experience of cyberbullying and being 'been mentioned in a message to a friend or relative in a way that is mocking or otherwise makes you feel uncomfortable or upset', 'bullied or picked up on a friend or relative, while online', and 'been talked about online by a friend or relative, in ways that make you feel uncomfortable or upset' is 43.6%, 43.4%, and 42.2% and respectively. This means these independent variables accounted for 43.6%, 43.4%, and 42.2% of the total variation in the dependent variable i.e. involvement in or experience of cyberbullying. These three independent variables are the main indicators of misinterpreted form of cyberbullying based on frequency, whereas the R^2 between involvement or experience of cyberbullying and all the five indicators of Q13 is 47.7%, as shown in Table 12.

Research demonstrates that the differentiation between cyberbullying and cyber-teasing depends on the subjective difference between the ways messages were intended versus how they were perceived. Given that the use of coarse or rude language is often a common phenomenon among close friends or those in close relationships, without intent to hurt each other. Of the total, 43% of respondents agreed that they had experienced this type of bullying behaviour 'A few times'.

Therefore, participants were asked for their reaction while experiencing this behaviour, through multiple-choice questions. Of the total, 44.4% of respondents said that they 'took it seriously and replied with a bullying message', and 46.3% mentioned that they 'took it seriously and never replied'. Here, based on the frequency, we formed a rule by comput-

Table 12. Regression (stepwise) analysis, model summary (Q12 & Q13)

	Coefficients[a]					
S. No.	**Model**	**Unstandardised Coefficients**		**Standardised Coefficients**	**t**	**Sig.**
		B	**Std. Error**	**Beta**		
	(Constant)	0.170	0.046		3.729	0.170
a.	You have bullied or picked up by a friend or relative, while online.	0.154	0.046	0.350	3.346	0.154
b.	You have been talked about online by a friend or relative, in ways that make you feel uncomfortable or upset.	0.063	0.064	0.134	0.991	0.063
c.	You have talked about a friend or relative, in ways that would make them feel uncomfortable or upset.	0.087	0.082	0.140	1.056	0.087
d.	You have been mentioned in a message to a friend or relative in a way that is mocking or otherwise makes you feel uncomfortable or upset.	0.136	0.066	0.290	2.059	0.136
e.	You have mentioned by a friend or relative in a message in a way that was mocking or otherwise makes them feel uncomfortable or upset.	-0.110	0.086	-0.179	-1.287	-0.110
	R	**R^2**	**Adjusted R^2**	**d.f.1**	**d.f.2**	**Significance F**
	0.701[a]	0.492	0.477	5	169	0.000**
	a. Dependent Variable: Have you experienced or been involved in cyberbullying?					

N=422

**Significant at $p \leq 0.01$

*Significant at $p \leq 0.05$

ing the likelihood of the given rude or hurtful messages, m, sent between friends, so the probability that m is cyberbullying ($y = 1$) or not ($y = -1$) can be defined as:

$$y = X(m, f);\ y \in \{1, -1\} \tag{1}$$

$$y = \begin{cases} 1 & if \quad 0.06 < f < 0.23; \\ -1 & if \quad 0.23 \leq f \leq 1 \quad or\ 0.0 \leq f \leq 0.06 \end{cases} \tag{2}$$

where, f is the frequency of the hurtful message over the total number of messages, over a period of one month ($n = 30$), and range of f is given as $0 \leq f \leq 1$.

This demonstrates that people ignore rude or coarse behaviour between close friends or in close relationships for 'A few times', but as the frequency of such occurrences increases, it may result in more serious cases of cyberbullying and not just jokes or intentional acts of poking fun at a friend. Similarly, it is also not classified as cyberbullying if it happens so frequently that it can be considered as the usual way of communication between two good friends who have a mutual understanding of the comments made. However, unusual patterns can indicate that there is something wrong and the behaviour could be an intentional act to hurt a friend. Also research demonstrates that cyberbullying victimisation is more frequent among peer groups [20].

These inconsistent results clearly indicate that not all online variants of cyberbullying (or what appears to be cyberbullying) are considered as real cyberbullying cases [22]. It is a matter of perception of the message sender as well as the message recipient whether they consider the message or behaviour as 'funny' or 'hurtful' [22]. Similarly, findings from the study regarding cyberbullying behaviours of teenagers from different socio-economic backgrounds among public and private school students revealed that participants from private schools did not mind cyberbullying because they thought it was a joke, whereas participants from public schools reported that they felt angry when faced with cyberbullying [21].

4. Conclusion

With regards to the prevalence of cyberbullying in social networks, the following observation seems to be especially relevant in light of the development of the cyberbullying indicators from the user-generated content: For *direct cyberbullying*, 'presence of loud language' and 'teasing - repeated comments or messages that may upset someone' are the main indicators in social networks. For *indirect cyberbullying*, 'bullied or picked on by someone indirectly, as a third person, while online', 'been talked about online, in ways that make you feel uncomfortable or upset', and 'been mentioned in a message to someone else in a way that is mocking or otherwise makes you feel uncomfortable or upset' are the main indicators. For *misinterpreted form of cyberbullying*, 'bullied or picked up on a friend or relative, while online', 'been talked about online by a friend or relative, in ways that make you feel uncomfortable or upset' and 'been mentioned in a message to a friend or relative in a way that is mocking or otherwise makes you feel uncomfortable or upset' are the main indicators.

References

[1] Osman Tolga Aricak. Psychiatric symptomatology as a predictor of cyberbullying among university students. *Eurasian Journal of Educational Research*, 34:167–184, 2009.

[2] Tanya Beran and Qing Li. Cyber-harassment: A study of a new method for an old behavior. *Journal of Educational Computing Research*, 32(3):265–277, 2005.

[3] Wanda Cassidy, Margaret Jackson, and Karen N. Brown. Sticks and stones can break my bones, but how can pixels hurt me? Students' experiences with cyber-bullying. *School Psychology International*, 30(4):383–402, 2009.

[4] Maral Dadvar, Franciska de Jong, Roeland Ordelman, and Dolf Trieschnigg. Improved cyberbullying detection using gender information. In *Proceedings of the 12th Dutch-Belgian Information Retrieval Workshop*, pages 23–25, 2012.

[5] Karthik Dinakar, Roi Reichart, and Henry Lieberman. Modeling the detection of textual cyberbullying. In *International Conference on Weblog and Social Media - Social Mobile Web Workshop*, pages 11–17, 2011.

[6] Jaana Juvonen and Elisheva F. Gross. Extending the school grounds?-bullying experiences in cyberspace. *Journal of School Health*, 78(9):496–505, 2008.

[7] April Kontostathis. Chatcoder: Toward the tracking and categorization of internet predators. In *Proceedings in Applied Mathematics - 9th SIAM International Conference on Data Mining, Text Mining Workshop*, pages 1327–1334, 2009.

[8] Robin M. Kowalski and Susan P. Limber. Electronic bullying among middle school students. *Journal of Adolescent Health*, 41(6):22–30, 2007.

[9] Qing Li. Cyberbullying in schools. a research of gender differences. *School Psychology International*, 27(2):157–170, 2006.

[10] India McGhee, Jennifer Bayzick, April Kontostathis, Lynne Edwards, Alexandra McBride, and Emma Jakubowski. Learning to identify internet sexual predation. *International Journal on Electronic Commerce*, 15(3):103–122, 2011.

[11] Vinita Nahar, Sanad Al-Maskari, Xue Li, and Chaoyi Pang. Semi-supervised learning for cyberbullying detection in social networks. In *the 25th Australasian Database Conference (ADC) (In press)*, 2014.

[12] Vinita Nahar, Xue Li, and Chaoyi Pang. An effective approach for cyberbullying detection. *Journal of Communications in Information Science and Management Engineering (CISME'13)*, 3(5):238–247, 2013.

[13] Vinita Nahar, Xue Li, Chaoyi Pang, and Yang Zhang. Cyberbullying detection based on text-stream classification. In *the 11th Australasian Data Mining Conference (AusDM'13) (In press)*, 2013.

[14] Vinita Nahar, Xue Li, Hao Lan Zhang, and Chaoyi Pang. Detecting cyberbullying in social networks using multi-agent system. *International Journal of Web Intelligence and Agent Systems, Special Issue on Multi-agent-based problem solving methods in Big Data Environment and Agent-based Data Mining (WIAS'13) (In press)*, 2014.

[15] Vinita Nahar, Sayan Unankard, Xue Li, and Chaoyi Pang. Sentiment analysis for effective detection of cyber bullying. In *Proceedings of the 14th Asia-Pacific Web Conference (APWeb'12)*, pages 767–774, 2012.

[16] Leandra Parris, Kris Varjas, Joel Meyers, and Hayley Cutts. High school students' perceptions of coping with cyberbullying. *Youth & Society*, 44(2):248–306, 2012.

[17] Michal Ptaszynski, Pawel Dybala, Tatsuaki Matsuba, Fumito Masui, Rafal Rzepka, and Kenji Araki. Machine learning and affect analysis against cyber-bullying. In *Proceedings of the Linguistic And Cognitive Approaches To Dialog Agents Symposium*, pages 7–16, 2010.

[18] Kelly Reynolds, April Kontostathis, and Lynne Edwards. Using machine learning to detect cyberbullying. In *Proceedings of the 10th International Conference on Machine Learning and Applications and Workshops - Volume 02 (ICMLA'11)*, pages 241–244, 2011.

[19] Peter K. Smith, Jess Mahdavi, Manuel Carvalho, Sonja Fisher, Shanette Russell, and Neil Tippett. Cyberbullying: its nature and impact in secondary school pupils. *Journal of Child Psychology and Psychiatry*, 49(4):376–385, 2008.

[20] Paris S. Strom and Robert D. Strom. Cyberbullying by adolescents: A preliminary assessment. *The Educational Forum*, 70(1):21–36, 2006.

[21] Cigdem Topcu, Ozgur Erdur-Baker, and Yesim Capa-Aydin. Examination of cyberbullying experiences among turkish students from different school types. *Cyberpsychology and Behavior*, 11(6):643–648, 2008.

[22] Heidi Vandebosch and Katrien Van Cleemput. Cyberbullying among youngsters: profiles of bullies and victims. *New Media and Society*, 11(8):1349–1371, 2009.

[23] Nancy Willard. Educator's guide to cyberbullying and cyberthreats, Retrieved on: 10 January 2011. *http://www.accem.org/pdf/cbcteducator.pdf*, pages 1–16, 2007.

[24] Michele L. Ybarra, Kimberly J. Mitchell, Janis Wolak, and David Finkelhor. Examining characteristics and associated distress related to internet harassment: Findings from the second youth internet safety survey. *Pediatrics*, 118(4):1169–1177, 2006.

[25] Dawei Yin, Zhenzhen Xue, Liangjie Hong, Brian D. Davisoni, April Kontostathis, and Lynne Edwards. Detection of harassment on web 2.0. In *Proceedings of the Content Analysis in the WEB 2.0 (CAW2.0) Workshop at WWW'09*, 2009.

[26] Jina Yoon, Sheri Bauman, Taesan Choi, and Alisa S. Hutchinson. How south korean teachers handle an incident of school bullying. *School Psychology International*, 32:312–329, 2011.

In: Handbook on Bullying
Editor: Phoebe Triggs

ISBN: 978-1-63463-023-8

Chapter 15

Cyberbullying Prevalence - Medium, Motive and Reaction

Vinita Nahar*, Xue Li†, and Chaoyi Pang‡
School of Information Technology and Electrical Engineering
The University of Queensland, Australia
The Australian E-Health Research Center, CSIRO, Australia

Abstract

Nowadays, cyberbullying is becoming an increasingly obvious concern, especially among children and teenagers. Cyberbullying can have an extremely negative impact on victims and in the worst scenarios, it can actually result in suicidal attempts.

In this Chapter, we present the results of an online survey, which is conducted to study the sources, motives and reaction to cyberbullying. The study focuses on obtaining feedback on the nature and prevalence of cyberbullying from the Internet users of different age groups and genders, based on the frequency of offensive posts received. Findings reveal that in social networking websites, instance messaging and chat rooms are the main sources of cyberbullying. Items 'to show hate', 'to make fun of someone', and 'to copycat others in cyberbullying activities' are the main motives of cyberbullying. The main reactions to cyberbullying are 'replied in a bullying manner', 'never replied' and 'blocked someone'. To differentiate real bullying from cyberbullying-like or non-bullying messages, the frequency between sender and receiver over a long period of a time can be seen to demonstrate whether it is an unusual (intentional) act of teasing, or a usual (unintentional) act that generally exists between good friends or those in close relationships. However, it is important to note that a frequent pattern should not be confused with frequent coarse language at one particular time. The unusual patterns over a long period of time should be considered as clear indicators of true bullying.

Keywords: cyberbullying, victimization, prevalence, social networks, cyberbullying indicators

---

*E-mail address: v.nahar@uq.edu.au
†E-mail address: xueli@itee.uq.edu.au
‡E-mail address: Chaoyi.Pang@csiro.au

1. Introduction

Though cyberbullying is a common phenomenon among adolescents and children, breakthrough advancements in information and web-based technologies, such as social networking sites, straddle age groups where non-physical aggression is often observed among different age group users. Research conducted in various countries, including Serbia, the UK, the USA, Korea, Turkey, Italy, and Australia clearly indicate that nearly 90% of school-aged students access the Internet at home, with over 50% reporting daily use [3, 10, 13, 14], which they use to interact in cyberspace. Teachers and administrators have recognized students' use of information and communication technology, particularly in their social interaction via the expanding use of electronic communication in school classrooms [2, 6]. Worldwide, studies reveal that most school-aged students now own a mobile phone and this increases with age [3, 10]. An empirical study conducted by Aricak [1] in the Turkish environment reveals the fact that ease of maintaining anonymity in cyberspace is one of the most significant causes of cyberbullying. He also found that males are more likely than females to validate that they would engage in cyberbullying in the future. Furthermore, this study also suggests that cyberbullying is not limited to children and adolescents, but extends to adults as well.

The very act of a bullying activity is harmful in some way or the other and its implications are so dangerous that it may destroy the precious lives of youths when they fail to cope with the unbearable pressure of insulting or humiliating messages, especially on the Internet, where the potential audience of cyberbullying is limitless [5]. In such settings, it is beneficial to have an automatic system which can monitor such harmful messages and alert users of its repetitive occurrence. This will help to maintain a safe and healthy online environment for all users and endorses the need for detection software.

In light of the facts that (i) young people have fully embraced the Internet as both an environment and a tool for socialising [12] on place like social networks; (ii) there is growing evidence of the existence of cyberbullying, including cases which have resulted in suicide; (iii) bullying in virtual reality is a difficult phenomenon for adults to monitor young children/students' actions [9]; (iv) young people (especially teenagers) do not tell adults about cyberbullying incidents and only a minority of participants use digital tools to prevent online bullying incidents [4]. This chapter aims to study the online users' understanding of the prevalence of cyberbullying.

Based on the frequency of sent and received messages under various conditions, such as involvement in direct, indirect and the misinterpreted form of cyberbullying, this chapter investigates the cyberbullying indicators in user-generated content that can be used towards cyberbullying detection in social networks. While cyberbullying is a problem that receives a lot of attention from the social science perspective, it has received much less research attention from the automatic detection perspective. Various definitions of cyberbullying, revealing the attributes which are inherent in the act of cyberbullying are: intentional hurt, repetitive patterns, an imbalance of power, and where a victim is unable to defend him/herself.

The differentiation between cyberbullying and cyber-teasing depends on the subjective difference between the ways messages were intended versus how they were perceived, and as a consequence automatic detection poses an important research challenge. The aim of this study is to develop rules, which can be incorporated within cyberbullying detection tools. Rules will be based on the frequency of offensive messages and the communication patterns between online users engaging in harassing /cruel or offensive messaging. In this chapter, we study various indicators in user-generated content which makes the online content appear as bullying content. We consider the frequency by which offensive or hurtful messages are sent and received as a basis to predict the communication pattern of an intentionally hurtful act.

As a part of this research, we conducted an online survey where we examined users understanding on how they consider cyberbullying-like posts as real-cyberbullying or non-cyberbullying. Previous investigations have been conducted based on the formal definitions of cyberbullying, indicators of cyberbullying, opinions of the people who are actually involved in or who have experienced cyberbullying, and their reactions to the cyberbullying incidents. Based on the above-mentioned literature relating to the prevalence of cyberbullying and involvement of the Internet users in cyberbullying activities, the current studies sources and causes of cyberbullying as well as the reaction to cyberbullying.

2. Methodology

2.1. Participants and Settings

The study focuses on obtaining feedback on the nature and prevalence of cyberbullying from the Internet users of different age groups and genders, based on the frequency of offensive posts received. Therefore, in this study, an anonymous online survey via *SurveyMonkey* [1] was conducted through social networks. A link to the questionnaire was distributed on social networks including Twitter and Facebook, and participants were randomly invited to take part.

Voluntary participants included, but were not limited to, students/staff/members of the University of Queensland (UQ) community. Students, academics and research peers were also approached to fill out the online questionnaire. Although not specifically targeted, people from communities outside of the UQ have also participated. As a strategy to obtain informed consent, it was requested that people under 18 years seek the permission from a parent or guardian before participating in the survey. Prior to the research being conducted, the study had been cleared in accordance with the ethical review processes of the University of Queensland, Australia.

2.2. Procedure

To examine the extent of cyberbullying and cyber-harassment, we selected different age groups (12-17 years, 18-21 years, 22-25 years, 25-30 years) and grouped users above 30 years as a single entity. In addition, we assumed that these Internet users have accounts on social networks such as Facebook and Twitter, which are the most popular social networks, and the mode through which the survey was conducted. The questionnaire was divided into five parts:

[1] http://www.surveymonkey.com (last visited [13 May 2014])

Part A: Relating to demographic factors;
Part B: Relating to direct cyberbullying;
Part C: Relating to indirect cyberbullying;
Part D: Relating to misinterpreted form of cyberbullying;
Part E: General questions about cyberbullying.

The pilot survey was conducted by interviewing a few UQ students and academics. After this, modifications were made based on the feedback and the revised questionnaire was posted on the *SurveyMonkey* website. A filter question *'Have you experienced or been involved in cyberbullying?'* was employed to filter out participants who have never been involved in or experienced any form of cyberbullying. In order to determine the best indicators of direct, indirect and misinterpreted form of cyberbullying; an explicit definition of each type of cyberbullying was provided. Also, indicators were independently prepared for each type of cyberbullying. Respondents were asked to answer each item about what constitutes cyberbullying, and the frequency by which they have experienced or been involved in these three types of cyberbullying. The statistical analysis of data is done by computing the Cronbach's alpha, the Spearman's Correlation Coefficient, Linear Regression Analysis and the Coefficient of determination using SPSS. Significance is calculated at 5% and 1% levels.

2.2.1. General Questions about Cyberbullying

This chapter focuses on the Part E of the questionnaire (for the details of Part A, B, C, and D of the questionnaire, please refer [7, 8]. In Part E, three multiple-choice questions were developed regarding the general questions about cyberbullying, such as main sources of cyberbullying, motives of cyberbullying, and participants' reactions to cyberbullying messages. A question to measure the level of severity of cyberbullying based on the percentage of cyberbullying was developed. Four severity levels were defined including 'Severe', 'Moderate', 'Normal', and 'Non-bullying'. Participants were also asked to provide five unusual bullying words they have encountered for the first time.

3. Results and Discussions

3.1. Cyberbullying Prevalence – Medium, Motive and Reaction

Through the multiple-choice questions, participants were asked to indicate the mediums, causes, and their reactions based on their experience while involved in cyberbullying.

3.1.1. Involvement or Experience of Cyberbullying versus Sources of Cyberbullying (Q6 & Q15)

Given the list of communication tools as a medium through which cyberbullying takes place, as shown in Table 1, 'Social networking websites *(SNs)*', 'Chat rooms *(CR)*' and 'Instant Messaging *(TM)*' are identified as the most common sources for the involvement in cyberbullying activities. The most prevalent tool is social networking websites among

Table 1. Involvement or experience of cyberbullying and sources of cyberbullying (Q6 & Q15)

S. No.	Indicators	Percent	Mean	Standard Deviation	Correlation (R)	R^2	Adjusted R^2
a.	Text messages (TM)	12.8	0.05	0.21	0.261**	0.068	0.066
b.	Phone calls via mobile phones	4.5	0.02	0.013	0.169**	0.029	0.026
c.	Chat rooms (CR)	51.9	0.19	0.39	0.644**	**0.415**	0.413
d.	Social networking websites (SNs)	75.0	0.28	0.45	0.704**	**0.495**	0.494
e.	Images or videos via mobile phone camera	4.5	0.02	0.13	0.127*	0.016	0.014
f.	Emails	17.9	0.07	0.25	0.110*	0.012	0.010
e.	Instant messaging (IM)	49.4	0.18	0.39	0.679**	**0.461**	0.460

N=422
**Correlation is significant at the 0.01 level (2-tailed)
*Correlation is significant at the 0.05 level (2-tailed)
[a]Correlation between involvement or experience of cyberbullying and sources of cyberbullying

76.3% male and 74.2% female participants of those who have been involved in cyberbullying across all age groups. CR was the second most common medium selected by 68% male and 42% female, with the majority from 12-17 years old candidates, while IM was also an equally likely place for 64% male and 40% females, especially among the 12-17 years olds.

Vandebosch *et al.* [11] conducted a study on cyberbullying in Flanders (Belgium) among primary school children and students in secondary education. On asking respondents directly whether they had been actively or passively involved in bullying via Internet or mobile phone, they found 10% were victims and 20% were perpetrators in this category. In addition, 61.9% of respondents had been victims and 52.5% had been perpetrators of at least one potentially offensive practice via the Internet or a mobile phone, which are generally considered as a 'form of bullying'.

The internal reliability of the seven sources and experiences of or involvement in cyberbullying is calculated using Cronbach's alpha. The overall alpha coefficient is 0.772 (range if one item deleted, from 0.681 to 0.790), suggested acceptable reliability. The experience and involvement in cyberbullying is a dichotomous variable coded 1 if the respondent answered 'Yes', 2 if a respondent answered 'No'. As shown in Table 1, the correlation coefficients between experience of or involvement in cyberbullying and for *TM*, *phonecalls*, *CR*, *SNs* and *IM* is highly significant at the 0.01 level (2-tailed), which shows a strong relationship existed, whereas it is significant for images and emails at the 0.05 level (2-tailed). However, linear regression analysis between dependent variables (experience or involvement of cyberbullying) and independent variables (as given in Table 1 from serial number '1' to '7') suggests that the coefficient of determination (R^2), between involvement or experience of cyberbullying and SNs, IM and CR is 49.5%, 46.1% and 41.5% respectively.

Table 2. Regression (stepwise) analysis, model summary (Q6 & Q15)

S. No.	Coefficients[a]					
	Model	**Unstandardised Coefficients**		**Standardised Coefficients**	**t**	**Sig.**
		B	**Std. Error**	**Beta**		
	(Constant)	0.049	0.017		2.996	0.003
a.	Text message	0.201	0.067	0.097	3.019	0.003*
b.	Phone calls via mobile phones	-0.013	0.119	-0.004	-0.114	0.910
c.	Chat rooms	0.198	0.051	0.176	3.894	0.000**
d.	Social networking websites	0.423	0.039	0.424	10.919	0.000**
e.	Images or videos via mobile phone camera	0.116	0.116	0.033	0.996	0.320
f.	Emails	-0.020	0.055	-0.011	-0.372	0.710
g.	Instant messaging (IM)	0.337	0.052	0.292	6.446	0.000**
	R	**R^2**	**Adjusted R^2**	**d.f.1**	**d.f.2**	**Significance F**
	0.798[a]	0.637	0.631	7	398	0.000**
	a. Dependent Variable: Have you experienced or been involved in cyberbullying?					

**Significant at p≤ 0.01
*Significant at p ≤ 0.05

This means these independent variables accounted for 49.5%, 46.1% and 41.5% of the total variation in the dependent variable i.e. involvement or experience of cyberbullying. These three independent variables are the main sources of cyberbullying, whereas the R^2 between involvement or experience of cyberbullying and all the seven indicators of Q15 is 63.7%, as given in Table 2.

3.1.2. Involvement or Experience of Cyberbullying versus Motives of Cyberbullying (Q6 & Q16)

Participants were then asked for their opinion for the most significant motive for cyberbullying in which they were involved, as given in Table 3. 'To make fun of someone', 'To show hate', 'To copycat others in bullying activities' and 'To show superiority' were the various motives given for bullying others. The most common cause of cyberbullying among males (73.8%) and females (74.2%) between 12 to 30 years of age was 'to make fun of someone'. 'To show hate' was the second most prevalent cause selected by 60.7% of males and 39.8% of females between 12 to 30 years of age. Of the total, 33.0% of participants mentioned that 'copycat others in bullying activities' was also a common cause, with the majority of respondents (66.7%) belonging to the 22-25 years of age group. Double the number of females than males in the age group 26-25 years and over 30 years said 'To show superiority' as the fourth most common cause of bullying others online.

The internal reliability of the six motives and involvement in and experience of cy-

Table 3. Involvement or experience of cyberbullying and motives of cyberbullying (Q6 & Q16)

S. No.	Motives	Percent	Mean	Standard Deviation	Correlation (R)	R^2	Adjusted R^2
a.	To make fun of someone	69.8	0.263	0.441	0.626**	**0.391**	0.390
b.	To show superiority	32.7	0.123	0.330	0.234**	0.055	0.052
c.	To show hate	47.8	0.180	0.385	0.625**	**0.424**	0.423
d.	To take revenge	17.0	0.064	0.245	0.282**	0.080	0.077
e.	To copycat others in bullying activities	33.3	0.126	0.333	0.503**	**0.253**	0.251
f.	To show anger	22.0	0.083	0.276	0.333**	0.111	0.109

N=422

**Correlation is significant at the 0.01 level (2-tailed)

*Correlation is significant at the 0.05 level (2-tailed)

[b]Correlation between involvement or experience of cyberbullying and sources of cyberbullying

Table 4. Regression (stepwise) analysis, model summary (Q6 & Q16)

S. No.	Model	Coefficients[a] Unstandardised Coefficients B	Std. Error	Standardised Coefficients Beta	t	Sig.
	(Constant)	0.070	0.019		3.782	0.000
a.	To make fun of someone	0.309	0.046	0.305	6.664	0.000**
b.	To show superiority	0.092	0.048	0.068	1.932	0.054
c.	To show hate	0.333	0.063	0.288	5.313	0.000**
d.	To take revenge	0.183	0.067	0.099	2.711	0.007**
e.	To copycat others in bullying activities	0.223	0.059	0.167	3.810	0.000**
d.	To show anger	0.162	0.066	0.101	2.467	0.014*
	R	**R^2**	**Adjusted R^2**	**d.f.1**	**d.f.2**	**Significance F**
	0.735[a]	0.540	0.533	6	400	0.000**
	a. Dependent Variable: Have you experienced or been involved in cyberbullying?					

**Significant at p≤ 0.01

*Significant at p≤ 0.05

berbullying is calculated using Cronbach's alpha. The overall alpha coefficient is 0.781 (range if one item deleted, from 0.701 to 0.797), which indicates acceptable reliability. The experience and involvement in cyberbullying is a dichotomous variable coded 1 if the respondent answered 'Yes', 2 if a respondent answered 'No'. As shown in Table 3, the cor-

Table 5. Involvement or experience of cyberbullying and reactions to cyberbullying (Q6 & Q17)

S. No.	Reactions	Percent	Mean	Standard Deviation	Correlation (R)	R^2	Adjusted R^2
a.	Didn't take it seriously and reply in normal way	16.6	0.062	0.241	0.082	0.007	0.004
b.	Replied in bullying manner	46.5	0.173	0.379	0.682**	**0.464**	0.463
c.	Never replied	55.4	0.206	0.405	0.538**	**0.289**	0.288
d.	Blocked someone	47.1	0.175	0.381	0.454**	**0.206**	0.204
e.	Changed User ID	3.8	0.014	0.119	0.150**	0.022	0.020
f.	Discussed it with parents/close friend/someone	12.7	0.0474	0.213	0.135**	0.018	0.016
g.	Reported it to the service provider or to police	3.2	0.0118	0.108	-0.020	0.000	-0.002

N=422

**Correlation is significant at the 0.01 level (2-tailed)

*Correlation is significant at the 0.05 level (2-tailed)

[c]Correlation between involvement or experience of cyberbullying and sources of cyberbullying

relation coefficient between 'involvement or experience of cyberbullying' and motives of cyberbullying from serial number '1' to '6' in Table 3 is highly significant at the 0.01 level (2-tailed), which shows a strong relationship existed. However, linear regression analysis between the dependent variables (involvement or experience of cyberbullying) and independent variables (as given in Table 5.14 from serial number '1' to '6') suggests that the coefficient of determination (R^2), between involvement or experience of cyberbullying and 'to show hate', 'to make fun of someone' and 'to copycat others in bullying activities', is 42.4%, 39.1% and 25.3% respectively. This means these independent variables accounted for 42.4%, 39.1% and 25.3% of the total variation in the dependent variable i.e. experience of or involvement in cyberbullying. These three independent variables are the main motives of cyberbullying, whereas the R^2 between involvement or experience of cyberbullying and all the six indicators of Q16 is 54.0%, as given in Table 4.

3.1.3. Involvement or Experience of Cyberbullying versus Reaction to Cyberbullying (Q6 & Q17)

Respondents were also asked how they have reacted while being involved in cyberbullying. As shown in Table 5 'never replied', 'blocked someone' and 'replied in a bullying manner' were the most common reactions among the participants. The majority of male participants (61%), who also belonged to the age range 12 to 25 years, indicated that they also replied in a bullying manner, while the majority of females (56.0%), generally of all ages, said that they never replied at all. Here we found two interesting things about the reaction to cyberbullying, in that only 12.7% of respondents 'Discussed it with parents/close friend/someone' and 3.2% 'Reported it to the service provider or to the police'. This shows that there is an urgent need to spread awareness about cyberbullying so that victims can easily and openly discuss this crucial issue with their parents or service provider, and take action against these activities.

The internal reliability of seven reactions to cyberbullying and experience of cyberbullying is calculated by using Cronbach's alpha. The overall alpha coefficient is 0.688 (range if one item deleted, from 0.564 to 0.717). The experience and involvement in cyberbullying is a dichotomous variable coded 1 if the respondent answered 'Yes', 2 if a respondent answered 'No'. As shown in Table 5, the correlation coefficient between involvement or experience of cyberbullying and all the reactions except 'didn't take it seriously and reply in normal way' and 'reported it to the service provider or to police', is highly significant at the 0.01 level (2-tailed), which shows a strong relationship existed. However, linear regression analysis between the dependent variable (involvement or experience of cyberbullying) and independent variables (as given in Table 5 from serial number '1' to '7') suggests that the coefficient of determination (R^2), between involvement or experience of cyberbullying and 'replied in a bullying manner', 'never replied' and 'blocked someone' is 46.4%, 28.9% and 20.6% respectively. This means these independent variables accounted for 46.4%, 28.9% and 20.6% of the total variation in the dependent variable i.e. involvement or experience of cyberbullying. These three independent variables are the main reactions to cyberbullying, whereas the R^2 between involvement or experience of cyberbullying and all the seven indicators of Q17 is 57.7%, as given in Table 6.

3.2. General Questions about Cyberbullying

Four severity levels of cyberbullying were defined including *'Severe'*, *'Moderate'*, *'Normal'*, and *'Non-bullying'*. Respondents were asked to select one suitable range based on the severity level of cyberbullying. The value in percentage terms shows the malevolence of a message. Out of the total, 59.1% respondents selected Severe (86%-100%), Moderate (51%-85%), Normal (16%-50%), and Non-bullying (1%-15%) category of cyberbullying. Participants were also asked to provide five unusual bullying words they had encountered for the first time. We were surprised to see that people were being targeted in the name of caste, religion, race, region, gender, and age etc. We have included these words in our swear-keyword list during the feature space modelling for the cyberbullying detection approaches.

4. Conclusion

'Social networking websites', 'instant messaging' and 'chat rooms' are the main sources of cyberbullying. Items 'to show hate', 'to make fun of someone', and 'to copycat others in cyberbullying activities' are the main motives of cyberbullying. The main reactions to cyberbullying are 'replied in a bullying manner', 'never replied' and 'blocked someone'. To differentiate real bullying from cyberbullying-like or non-bullying messages, the frequency between sender and receiver over a long period of a time can be seen to demonstrate whether it is an unusual (intentional) act of teasing or a usual (unintentional)

Table 6. Regression (stepwise) analysis, model summary (Q6 & Q17)

S. No.	Model	Coefficients[a] Unstandardised Coefficients B	Std. Error	Standardised Coefficients Beta	t	Sig.
	(Constant)	0.071	0.018		3.969	0.000
a.	Didn't take it seriously and reply in normal way	0.159	0.061	0.086	2.604	0.010**
b.	Replied in bullying manner	0.648	0.045	0.549	14.399	0.000**
c.	Never replied	0.342	0.043	0.311	7.952	0.000**
d.	Blocked someone	0.016	0.051	0.014	0.313	0.755
e.	Changed User ID	0.079	0.127	0.021	0.618	0.537
f.	Discussed it with parents/close friend/someone	0.269	0.072	0.129	3.742	0.000**
g.	Reported it to the service provider or to police	-0.267	0.138	-0.065	-1.936	0.054
	R	**R^2**	**Adjusted R^2**	**d.f.1**	**d.f.2**	**Significance F**
	0.760[a]	0.577	0.570	7	399	0.000**
	a. Dependent Variable: Have you experienced or been involved in cyberbullying?					

** Significant at $p \leq 0.01$
* Significant at $p \leq 0.05$

act that generally exists between good friends or those in close relationships. However, it is important to note that a too frequent pattern should not be confused with frequent coarse language at a particular time. The unusual patterns over a long period of time should be considered as a clear indicator of real cyberbullying.

References

[1] Osman Tolga Aricak. Psychiatric symptomatology as a predictor of cyberbullying among university students. *Eurasian Journal of Educational Research*, 34:167–184, 2009.

[2] Tanya Beran and Qing Li. Cyber-harassment: A study of a new method for an old behavior. *Journal of Educational Computing Research*, 32(3):265–277, 2005.

[3] Wanda Cassidy, Margaret Jackson, and Karen N. Brown. Sticks and stones can break my bones, but how can pixels hurt me? Students' experiences with cyber-bullying. *School Psychology International*, 30(4):383–402, 2009.

[4] Jaana Juvonen and Elisheva F. Gross. Extending the school grounds?-bullying experiences in cyberspace. *Journal of School Health*, 78(9):496–505, 2008.

[5] Robin M. Kowalski and Susan P. Limber. Electronic bullying among middle school students. *Journal of Adolescent Health*, 41(6):22–30, 2007.

[6] Qing Li. Cyberbullying in schools. a research of gender differences. *School Psychology International*, 27(2):157–170, 2006.

[7] Vinita Nahar, Xue Li, and Chaoyi Pang. A step towards combating cyberbullying: Automated detection. In *Proceedings of the No 2 Bullying Conference*, pages 54–73, 2013.

[8] Vinita Nahar, Xue Li, and Chaoyi Pang. Cyberbullying validation. *Nova Science Publishers, Inc. (In press)*, 2014.

[9] Leandra Parris, Kris Varjas, Joel Meyers, and Hayley Cutts. High school students' perceptions of coping with cyberbullying. *Youth & Society*, 44(2):248–306, 2012.

[10] Christina Salmivalli, Kirsti Lagerspetz, Kaj Björkqvist, Karin Österman, and Ari Kaukiainen. Bullying as a group process: Participant roles and their relations to social status within the group. *Aggressive Behavior*, 22(1):1–15, 1996.

[11] Heidi Vandebosch and Katrien Van Cleemput. Cyberbullying among youngsters: profiles of bullies and victims. *New Media and Society*, 11(8):1349–1371, 2009.

[12] Nancy Willard. Educator's guide to cyberbullying and cyberthreats, Retrieved on: 10 January 2011. *http://www.accem.org/pdf/cbcteducator.pdf*, pages 1–16, 2007.

[13] Michele L. Ybarra, Kimberly J. Mitchell, Janis Wolak, and David Finkelhor. Examining characteristics and associated distress related to internet harassment: Findings from the second youth internet safety survey. *Pediatrics*, 118(4):1169–1177, 2006.

[14] Jina Yoon, Sheri Bauman, Taesan Choi, and Alisa S. Hutchinson. How south korean teachers handle an incident of school bullying. *School Psychology International*, 32:312–329, 2011.

INDEX

#

A

B

C

D

E

F

G

H

I

N

O

P

Q

R

S

T

U

V

W

X

Y